Incidents of Travel in Central America, Chiapas, and Yucatan

A Square Altar sculptured on the four sides and top.
B Statue erect.
C do.   do.
D do.   Fallen do. with many fragments on site of Pyramid.
E Colossal Head.
F,G Remains of sculptured figures.
H Colossal Head.
I Sepulchre and underground passage leading to the River.
J Remains of 2 circular Towers with Stairs.
K Statue and Altar, (Fallen.)
L Statue and Altar, (Erect.)
M do.   do.   do.
N do.   do.   do.
O do.   do.   (Fallen.)
P do.   do.   (Erect.)

Q Statue and Altar. (Erect.)
R do.   do.   (Fallen.)
S Statue of Female with Altar, (Erect.)
T do.   do.   (Fallen.)
U Beautiful Fragment, partly buried.
V Entrance with remains of Shafts of Columns.
W Court Yard, with steps on three sides.
X Pyramidal Building, Steps 10 ft. wide, and 6 ft. high
Y Y Y Area, overgrown with Trees.
Z Z Z Z Z Z Remains of Pyramidal Buildings.

The dotted line shows the boundaries of the survey.

Indian Rubber, Mahogany, Cedar, and other large trees are dispersed over the Ruins.

PLAN OF COPAN
Scale of English Feet

F. Catherwood.

No. 5.

is difficult to form a conception, must have passed within two days' march of this city.

The extent along the river, as ascertained by monuments still found, is more than two miles. There is one monument on the opposite side of the river, at the distance of a mile, on the top of a mountain 2,000 feet high. Whether the city ever crossed the river, and extended to that monument, it is impossible to say. I believe not. At the rear is an unexplored forest, in which there may be ruins. There are no remains of palaces or private buildings, and the principal part is that which stands on the bank of the river, and may, perhaps, with propriety be called the Temple.

This temple is an oblong enclosure. The front or river wall extends in a right line north and south 624 feet, and is from sixty to ninety feet in height. It is made of cut stones, from three to six feet in length, and a foot and a half in breadth. In many places the stones have been thrown down by bushes growing out of the crevices, and in one place there is a small opening, from which the ruins are sometimes called by the Indians Las Ventanas, or the windows. The other three sides consist of ranges of steps and pyramidal structures, rising from 30 to 140 feet in height on the slope. The whole line of survey is 2,866 feet, which, though gigantic and extraordinary for a ruined structure of the aborigines, that the reader's imagination may not mislead him, I consider it necessary to say, is not so large as the base of the great Pyramid of Ghizeh.

The engraving opposite gives the plan according to our survey, a reference to which will assist the reader to understand the description.

To begin on the right: Near the south-west corner of the river wall and the south wall is a recess, which was probably once occupied by a colossal monument fronting the water, no part of which is now visible; it may have fallen and been broken, and the fragments buried or washed away by the floods of the rainy season. Beyond are the remains of two small pyramidal structures, to the largest of which is attached a wall running along the right bank of the river: this appears to have been one of the principal walls of the city; and between the two pyramids there seems to have been a gateway or principal entrance from the water.

The south wall runs at right angles to the river, beginning with a range of steps about thirty feet high, and each step about eighteen inches square. At the south-east corner is a massive pyramidal structure, 120 feet high on the slope. On the right are other remains of terraces and pyramidal buildings; and here also was probably a gateway, by a passage about twenty feet wide, into a quadrangular

G

area 250 feet square, two sides of which are massive pyramids, 120 feet high on the slope.

At the foot of these structures, and in different parts of the quadrangular area, are numerous remains of sculpture. At the point marked E (see the plan) is a colossal monument, richly sculptured, fallen, and ruined. Behind it fragments of sculpture, thrown from their places by trees, are strewed and lying loose on the side of the pyramid, from the base to the top; and among them our attention was forcibly arrested by rows of death's heads of gigantic proportions, still standing in their places about half way up the side of the pyramid: the effect was extraordinary. The engraving which follows represents one of them.

At the time of our visit, we had no doubt that these were death's heads; but it has been suggested that the drawing is more like the skull of a monkey than that of a man. And, in connexion with this remark, I add what attracted our attention, though not so forcibly at the time. Among the fragments on this side were the remains of a colossal ape or baboon, strongly resembling in outline and appearance one of the four monstrous animals which once stood in front attached to the base of the obelisk of Luxor now in Paris,* and which, under the name of Cynocephali, were worshipped at Thebes. This fragment was about six feet high. The head was wanting; the trunk lay on the side of the pyramid, and we rolled it down several steps, when it fell among a mass of stones, from which we could not disengage it. We had no such idea at the time, but it is not absurd to suppose the sculptured skulls to be intended for the heads of monkeys,

* As it stands in Paris, these figures are wanting to make it complete as it stood at Thebes, the obelisk alone having been removed.

F. Catherwood.

8. STONE IDOL, 13 feet high, at Copan.

CHARACTER OF THE ENGRAVINGS. 83

and that these animals were worshipped as deities by the people who built Copan.

Among the fragments lying on the ground, near this place, is a remarkable portrait, of which the following engraving is a representation. It is probably the portrait of some king, chieftain, or sage.

The mouth is injured, and part of the ornament over the wreath that crowns the head. The expression is noble and severe, and the whole character shows a close imitation of nature.

At the point marked D stands one of the columns or "idols" which give the peculiar character to the ruins of Copan; to the front of which I particularly request the attention of the reader. It stands with its face to the east, about six feet from the base of the pyramidal wall. It is thirteen feet in height, four feet in front, and three deep, sculptured on all four of its sides from the base to the top, and one of the richest and most elaborate specimens in the whole extent of the ruins. Originally it was painted, the marks of red colour being still distinctly visible. Before it, at a distance of about eight feet, is a large block of sculptured stone, which the Indians call an altar. The subject in the front is a full-length figure, the face wanting beard,

G 2

and of a feminine cast, though the dress seems that of a man. On the two sides are rows of hieroglyphics, which probably recite the history of this mysterious personage.

As the monuments speak for themselves, it is unnecessary to give any verbal description; and there being so many to present to the reader, all differing very greatly in detail, it will be impossible, within reasonable limits, to present our own speculations as to their character. It need only be remarked that, from the beginning, our great object and effort was to procure true copies of the originals, adding nothing for effect as pictures. All the outlines were made with the camera lucida, and the minute parts afterwards filled in with the pencil.

Following the wall, at the place marked C is another monument or idol of the same size, and in many respects similar. The engraving No. 9, represents the back. The character of this image, as it stands at the foot of the pyramidal wall, with masses of fallen stone resting against its base, is grand, and it would be difficult to exceed the richness of the ornament and sharpness of the sculpture. This, too, was painted, and the red colour is still distinctly visible.

The whole quadrangle is overgrown with trees, and interspersed with fragments of fine sculpture, particularly on the east side; and at the northeast corner is a narrow passage, which was probably a third gateway.

On the right is a confused range of terraces, running off into the forest, ornamented with death's heads, some of which are still in position, and others lying about as they have fallen or been thrown down. Turning northward, the range on the left hand continues a high, massive pyramidal structure, with trees growing out of it to the very top. At a short distance is a detached pyramid, tolerably perfect, marked on the plan Z, about fifty feet square and thirty feet high. The range continues for a distance of about 400 feet, decreasing somewhat in height, and along this there are but few remains of sculpture.

The range of structures turns at right angles to the left, and runs to the river, joining the other extremity of the wall, at which we began our survey. The bank was elevated about thirty feet above the river, and had been protected by a wall of stone, most of which has fallen down. Among the fragments lying on the ground on this side is the portrait given on the next page.

The plan was complicated, and, the whole ground being overgrown with trees, difficult to make out. There was no entire pyramid, but, at most, two or three pyramidal sides, and these joined on to terraces or other structures of the same kind. Beyond the wall of enclosure were walls, terraces, and pyramidal elevations, running off into the forest, which sometimes confused us. Probably the whole was not

9. STONE STATUE—*Front View.*

II. FRONT OF STONE IDOL.

erected at the same time, but additions were made and statues erected by different kings, or, perhaps, in commemoration of important events in the history of the city. Along the whole line were ranges of steps with pyramidal elevations, probably crowned on the top with buildings or altars now ruined. All these steps and the pyramidal sides were

painted, and the reader may imagine the effect when the whole country was clear of forest, and priest and people were ascending from the outside to the terraces, and thence to the holy places within to pay their adoration in the temple.

Within this enclosure are two rectangular courtyards, having ranges of steps ascending to terraces. The area of each is about forty feet above the river. Of the larger and most distant from the river the steps have all fallen, and constitute mere mounds. On one side, at the foot of the pyramidal wall, is the monument or "idol" marked B, of which the engraving No. 11 represents the front. It is about the same height with the others, but differs in shape, being larger at the top than below. Its appearance and character are tasteful and pleasing, but the sculpture is in much lower relief; the expression of the hands is good, though somewhat formal. The back and sides are covered with hieroglyphics.

Near this, at the point marked A, is a remarkable altar, which perhaps presents as curious a subject of speculation as any monument in Copan. The altars, like the idols, are all monolithic, or of a single block of stone. In general they are not so richly ornamented, and are more faded and worn, or covered with moss; some were completely buried, and of others it was difficult to make out more than the form. All differed in fashion, and doubtless had some distinct and peculiar reference to the idols before which they stood. This stands on four globes cut out of the same stone; the sculpture is in bas-relief, and it is the only specimen of that kind of sculpture found at Copan, all the rest being in bold alto-relievo. It is six feet square and four feet high, and the top is divided into thirty-six tablets of hieroglyphics, which beyond doubt record some event in the history of the mysterious people who once inhabited the city. The lines are still distinctly visible, and a faithful copy appears in the following cut.

The engravings, Nos. 13, 14, exhibit the four sides of this altar. Each side represents four individuals. On the west side are the two principal personages, chiefs or warriors, with their faces opposite each other, and apparently engaged in argument or negotiation. The others are divided into two equal parties, and seem to be following their leaders. Each of the two principal figures is seated cross-legged, in the Oriental fashion, on a hieroglyphic which probably designates his

West Side.

F. Catherwood.

North Side.

13. ALTAR.

South Side.

F. Catherwood.   East Side.

14. ALTAR.

F. Catherwood.

15. GIGANTIC HEAD.

name and office, or character; and on three of which the serpent forms part. Between the two principal personages is a remarkable cartouche, containing two hieroglyphics, well preserved, which reminded us strongly of the Egyptian method of giving the names of the kings or heroes in whose honour monuments were erected. The headdresses are remarkable for their curious and complicated form: the figures have all breastplates, and one of the two principal characters holds in his hand an instrument, which may, perhaps, be considered a sceptre; each of the others holds an object which can be only a subject for speculation and conjecture. It may be a weapon of war; and, if so, it is the only thing of the kind found represented at Copan. In other countries, battle-scenes, warriors, and weapons of war are among the most prominent subjects of sculpture; and from the entire absence of them here, there is reason to believe that the people were not warlike, but peaceable, and easily subdued.

The other courtyard is near the river. By cutting down the trees, we discovered the entrance to be on the north side, by a passage thirty feet wide, and about three hundred feet long. On the right is a high range of steps rising to the terrace of the river wall. At the foot of this are six circular stones, from eighteen inches to three feet in diameter,—perhaps once the pedestals of columns or monuments now fallen and buried. On the left side of the passage is a high pyramidal structure, with steps six feet high and nine feet broad, like the side of one of the pyramids at Saccara, and one hundred and twenty-two feet high on the slope. The top is fallen, and has two immense Ceiba trees growing out of it, the roots of which have thrown down the stones, and now bind the top of the pyramid. At the end of the passage is the area or courtyard, probably the great circus of Fuentes; but which, instead of being circular, is rectangular, one hundred and forty feet long and ninety broad, with steps on all the sides. This was probably the most holy place in the temple. Beyond doubt it had been the theatre of great events, and of imposing religious ceremonies; but what those ceremonies were, or who were the actors in them, or what had brought them to such a fearful close, were mysteries which it was impossible to fathom. There was no idol or altar, nor were there any vestiges of them. On the left, standing alone, two-thirds of the way up the steps, is the gigantic head represented in Plate No. 15. It is moved a little from its place, and a portion of the ornament on one side has been thrown down some distance by the expansion of the trunk of a large tree, as shown by the drawing. The head is about six feet high, and the style good. Like many of the others, with the great expansion of the eyes it seems intended to inspire awe. On either side of it, distant about thirty or forty feet, and rather lower down, are other fragments of sculpture of colossal dimensions and good design; and at the foot are two colossal heads, turned over and partly buried, well worthy the attention of future travellers and artists. The whole area is overgrown with trees and encumbered with decayed vegetable matter, with fragments of curious sculpture protruding above the surface, which, probably, with many others completely buried, would be brought to light by digging.

On the opposite side, parallel with the river, is a range of fifteen steps to a terrace twelve feet wide; and then fifteen steps more to another terrace twenty feet wide, extending to the river wall. On each side of the centre of the steps is a mound of ruins, apparently of a circular tower. About half way up the steps on this side is a pit five feet square and seventeen feet deep, cased with stone. At the bottom is an opening two feet four inches high, with a wall one foot nine inches thick, which leads into a chamber ten feet long, five feet eight inches wide, and four feet high. At each end is a niche one foot nine inches high, one foot eight inches deep, and two feet five inches long. Col. Galindo first broke into this sepulchral vault, and found the niches and the ground full of red earthenware dishes and pots, more than fifty of which, he says, were full of human bones packed in lime; also several sharp-edged and pointed knives of chaya, a small death's head, carved in a fine green stone, its eyes nearly closed, the lower features distorted, and the back symmetrically perforated by holes, the whole of exquisite workmanship. Immediately above the pit which leads to this vault is a passage leading through the terrace to the river wall, from which, as before mentioned, the ruins are sometimes called Las Ventanas, or the windows. It is one foot eleven inches at the bottom, and one foot at the top, in this form, and barely large enough for a man to crawl through on his face.

There were no remains of buildings. In regard to the stone hammock mentioned by Fuentes, and which, in fact, was our great inducement to visit these ruins, we made special inquiry and search, but saw nothing of it. Colonel Galindo does not mention it. Still it may have existed, and may be there still, broken and buried. The padre of Gualan told us that he had seen it; and in our inquiries among the Indians, we met with one who told us that he had heard his father say that *his* father, two generations back, had spoken of such a monument.

I have omitted the particulars of our survey: the difficulty and labour of opening lines through the trees—climbing up the sides of the ruined pyramids—measuring steps,—and the aggravation of all these, from our want of materials and help, and our imperfect knowledge of the language. The people of Copan could not comprehend what we were about, and thought we were practising some black art to discover hidden treasure. Bruno and Francisco, our principal coadjutors, were completely mystified, and even the monkeys seemed embarrassed and confused; these counterfeit presentments of ourselves aided not a little in keeping alive the strange interest that hung over the place. They had no "monkey-tricks," but were grave and solemn, as if officiating as the guardians of consecrated ground. In the morning they were quiet, but in the afternoon they came out for a promenade on the tops of the trees; and sometimes, as they looked steadfastly at us, they seemed on the point of asking us why we disturbed the repose of the ruins. I have omitted, too, what aggravated our hardships and disturbed our sentiment: apprehensions from scorpions, and bites of mosquitos and garrapatas or ticks, the latter of which, in spite of precautions (pantaloons tied tight over our boots, and coats buttoned close in the throat), got under our clothes, and buried themselves in the flesh; at night, moreover, the hut of Don Miguel was alive with fleas, to protect ourselves against which, on the third night of our arrival, we sewed up the sides and one end of our sheets, and thrust ourselves into them as we would into a sack. And while in the way of mentioning our troubles I may add, that during this time the flour of the hacienda gave out, we were cut off from bread, and brought down to tortillas.

The day after our survey was finished, as a relief, we set out for a walk to the old stone quarries of Copan. Very soon we abandoned the path along the river, and turned off to the left. The ground was broken, the forest thick, and all the way we had an Indian before us with his machete, cutting down branches and saplings. The range lies about two miles north from the river, and runs east and west. At the foot of it we crossed a wild stream. The side of the mountain was overgrown with bushes and trees. The top was bare, and commanded a magnificent view of a dense forest, broken only by the winding of the Copan River, and the clearings for the haciendas of Don Gregorio and Don Miguel. The city was buried in forest, and entirely hidden from sight. Imagination peopled the quarry with workmen, and laid bare the city to their view. Here, as the sculptor worked, he turned to the theatre of his glory, as the Greek did to the Acropolis of Athens, and dreamed of immortal fame. Little did he imagine that the time would come when his works would perish, his race be extinct, his city a desolation and abode for reptiles,—for strangers to gaze at, and wonder by what race it had once been inhabited.

The stone is of a soft grit. The range extended a long distance, seemingly unconscious that stone enough had been taken from its sides to build a city. How the huge masses were transported over the irregular and broken surface we had crossed, and particularly how one of them was set up on the top of a mountain 2,000 feet high, it was impossible to conjecture. In many places were blocks which had been quarried out, and rejected for some defect; and at one spot, midway in a ravine leading toward the river, was a gigantic block, much larger than any we saw in the city, which was probably on its way thither, to be carved and set up as an ornament, when the labours of the workmen were arrested. Like the unfinished blocks in the quarries at Assouan and on the Pentelican Mountain, it remains as a memorial of baffled human plans.

We remained all day on the top of the range. The close forest in which we had been labouring made us feel more sensibly the beauty of the extended view. On the top of the range was a quarried block. With the chay stone found among the ruins, and supposed to be the instrument of sculpture, we wrote our names upon it. They stand alone, and few will ever see them. Late in the afternoon we returned, and struck the river above the ruins, near a stone wall with a circular building and a pit, apparently for a reservoir.

As we approached our hut we saw two horses with side-saddles tied outside, and heard the cry of a child within. A party had arrived, consisting of an old woman and her daughter, son, and his wife and child, and their visit was to the medicos. We had had so many applications for remedios, our list of patients had increased so rapidly; and we had been so much annoyed every evening with weighing and measuring medicines, that, influenced also by the apprehensions before referred to, we had given out our intention to discontinue practice; but our fame had extended so far, that these people had actually come from beyond San Antonio, more than thirty miles distant, to be cured, and it was hard to send them away without doing something for them. As Mr. C. was the medico in whom the public had most confidence, I scarcely paid any attention to them, unless to observe that they were much more respectable in dress and appearance than any patients we had had, except the members of Don Gregorio's family; but during the evening I was attracted by the tone in which the mother spoke of the daughter, and for the first time noticed in the latter an extreme delicacy of figure and a pretty foot, with a neat shoe and clean stocking. She had a shawl drawn over her head, and on speaking to her she removed the shawl, and turned up a pair of the most soft and dove-like eyes that mine ever met. She was the first of our patients in whom I took any interest, and I could not deny myself the physician's privilege of taking her hand in mine. While she thought we were consulting in regard to her malady, we were speaking of her interesting face; but the interest which we took in her was melancholy and painful, for we felt that she was a delicate flower, born to bloom but for a season, and, even at the moment of unfolding its beauties, doomed to die.

The reader is aware that our hut had no partition walls. Don Miguel and his wife gave up their bed to two of the women; she herself slept on a mat on the ground with the other. Mr. C. slept in his hammock, I on my bed of Indian corn, and Don Miguel and the young men under a shed out of doors.

I passed two or three days more in making the clearings and preparations, and then Mr. Catherwood had occupation for at least a month. When we turned off to visit these ruins, we did not expect to find employment for more than two or three days, and I did not consider myself at liberty to remain longer. I apprehended a desperate chase after a government; and fearing that among these ruins I might wreck my own political fortunes, and bring reproach upon my political friends, I thought it safer to set out in pursuit. A council was called at the base of an idol, at which Mr. C. and I were both present. It was resumed in Don Miguel's hut. The subject was discussed in all its bearings. All the excitement in the village had died away; we were alone and undisturbed; Mr. C. had under his dominion Bruno and Francisco, Don Miguel, his wife, and Bartolo. We were very reluctant to separate, but it was agreed, *nem. con*, for me to go on to Guatimala, and for Mr. Catherwood to remain and finish his drawings. Mr. Catherwood did remain, and, after many privations and difficulties, was compelled to leave on account of illness. He returned a second time and completed them, and we now give the result of the whole.

At a short distance from the Temple, within terraced walls, probably once connected with the main building, are the "idols" which give the distinctive character to the ruins of Copan; and if the reader will look at the map, and follow the line marked "pathway to Don Miguel's house," toward the end on the right he will see the place where they stand. Near as they are, the forest was so dense that one could not be seen from the other. In order to ascertain their juxtaposition, we cut vistas through the trees, and took the bearings and distances, and I introduce them in the order in which they stand. The first is on the left of the pathway, at the point marked K. This statue is fallen and the face destroyed. It is twelve feet high, three feet three inches on one side, and four feet on the other. The altar is sunk in the earth, and we give no drawing of either.

At a distance of 200 feet stands the one marked S. It is eleven feet eight inches high, three feet four inches on each side, and stands with its front to the east on a pedestal six feet square, the whole resting on a circular stone foundation sixteen feet in diameter. Before it, at a distance of eight feet ten inches, is an altar, partly buried, three feet three inches above the ground, seven feet square, and standing diagonally to the "idol." It is in high relief, boldly sculptured, and in a good state of preservation.

The engravings which follow, Nos 16 and 17, represent the front and back view. The front, from the absence of a beard and from the dress, we supposed to be the figure of a woman, and the countenance presents traits of individuality, leading to the supposition that it is a portrait.

The back is a different subject. The head is in the centre, with complicated ornaments over it, the face broken, the border gracefully disposed, and at the foot are tablets of hieroglyphics. The altar is introduced on one side, and consists of four large heads strangely grouped together, so as not to be easily made out. It could not be introduced in its proper place without hiding the lower part of the "idol." In drawing the front, Mr. Catherwood always stood between the altar and the "idol."

A little behind this is the monument marked T, No. 18. It is one of the most beautiful in Copan, and in workmanship is equal to the finest Egyptian sculpture. Indeed, it would be impossible, with the best instruments of modern times, to cut stones more perfectly. It stands at the foot of a wall of steps, with only the head and part of the breast rising above the earth. The rest is buried, and probably as perfect as the portion which is now visible. When we first discovered it, it was buried up to the eyes. Arrested by the beauty of the sculpture, and by its solemn and mournful position, we commenced excavating. As the ground was level up to that mark, the excavation was made by loosening the earth with the machete, and scooping it out with the hands. As we proceeded, the earth formed a wall around and increased the labour. The Indians struck so carelessly with their machetes, that, afraid to let them work near the stone, we cleared it with our own hands. It was impossible, however, to continue; the earth was matted together by roots which entwined and bound the monument. It required a complete throwing out of the earth for ten or twelve feet around; and without proper tools, and afraid of

16. STONE IDOL.—*Front View.*

F. Catherwood.

17. STONE IDOL—Back View.

F. Catherwood.

13. IDOL HALF BURIED.

18. IDOL.—Front View.

F. Catherwood.

29. IDOL—Back View.

F. Catherwood.

21. IDOL—*Front View.*

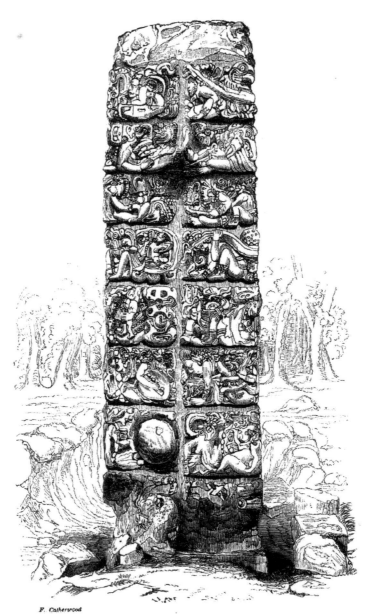

F. Catherwood.

22.—IDOL.—Back View.

injuring the sculpture, we preferred to let it remain, to be excavated by ourselves at some future time, or by some future traveller. Whoever he may be, I almost envy him the satisfaction of doing it. The outline of the trees growing around it is given in the engraving.

Toward the south, at a distance of fifty feet, is a mass of fallen sculpture, with an altar, marked R on the map; and at ninety feet distance is the statue marked Q, No. 19, standing with its front to the east, twelve feet high and three feet square, on an oblong pedestal seven feet in front and six feet two inches on the sides. Before it, at a distance of eight feet three inches, is an altar five feet eight inches long, three feet eight inches broad, and four feet high.

The face of this idol is decidedly that of a man. The beard is of a curious fashion, and joined to the mustache and hair. The ears are large, though not resembling nature; the expression is grand, the mouth partly open, and the eyeballs seem starting from the sockets; the intention of the sculptor seems to have been to excite terror. The feet are ornamented with sandals, probably of the skins of some wild animals, in the fashion of that day.

The back of this monument, No. 20, contrasts remarkably with the horrible portrait in front. It has nothing grotesque or pertaining to the rude conceits of Indians, but is noticeable for its extreme grace and beauty. In our daily walks we often stopped to gaze at it, and the more we gazed the more it grew upon us. Others seemed intended to inspire terror, and with their altars before them, sometimes suggested the idea of a blind, bigoted, and superstitious people, and sacrifices of human victims. This always left a pleasing impression; and there was a higher interest, for we considered that in its medallion tablets, the people who reared it had published a record of themselves, through which we might one day hold conference with a perished race, and unveil the mystery that hung over the city.

At a distance of 142 feet in a south-easterly direction is the idol marked P. It stands at the foot of a wall rising in steps to the height of thirty or forty feet; originally much higher, but the rest fallen and in ruins. Its face is to the north; its height eleven feet nine inches, the breadth of its sides three feet, and the pedestal is seven feet square. Before it, at a distance of twelve feet, is a colossal altar. It is of good workmanship, and has been painted red, though scarcely any vestige of the paint remains, and the surface is time-worn. The two engravings, Nos. 21 and 22, represent the front and back view. The former appears to represent the portrait of a king or hero, perhaps erected into a deity. It is judged to be a portrait, from certain marks of individuality in the features, also observable in most of the others, and its sex is ascertained by the beard, as in the Egyptian monuments, though this has a mustache, which is not found in Egyptian portraits.

The back of this idol, again, presents an entirely different subject, consisting of tablets, each containing two figures oddly grouped together, ill-formed, in some cases with hideous heads, while in others the natural countenance is preserved. The ornaments, diadems, and dresses are interesting, but what these personages are doing or suffering it is impossible to make out. This statue had suffered so much from the action of time and weather, that it was not always easy to make out the characters, the light being in all cases very bad, and coming through irregular openings among the branches of trees.

The stone of which all these altars and statues are made is a soft grit-stone from the quarries before referred to. At the quarries we observed many blocks with hard flint-stones distributed through them, which had been rejected by the workmen after they were quarried out. The back of this monument had contained two. Between the second and third tablets the flint has been picked out, and the sculpture is blurred; the other, in the last row but one from the bottom, remains untouched. An inference from this is, that the sculptor had no instruments with which he could cut so hard a stone, and, consequently that iron was unknown. We had, of course, directed our searches and inquiries particularly to this point, but did not find any pieces of iron or other metal, nor could we hear of any having ever been found there. Don Miguel had a collection of chay or flint stones, cut in the shape of arrow-heads, which *he* thought—and Don Miguel was no fool—were the instruments employed. They were sufficiently hard to scratch into the stone. Perhaps by men accustomed to the use of them, the whole of these deep relief ornaments might have been scratched, but the chay stones themselves looked as if they had been cut by metal.

The engraving No. 23, represents the altar as it stands before the last monument. It is seven feet square and four feet high, richly sculptured all around. The front represents a death's head. The top is sculptured, and contains grooves, perhaps for the passage of the blood of victims, animal or human, offered in sacrifice. The trees in the engraving give an idea of the forest in which these monuments are buried.

At the distance of 120 feet north is the monument marked O, No. 24, which, unhappily, is fallen and broken. In sculpture it is the same with the beautiful half-buried monument before given, and, I repeat it, in workmanship equal to the best remains of Egyptian art. The fallen part was completely bound to the earth by vines and creepers, and before it could be drawn it was necessary to unlace them,

23. IDOL AND ALTAR.

F. Catherwood.   24. FALLEN IDOL.

25. FRONT OF IDOL.

F. Catherwood.

26. BACK OF IDOL.

27. SIDE OF IDOL.

IDOLS ORIGINALLY PAINTED.

and tear the fibres out of the crevices. The paint is very perfect, and has preserved the stone, which makes it more to be regretted that it is broken. The altar is buried with the top barely visible, which, by excavating, we made out to represent the back of a tortoise.

The next engravings, Nos. 25, 26, 27, exhibit the front, back, and one of the sides of the monument N, distant twenty feet from the last. It is twelve feet high, four feet on one side, three feet four inches on the other, and stands on a pedestal seven feet square, with its front to the west. There is no altar visible; probably it is broken and buried. The front view seems a portrait, probably, of some deified king or hero. The two ornaments at the top look like the trunks of elephants, an animal unknown in that country. The crocodile's head is seven feet from it, but appears to have no connexion with it. This is four feet out of the ground, and is given in the plate as one of the many fragments found among the ruins.

The back presents an entirely different subject from the front. At the top is a figure sitting cross-legged, almost buried under an enormous head-dress, and three of the compartments contain tablets of hieroglyphics.

Not to multiply engravings, we have omitted side views, as they are, in general, less interesting. This is particularly beautiful. The tablets of hieroglyphics are very distinct.

At a distance of twenty-eight feet in the same direction is the statue

marked M, which is fallen, and lies on its back, with a tree across it nearly lengthwise, leaving visible only the outline, feet, and sandals, both of which are well sculptured. The preceding engraving is a representation of it.

Opposite is a circular altar with two grooves on the top, three feet high, and five feet six inches in diameter, an engraving of which is here given.

The next three engravings, Nos. 30, 31, and 32, are the front, back, and side view of the monument marked L, distant seventy-two feet north from the last, with its front toward the west, twelve feet high, three feet in front, two feet eight inches on the side, and the pedestal is six feet square. Before it, at a distance of eleven feet, is an altar very much defaced, and buried in the earth.

The front view is a portrait. The back is entirely made up of hieroglyphics, and each tablet has two hieroglyphics joined together, an arrangement which afterwards we observed occasionally at Palenque. The side presents a single row of hieroglyphics, joined in the same manner. The tablets probably contain the history of the king or hero delineated, and the particular circumstances or actions which constituted his greatness.

We have now given engravings of all the most interesting monuments of Copan, and they may be relied on as accurate and faithful representations. We have purposely abstained from all comment. If the reader can derive from them but a small portion of the interest that we did, he will be repaid for whatever he may find unprofitable in these pages.

Of the moral effect of the monuments themselves, standing as they

F. Catherwood.

30. STONE IDOL—*Front View.*

31. STONE IDOL.—*Back View.*

32. STONE IDOL—*Side View.*

We did not wake till nearly ten o'clock. It was Sunday; the morning was bright and beautiful, the arches and flowers still adorned the streets, and the Indians, in their clean clothes, were going to Sunday mass. None except the immediate parties knew or cared for the events of the night. Crossing the plaza, we met a tall, dashing fellow on horseback, with a long sword by his side, who bowed to Mr. Pavon, and rode on past the house of Chico. This was Espinoza. No one attempted to molest him, and no notice whatever was taken of the circumstance by the authorities.

The door of the church was so crowded that we could not enter; and passing through the curate's house, we stood in a doorway on one side of the altar. The curate, in his richest vestments, with young Indian assistants in sacerdotal dresses, their long black hair and sluggish features contrasting strangely with their garb and occupations, was officiating at the altar. On the front steps, with their black mantas drawn over their heads, and their eyes bent on the ground, were the dancers of our party the preceding night; kneeling along the whole floor of the immense church was a dense mass of Indian women, with red head-dresses; and leaning against the pillars, and standing up in the background, were Indians wrapped in black chamarros.

We waited till mass was over, and then accompanied the ladies to the house and breakfasted. Sunday though it was, the occupations for the day were a cockfight in the morning and bullfight in the afternoon. Our party was increased by the arrival of a distinguished family from Guatimala, and we all set out for the former. It was in the yard of an unoccupied house, which was already crowded; and I noticed, to the honour of the Indians and the shame of the better classes, that they were all Mestitzoes or white men, and, always excepting Carrera's soldiers, I never saw a worse looking or more assassin-like set of men. All along the walls of the yard were cocks tied by one leg, and men running about with other cocks under their arms, putting them on the ground to compare size and weight, regulating bets, and trying to cheat each other. At length a match was made; the ladies of our party had seats in the corridor of the house, and a space was cleared before them. The gaffs were murderous instruments, more than two inches long, thick, and sharp as needles, and the birds were hardly on the ground before the feathers of the neck were ruffled and they flew at each other. In less time than had been taken to gaff them, one was lying on the ground with its tongue hanging out, and the blood running from its mouth, dead. The eagerness and vehemence, noise and uproar, wrangling, betting, swearing, and scuffling of the crowd, exhibited a dark picture of human nature and a sanguinary people. I owe it to the ladies to say, that in the city they never are present at such scenes. Here they went for no other reason that I could see than because they were away from home, and it was part of the fête. We must make allowances for an education and state of society every way different from our own. They were not wanting in sensibility or refinement; and though they did not turn away with disgust, they seemed to take no interest in the fight, and were not disposed to wait for a second.

Leaving the disgusting scene, we walked around the suburbs, one point of which commands a noble view of the plain and city of Guatimala, with the surrounding mountains, and suggests a wonder, that, amid objects so grand and glorious, men can grow up with tastes so grovelling. Crossing the plaza, we heard music in a large house belonging to a rich muleteer; and, entering, we found a young harpist, and two mendicant friars, with shaved crowns, dressed in white, with long white mantles and hoods, of an order newly revived in Guatimala, and drinking agua ardiente. Mantas and hats were thrown off, tables and seats placed against the wall, and in a few moments my friends were waltzing.

This over, the young men brought out the ladies' mantas, and again we sallied for a walk; but, reaching the plaza, the young men changed their minds, and seating the ladies, to whom I attached myself, in the shade, commenced prisoner's base. All who passed stopped, and the villagers seemed delighted with the gaiety of our party. The players tumbled each other in the dust, to the great amusement of the lookers-on; and this continued till we saw trays coming across the plaza, which was a sign of dinner. This over, and thinking that I had seen enough for one Sunday, I determined to forego the bullfight; and in company with Don Manuel and another prominent member of the Assembly, and his family, I set out on my return to the city. Their mode of travelling was primitive. All were on horseback, he himself with a little son behind him; his daughter alone; his wife on a pillion, with a servant to support her; a servant-maid with a child in her arms, and a servant on the top of the luggage. It was a beautiful afternoon, and the plain of Guatimala, with its green grass and dark mountains, was a lovely scene. As we entered the city we encountered a religious procession, with priests and monks all bearing lighted candles, and preceded by men throwing rockets. We avoided the plaza on account of the soldiers, and in a few minutes I was in my house, alone.

CHAPTER XIII.

EXCURSION TO LA ANTIGUA AND THE PACIFIC OCEAN—SAN LUCAS—MOUNTAIN SCENERY—EL RIO PENSATIVO—LA ANTIGUA—ACCOUNT OF ITS DESTRUCTION—AN OCTOGENARIAN—THE CATHEDRAL—SAN JUAN OBISPO—SANTA MARIA—VOLCANO DE AGUA—ASCENT OF THE MOUNTAIN—THE CRATER—A LOFTY MEETING-PLACE—THE DESCENT—RETURN TO LA ANTIGUA—CULTIVATION OF COCHINEAL—CLASSIC GROUND—CIUDAD VIEJA—ITS FOUNDATION—VISIT FROM INDIANS—DEPARTURE FROM CIUDAD VIEJA—FIRST SIGHT OF THE PACIFIC—ALOTENANGO—VOLCAN DEL FUEGO—ESCUINTLA—SUNSET SCENE—MASAGUA—PORT OF ISTAPA—ARRIVAL AT THE PACIFIC.

On Tuesday, the 17th of December, I set out on an excursion to La Antigua Guatimala and the Pacific Ocean. I was accompanied by a young man who lived opposite, and wished to ascend the Volcano de Agua. I had discharged Augustin, and with great difficulty procured a man who knew the route. Rumaldo had but one fault—he was married: like some other married men, he had a fancy for roving; but his wife set her face against this propensity; she said that I was going to El Mar, the sea, and might carry him off, and she should never see him again, and the affectionate woman wept at the bare idea; but upon my paying the money into her hands before going, she consented. My only luggage was a hammock and pair of sheets, which Rumaldo carried on his mule, and each had a pair of alforjas, or saddle-bags. At the gate we met Don José Vidaurre, whom I had first seen in the president's chair of the Constituent Assembly, and was going to visit his hacienda at the Antigua. Though it was only a journey of five or six hours, Señor Vidaurre, being a very heavy man, had two led horses, one of which he insisted on my mounting; and when I expressed my admiration of the animal, he told me, in the usual phrase of Spanish courtesy, that the horse was mine. It was done in the same spirit in which a Frenchman, who had been entertained hospitably in a country house in England, offered himself to seven of the daughters, merely for the compliment; and my worthy friend would have been very much astonished if I had accepted his offer.

The road to Mixco I have already described. In the village I stopped to see Chico. His hand had been cut off, and he was doing well. Leaving the village, we ascended a steep mountain, from the top of which we had a fine view of the village at its foot, the plain and city of Guatimala, and the Lake of Amatitan, enclosed by a belt of mountains. Descending by a wild and rugged road, we reached a plain, and saw on the left the village of San Lucas, and on the right, at some distance, San Mateo. We then entered a piece of woodland, and first ascending, then again descended by the precipitous side of a mountain, with a magnificent ravine on our right, to a beautiful stream. At this place mountains rose all around us; but the banks of the stream were covered with delicate flowers, and parrots with gay plumage were perched on the trees and flying over our heads, making, in the midst of gigantic scenery, a fairy spot. The stream passed between two ranges of mountains so close together that there was barely room for a single horsepath by its side. As we continued, the mountains turned to the left, and on the other side of the stream were a few openings, cultivated with cochineal, into the very hollow of the base. Again the road turned, and then ran straight, making a vista of more than a mile between the mountains, at the end of which was the Antigua, standing in a delightful valley, shut in by mountains and hills that always retain their verdure, watered by two rivers that supply numerous fountains, with a climate in which heat or cold never predominates; yet this city, surrounded by more natural beauty than any site I ever saw, has perhaps undergone more calamities than any city that was ever built. We passed the gate, and rode through the suburbs, in the opening of the valley, on one side of which was a new house, that reminded me of an Italian villa, with a large cochineal plantation extending to the base of the mountain. We crossed a stream bearing the poetical name of El Rio Pensativo; on the other side was a fine fountain, and at the corner of the street was the ruined church of San Domingo, a monument of the dreadful earthquakes which had prostrated the old capital, and driven the inhabitants from their homes.

On each side were the ruins of churches, convents, and private residences, large and costly, some lying in masses, some with fronts still standing, richly ornamented with stucco, cracked and yawning, roofless, without doors or windows, and trees growing inside above the walls. Many of the houses have been repaired, the city is repeopled, and presents a strange appearance of ruin and recovery. The inhabitants, like the dwellers over the buried Herculaneum, seemed to entertain no fears of renewed disaster. I rode up to the house of Don Miguel Manrique, which was occupied by his family at the time of the destruction of the city, and, after receiving a kind welcome, in company with Señor Vidaurre walked to the plaza. The great volcanoes of Agua and Fuego look down upon it; in the centre is a noble stone fountain, and the buildings which face it, especially the palace of the captain-general, displaying on its front the armorial bearings granted by the

F. Catherwood. 334. ANTIGUA GUATIMALA.

Emperor Charles the Fifth to the loyal and noble city, and surmounted by the Apostle St. James on horseback, armed, and brandishing a sword; and the majestic but roofless and ruined cathedral, 300 feet long, 120 broad, nearly 70 high, and lighted by 50 windows, show at this day that La Antigua was once one of the finest cities of the New World, deserving the proud name which Alvarado gave it, the city of the Knights of St. James.

This was the second capital of Guatimala, founded in 1542 on account of the destruction of the first by a water volcano. Its history is one of uninterrupted disasters. "In 1558 an epidemic disorder, attended with a violent bleeding at the nose, swept away great numbers of people; nor could the faculty devise any method to arrest the progress of the distemper. Many severe shocks of earthquake were felt at different periods; the one in 1565 seriously damaged many of the principal buildings; those of 1575, 76, and 77 were not less ruinous. On the 27th of December, 1581, the population was again alarmed by the volcano, which began to emit fire; and so great was the quantity of ashes thrown out and spread in the air, that the sun was entirely obscured, and artificial light was necessary in the city at mid-day."

"The years 1585 and 1586 were dreadful in the extreme. On January 16th of the former, earthquakes were felt, and they continued through that and the following year so frequently, that not an interval of eight days elapsed during the whole period without a shock more or less violent. Fire issued incessantly, for months together, from the mountain, and greatly increased the general consternation. The greatest damage of this series took place on the 23d of December, 1586, when the major part of the city again became a heap of ruins, burying under them many of the unfortunate inhabitants; the earth shook with such violence that the tops of the high ridges were torn off, and deep chasms formed in various parts of the level ground.

"In 1601 a pestilential distemper carried off great numbers. It raged with so much malignity that three days generally terminated the existence of such as were affected by it."

"On the 18th of February, 1651, about one o'clock in the afternoon, a most extraordinary subterranean noise was heard, followed immediately by three violent shocks, at very short intervals from each other, which threw down many buildings and damaged others; the tiles from the roofs of the houses were dispersed in all directions, like light straws by a gust of wind; the bells of the churches were rung by the vibrations; masses of rock were detached from the mountains; and even the wild beasts were so terrified, that, losing their natural instinct, they quitted their retreats, and sought shelter in the habitations of men."

"The year 1686 brought with it another dreadful epidemic, which in three months swept away a tenth part of the inhabitants." ... "From the capital the pestilence spread to the neighbouring villages, and thence to the more remote ones, causing dreadful havoc, particularly among the most robust of the inhabitants."

"The year 1717 was memorable; on the night of August 27th the mountain began to emit flames, attended by a continued subterranean rumbling noise. On the night of the 28th the eruption increased to great violence, and very much alarmed the inhabitants. The images of saints were carried in procession, public prayers were put up, day after day; but the terrifying eruption still continued, and was followed by frequent shocks, at intervals, for more than four months. At last, on the night of September 29th, the fate of Guatimala appeared to be decided, and inevitable destruction seemed to be at hand. Great was the ruin among the public edifices; many of the houses were thrown down, and nearly all that remained were dreadfully injured; but the greatest devastation was seen in the churches."

"The year 1773 was the most melancholy epoch in the annals of this metropolis; it was then destroyed, and, as the capital, rose no more from its ruins." .... "About four o'clock, on the afternoon of July 29, a tremendous vibration was felt, and shortly after began the dreadful convulsion that decided the fate of the unfortunate city." ... "On the 7th September there was another, which threw down most of the buildings that were damaged on the 29th of July; and on the 13th December, one still more violent terminated the work of destruction." ....

"The people had not well recovered from the consternation inflicted by the events of the fatal 29th of July, when a meeting was convoked for the purpose of collecting the sense of the inhabitants on the subject of removal." ... "At this meeting it was determined that all the public authorities should remove provisionally to the little village of La Hermita, until the valleys of Jalapa and Las Vacas could be surveyed, and until the king's pleasure could be ascertained on the subject." ...

"On the 6th of September the governor and all the tribunals withdrew to La Hermita; the surveys of the last-mentioned places being completed, the inhabitants were again convoked, to decide upon the transfer. This congress was held in the temporary capital, and lasted from the 12th to the 16th of January, 1774: the report of the commissioners was read, and, by a plurality of votes, it was resolved to make a formal translation of the city of Guatimala to the Valley of Las Vacas. The king gave his assent to this resolution on the 21st of July, 1775; and, by a decree of the 21st September following, approved most of the plans that were proposed for carrying the determination into effect; granting very liberally the whole revenue arising from the customs, for the space of ten years, toward the charges of building, &c. In virtue of this decree, the ayuntamiento was in due form established in the new situation on the 1st of January, 1776; and on the 29th of July, 1777, a proclamation was issued in Old Guatimala, commanding the population to remove to the new city within one year, and totally abandon the remains of the old one."

Such is the account given by the historian of Guatimala concerning the destruction of this city; besides which, I saw on the spot Padre Antonio Croquer, an octogenarian, and the oldest canonigo in Guatimala, who was living in the city during the earthquake which completed its destruction. He was still vigorous in frame and intellect, wrote his name with a free hand in my memorandum-book, and had vivid recollections of the splendour of the city in his boyhood, when, as he said, carriages rolled through it as in the streets of Madrid. On the fatal day he was in the Church of San Francisco with two padres, one of whom, at the moment of the shock, took him by the hand and hurried him into the patio; the other was buried under the ruins of the church. He remembered that the tiles flew from the roofs of the houses in every direction; the clouds of dust were suffocating, and the people ran to the fountains to quench their thirst. The fountains were broken, and one man snatched off his hat to dip for water. The archbishop slept that night in his carriage in the plaza. He described to me the ruins of individual buildings, the dead which were dug from under them, and the confusion and terror of the inhabitants; and though his recollections were only those of a boy, he had material enough for hours of conversation.

In company with the cura we visited the interior of the cathedral. The gigantic walls were standing, but roofless; the interior was occupied as a burying-ground, and the graves were shaded by a forest of dahlias and trees 70 or 80 feet high, rising above the walls. The grand altar stood under a cupola supported by 16 columns faced with tortoise-shell, and adorned with bronze medallions of exquisite workmanship. On the cornice were once placed statues of the Virgin and the twelve apostles, in ivory; but all these are gone; and more interesting than the recollections of its ancient splendour or its mournful ruins, was the empty vault where once reposed the ashes of Alvarado the Conqueror.

Toward evening my young companion joined me, and we set out for Santa Maria, an Indian village at two leagues' distance, situated on the side of the Volcano de Agua, with the intention of ascending the next day to the summit. As we entered the valley, the scene was so beautiful I did not wonder that even earthquakes could not make it desolate. At the distance of a league we reached the village San Juan del Obispo, the church and convent of which are conspicuous from below, and command a magnificent view of the valley and city of the Antigua. At dark we reached the village of Santa Maria, perched at a height of 2,000 feet above the Antigua, and 7,000 feet above the level of the Pacific. The church stands in a noble court with several gates, and before it is a gigantic white cross. We rode up to the convent, which is under the care of the cura of San Juan del Obispo, but it was unoccupied, and there was no one to receive us except a little talkative old man, who had only arrived that morning. Very soon there was an irruption of Indians, with the alcalde and his alguazils, who came to offer their services as guides up the mountain. They were the first Indians I had met who did not speak Spanish, and their eagerness and clamour reminded me of my old friends the Arabs. They represented the ascent as very steep, with dangerous precipices, and the path extremely difficult to find, and said it was necessary for each of us to have sixteen men with ropes to haul us up, and to pay twelve dollars for each man. They seemed a little astonished when I told them that we wanted two men each, and would give them half a dollar apiece, but fell immediately to eight men for each, and a dollar apiece; and, after a noisy wrangling, we picked out six from forty, and they all retired. In a few minutes we heard a violin out of doors, which we thought was in honour of us; but it was for the little old man, who was a titiritero or puppet-player, and intended giving an exhibition that night. The music entered the room, and a man stationed himself at the door to admit visitors. The price of admission was three halfpence, and there were frequent wranglings to have one halfpenny taken off, or two admitted for three halfpence. The high price preventing the entrance of common people, the company was very select, and all sat on the floor. The receipts, as I learned from the doorkeeper, were upward of 2s. 6d. Rumaldo, who was a skilful amateur, led the orchestra, that is, the other fiddler. The puppet was in an adjoining room, and when the door opened disclosed a black chamarro hanging as a curtain, the rising of which discovered the puppet-player sitting at a table with his little figures before him. The sports of the puppets were carried on with ventriloquial conversations, in the midst of which I fell asleep.

We did not get off till seven o'clock the next morning. The day was very unpromising, and the whole mountain was covered with clouds. As yet the side of the volcano was cultivated. In half an hour the road became so steep and slippery that we dismounted, and commenced the ascent on foot. The Indians went on before, carrying water and provisions, and each of us was equipped with a strong staff. At a quarter before eight we entered the middle region, which is covered with a broad belt of thick forest; the path was steep and muddy, and every three and four minutes we were obliged to stop and rest. At a quarter before nine we reached a clearing, in which stood a large wooden cross. This was the first resting-place, and we sat down at the foot of the cross and lunched. A drizzling rain had commenced, but, in the hope of a change, at half-past nine we resumed our ascent. The path became steeper and muddier, the trees so thickly crowded together that the sun never found its way through them, and their branches and trunks covered with green excrescences. The path was made and kept open by Indians, who go up in the winter-time to procure snow and ice for Guatimala. The labour of toiling up this muddy acclivity was excessive, and very soon my young companion became fatigued, and was unable to continue without help. The Indians were provided with ropes, one of which was tied around his waist, and two Indians went before with the rope over their shoulders

At half-past ten we were above the region of forest, and came out upon the open side of the volcano. There were still scattering trees, long grass, and a great variety of curious plants and flowers, furnishing rich materials for the botanist. Among them was a tree, growing to the height of 40 to 50 feet, bearing a red flower, called the *mano del mico*, or hand-flower, but more like a monkey's paw, the inside a light vermillion colour, and the outside vermillion with stripes of yellow. My companion, tired with the toil of ascending, even with the aid of the rope, at length mounted an Indian's shoulders. I was obliged to stop every two or three minutes, and my rests were about equal to the actual time of walking. The great difficulty was on account of the wet and mud, which, in ascending, made us lose part of every step. It was so slippery that, even with the staff, and the assistance of branches of trees and bushes, it was difficult to keep from falling. About half an hour before reaching the top, and, perhaps, 1,000 or 1,500 feet from it, the trees became scarce, and seemed blasted by lightning or withered by cold. The clouds gathered thicker than before, and I lost all hope of a clear day. At half an hour before twelve we reached the top, and descended into the crater. A whirlwind of cloud and vapour was sweeping around it. We were in a perspiration; our clothes were saturated with rain and mud; and in a few moments the cold penetrated our very bones. We attempted to build a fire, but the sticks and leaves were wet, and would not burn. For a few moments we raised a feeble flame, and all crouched around it; but a sprinkling of rain came down, just enough to put it out. We could see nothing, and the shivering Indians begged me to return. On rocks near us were inscriptions, one of which bore date in 1548; and on a stone were cut the words,

> Alexandro Ldvert,
> De San Petersbrgo;
> Edvardo Legh Page,
> De Inglaterra;
> *Jose Croskey,*
> *De Fyladelfye,*
> Bibymos aqui unas Boteas
> De Champana, el dia 26
> de Agosto de 1834.

It seemed strange that three men from such distant and different parts of the world, St. Petersburgh, England and *Philadelphia*, had met to drink Champagne on the top of this volcano. While I was blowing my fingers and copying the inscription, the vapour cleared away a little, and gave me a view of the interior of the crater. It was a large oval basin, the area level and covered with grass. The sides were sloping, about 100 or 150 feet high, and all around were masses of rock piled up in magnificent confusion, and rising to inaccessible peaks. There is no tradition of this mountain having

ever emitted fire, and there is no calcined matter or other mark of volcanic eruption anywhere in its vicinity. The historical account is, that in 1541 an immense torrent, not of fire, but of water and stones, was vomited from the crater, by which the old city was destroyed. Father Remesal relates that on this occasion the crown of the mountain fell down. The height of this detached part was one league, and from the remaining summit to the plain was a distance of three leagues, which he affirms he measured in 1615. The area, by my measurement, is 83 paces long and 60 wide. According to Torquemada (and such is the tradition according to Padre Alcantara, of Ciudad Vieja), this immense basin, probably the crater of an extinct volcano, with sides much higher than they are now, became filled with water by accumulations of snow and rain. There never was any eruption of water, but one of the sides gave way, and the immense body of fluid rushed out with horrific force, carrying with it rocks and trees, inundating and destroying all that opposed its progress. The immense barranca or ravine by which it descended, was still fearfully visible on the side of the mountain. The height of this mountain has been ascertained by barometrical observation to be 14,450 feet above the level of the sea. The edge of the crater commands a beautiful view of the old city of Guatimala, 32 surrounding villages, and the Pacific Ocean; at least so I am told, but I saw nothing of it. Nevertheless, I did not regret my labour; and though drenched with rain and plastered with mud, I promised myself in the month of February, when the weather is fine, to ascend again, prepared for the purpose, and pass two or three days in the crater.*

At one o'clock we began our descent. It was rapid, and sometimes dangerous, from the excessive steepness and slipperiness, and the chance of pitching head foremost against the trunk of a tree. At two o'clock we reached the cross; and I mention, as a hint for others, that, from the pressure of heavy water-proof boots upon the toes, I was obliged to stop frequently; and, after changing the pressure by descending sidewise and backward, catching at the branches of trees, I was obliged to pull off my boots and go down barefooted, ankle deep in mud. My feet were severely bruised by the stones, and I could hardly walk at all, when I met one of the Indians pulling my horse up the mountain to meet me. At four o'clock we reached Santa Maria, at five the Antigua, and at a quarter past I was in bed.

The next morning I was still asleep when Señor Vidaurre rode into the courtyard to escort me on my journey. Leaving Rumaldo to follow, I was soon mounted; and emerging from the city, we entered the open plain, shut in by mountains, and cultivated to their base with cochineal. At about a mile's distance we turned in to the hacienda of Señor Vidaurre. In the yard were four oxen grinding

* I ascended this volcano, shortly after Mr. Stephens, during perfectly clear weather, and beheld from its summit one of the most extensive and beautiful views I ever beheld, reminding me much of the view from the top of Mount Etna. The thermometer fell from 74° to 34° in less than ten minutes.—F. C.

sugar-cane, and behind was his nopal, or cochineal plantation, one of the largest in the Antigua. The plant is a species of cactus, set out in rows like Indian corn, and, at the time I speak of, it was about four feet high. On every leaf was pinned with a thorn a piece of cane, in the hollow of which were 30 or 40 insects. These insects cannot move, but breed, and the young crawl out and fasten upon the leaf; when they have once fixed they never move; a light film gathers over them, and as they feed the leaves become mildewed and white. At the end of the dry season some of the leaves are cut off and hung up in a storehouse for seed, the insects are brushed off from the rest and dried in ovens, and are then sent abroad to minister to the luxuries and elegances of civilized life, and enliven with their bright colours the *salons* of London, Paris, and St. Louis in Missouri. The crop is valuable, but uncertain, as an early rain may destroy it; and sometimes all the workmen of a hacienda are taken away for soldiers at the moment when they are most needed for its culture. The situation was ravishingly beautiful, at the base and under the shade of the Volcano de Agua, and the view was bounded on all sides by mountains of perpetual green; the morning air was soft and balmy, but pure and refreshing. With good government and laws, and one's friends around, I never saw a more beautiful spot on which man could desire to pass his allotted time on earth.

Resuming our ride, we came out upon a rich plain covered with grass, on which cattle and horses were pasturing, between the bases of the two great volcanoes; and on the left, at a distance, on the side of the Volcano de Agua, saw the Church of Ciudad Vieja, the first capital of Guatimala, founded by Alvarado the Conqueror. I was now on classic ground. The fame of Cortez and his exploits in Mexico spread among the Indian tribes to the south, and the Kachiquel kings sent an embassy offering to acknowledge themselves vassals of Spain. Cortez received the ambassadors with distinction, and sent Pedro de Alvarado, an officer distinguished in the conquest of New Spain, to receive the submission of the native kings, and take possession of Guatimala. On the 13th of November, 1523, Alvarado left the city of Mexico with 300 Spaniards, and a large body of Tlascaltecas, Cholotecas, Chinapas, and other auxiliary Mexican Indians, fought his way through the populous provinces of Soconusco and Tonala, and on the 14th of May, by a decisive victory over the Quiché Indians, he arrived at the capital of the Kachiquel kingdom, now known as the village of Tecpan Guatimala. After remaining a few days to recover from their fatigues, the conquering army continued their route by the villages on the coast, overcoming all that disputed their progress; and on the 24th of July, 1524, arrived at a place called by the Indians Almolonga, meaning, in their language, a spring of water (or the mountain from which water flows), situated at the base of the Volcano de Agua. The situation, says Remesal, pleased them so much by its fine climate, the beauty of the meadows, delightfully watered by running streams, and particularly from its lying between two lofty mountains, from one of which descended runs of water in every direction, and from the summit of the other issued volumes of smoke and fire, that they determined to build a city which should be the capital of Guatimala.

On the 25th of July, the festival of St. James, the patron of Spain, the soldiers, with martial music, splendid armour, waving plumes, horses superbly caparisoned in trappings glittering with jewels and plates of gold, proceeded to the humble church which had been constructed for that purpose, where Juan Godines, the chaplain to the army, said mass. The whole body invoked the protection of the apostle, and called by his name the city they had founded. On the same day Alvarado appointed alcaldes, regidors, and the chief alguazil. The appearance of the country harmonized with the romantic scenes of which it had been the theatre; and as I rode over the plain I could almost imagine the sides of the mountains covered with Indians, and Alvarado and his small band of daring Spaniards, soldiers and priests, with martial pride and religious humility, unfurling the banners of Spain and setting up the standard of the cross.

As we approached the town its situation appeared more beautiful; but very early in its history dreadful calamities befell it. "In 1532 the vicinity of the city was ravaged, and the inhabitants thrown into consternation by a lion of uncommon magnitude and ferocity, that descended from the forests on the mountain called the Volcan de Agua, and committed great devastation among the herds of cattle. A reward of 25 gold dollars, or 100 bushels of wheat, was offered by the town council to any person that could kill it; but the animal escaped, even from a general hunting-party of the whole city, with Alvarado at the head of it. After five or six months' continual depredations, it was killed on the 13th of July by a herdsman, who received the promised reward. The next great disaster was a fire that happened in February 1536, and caused great injury; as the houses were at that time nearly all thatched with straw, a large portion of them was destroyed before it could be extinguished. The accident originated in a blacksmith's shop; and to prevent similar misfortunes in future, the council prohibited the employment of forges within the city.

"The most dreadful calamity that had as yet afflicted this unfortunate place occurred on the morning of September 11, 1541. It had rained incessantly, and with great violence, on the three preceding days, particularly on the night of the 10th, when the water descended more like the torrent of a cataract than rain; the fury of the wind, the incessant appalling lightning, and the dreadful thunder, were indescribable." . . . "At two o'clock on the morning of the 11th, the vibrations of the earth were so violent that the people were unable to stand; the shocks were accompanied by a terrible subterranean noise, which spread universal dismay; shortly afterward, an immense torrent of water rushed down from the summit of the mountain, forcing away with it enormous fragments of rocks and large trees, which, descending upon the ill-fated town, overwhelmed and destroyed almost all the houses, and buried a great number of the inhabitants under the ruins; among the many, Doña Beatricè de la Cuéba, the widow of Pedro Alvarado, lost her life."

All the way down the side of the volcano we saw the seams and gullies made by the torrents of water which had inundated the city. Again we crossed the beautiful stream of El Rio Pensativo, and rode up to the convent. It stands adjoining the gigantic and venerable church of the Virgin. In front was a high stone wall; a large gate opened into a courtyard, at the extremity and along the side of which were the spacious corridors of the convent, and on the left the gigantic wall of the church, with a door of entry from one end of the corridor. The patio was sunk about four feet below the level of the corridor, and divided into parterres, with beds of flowers, and in the centre was a large white circular fountain, with goldfish swimming in it, and rising out of it, above a jet d'eau, an angel with a trumpet and flag.

Señor Vidaurre had informed Padre Alcantara of my intended visit, and he was waiting to receive us. He was about thirty-three years of age, intelligent, educated, and energetic, with a passion for flowers, as was shown by the beautiful arrangements of the courtyard. He had been banished by Morazan, and only returned to his curacy about a year before. On a visit to him was his friend and neighbour Don Pepe Asteguieta, proprietor of a cochineal hacienda, and a man of the same stamp and character. They were among the few whom I met who took any interest in the romantic events connected with the early history of the country. After a brief rest in the convent, with a feeling more highly wrought than any that had been awakened in me except by the ruins of Copan, we visited a tree standing before the church, and extending wide its branches, under whose shade, tradition says, Alvarado and his soldiers first encamped; the fountain of Almolonga, or, in the Indian language, the mountain from which water flows, which first induced him to select this spot as the site for the capital; and the ruined cathedral, on the spot where Juan Godines first said mass. The fountain is a large natural basin of clear and beautiful water, shaded by trees, under which thirty or forty Indian women were washing. The walls of the cathedral were standing, and in one corner was a chamber filled with the skulls and bones of those destroyed by the inundation from the volcano.

After breakfast we visited the church, which was very large, and more than 200 years old; its altar is rich in ornaments of gold and silver, among which is a magnificent crown of gold, studded with diamonds and emeralds, presented by one of the Philips to the Virgin, to whom the church was consecrated. Returning to the house, I found that Padre Alcantara had prepared for me a visit from a deputation of Indians, consisting of the principal chiefs and women, descendants of caciques of the Mexican auxiliaries of Alvarado, calling themselves, like the Spaniards, Conquistadores, or Conquerors; they entered, wearing the same costumes which their ancestors had worn in the time of Cortez, and bearing on a salver covered with velvet a precious book bound in red velvet, with silver corners and clasp, containing the written evidence of their rank and rights. It was written on parchment, dated in 1639, and contained the order of Philip the First, acknowledging them as conquerors, and exempting them, as such, from the tribute paid by the native Indians. This exemption continued until the revolution of 1825, and even yet they call themselves descendants of the conquerors, and the head of the Indian aristocracy. The interest which I felt in these memorials of the conquerors was increased in no small degree by the beauty and comfort of the convent, and Padre Alcantara's kindness. In the afternoon, we walked down to the bridge across the Rio Pensativo. The plain on which the Spanish soldiers had glittered in armour was shaded by the high volcanoes, and the spirit of romance rested upon it.

The day which I passed at the "old city" is one of those upon which I look back with pleasure. Señor Vidaurre and Don Pepe remained with us all day. Afterward, when Padre Alcantara had again been obliged to fly from the convent at the approach of an invading army, and we had all passed through the crash of the revolution, on leaving Guatimala to return home, I diverged from my road to pay them a visit, and they were the last friends to whom I said farewell.

In the morning, with great regret, I left Ciudad Vieja. Padre Alcantara and Don Pepe accompanied me, and to help me on my journey, the latter lent me a noble mule, and the padre an excellent servant. The exit from this mountain-girt valley was between the two great volcanoes of Agua and Fuego, rising on each side nearly 15,000 feet high; and from between the two, so unexpectedly to me as almost to induce a burst of enthusiasm, we overlooked an immense plain, and saw the Pacific Ocean. At a league's distance we reached the village of Alotenango, where, among Indian huts, stood another gigantic church, roofless, and ruined by an earthquake, and where, with the hope, in which I was not disappointed, of seeing them again, I took leave of the cura and Don Pepe. The road between the two great volcanoes was singularly interesting; one with its base cultivated, girt by a belt of thick forests, and verdant to the very summit; the other with three bare and rugged peaks, covered with dried lava and ashes, shaken by the strife of the elements within, the working of internal fires, and emitting constantly a pale blue smoke. The road bears marks of the violent convulsions to which it has been subject. In one place the horse-path lies through an immense chasm, rent asunder by a natural convulsion, over which huge stones, hurled in every direction, lay in the wildest confusion; in another it crosses a deep bed of ashes, and cinders, and scorified lava; and a little farther on, strata of decomposed vegetable matter cover the volcanic substances, and high shrubs and bushes have grown up, forming a thick shady arbour, fragrant as the fields of Araby the Blessed. At every step there was a strange contrast of the horrible and beautiful. The last eruption of the Volcan del Fuego took place about twelve years ago, when flames issued from the crater and ascended to a great height; immense quantities of stones and ashes were cast out, and the race of monkeys inhabiting the neighbouring woods was almost extirpated; but it can never burst forth again; its crater is no longer la Boca del Infierno, or the Mouth of the Infernal Regions, for, as a very respectable individual told me, it has been blessed by a priest.

After a beautiful ride under a hot sun, but shaded nearly all the way, at three o'clock we reached Escuintla, where was another magnificent church, roofless, and again with its rich façade cracked by an earthquake. Before it were two venerable Ceiba trees, and the platform commanded a splendid panoramic view of the volcanoes and mountains of the Antigua.

In the streets were soldiers and drunken Indians. I rode to the house of the corregidor, Don Juan Dios de Guerra, and, with Rumaldo for a guide, I walked down to the banks of a beautiful stream, which makes Escuintla, in the summer months of January and February, the great watering-place of Guatimala. The bank was high and beautifully shaded, and, descending to the river through a narrow passage between perpendicular rocks, in a romantic spot, where many a Guatimala lover has been hurried, by the charming influences around, into a premature outpouring of his hopes and fears, I sat down on a stone and washed my feet.

At two o'clock, under a brilliant moonlight, and with a single guide, we started for the Pacific. The road was level and wooded. We passed a trapiche or sugar-mill, worked by oxen, and before daylight reached the village of Masagua, four leagues distant, built in a clearing cut out of the woods, at the entrance of which we stopped under a grove of orange-trees, and by the light of the moon filled our pockets and alforgas with the shining fruit. Daylight broke upon us in a forest of gigantic trees, from 75 to 100 feet high, and from 20 to 25 feet in circumference, with creepers winding around their trunks and hanging from the branches. The road was merely a path through the forest, formed by cutting away shrubs and branches. The freshness of the morning was delightful. We had descended from the table land called the tierras templadas, and were now in the tierras calientes; but at nine o'clock the glare and heat of the sun did not penetrate the thick shade of the woods. In some places the branches of the trees, trimmed by the machete of a passing muleteer, and hung with a drapery of vines and creepers, bearing red and purple flowers, formed for a long distance natural arches more beautiful than any ever fashioned by man; and there were parrots and other birds of beautiful plumage flying among the trees; among them Guacamayas, or great macaws, large, clothed in red, yellow and green, and when on the wing displaying a splendid plumage. But there were also vultures and scorpions, and, running across the road and up the trees, innumerable iguanas or lizards, from an inch to three feet long. The road was a mere track among the trees, perfectly desolate, though twice we met muleteers bringing up goods from the port. At the distance of twelve miles we reached the hacienda of Naranjo, occupied by a major-domo, who looked after the cattle of the proprietor, roaming wild in the woods; the house stood alone in the midst of a clearing, built of poles, with a cattle-yard in front; and I spied a cow with a calf, which was a sign of milk. But you must catch a cow before you can milk her. The major-domo went out with a lazo, and, playing upon the chord of nature, caught the calf first, and then the cow, and hauled her up by the horns to a post. The hut had but one guacal, or drinking-shell, made of a gourd, and it was so small that we sat down by the cow so as not to lose much time. We had bread, chocolate, and sausages, and after a ride of twenty-four miles, made a glorious breakfast; but we exhausted the poor cow, and I was ashamed to look the calf in the face.

Resuming our journey, at a distance of nine miles we reached the solitary hacienda of Overo. The whole of this great plain was densely wooded and entirely uncultivated, but the soil was rich, and capable of maintaining, with very little labour, thousands of people. Beyond Overo the country was open in places, and the sun beat down with scorching force. At one o'clock we crossed a rustic bridge, and through the opening in the trees saw the river Michatoyal. We followed along its bank, and very soon heard breaking on the shore the waves of the great Southern Ocean. The sound was grand and solemn, giving a strong impression of the immensity of those waters, which had been rolling from the creation, for more than 5,000 years, unknown to civilized man. I was loth to disturb the impression, and rode slowly through the woods, listening in profound silence to the grandest music that ever fell upon my ear. The road terminated on the bank of the river, and I had crossed the Continent of America.

On the opposite side was a long sandbar, with a flagstaff, two huts built of poles and thatched with leaves, and three sheds of the same rude construction; and over the bar were seen the masts of a ship riding on the Pacific. This was the port of Istapa. We shouted above the roar of the waves, and a man came down to the bank, and loosing a canoe, came over for us. In the meantime, the interest of the scene was somewhat broken by a severe assault of mosquitoes and sandflies. The mules suffered as much as we; but I could not take them across, and was obliged to tie them under the trees. Neither Rumaldo nor my guide could be prevailed upon to remain and watch them; they said it would be death to sleep there. The river is the outlet of the Lake of Amatitan, and is said to be navigable from the Falls of San Pedro Martyr, seventy miles from its mouth; but there are no boats upon it, and its banks are in the wildness of primeval nature. The crossing-place was at the old mouth of the river. The sandbar extends about a mile further, and has been formed since the conquest. Landing, I walked across the sand to the house or hut of the captain of the port, and a few steps beyond saw the object of my journey, the boundless waters of the Pacific. When Nunez de Balboa, after crossing swamps and rivers, mountains and woods, which had never been passed but by straggling Indians, came down upon the shores of this newly-discovered sea, he rushed up to the middle in the waves with his buckler and sword, and took possession of it in the name of the king his master, vowing to defend it in arms against all his enemies. But Nunez had the assurance that beyond that sea "he would find immense stores of gold, out of which people did eat and drink." I had only to go back again. I had ridden nearly sixty miles; the sun was intensely hot, the sand burning, and very soon I entered the hut and threw myself into a hammock. The hut was built of poles set up in the sand, thatched with the branches of trees; furnished with a wooden table, a bench, and some boxes of merchandise, and swarming with mosquitoes. The captain of the port, as he brushed them away, complained of the desolation and dreariness of the place, its isolation and separation from the world, its unhealthiness, and the misery of a man doomed to live there; and yet he feared the result of the war, a change of administration, and being turned out of office!

Toward evening, rested and refreshed, I walked out upon the shore. The port is an open roadstead, without bay, headland, rock, or reef, or anything whatever to distinguish it from the line of the coast. There is no light at night, and vessels at sea take their bearings from the great volcanoes of the Antigua, more than sixty miles inland. A buoy was anchored outside of the breakers, with a cable attached, and under the sheds were three large launches for embarking and disembarking cargoes. The ship, which was from Bordeaux, lay off more than a mile from the shore. Her boat had landed the supercargo and passengers, since which she had had no communication with the land, and seemed proudly independent of so desolate a place. Behind the sandbar were a few Indian huts, and Indians nearly naked were sitting by me on the shore. Yet this desolate place was once the focus of ambitious hopes, high aspirations, lust of power and gold, and romantic adventure. Here Alvarado fitted out his armament, and embarked with his followers to dispute with Pizarro the riches of Peru. The sun was sinking, and the red globe touched the ocean; clouds were visible on its face, and when it disappeared, ocean and land were illuminated with a ruddy haze. I returned to the hut, and threw myself into my hammock. Could it be that I was again so far from home, and that these were the waves of the great Southern Ocean breaking on my ears?

CHAPTER XIV.

THE RETURN—HUNT FOR A MULE—OVERO—MASAGUA—ESCUINTLA—FALLS OF SAN PEDRO MARTYR—MICHATOYAL RIVER—VILLAGE OF SAN PEDRO—A MAJOR-DOMO—SAN CRISTOVAL—AMATITAN—A ROVING AMERICAN—ENTRY INTO GUATIMALA—LETTER FROM MR CATHERWOOD—CHRISTMAS EVE—ARRIVAL OF MR. CATHERWOOD—PLAZA DE TOROS—A BULLFIGHT—THE THEATRE—OFFICIAL BUSINESS—THE ARISTOCRACY OF GUATIMALA—STATE OF THE COUNTRY—NEW YEAR'S DAY—FEROCITY OF PARTY.

At three o'clock Rumaldo woke me to set out on my return. The moonbeams were glancing over the water, and the canoe was ready. I bade farewell to my host as he lay in his hammock, and crossed the river. Here I found an unexpected difficulty. My spare mule had broken her halter, and was nowhere to be seen. We beat about among the woods till daylight, and concluding that she must have taken the only path open, and set out for home on her own account, we saddled and rode on to Overo, a distance of twenty miles. But no stray mule had passed the hacienda, and I stopped and sent Rumaldo back to the port.

Very soon I became tired of waiting at the miserable hacienda, saddled my mule, and started alone. The road was so shaded that I did not stop for the noonday heat. For twenty-one miles further the road was perfectly desolate, the only sound being occasionally the crash of a falling tree. At the village of Masagua I rode up to a house, at which I saw a woman under the shed, and, unsaddling my mule, got her to send a man out to cut sacate, and to make me some chocolate. I was so pleased with my independence that I almost resolved to travel altogether by myself, without servant or change of apparel. In half an hour I resumed my journey. Towards evening I met drunken Indians coming out from Escuintla, and, looking forward, saw towering to the skies the two volcanoes of Fire and Water, and the intervening country glowing in the bright colours of the setting sun. Some time after dark I rode up to the house of the corregidor, having performed in the two days 110 miles. Unfortunately, there was no sacate for my mule. This article is brought into the towns by the Indians daily, and every person buys just enough for the night, and no more. There was not a spare lock of grass in the place. With a servant of the corregidor's I made an exploring expedition through the town, and by an affecting appeal to an old woman, enforced by treble price, bought from under their very noses the portion of two mules, and left them supperless.

I waited till two o'clock the next day for Rumaldo and the mule, and, after a vain endeavour to procure a guide to the falls of San Pedro Martyr, set out alone direct for Guatimala. At the distance of two leagues, ascending a steep hill, I passed a trapiche or sugar-mill, in a magnificent situation, commanding a full view of the plain I had

P. Catherwood. 33. ESQUINTLA.

crossed and the ocean beyond. Two oxen were grinding sugar-cane, and under a shed was a large boiling caldron for making panela, a brown sugar, in lumps of about two pounds each, an enormous quantity of which is consumed in the country. Here the humour seized me to make some inquiries about the falls of San Pedro Martyr. A man out at elbows, and every other mentionable and unmentionable part of his body, glad to get rid of regular work, offered to conduct me. I had passed, a league back, the place where I ought to have turned off; and proceeding onward to the village of San Pedro, he turned off to the right, and went back almost in the same direction by a narrow path descending through thick woods choked with bushes, and in a ravine reached the Michatoyal River, which I had crossed at Istapa. It was narrow and rapid, breaking wildly over a stony bed, with a high mountain on the opposite side. Following it, we reached the cataract, consisting of four streams separated by granite rock, partly concealed by bushes, and precipitated from a height of about 200 feet, forming with the wild scenery around a striking and romantic view. A little below it were a sugar-mill worked by water, and an uncommonly fine hacienda, which commanded a view of the falls, and at which I was very much disposed to pass the night. The major-domo, a black man, was somewhat surprised at my visit; but when he learned that I did not come to see the mill, but only the falls, he seemed to suspect that I was no better than I should be; and when I asked him if I could reach San Cristoval before dark, he answered that I could if I started immediately. This was not exactly an invitation to stay, and I left him. It shows the want of curiosity and indolence of the people, that, though these falls are but a pleasant afternoon's ride from Escuintla, which for two months is thronged with visitors from Guatimala, nobody ever visits them.

Hurrying back by the same wild path, we reached the main road, and, as it was late, I hired my guide to go on with me to San Cristoval. We passed through the village of San Pedro, which was a collection of miserable huts, with an estanco or place for the sale of agua ardiente, and thronged with half-intoxicated Indians. As we advanced, clouds began to gather around the mountains, and there was every appearance of heavy rain. I had no cloak or greatcoat, and, being particularly apprehensive of fevers and rheumatisms, after riding about a mile, I returned to San Pedro. The most respectable citizens of the place were reeling round the estanco, and urged me stop; but my guide said they were a bad set, and advised me to return and pass the night at the sugar-mill. Presuming that he knew the people of whom he spoke better than I did, I was no way inclined to disregard his caution. It was after dark when we reached the trapiche; some of the workmen were sitting around a fire smoking; others were lying asleep under a shed, and I had but to

> "Look around and choose *my* ground,
> And take my rest."

I inquired for the major-domo, and was escorted to a mud house, where in the dark I heard a harsh voice, and presently by the light of a pine stick, saw an old and forbidding face corresponding, and by its side that of a young woman, so soft and sweet that it seemed to appear expressly for the sake of contrast; and these two were one. I was disposed to pity her; but the old major-domo was a noble fellow in heart, and she managed him so beautifully that he never suspected it. He was about going to bed, but sent men out to cut sacate, and both he and his wife were pleased that accident had brought me to their hut. The workmen sympathised in their humour, and we sat for two hours around a large table under the shed, with two candles sticking up in their own tallow. They could not comprehend that I had been to the top of the Volcano de Agua, and then ridden down to the coast merely to see the Pacific. A fine, open-faced young man had a great desire to travel, only he did not like to go away from home. I offered to take him with me and give him good wages. The subject was discussed aloud. It was an awful thing to go away from home, and among strangers, where no one would care for him. His house was the outside of the major-domo's hut, but his home was in the hearts of his friends, and perhaps some of them would be dead before he returned. The wife of the major-domo seemed a good spirit in tempering the hearts and conduct of these wild and half-naked men. I promised to give him money to pay his expenses home when he should wish to return, and he agreed to go with me. At three o'clock the old major-domo was shouting in my ears. I was not familiar with my own name with the don prefixed, and thought he had "waked up the wrong passenger." The courage of the young man who wished to travel failed him, and he did not make his appearance; in the expectation of his going my guide did not come, and I set out alone. Before daylight I passed for the third time through the village of San Pedro, and a little beyond overtook a bundle on horseback, which proved to be a boy and a woman, with one poncha over both.

The River Michatoyal was foaming and breaking in a long succession of rapids on our right, and we rode on together to San Cristoval. I rode up to the convent, pounced upon the cura at the witching hour of breakfast, mounted again, and rode around the base of the Volcano de Agua, with its cultivated fields and belt of forest and verdure to the top. Opposite was another volcano, its sides covered with immense forests. Between the two I passed a single trapiche belonging to a convent of Dominican friars, traversed a large and beautiful valley, passed hot springs, smoking for more than a mile along the road, and entered among the nopals or cochineal plantations of Amatitan. On both sides were high clay fences, and the nopals were more extensive than those of the Antigua, and more valuable, as, though only twenty-five miles from it, the climate is so different that they produce two crops in each season.

The road lay across a plain, with a high, precipitous, and verdant wall on the left. At a distance of a league we ascended a steep hill to the table-land of Guatimala. I regret that I cannot communicate to the reader the highest pleasure of my journey in Central America, that derived from the extraordinary beauty of scenery constantly changing. At the time I thought this the most delightful ride I had had in the country. On the way I overtook a man and his wife on horseback, he with a game-cock under his arm, and she with a guitar; a little boy was hidden away among bedding on a luggage-mule, and four lads were with them on foot, each with a game-cock wrapped in matting, with the head and tail only visible. They were going to Guatimala to pass the Christmas holydays, and with this respectable party I entered the gate of the city, on the eighth day after my departure. I found a letter from Mr. Catherwood, dated at Esquipulas, informing me that he had been robbed by his servant, taken ill, had left the ruins, gone to Don Gregorio's, and was then on his journey to Guatimala. My messenger had passed through Copan, and gone on he did not know where. I was in great distress, and resolved, after a day's rest, to set off in search of him.

I dressed myself and went to a party at Señor Zebadua's, formerly minister to England, where I surprised the Guatimaltecos by the tour I had made, and particularly by having come alone from Istapa. Here I met Mr. Chatfield, her Britannic majesty's consul-general, and Mr. Skinner, who had arrived during my absence. It was Christmas Eve, the night of El Nacimiento, or birth of Christ. At one end of the sala was a raised platform, with a green floor, and decorated with branches of pine and cypress, having birds sitting upon them, and looking-glass, and sandpaper, and figures of men and animals, representing a rural scene, with an arbour, and a wax doll in a cradle; in short, the grotto of Bethlehem and the infant Saviour. Always, at this season of the year, every house in Guatimala has its Nacimiento, according to the wealth and taste of the proprietor, and in time of peace the figure of the Saviour is adorned with family jewels, pearls, and precious stones, and at night every house is open, and the citizens, without acquaintance or invitation, or distinction of rank or persons, go from house to house visiting; and the week of El Nacimiento is the gayest in the year; but unfortunately, at this time it was observed only in form; the state of the city was too uncertain to permit general opening of houses and running in the streets at night. Carrera's soldiers might enter.

The party was small, but consisted of the élite of Guatimala, and commenced with supper, after which followed dancing, and, I am obliged to add, smoking. The room was badly lighted, and the company, from the precarious state of the country, not gay; but the dancing was kept up till twelve o'clock, when the ladies put on their mantillas, and we all went to the Cathedral, where were to be performed the imposing ceremonies of the Christmas Eve. The floor of the church was crowded with citizens, and a large concourse from the villages around. Mr. Savage accompanied me 'home,' and we did not get to bed till three o'clock in the morning.

The bells had done ringing, and Christmas mass had been said in all the churches before I awoke. In the afternoon was the first bull-fight of the season. My friend Vidaurre had called for me, and I was in the act of going to the Plaza de Toros, when there was a loud knock at the puerta cochèra, and in rode Mr. Catherwood, armed to the teeth, pale and thin, most happy at reaching Guatimala, but not half so happy as I was to see him. He was in advance of his luggage, but I dressed him up and carried him immediately to the Plaza de Toros.

It stands near the church of El Calvario, at the end of the Calle Real, in shape and form like the Roman amphitheatre, about 350 feet long, and 250 broad, capable of containing, as we supposed, about 8,000 people, at least one-fourth of the population of Guatimala, and was then crowded with spectators of both sexes and all classes, the best and the vilest in the city, but all conducting themselves with perfect propriety. We recognised several parties; in fact, the greater part of our Guatimala acquaintances were present.

The seats commenced about 10 feet above the area, with a corridor and open wooden fence in front to protect the spectators, astride which sat Carrera's disorderly soldiers to keep order. At one end, underneath the corridor, was a large door, through which the bull was to be let in. At the other end, separated by a partition from the part occupied by the rest of the spectators, was a large box, empty, formerly intended for the captain general and other principal officers of government, and now reserved for Carrera. Underneath was a military band, composed mostly of Indians. Notwithstanding the collection of people, and the expectation of an animating sport, there was no clapping or stamping, or other expression of impatience and anxiety for the performance to begin. At length Carrera entered the captain general's box, dressed in a badly-fitting blue military frock-coat, embroidered with gold, and attended by Monte Rosa and other officers, richly dressed, the alcalde and members of the municipality. All eyes were turned towards him, as when a king or emperor enters his box at the theatre in Europe. A year before he was hunted among the mountains, under a reward for his body, "dead or alive," and nine-tenths of those who now looked upon him would then have shut the city against him as a robber, murderer and outcast.

Soon after the picadores entered, eight in number, mounted, and each carrying a lance and a red poncha; they galloped round the area, and stopped with their lances opposite the door at which the bull was to enter. The door was pulled open by a padre, a great cattle-proprietor, who owned the bulls of the day, and the animal rushed out into the area, kicking up his heels as if in play, but at sight of the line of horsemen and lances turned about and ran back quicker than he entered. The padre's bull was an ox, and, like a sensible beast, would rather run than fight; but the door was closed upon him, and perforce he ran round the area, looking up to the spectators for mercy, and below for an outlet of escape. The horsemen followed, "prodding" him with their lances; and all around the area, men and boys on the fence threw barbed darts with ignited fireworks attached, which, sticking in his flesh and exploding on every part of his body, irritated him, and sometimes made him turn on his pursuers. The picadores led him on by flaring ponchas before him, and as he pressed them, the skill of the picadore consisted in throwing the poncha over his horns so as to blind him, and then fixing in his neck, just behind his jaw, a sort of balloon of fireworks; when this was done successfully it created shouts of applause. The government, in an excess of humanity, had forbidden the killing of bulls, and restricted the fight to worrying and torturing. Consequently, it was entirely different from the bullfight in Spain, and wanted even the exciting interest of a fierce struggle for life, and the chance of the picadore being gored to death or tossed over among the spectators. But, watching the earnest gaze of thousands, it was easy to imagine the intense excitement in a martial age, when gladiators fought in the arena before the nobility and beauty of Rome. One poor ox, after being tired out, was allowed to withdraw. Others followed, and went through the same round. All the padre's bulls were oxen. Sometimes a picadore on foot was chased to the fence under a general laugh of the spectators. After the last ox had run his rounds, the picadores withdrew, and men and boys jumped over into the arena in such numbers that they fairly hustled the ox. The noise and confusion, the flaring of coloured ponchas, the running and tumbling, attacking and retreating, and clouds of dust, made this the most stirring scene of any; but altogether it was a puerile exhibition, and the better classes regarded it merely as an occasion for meeting acquaintance.

In the evening we went to the theatre, which opened for the first time. A large building had been commenced in the city, but in one of the revolutions it had been demolished, and the work was abandoned. The performance was in the courtyard of a house. The stage was erected across one of the corners; the patio was the pit, and the corridor was divided by temporary partitions into boxes; the audience sent beforehand, or servants brought with them, their own seats. We had invitations to the box of Señor Vidaurre. Carrera was there, sitting on a bench a little elevated against the wall of the house, and at the right hand of Rivera Paz, the chief of the state. Some of his officers were with him in their showy uniforms, but he had laid his aside, and had on his black bombazet jacket and pantaloons, and was very unpretending in his deportment. The first piece was Saide, a tragedy. The company consisted entirely of Guatimaltecos, and their performance was very good. There was no change of scenery; when the curtain fell, all lighted cigars, ladies included, and, fortunately, there was an open court yard for the escape of the smoke. When the performance was over, the boxes waited till the pit was emptied. Special care had been taken in placing sentinels, and all went home quietly.

During the week there was an attempt at gaiety, but all was more or less blended with religious solemnities. One was that of the Novena, or term of nine days' praying to the Virgin. One lady, who was distinguished for the observance of this term, had an altar built across the whole end of the sala, with three steps, decorated with flowers, and a platform adorned with looking-glasses, pictures, and figures, in the centre of which was an image of the Virgin richly dressed, the whole ornamented in a way impossible for me to describe, but that may be imagined in a place where natural flowers are in the greatest profusion, and artificial ones made more perfect than in Europe, and where the ladies have extraordinary taste in the disposition of them. When I entered the gentlemen were in an ante-room, with hats, canes, and small swords; and in the sala the ladies, with female servants cleanly dressed, were on their knees praying; in front of the fairy altar was one who seemed a fairy herself; and while her lips moved, her bright eye was roving, and she looked more worthy of being kneeled to than the pretty image before her, and as if she thought so too.

In regard to my official business I was perfectly at a loss what to do. In Guatimala all were on one side; all said that there was no Federal Government; and Mr. Chatfield, the British consul-general, whose opinion I respected more, concurred, and had published a circular, denying its existence. But the Federal Government claimed to be in existence; and the bare suggestion of General Morazan's marching against Guatimala excited consternation. Several times there were rumours to that effect, and one that he had actually determined to do so; that not a single priest would be spared, and that the streets would run with blood. The boldest partisans trembled for their lives. Morazan had never been beaten; Carrera had always run before him; they had no faith in his being able to defend them, and could not defend themselves. At all events, I had as yet heard only one side, and did not consider myself justified in assuming that there was no government. I was bound to make "diligent search," and then I might return, in legal phrase, "cepi corpus," or "non est inventus," according to circumstances.

For this purpose I determined to go to San Salvador, which was formerly, and still claimed to be, the capital of the Confederation and the seat of the Federal Government, or, rather, to Cojutepeque, to which place the government had been then lately transferred, on account of earthquakes at San Salvador. This project was not without its difficulties. One Rascon, with an insurgent and predatory band, occupied an intervening district of country, acknowledging neither party, and fighting under his own flag. Mr. Chatfield and Mr. Skinner had come by sea, a circuitous route, to avoid him, and Captain de Nouvelle, master of a French ship lying at the port of San Salvador, arrived in Guatimala almost on a run, having ridden sixty miles the last day over a mountainous country, who reported horrible atrocities, and three men murdered near San Vicente, on their way to the fair at Esquipulas, and their faces so disfigured that they could not be recognised. Immediately on his arrival, he sent a courier to order his ship up to Istapa, merely to take him back, and save him from returning by land. I had signified my intention to the state government, which was dissatisfied with my going to San Salvador at all, but offered me an escort of soldiers, suggesting, however, that if we met any of Morazan's, there would certainly be a fight. This was not at all pleasant. I was loth to travel a third time the road to Istapa, but, under the circumstances, accepted Captain de Nouvelle's invitation to take a passage in his ship.

Meanwhile I passed my time in social visiting. In our own city the aristocracy is called by the diplomatic corps at Washington the aristocracy of streets. In Guatimala it is the aristocracy of houses, as certain families live in the houses built by their fathers at the foundation of the city, and they are really aristocratic old mansions. These families, by reason of certain monopolies of importation, acquired under the Spanish dominion immense wealth and rank as "merchant princes." Still they were excluded from all offices and all part in the government. At the time of the revolution one of these families was noble, with the rank of marquisate, and its head tore off the insignia of his rank, and joined the revolutionary party. Next in position to the officers of the crown, they thought that, emancipated from the yoke of Spain, they would have the government in their own hands; and so they had, but it was only for a short time. The principles of equal rights began to be understood, and they were put aside. For ten years they had been in obscurity, but accidentally they were again in power, and at the time of my visit ruled in social as well as political life. I do not wish to speak harshly of them, for they were the only people who constituted society; my intercourse was almost exclusively with them; my fair countrywoman was one of them; I am indebted to them for much kindness; and, besides, they are personally amiable; but I speak of them as public men. I did not sympathise with them in politics.

To me the position of the country seemed most critical, and from a cause which in all Spanish America had never operated before. At the time of the first invasion a few hundred Spaniards, by superior bravery and skill, and with more formidable arms, had conquered the whole Indian population. Naturally peaceable, and kept without arms, the conquered people had remained quiet and submissive during the three centuries of Spanish dominion. In the civil wars following the independence they had borne but a subordinate part; and down to the time of Carrera's rising they were entirely ignorant of their own physical strength. But this fearful discovery had now been made. The Indians constituted three-fourths of the inhabitants of Guatimala; were the hereditary owners of the soil; for the first time since they fell under the dominion of the whites, were organized and armed under a chief of their own, who chose for the moment to sustain the Central party. I did not sympathise with that party, for I believed that in their hatred of the Liberals they were courting a third power that might destroy them both; consorting with a wild animal which might at any moment turn and rend them in pieces I believed that they were playing upon the ignorance and prejudices of the Indians, and, through the priests, upon their religious fanaticism; amusing them with fêtes and Church ceremonies, persuading them that the Liberals aimed at a demolition of churches, destruction of the priests, and hurrying back the country into darkness; and in the general heaving of the elements there was not a man of nerve enough among them, with the influence of name and station, to rally round him the strong and honest men of the country, reorganize the shattered republic, and save them from the disgrace and danger of truckling to an ignorant uneducated Indian boy.

Such were my sentiments; of course I avoided expressing them; but because I did not denounce their opponents, some looked coldly upon me. With them political differences severed all ties. Our worst party abuse is moderate and mild compared with the terms in which they speak of each other. We seldom do more than call men ignorant, incompetent, dishonest, dishonourable, false, corrupt, subverters of the Constitution, and bought with British gold; there a political opponent is a robber, an assassin; it is praise to admit that he is not a bloodthirsty cut-throat. We complain that our ears are constantly offended, and our passions roused by angry political discussions. There it would have been delightful to hear a good, honest, hot, and angry political dispute. I travelled in every State, and I never heard one; for I never met two men together who differed in political opinions. Defeated partisans are shot, banished, run away, or get a moral lockjaw, and never dare express their opinions before one of the dominant party.* We have just passed through a violent political struggle; twenty millions of people have been divided almost man to man, friend against friend, neighbour against neighbour, brother against brother, and son against father; besides honest differences of opinion, ambition, want, and lust of power and office have roused passions sometimes to fierceness. Two millions of men highly excited have spoken out their thoughts and sentiments fearlessly and openly. They have all been counted, and the first rule in arithmetic has decided between them; and the defeated party are still permitted to live in the country; their wives and children are spared; nay, more, they may grumble in the streets, and hang out their banners of defiance, of continued and determined opposition: and, more than all, the pillars of the republic are not shaken! Among a million of disappointed men, never, with all the infirmities of human passion, has one breathed resistance to the Constitution and laws. The world has never presented such a spectacle, such a proof of the capacity of the people for self-government. Long may it continue! May the tongue wither that dares preach resistance to the ballot-boxes; and may the moral influence of our example reach our distracted sister republics, staying the sword of persecution in the hands of victors, and crushing the spirit of revolution in a defeated party.

January 1, 1840.—This day, so full of home associations—snow, and red noses, and blue lips out of doors, and blazing fires, and beauteous faces within—opened in Guatimala like a morning in spring. The sun seemed rejoicing in the beauty of the land it shone upon. The flowers were blooming in the courtyards, and the mountains, visible above the tops of the houses, were smiling in verdure. The

* This was written in 1840.

bells of thirty-eight churches and convents proclaimed the coming of another year. The shops were shut as on a Sunday; there was no market in the plaza. Gentlemen well dressed, and ladies in black mantas, were crossing it to attend grand mass in the Cathedral. Mozart's music swelled through the aisles. A priest in a strange tongue proclaimed morality, religion, and love of country. The floor of the church was thronged with whites, Mestitzoes, and Indians. On a high bench opposite the pulpit sat the chief of the state, and by his side Carrera, again dressed in his rich uniform. I leaned against a pillar opposite, and watched his face; and if I read him right, he had forgotten war and the stains of blood upon his hands, and his very soul was filled with fanatic enthusiasm; exactly as the priests would have him I did verily believe that he was honest in his impulses, and would do right if he knew how. They who undertake to guide him have a fearful responsibility. The service ended, a way was cleared through the crowd. Carrera, accompanied by the priests and the chief of the state, awkward in his movements, with his eyes fixed on the ground, or with furtive glances, as if ill at ease in being an object of so much attention, walked down the aisle. A thousand ferocious-looking soldiers were drawn up before the door. A wild burst of music greeted him, and the faces of the men glowed with devotion to their chief. A broad banner was unfurled, with stripes of black and red, a device of a death's head and legs in the centre, and on one side the words "Viva la religion!" and on the other, "Paz o muerte a los Liberales!" Carrera placed himself at their head, and with Rivera Paz by his side, and the fearful banner floating in the air, and wild and thrilling music, and the stillness of death around, they escorted the chief of the state to his house. How different from New Year's Day at home!

Fanatic as I knew the people to be in religion, and violent in political animosities, I did not believe that such an outrage would be countenanced as flaunting in the plaza of the capital a banner linking together the support of religion and the death or submission of the Liberal party. Afterwards, in a conversation with the chief of the state, I referred to this banner. He had not noticed it, but thought that the last clause was "Paz o muerte *a los qui no lo quieron*," "to those who do not wish it." This does not alter its atrocious character, and only adds to fanaticism what it takes from party spirit. I think, however, that I am right; for on the return of the soldiers to the plaza, Mr. C. and I followed it, till, as we thought, the standard-bearer contracted its folds expressly to hide it, and some of the officers looked at us so suspiciously that we withdrew.

CHAPTER XV.

HUNT FOR A GOVERNMENT—DIPLOMATIC DIFFICULTIES—DEPARTURE FROM GUATIMALA—LAKE OF AMATITAN—ATTACK OF FEVER AND AGUE—OVERO—ISTAPA—A FRENCH MERCHANT SHIP—PORT OF ACAJUTLA—ILLNESS—ZONZONATE—THE GOVERNMENT FOUND—VISIT TO THE VOLCANO OF IZALCO—COURSE OF THE ERUPTIONS—DESCENT FROM THE VOLCANO.

On Sunday, the fifth of January, I rose to set out in search of a government. Don Manuel Pavon, with his usual kindness, brought me a packet of letters of introduction to his friends in San Salvador. Mr. Catherwood intended to accompany me to the Pacific. We had not packed up, the muleteer had not made his appearance, and my passport had not been sent. Captain de Nouvelle waited till nine o'clock, and then went on in advance. In the midst of my confusion I received a visit from a distinguished ecclesiastic. The reverend prelate was surprised at my setting out on that day. I was about pleading my necessities as an excuse for travelling on the sabbath; but he relieved me by adding that there was to be a dinner-party, a bull-fight, and a play, and he wondered that I could resist such temptations. At eleven o'clock the muleteer came, with his mules, his wife, and a ragged little son; but owing to various delays we did not get off until the afternoon, and late as it was, diverged from the regular road for the purpose of passing by the Lake of Amatitan, but it was dark when we reached the top of the high range of mountains which bounds that beautiful water.

Looking down, it seemed like a gathering of fog in the bottom of a deep valley. The descent was by a rough zigzag path on the side of the mountain, very steep, and, in the extreme darkness, difficult and dangerous. We felt happy when we reached the bank of the lake, though still a little above it. The mountains rose round it like a wall, and cast over it a gloom deeper than the shade of night. We rode for some distance with the lake on our left, and a high and perpendicular mountain-side on our right. A cold wind had succeeded the intense heat of the day, and when we reached Amatitan I was perfectly chilled. We found the captain in the house he had indicated. It was nine o'clock, and, not having touched anything since seven in the morning, we were prepared to do justice to the supper he had provided for us.

To avoid the steep descent to the lake with the cargo-mules, our muleteer had picked up a guide for us on the road, and gone on himself direct; but, to our surprise, he had not yet arrived. While at supper we heard an uproar in the street, and a man ran in to tell us that a mob was murdering our muleteer. The captain, a frequent visitor to the country, said it was probably a general sword fight, and cautioned us against going out. While in the corridor, hesitating, the uproar was hurrying toward us; the gate burst open, and a crowd rushed in, dragging with them our muleteer, that respectable husband and father, with his machete drawn, and so tipsy that he could hardly stand, but wanting to fight all the world. With difficulty we got him entangled among some saddle-gear, when he dropped down, and, after vain efforts to rise, fell asleep.

I awoke the next morning with violent headache and pain in all my bones. Nevertheless, we started at daylight, and rode till five o'clock. The sun and heat increased the pain in my head, and for three hours before reaching Escuintla I was in great suffering. I avoided going to the corregidor's, for I knew that his sleeping apartment was open to all who came, and I wanted quiet; but I made a great mistake in stopping at the house of the captain's friend. He was the proprietor of an estanco, or distillery for making agua ardiente, and gave us a large room directly back of a store, and separated from it by a low board partition open over the top; and this store was constantly filled with noisy, wrangling, and drinking men and women. My bed was next to the partition, and we had eight or ten men in our room. All night I had a violent fever, and in the morning I was unable to move. Captain de Nouvelle regretted it, but he could not wait, as his ship was ordered to lie off and on without coming to anchor. Mr. Catherwood had me removed to a store-room filled with casks and demijohns, where, except from occasional entries to draw off liquor, I was quiet; but the odour was sickening.

In the afternoon the fever left me, and we rode to Masaya, a level and shady road of four leagues, and, to our surprise and great satisfaction, found the captain at the house at which I had stopped on my return from Istapa. He had advanced two leagues beyond, when he heard of a band of robbers at some distance further on, and returned to wait for company, sending, in the mean time, to Escuintla for a guard of soldiers. We afterwards learned that they were a body of exiles who had been expelled from Guatimala, and were crossing from Quezaltenango to San Salvador; but, being in desperate circumstances, they were dangerous persons to meet on the road.

The hut at which we stopped was hardly large enough for the family that occupied it, and our luggage, with two hammocks and a catré, drove them into a very small space. Crying children are said to be healthy; if so, the good woman of the house was blessed: besides this, a hen was hatching a brood of chickens under my head. During the night a party of soldiers entered the village, in pursuance of the captain's requisition, and passed on to clear the road. We started before daylight: but as the sun rose my fever returned, and at eleven o'clock, when we reached Overo, I could go no further.

I have before remarked that this hacienda is a great stopping-place from Istapa and the salt-works; and unfortunately for me, several parties of muleteers, in apprehension of the robbers, had joined together, and starting at midnight, had already finished their day's labour. In the afternoon a wild pig was hunted, which our muleteer, with my gun, killed. There was a great feast in cooking and eating him, and the noise racked my brain. Night brought no relief. Quiet was all I wanted, but that it seemed impossible to have; besides which, the rancho was more than usually abundant in fleas. All night I had violent fever. Mr. Catherwood, who, from not killing any one at Copan, had conceived a great opinion of his medical skill, gave me a powerful dose of medicine, and toward morning I fell asleep.

At daylight we started, and arrived at Istapa at nine o'clock. Captain de Nouvelle had not yet gone on board. Two French ships were then lying off the port: the Belle Poule and the Melanie, both from Bordeaux, the latter being the vessel of Captain de Nouvelle. He had accounts to arrange with the captain of the Belle Poule, and we started first for his vessel.

As I have before said, Istapa is an open roadstead, without bay, headland, rock, reef, or any protection whatever from the open sea. Generally the sea is, as its name imports, pacific, and the waves roll calmly to the shore; but in the smoothest times there is a breaker, and to pass this, as a part of the fixtures of the port, an anchor is dropped outside, with a buoy attached, and a long cable passing from the buoy is secured on shore. The longboat of the Melanie lay hard ashore, stern first, with a cable run through a groove in the bows, and passing through the skulling hole in the stern. She was filled with goods, and among them we took our seats. The mate sat in the stern, and, taking advantage of a wave that raised the bows, gave the order to haul. The wet rope whizzed past, and the boat moved till, with the receding wave, it struck heavily on the sand. Another wave and another haul, and she swung clear of the bottom; and meeting the coming, and hauling fast on the receding wave, in a few minutes we passed the breakers, the rope was thrown out of the groove, and the sailors took to their oars.

It was one of the most beautiful of those beautiful days on the Pacific. The great ocean was as calm as a lake; the freshness of the morning still rested upon the water, and already I felt revived. In a few minutes we reached the Belle Poule, one of the most beautiful ships that ever floated, and considered a model in the French commercial marine. The whole deck was covered with an awning, having a border trimmed with scarlet, and fluttering in the wind. The quarter-deck was raised, protected by a fanciful awning, furnished with settees, couches, and chairs, and on a brass railing in front sat two beautiful Peruvian parrots. The door of the cabin was high enough to admit a tall man without stooping. On each side were four cabins, and the stern was divided into two chambers for the captain and super-cargo, each with a window in it, and furnished with a bed (not a berth), a sofa, books, drawers, writing desk, everything necessary for luxurious living on ship-board; just the comforts with which one would like to circumnavigate the world. She was on a trading voyage from Bordeaux, with an assorted cargo of French goods; had touched at the ports in Peru, Chili, Panama, and Central America, and left at each place merchandise to be sold, and the proceeds to be invested in the products of the country; and was then bound to Mazatlan, on the coast of Mexico, whence she would return and pick up her cargo, and in two years return to Bordeaux. We had a déjeuner à la fourchette, abounding in Paris luxuries, with wines and café, as in Paris, to which, fortunately for the ships stores, I did not bring my accustomed vigour; and there was style in everything, even to the name of the steward, who was called the maître d'hôtel.

At two o'clock we went on board the Melanie. She was about the same size, and if we had not seen the Belle Poule first, we should have been delighted with her. The comfort and luxury of these "homes on the sea" were in striking contrast with the poverty and misery of the desolate shore. The captain of the Belle Poule came on board to dine, It was a pleasure to us to see the delight with which these two Bordeaux men and their crews met on this distant shore. Cape Horn, Peru, and Chili were the subjects of conversation, and we found on board a file of papers, which gave us the latest news from our friends in the Sandwich Islands. Mr. C. and the captain of the Belle Poule remained on board till we got under way. We bade them good-bye over the railing; the evening breeze filled our sails; for a few moments we saw them, a dark spot on the water; the wave sank, and we lost sight of them entirely.

I remained on deck but a short time. I was the only passenger, and the maître d'hôtel made me a bed with settees directly under the stern windows, but I could not sleep. Even with windows and doors wide open the cabin was excessively warm; the air was heated, and it was full of mosquitoes. The captain and mates slept on deck. I was advised not to do so, but at twelve o'clock I went out. It was bright starlight; the sails were flapping against the mast; the ocean was like a sheet of glass, and the coast dark and irregular, gloomy, and portentous with volcanoes. The great bear was almost upon me, the north star was lower than I had ever seen it before, and, like myself, seemed waning. A young sailor of the watch on deck spoke to me of the deceitfulness of the sea, of shipwrecks, of the wreck of an American vessel which he had fallen in with on his first cruise in the Pacific, and of his beautiful and beloved France. The freshness of the air was grateful; and while he was entertaining me, I stretched myself on a settee and fell asleep.

The next day I had a recurrence of fever, which continued upon me all day, and the captain put me under ship's discipline. In the morning the maître d'hôtel stood by me with cup and spoon,—" Monsieur, un vomitif;" and in the afternoon, "Monsieur, une purge." When we arrived at Acajutla I was unable to go ashore. As soon as we cast anchor the captain landed, and before leaving for Zonzonate engaged mules and men for me. The port of Acajutla is not quite so open as that of Istapa, having on the south a slight projecting headland of rock. In the offing were a goelette brig for a port in Peru, a Danish schooner for Guayaquil, and an English brig from London. All the afternoon I sat on the upper deck. Some of the sailors were asleep, and others playing cards. In sight were six volcanoes; one constantly emitting smoke, and another flames. At night the Volcano of Izalco seemed a steady ball of fire.

The next morning the mate took me ashore in the launch. The process was the same as at Istapa, and we were detained some time by the boat of the English vessel occupying the cable. As soon as we struck, a crowd of Indians, naked except a band of cotton cloth around the loins and passing between the legs, backed up against the side of the boat. I mounted the shoulders of one of them; as the wave receded he carried me several paces onward, then stopped and braced himself against the coming wave. I clung to his neck, but was fast sliding down his slippery sides, when he deposited me on the shore of San Salvador, called by the Indians "Cuscatlan," or the land of riches. Alvarado, on his voyage to Peru, was the first Spaniard who ever set foot upon this shore; and as I took special care to keep my feet from getting wet, I could not but think of the hardy frames as well as iron nerves of the conquerors of America.

The mate and sailors took leave of me and returned to the ship. I walked along the shore and up a steep hill. It was only eight o'clock, and already excessively hot. On the bank fronting the sea were the ruins of large warehouses, occupied as receptacles for merchandise under the Spanish dominion, when all the ports of America were closed against foreign vessels. In one corner of the ruined building was a sort of guard-room, where a few soldiers were eating tortillas, and one was cleaning his musket. Another apartment was occupied by the captain of the port, who told me that the mules engaged for me had got loose, and the muleteers were looking for them. Here I had the pleasure to meet Dr. Drivon, a gentleman from the island of St. Lucia, who had a large sugar hacienda a few leagues distant, and was at the port to superintend the disembarkation of machinery for a mill from the English brig. While waiting for the mules he conducted me to a hut where he had two Guayaquil hammocks hung, and feeling already the effect of my exertions, I took possession of one of them.

The woman of the rancho was a sort of ship's husband; and there being three vessels in port, the rancho was encumbered with vegetables, fruit, eggs, fowls, and ship's stores. It was close and hot, but very soon I required all the covering I could get. I had a violent ague, followed by a fever, in comparison with which all I had suffered before was nothing. I called for water till the old woman was tired of giving it to me, and went out and left me alone. I became light-headed, wild with pain, and wandered among the miserable huts with only the consciousness that my brain was scorching. I have an indistinct recollection of speaking English to some Indian women, begging them to get me a horse to ride to Zonzonate; of some laughing, others looking at me with pity, and others leading me out of the sun, and making me lie down under the shade of a tree. At three o'clock in the afternoon the mate came ashore again. I had changed my position, and he found me lying on my face asleep, and almost withered by the sun. He wanted to take me back on board the ship, but I begged him to procure mules and take me to Zonzonate, within the reach of medical assistance. It is hard to feel worse than I did when I mounted. I passed three hours of agony, scorched by the intense heat, and a little before dark arrived at Zonzonate, fortunate, as Dr. Drivón afterward told me, in not having suffered a stroke of the sun. Before entering the town and crossing the bridge over the Rio Grande, I met a gentleman well mounted, having a scarlet Peruvian pellon over his saddle, with whose appearance I was struck, and we exchanged low bows. This gentleman, as I afterward learned, was the government I was looking after.

I rode to the house of Captain de Nouvelle's brother, one of the largest in the place, where I had that comfort, seldom known in Central America, a room to myself, and everything else necessary. For several days I remained within doors. The first afternoon I went out I called upon Don Manuel de Aguilar, formerly chief of the State of Costa Rica, but about a year before driven out by a revolution and banished for life. At his house I met Don Diego Vigil, the vice-president of the republic, the same gentleman whom I had met on the bridge, and the only existing officer of the Federal Government.

His business at Zonzonate showed the wretched state of the country. He had come expressly to treat with Rascon, the head of the band which had prevented my coming from Guatimala by land. Chico Rascon, as he was familiarly called in Zonzonate, was of an old and respectable family, who had spent a large fortune in dissipation in Paris, and returning in desperate circumstances, had turned patriot. About six months before, he had made a descent upon Zonzonate, killed the garrison to a man, robbed the custom-house, and retreated to his hacienda. He was then on a visit in the town, publicly, by appointment with Señor Vigil, and demanded, as the price of disbanding his troops, a colonel's commission for himself, other commissions for some of his followers, and 4,000 dollars in money. Vigil assented to all except the 4,000 dollars in money, but offered instead the credit of the State of San Salvador, which Rascon agreed to accept. Papers were drawn up, and that afternoon was appointed for their execution; but, while Vigil was waiting for him, Rascon and his friends, without a word of notice, mounted their horses and rode out of town. The place was thrown into great excitement, and in the evening I saw the garrison busily engaged in barricading the plaza, in apprehension of another attack.

While these occurrences were taking place, I remained in Zonzonate recruiting. The town is situated on the banks of the Rio Grande, which is formed by almost innumerable springs, and in the Indian language its name means 400 springs of water. It stands in one of the richest districts of the rich State of San Salvador, and has its plaza, with streets at right angles, and white houses of one story, some of them very large; but it has borne its share of the calamities which have visited the unfortunate Republic. The best houses are deserted, and their owners in exile. There are seven costly churches, and but one cura.

I was unable to undertake any journey by land, and feeling the enervating effect of the climate, swung all day in a hammock. Fortunately, the proprietors of the brig which I had seen at Acajutla, bound for Peru, changed her destination, and determined to send her to Costa Rica, the southernmost state of the Confederacy. At the same time, a man offered as a servant, very highly recommended, and whose appearance I liked; and I resolved to have the benefit of the sea voyage, and, in returning by land, explore the canal route between the

Atlantic and Pacific by the Lake of Nicaragua, a thing which I had desired much, but despaired of being able to accomplish.

Before leaving I roused myself for an excursion. The window of my room opened upon the Volcano of Izalco. All day I heard at short intervals the eruptions of the burning mountain, and at night saw the column of flame bursting from the crater, and streams of fire rolling down its side. Fortunately, Mr. Blackwood, an Irish merchant, for many years resident in Peru, arrived, and agreed to accompany me. The next morning before five o'clock we were in the saddle. At the distance of a mile we forded the Rio Grande, here a wild river, and riding through a rich country, in half an hour reached the Indian village of Naguisal, a lovely spot, and literally a forest of fruits and flowers. Large trees were perfectly covered with red, and at every step we could pluck fruit. Interspersed among these beautiful trees were the miserable huts of Indians, and lying on the ground, or at some lazy work, were the miserable Indians themselves. Before us, at the extreme end of a long street, was the church of Izalco, standing out in strong relief against the base of the volcano, which at that moment, with a loud report like the rolling of thunder, threw in the air a column of black smoke and ashes, lighted by a single flash of flame.

With difficulty we obtained a guide, but he was so tipsy that he could scarcely guide himself along a straight street; and he would not go till the next day, as he said it was so late that we should be caught on the mountain at night, and that it was full of tigers. In the meantime the daughter of our host found another, and, stowing four green cocoa-nuts in his alforjas, we set out. Soon we came out upon an open plain, and, without a bush to obstruct the view, saw on our left the whole volcano from its base to its top. It rose from near the foot of a mountain, to a height perhaps of 6,000 feet, its sides brown and barren, and all around for miles the earth was covered with lava. Being in a state of eruption, it was impossible to ascend it, but behind it is a higher mountain, which commands a view of the burning crater. The whole volcano was in full sight, spouting into the air a column of black smoke and an immense body of stones, while the earth shook under our feet Crossing the plain, we commenced ascending the mountain. At eleven o'clock we sat down by the bank of a beautiful stream to breakfast. My companion had made abundant provision, and for the first time since I left Guatimala I felt the keenness of returning appetite. In half an hour we mounted, and soon after twelve o'clock entered the woods, having a very steep ascent by a faint path, which we soon lost altogether. Our guide changed his direction several times, and at length got lost, tied his horse, and left us to wait while he searched the way. We knew that we were near the volcano, for the explosions sounded like the deep mutterings of dreadful thunder. Shut up as we were in the woods, these reports were awful. Our horses snorted with terror, and the mountain quaked beneath our feet. Our guide returned, and in a few minutes we came out suddenly upon an open point, higher than the top of the volcano, commanding a view of the interior of the crater, and so near it that we saw the huge stones as they separated in the air, and fell pattering around the sides of the volcano. In a few minutes our clothes were white with ashes, which fell around us with a noise like the sprinkling of rain.

The crater had three orifices, one of which was inactive; another emitted constantly a rich blue smoke; and after a report, deep in the huge throat of the third, appeared a light blue vapour, and then a mass of thick black smoke, whirling and struggling out in enormous wreaths, and rising in a dark majestic column, lighted for a moment by a sheet of flame; and when the smoke dispersed, the atmosphere was darkened by a shower of stones and ashes. This over, a moment of stillness followed, and then another report and eruption, and these continued regularly, at intervals, as our guide said, of exactly five minutes, and really he was not much out of the way. The sight was fearfully grand. We refreshed ourselves with a draught of cocoa-nut milk, and thought how this grandeur would be heightened when the stillness and darkness of night were interrupted by the noise and flame, and forthwith resolved to sleep upon the mountain.

The cura of Zonzonate, still in the vigour of life, told me that he remembered when the ground on which this volcano stands had nothing to distinguish it from any other spot around. In 1798 a small orifice was discovered puffing out small quantities of dust and pebbles. He was then living at Izalco, and, as a boy, was in the habit of going to look at it; and he had watched it, and marked its increase from year to year, until it had grown into what it is now. Captain de Nouvelle told me he could observe from the sea, that it had grown greatly within the last two years. Two years before, its light could not be seen at night on the other side of the mountain on which I stood. Night and day it forces up stones from the bowels of the earth, spouts them into the air, and receives them upon its sides. Every day it is increasing, and probably it will continue to do so until the inward fires die, or by some violent convulsion the whole is rent to atoms.

Old travellers are not precluded occasional bursts of enthusiasm, but they cannot keep it up long. In about an hour we began to be critical and even captious. Some eruptions were better than others, and some were comparatively small affairs. In this frame of mind we summed up our want of comforts for passing the night on the mountain, and determined to return. Mr. Blackwood and I thought that we could avoid the circuit of the mountain, by descending directly to the base of the volcano, and crossing it, reach the camino real; but our guide said it was a tempting of Providence, and refused to accompany us. We had a very steep descent on foot, and in some places our horses slid down on their haunches. An immense bed of lava, stopped in its rolling course by the side of the mountain, filled up the wide space between us and the base of the volcano. We stepped directly upon this black and frightful bed, but we had great difficulty in making our horses follow. The lava lay in rolls as irregular as the waves of the sea, sharp, rough, and with huge chasms, difficult for us, and dangerous for the horses. With great labour we dragged them to the base and around the side of the volcano. Massive stones, hurled into the air, fell and rolled down the sides, so near, that we dared not venture further. We were afraid of breaking our horses' legs in the holes into which they were constantly falling, and turned back. On the lofty point from which we had looked down into the crater of the volcano sat our guide, gazing, and, as we could imagine, laughing at us. We toiled back across the bed of lava and up the side of the mountain, and when we reached the top, both my horse and I were almost exhausted. Fortunately, the road home was down hill. It was long after dark when we passed the foot of the mountain and came out upon the plain. Every burst of the volcano sent forth a pillar of fire; in four places were steady fires, and in one a stream of fire was rolling down its side. At eleven o'clock we reached Zonzonate, besides toiling around the base of the volcano, having ridden upwards of fifty miles; and such had been the interest of the day's work, that, though my first effort, I never suffered from it.

The arrangements for my voyage down the Pacific were soon made. The servant to whom I referred was a native of Costa Rica, then on his way home, after a long absence, with a cargo of merchandise belonging to himself. He was a tall, good-looking fellow, dressed in a Guatimala jacket or coton, a pair of Mexican leather trousers, with buttons down the sides, and a steeple-crowned, broad-brimmed, drab wool hat, altogether far superior to any servant I saw in the country; and I think if it had not been for him I should not have undertaken the journey. The reader will perhaps be shocked to hear that his name was *Jesus*, pronounced in Spanish 'Hezoos, by which latter appellation, to avoid what might be considered profanity, I shall hereafter call him.

CHAPTER XVI.

SICKNESS AND MUTINY—ILLNESS OF CAPTAIN JAY—CRITICAL SITUATION—ROUGH NURSING—DOLPHINS — SUCCESSION OF VOLCANOES — GULF OF NICOTA — HARBOUR OF CALDERA — ANOTHER PATIENT—HACIENDA OF SAN FELIPPE—MOUNTAIN OF AGUACATE—"ZILLENTHAL PATENT SELF-ACTING COLD AMALGAMATION MACHINE"—GOLD MINES—VIEW FROM THE MOUNTAIN TOP.

On Monday, the twenty-second of January, two hours before daylight, we started for the port. 'Hezoos led the way, carrying before him all my luggage, rolled up in a baquette, being simply a cowhide, after the fashion of the country. At daylight we heard behind us the clattering of horses' hoofs, and Don Manuel de Aguila, with his two sons, overtook us. Before the freshness of the morning was past, we reached the port, and rode up to the old hut, which I had hoped never to see again. The hammock was swinging in the same place. The miserable rancho seemed destined to be the abode of sickness. In one corner lay Señor D'Yriarte, my captain, exhausted by a night of fever, and unable to sail that day.

Dr. Drivon was again at the port. He had not yet disembarked his machinery: in fact, the work was suspended by a mutiny on board the English brig, the ringleader of which, as the doctor complained to me, was an American. I passed the day on the seashore. In one place, a little above high-water mark, almost washed by the waves, were rude wooden crosses, marking the graves of unhappy sailors who had died far from their homes. Returning, I found at the hut Captain Jay, of the English brig, who also complained to me of the American sailor. The captain was a young man, making his first voyage as master; his wife, whom he had married a week before sailing, accompanied him. He had had a disastrous voyage of eight months from London; in doubling Cape Horn, his crew were all frostbitten, and his spars carried away. With only one man on deck, he had worked up to Guayaquil, where he incurred great loss of time and money in making repairs, and shipped an entirely new crew. At Acajutla, he found that his boats were not sufficient to land the doctor's machinery, and was obliged to wait until a raft could be constructed. In the meantime his crew mutinied, and part of them refused to work. His wife was then at the doctor's hacienda; and I noticed that, while writing her a note with pencil, his sunburned face was pale, and large drops of perspiration stood on his forehead. Soon after he threw himself into the hammock, and, as I thought, fell asleep; but in a few minutes I saw the hammock shake, and, remembering my own shaking there, thought it was at its old tricks of giving people the fever and ague; but very soon I saw that the poor captain was in convulsions. Excepting Captain D'Yriarte, who was lying against the wall perfectly helpless, I was the only man in the hut; and as there was danger of his throwing himself out of the hammock, I endeavoured to hold him in; but with one convulsive effort he threw me to the other side of the hut, and hung over the side of the hammock, with one hand entangled in the cords, and his head almost touching the ground. The old woman said that the devil had taken possession of him, and ran out of doors, screaming. Fortunately, this brought in a man whom I had not seen before, Mr. Warburton,* an engineer, who had come out to set up the machinery, and who was himself a machine of many horsepower, having a pair of shoulders that seemed constructed expressly for holding men in convulsions. At first he was so shocked that he did not know what to do. I told him that the captain was to be held, whereupon, opening his powerful arms, he closed them around the captain's with the force of a hydraulic press, turning the legs over to me. These legs were a pair of the sturdiest that ever supported a human body; and I verily believe that if the feet had once touched my ribs, they would have sent me through the wall of the hut. Watching my opportunity, I wound the hammock around his legs, and my arms around the hammock. In the meantime he broke lose from Mr. Warburton's hug, who, taking the hint from me, doubled his part in with the folds of the hammock, and gave his clinch from the outside. The captain struggled, and, worming like a gigantic snake, slipped his head out of the top of the hammock, and twisted the cords around his neck, so that we were afraid of his strangling himself. We were in utter despair, when two of his sailors rushed in, who, being at home with ropes, extricated his head, shoved him back into the hammock, wrapped it around him as before, and I withdrew, completely exhausted.

The two recruits were Tom, a regular tar of about forty, and the cook, a black man, and particular friend of Tom, who called him "Darkey." Tom undertook the whole direction of securing the captain; and, although Dr. Drivon and several Indians came in, Tom's voice was the only one heard, and addressed only to "Darkey".— "Stand by his legs, Darkey!"—"Hold fast, Darkey!"—"Steady, Darkey!" but all together could not hold him. Turning on his face,

* Died at Mazatlan about six months afterwards.

and doubling himself inside, he braced his back, and drove both legs through the hammock, striking his feet violently against the ground; his whole body passed through. His struggles were dreadful. Suddenly the mass of bodies on the floor rolled against Captain D'Yriarte's bed, which broke down with a crash, and, with a fever upon him, he was obliged to scramble out of the way. In the interval of one of the most violent struggles, we heard a strange idiotic noise, which seemed like an attempt to crow. The Indians who crowded the hut laughed; and Dr. Drivon was so indignant at their heartlessness, that he seized a club and drove them all out of doors. An old naked African, who had been a slave at Balize, and had lost his own language without acquiring much of any other, returned with a bunch of feathers, which he wished to stick in the captain's nose and set fire to, saying it was the remedy of his country; but the doctor showed him his stick, and he retreated.

The convulsions continued for three hours, during which time the doctor considered the captain's situation very critical. The old woman persisted that the devil was in him, and would not give him up, and that he must die; and I could not but think of his young wife, who was sleeping a few miles off, unconscious of the calamity that threatened her. The fit was brought on, as the doctor said, by anxiety and distress of mind occasioned by his unfortunate voyage, and particularly by the mutiny of his crew. At eleven o'clock he fell asleep, and now we learned the cause of the strange noise which had affected us so unpleasantly. Tom was just preparing to go on board the vessel, when the African ran down to the shore, and told him that the captain was at the hut drunk. Tom, being himself in that state, felt that it was his duty to look after the captain; but he had just bought a parrot, for which he had paid a dollar, and, afraid to trust him in other hands, hauled his baggy shirt a foot more out of his trousers, and thrust the parrot into his bosom, almost smothering it with his neckcloth. The parrot, indignant at this confinement, was driving his beak constantly into Tom's breast, which was scarified and covered with blood; and once, when Tom thought it was going too far, he put his hand inside and pinched it, which produced the extraordinary sounds we had heard.

In a little while Tom and Darkey got the Indians to relieve them, and went out to drink the captain's health. On their return they took their places on the ground, one on each side of their commander. I threw myself into the broken hammock; and Dr. Drivon, charging them, if the captain awoke, not to say anything that could agitate him, went off to another hut.

It was not long before the captain, raising his head, called out, "What the devil are you doing with my legs?" which was answered by Tom's steady cry, "Hold on, Darkey?" Darkey and an Indian were holding the captain's legs, two Indians his arms, and Tom was spread over his body. The captain looked perfectly sensible, and utterly amazed at being pinned to the ground. "Where am I?" said he. Tom and Darkey had agreed not to tell him what had happened; but, after the most extraordinary lying on the part of Tom, while the captain was looking at him and us in utter amazement, the poor fellow became so entangled, that, swearing the doctor might stay and tell his own stories, he began where he and Darkey came in, and found the captain kicking in the hammock; and the captain was given to understand that if it had not been for him and Darkey he would have kicked his own brains out. I relieved Tom's story from some obscurity, and a general and noisy conversation followed, which was cut short by poor Captain D'Yriarte, who had not had a wink of sleep all night, and begged us to give him a chance.

The next evening I embarked on board "La Cosmopolita," a small goelette brig, and my first night on board was not particularly agreeable. I was the only cabin passenger; but, besides the bugs that always infest an old vessel, I had in my berth mosquitoes, spiders, ants, and cockroaches. Yet there is no part of my tour upon which I look back with so much quiet satisfaction as this voyage on the Pacific. I had on board Gil Blas and Don Quixote in the original, and all day I sat under an awning, my attention divided between them and the great range of gigantic volcanoes which stud the coast. Before this became tedious we reached the Gulf of Papajayo, the only outlet by which the winds of the Atlantic pass over to the Pacific. The dolphin, the most beautiful fish that swims, played under our bows and stern, and accompanied us slowly alongside. But the sailors had no respect for his golden back. The mate, a murderous young Frenchman, stood for hours with a harpoon in his hand, drove it into several, and at length brought one on board. The king of the sea seemed conscious of his fallen state; his beautiful colours faded, and he became spotted, and at last heavy and lustreless, like any other dead fish.

We passed in regular succession the volcanoes of San Salvador, San Vicente, San Miguel, Telega, Momotombo, Managua, Nindiri, Masaya, and Nicaragua, each one a noble spectacle, and all together forming a chain with which no other in the world can be compared; indeed, this coast has been described as "bristling with volcanic cones." For two days we lay with sails flapping in sight of Cape Blanco, the upper headland of the Gulf of Nicoya. On the afternoon of the 31st we entered the gulf. On a line with the point of the cape was an island of rock, with high, bare, and precipitous sides, and the top covered with verdure. It was about sunset; for nearly an hour the sky and sea seemed blazing with the reflection of the departing luminary, and the island of rocks seemed like a fortress with turrets. It was a glorious farewell view. I had pased my last night on the Pacific, and the highlands of the Gulf of Nicoya closed around us.

Early in the morning we had the tide in our favour, and very soon leaving the main body of the gulf, turned off to the right, and entered a beautiful little cove, forming the harbour of Caldera. In front was the range of mountains of Aguacate, on the left the old port of Pont Arenas, and on the right the volcano of San Pablo. On the shore was a long low house set upon piles, with a tile roof, and near it were three or four thatched huts and two canoes. We anchored in front of the houses, and apparently without exciting the attention of a soul on shore.

All the ports of Central America on the Pacific are unhealthy, but this was considered deadly. I had entered without apprehension cities where the plague was raging, but here, as I looked ashore, there was a deathlike stillness that was startling. To spare me the necessity of sleeping at the port, the captain sent the boat ashore with my servant, to procure mules with which I could proceed immediately to a hacienda two leagues beyond.

In the afternoon the captain took me ashore. At the first house we saw two candles lighted to burn at the body of a dead man. All whom we saw were ill, and all complained that the place was fatal to human life. In fact, it was almost deserted; and, notwithstanding its advantages as a port, government, a few days afterward, issued an order for breaking it up, and removing back to the old port of Pont Arenas. The captain was still suffering from fever and ague, and would not on any account remain after dark. I was so rejoiced to find myself on shore, that if I had met a death's head at every step it would hardly have turned me back.

Determined not to lose sight of my friend, the captain of the port, with my luggage at my heels I walked down the beach for the custom-house. It was a frame building, about 40 feet long, and stood at a little distance above high-water mark, on piles about 6 feet above ground. It was the gathering-place of different persons in the employ of the government, civil and military, and of two or three women employed by them. The military force consisted of the captain of the port and the soldier who boarded us, so that I had not much fear of being sent back at the point of the bayonet. My host gave me a bedstead, with a bull's hide for a bed. It was a warm night, and I placed it opposite an open door, and looked out upon the water of the gulf. The waves were breaking gently upon the shore, and it was beautiful to see the Cosmopolita riding quietly at her anchor, without even 'Hezoos or the luggage in her.

At two o'clock in the morning we rose, and before three we started. The tide was low, and for some distance we rode along the shore by moonlight. At daylight we overtook the courier sent to give advice of my coming; in an hour crossed the river of Jesus Maria; and at seven o'clock stopped to breakfast at the hacienda of the same name.

While breakfasting, the woman of the house told me of a sick daughter, asked me for remedios, and finally requested me to go in and see her. The door opened from the shed, and all the apertures in the room were carefully closed, so as to exclude even a breath of air. The invalid lay in a bed in one corner, with a cotton covering over it like a mosquito-netting, but lower, and pinned close all around; and when the mother raised the covering, I encountered a body of hot and unwholesome air that almost overcame me. The poor girl lay on her back, with a cotton sheet wound tightly around her body; and already she seemed like one laid out for burial. She was not more than eighteen; the fever had just left her, her eye still sparkled, but her face was pale, and covered with spots, seams, and creases of dirt. She was suffering from intermitting fever, that scourge which breaks down the constitution and carries to the grave thousands of the inhabitants of Central America; and, according to the obstinate prejudice of the country, her face had not been washed for more than two months! I had often been disgusted with the long beards and unwashed faces of fever and ague subjects, and the ignorance and prejudice of the people on medical subjects; in illustration of which Dr. Drivon told me of a case of practice by an old quack woman, who directed her patient, a rich cattle proprietor, to be extended on the ground naked every morning, and a bullock to be slaughtered over him, so that the blood could run warm upon his body. The man submitted to the operation more than a hundred times, and was bathed with the blood of more than a hundred bullocks; afterward he underwent a much more disgusting process, and, strange to say, he lived.

But to return: in general my medical practice was confined to men, and with them I considered myself a powerful practitioner. I did not like prescribing for women; and in this case I struck at all the prejudices of the country, and cheapened my medical skill by directing, first, that the poor girl's face should be washed; but I saved myself somewhat by making a strong point that it should be washed with warm water. Whether they thanked me or not I do not know, but I had my reward, for I saw a lovely face, and long afterward I remembered the touching expression of her eyes, as she turned toward me, and listened to the advice I gave her mother.

At ten we resumed our journey. The road had been much improved lately, but the ascent was steep, wild, and rugged. As we toiled up a ravine, we heard before us a loud noise, that sounded like distant thunder, but regular and continued, and becoming louder as we advanced; and at length we came out on a small clearing, and saw on the side of the mountain a neat frame building of two stories, with a light and graceful balcony in front; and alongside was the thundering machine which had startled us by its noise. Strangers from the other side of the Atlantic were piercing the sides of the mountain, and pounding its stones into dust to search for gold. The whole range, the very ground which our horses spurned with their hoofs, contained that treasure for which man forsakes kindred and country.

I rode up to the house and introduced myself to Don Juan Bardh, the superintendent, a German from Friesburg. It was about two o'clock, and excessively hot. The house was furnished with chairs, sofa, and books, and had in my eyes a delightful appearance; but the view without was more so. The stream which turned the immense pounding-machine had made the spot, from time immemorial, a descansadera, or resting-place for muleteers. All around were mountains, and directly in front one rose to a great height, receding, and covered to the top with trees.

Don Juan Bardh had been superintendent of the Quebrada del Ingenio for about three years. The Company which he represented was called the Anglo Costa Rican Economical Mining Company. It had been in operation these three years without losing anything, which was considered doing so well that it had increased its capital, and was about continuing on a larger scale. The machine, which had just been set up, was a new German patent, called a *Machine for extracting Gold by the Zillenthal Patent Self-acting Cold Amalgamation Process* (I believe that I have omitted nothing), and its great value was, that it required no preliminary process, but by one continued and simple operation extracted the gold from the stone. It was an immense wheel of cast-iron, by which the stone, as it came from the mountain, was pounded into powder; this passed into troughs filled with water, and from them into a reservoir containing vases, where the gold detached itself from the other particles, and combined with the quicksilver with which the vases were provided.

There were several mines under Don Juan's charge, and after

dinner he accompanied me to that of Corrallio, which was the largest, and, fortunately, lay on my road. After a hot ride of half an hour, ascending through thick woods, we reached the spot.

According to the opinion of the few geologists who have visited that country, immense wealth lies buried in the mountain of Aguacate; and so far from being hidden, the proprietors say, its places are so well marked that all who search may find. The lodes or mineral veins run regularly north and south, in ranges of greenstone porphyry, with strata of basaltic porphyry, and average about 3 feet in width. In some places side-cuts or lateral excavations are made from east to west, and in others shafts are sunk until they strike the vein. The first opening we visited was a side-cut 4 feet wide, and penetrating 240 feet before it struck the lode; but it was so full of water that we did not enter. Above it was another cut, and higher still a shaft was sunk. We descended the shaft by a ladder made of the trunk of a tree, with notches cut in it, until we reached the vein, and followed it with a candle as far as it was worked. It was about a yard wide, and the sides glittered—but it was not with gold; they were of quartz and feldspar, impregnated with sulphuret of iron, and gold in such small particles as to be invisible to the naked eye. The most prominent objects in these repositories of wealth were naked workmen with pickaxes, bending and sweating under heavy sacks of stones.

It was late in the afternoon when I came out of the shaft. Don Juan conducted me by a steep path up the side of the mountain, to a small table-land, on which was a large building occupied by miners. The view was magnificent: below was an immense ravine; above, perched on a point, like an eagle's nest, the house of another superintendent; and on the opposite side the great range of the mountains of Candelaria. I waited till my mules came up, and with many thanks for his kindness, bade Don Juan farewell.

As we continued ascending, every moment the view became more grand and beautiful; and suddenly, from a height of 6,000 feet, I looked down upon the Pacific, the Gulf of Nicoya, and, sitting like a bird upon the water, our brig, La Cosmopolita. And here, on the very highest points, in the wildest and most beautiful spots that ever men chose for their abodes, were the huts of the miners. The sun touched the sea, lighted up the surface of the water, and softened the rugged mountains; it was the most beautiful scene I ever saw, and this loveliest view was the last; for suddenly it became dark, and very soon the darkest night I ever knew came on. As we descended, the woods were so thick that even in the daytime they shut out the light, and in some places the road was cut through steep hills higher than our heads, and roofed over by the dense foliage. 'Hezoos was before me, with a white hat and jacket, and had a white dog running by his side, but I could not see the outline of his figure. The road was steep but good, and I did not pretend to direct the mule. In one of the darkest passages 'Hezoos stopped, and, with a voice that made the woods ring, cried out, "A lion, a lion!" I was startled, but he dismounted and lighted a cigar. This was cool, I thought; but he relieved me by telling me that the lion was a different animal from the roarer of the African desert, small, frightened by a shout, and only ate children. Long as it seemed, our whole descent did not occupy three hours, and at ten o'clock we reached the house in the Boca de la Montagna. It was shut, and all were asleep; but we knocked hard, and a man opened the door, and, before we could ask any questions, disappeared. Once inside, however, we made noise enough to wake everybody, and got corn for the mules, and a light. There was a large room, open to all comers, with three bedsteads, all occupied, and two men were sleeping on the floor. The occupant of one of the beds, after eyeing me a few moments, vacated it, and I took his place. The reader must not suppose that I am perfectly unscrupulous; he took all his bedclothes, viz. his chamarro, with him. The bed and all its furniture consisted of an untanned bull's hide.

CHAPTER XVII.

LA GARITA—ALAJUELA—A FRIENDLY PEOPLE—HEREDIA—RIO SEGUNDO—COFFEE PLANTA-
TIONS OF SAN JOSE—THE SACRAMENT FOR THE DYING—A HAPPY MEETING—TRAVELLING
EMBARRASSMENTS—QUARTERS IN A CONVENT—SEÑOR CARILLO, CHIEF OF STATE—VICISSI-
TUDES OF FORTUNE—VISIT TO CARTAGO—TRES RIOS—AN UNEXPECTED MEETING—ASCENT OF
THE VOLCANO OF CARTAGO—THE CRATER—VIEW OF THE TWO SEAS—DESCENT—STROLL
THROUGH CARTAGO—A BURIAL—ANOTHER ATTACK OF FEVER AND AGUE—A VAGABOND—
CULTIVATION OF COFFEE.

THE next morning we ascended by a steep road to the top of a ravine, where a long house stood across the road, so as to prevent all passing except directly through it. It is called La Garita, and commands the road from the port to the capital. Officers are stationed here to take an account of merchandise, and to examine passports. The one then in command had lost an arm in the service of his country, *i. e.* in a battle between his own town and another fifteen miles off, and the place was given to him as a reward for his patriotic services.

At the entry of Alajuela, I stopped to inquire for one bearing a name immortal in the history of the Spanish conquest. It was the name of Alvarado. Whether he was a descendant or not I do not know, nor did he; and strange to say, though I met several bearing that name, not one attempted to trace his lineage to the conqueror. Don Ramon Alvarado, however, was recommended to me for qualities which allied him in character with his great namesake. He was the courier of the English Mining Company for Serapequea and the River St. Juan, one of the wildest roads in all Central America.

Next to the advantage of the sea voyage, my principal object in leaving Zonzonate was to acquire some information in regard to the canal route between the Atlantic and Pacific by means of the Lake of Nicaragua and the River San Juan, and my business with Alvarado was to secure him as a guide to the port of San Juan. In half an hour all these arrangements were made, the day fixed, and half the contract-money paid.

There are four cities in Costa Rica, all of which lie within the space of fifteen leagues; yet each has a different climate and different productions. Including the suburbs, Alajuela contains a population of about 10,000. The plaza was beautifully situated, and the church, the cabildo, and the houses fronting it were handsome. The latter were long and low, with broad piazzas and large windows, having balconies made of wooden bars. It was Sunday, and the inhabitants, cleanly dressed, were sitting on the piazzas, or, with doors wide open, reclining in hammocks, or on high-backed wooden settees inside. The women were dressed like ladies, and some were handsome, and all white. A respectable-looking old man, standing in the door of one of the best houses, called out "Amigo," "friend," and asked us who we were, whence we came, and whither we were going, recommending us to God at parting; and all along the street we were accosted in the same friendly spirit.

At a distance of three leagues we passed through Heredia without dismounting. I had ridden all day with a feeling of extraordinary satisfaction; and if such were my feelings, what must have been those of 'Hezoos? He was returning to his country, with his love for it increased by absence and hardship away from home. All the way he met old acquaintance and friends. He was a good-looking fellow, dashingly dressed, and wore a basket-hilted Peruvian sword more than six feet long. Behind him was strapped a valise of scarlet cloth, with black borders, part of the uniform of a Peruvian soldier. It would have been curious to remember how many times he told his story; of military service and two battles in Peru; of impressment for the navy and desertion; a voyage to Mexico, and his return to Guatimala by land; and always concluded by inquiring about his wife, from whom he had not heard since he left home, "la pobra" being regularly his last words. As we approached his home, his tenderness for la pobra increased. He could not procure any direct intelligence of her; but one good-natured friend suggested that she had probably married some one else, and that he would only disturb the peace of the family by his return.

On the top of the ravine we came upon a large table-land covered with the rich coffee-plantations of San José. It was laid out into squares of 200 feet, enclosed by living fences of trees bearing flowers, with roads 60 feet wide; and, except the small horsepath, the roads, had a sod of unbroken green. The deep green of the coffee-plantations, the sward of the roads, and the vistas through the trees at all the cross-roads, were lovely; at a distance on each side were mountains, and in front, rising above all, was the great Volcano of Cartago. It was about the same hour as when, the day before, from the top of the mountain of Aguacate, I had looked down into great ravines and over the tops of high mountains, and seen the Pacific Ocean. This was as soft as that was wild; and it addressed itself to other senses than the sight, for it was not, like the rest of Central America, retrograding and going to ruin, but smiling as the reward of industry. Seven years before the whole plain was an open waste.

At the end of this table-land we saw San José on a plain below us. On the top of the hill we passed a house with an arch of flowers before the door, indicating that within lay one waiting to receive the last sacrament before going to his final account in another world. Descending, we saw at a distance a long procession, headed by a cross with the figure of the Saviour crucified. It approached with the music of violins and a loud chorus of voices, and was escorting the priest to the house of the dying man. As it approached, horsemen pulled off their hats and pedestrians fell on their knees. We met it near a narrow bridge at the foot of the hill. The sun was low, but its last rays were scorching to the naked head. The priest was carried in a sedan chair. We waited till he passed, and taking advantage of a break in the procession, crossed the bridge, passed a long file of men, and longer of women, and being some distance ahead, I put on my hat. A fanatic fellow, with a scowl on his face, cried out, "Quita el sombrero," "take off your hat." I answered by spurring my horse, and at the same moment the whole procession was thrown into confusion. A woman darted from the line, and 'Hezoos sprang from his horse and caught her in his arms, and hugged and kissed her as much as decency in the public streets would allow. To my great surprise, the woman was only his cousin, and she told him that his wife, who was the principal milliner in the place, was on before in the procession. 'Hezoos was beside himself; ran back, returned, caught his horse, and dragged the beast after him; then mounting and spurring, begged me to hurry on and let him go back to his wife. Entering the town, we passed a respectable-looking house, where four or five well-dressed women were sitting on the piazza. They screamed, 'Hezoos drove his mule up the steps, and throwing himself off, embraced them all around. After a few hurried words, he embraced them all over again. Some male friends attempted to haul him off, but he returned to the women. In fact, the poor fellow seemed beside himself, though I could not but observe that there was method in his madness; for, after two rounds with the very respectable old ladies, he abandoned them, and dragging forward a very pretty young girl with his arms around her waist, and kissing her every moment, told me she was the apprentice of his wife; and though at every kiss he asked her questions about his wife, he did not wait for answers, and the kisses were repeated faster than the questions. During all this time I sat on my horse looking on. Doubtless it was very pleasant for him, but I began to be impatient; seeing which, he tore himself away, mounted, and, accompanied by half-a-dozen of his friends, he again led the way. As we advanced his friends increased. It was rather vexatious, but I could not disturb him in the sweetest pleasures in life,—the welcome of friends after a long absence. Crossing the plaza, two or three soldiers of his old company, leaning on the railing of the quartel, cried out "companero," and, with the sergeant at their head, passed over and joined us. We crossed the plaza with fifteen or twenty in our suite, or rather in his suite, some of whom, particularly the sergeant, in compliment to him, were civil to me.

While he had so many friends to welcome him, I had none. In fact, I did not know where I should sleep that night. 'Hezoos had told me that there was an old chapiton, *i.e.* a person from Spain, in whose house I could have a room to myself, and pay for it; but, unfortunately, time had made its changes, and the old Spaniard had been gone so long that the occupants of his house did not know what had become of him. I had counted upon him with so much certainty that I had not taken out my letters of recommendation, and did not even know the names of the persons to whom they were addressed. The cura was at his hacienda, and his house shut up; a padre who had been in the United States was sick, and could not receive any one; my servant's friends all recommended different persons, as if I had the whole town at my disposal; and principally they urged me to honour with my company the chief of the state. In the midst of this street consultation, I longed for a hotel at 100 dollars a-day, and the government for paymaster. 'Hezoos, who was all the time in a terrible hurry, after an animated interlude with some of his friends, spurred his mule and hurried me back, crossed a corner of the plaza, turned down a street to the right, stopped opposite a small house, where he dismounted, and begging me to do the same, in a moment the saddles were whipped off and carried inside. I was ushered into the house, and seated on a low chair in a small room, where a dozen women, friends of 'Hezoos and his wife, were waiting to welcome him to his home. He told me that he did not know where his house was, or that it had an extra room, till he learned it from his friends; and carrying my luggage into a little dark apartment, said that I could have that to myself, and that he, and his wife, and all his friends, would wait upon me, and that I could be more comfortable than in any house in San José. I was excessively tired, having made three days' journey in two, worn out with the worry of searching for a resting-place, and if I had been younger, and had no character to lose, I should not have given myself any further trouble; but, unfortunately, the dignity of office might have been touched by remaining in the house of my servant; and, besides, I could not move without running against a woman; and, more than all, 'Hezoos threw his arms around any one he chose, and kissed her as much as he pleased. In the midst of my irresolution, "la pobra" herself arrived, and half the women in the procession, amateurs of tender scenes, followed. I shall not attempt to describe the meeting. 'Hezoos, as in duty bound, forsook all the rest, and notwithstanding all that he had done, wrapped her little figure in his arms as tightly as if he had not looked at a woman for a month; and "la pobra" lay in his arms as happy as if there were no pretty cousins or apprentices in the world.

All this was too much for me: I worked my way out of doors, and after a consultation with the sergeant, ordered my horse to be saddled, and riding a third time across the plaza, stopped before the convent of Don Antonio Castro. The woman who opened the door said that the padre was not at home. I answered that I would walk in and wait, and ordered my luggage to be set down on the portico. She invited me inside, and I ordered the luggage in after me. The room occupied nearly the whole front of the convent, and besides some pictures of saints, its only furniture was a large wooden table, and a long, high-backed, wooden-bottomed settee. I laid my pistols and spurs upon the table, and stretching myself upon the settee, waited to welcome the padre to his house.

It was some time after dark when he returned. He was surprised, and evidently did not know what to do with me, but seemed to recognise the principle that possession is nine points of the law. I saw, however, that his embarrassment was not from want of hospitality, but from a belief that he could not make me comfortable. In Costa Rica the padres are poor, and I afterward learned that there it is unusual for a stranger to plant himself upon one. I have since thought that the Padre Castro must have considered me particularly cool; but, at all events, his nephew coming in soon after, they forthwith procured me chocolate. At each end of the long room was a small one, one occupied by the padre and the other by his nephew. The latter vacated his; and with a few pieces from the padre's, they fitted me up so well, that when I lay down I congratulated myself upon my forcible entry; and probably before they had recovered from their surprise I was asleep.

My arrival was soon known, and the next morning I received several invitations to the houses of residents—one from the lady of Don Manuel de Aguila; but I was so well pleased with the convent that I was not disposed to leave it. As a matter of course, I soon became known to all the foreign residents, who, however, were but four; Messrs Steipel and Squire, a German and an Englishman, associated in business;

Mr. Wallenstein, German; and the fourth was a countryman, Mr. Lawrence, from Middletown, Connecticut. All lived with Mr. Steipel; and I had immediately a general invitation to make his house my home.

In the afternoon I dined with the foreign residents at the house of Mr. Steipel. This gentleman is an instance of the vicissitudes of fortune. He is a native of Hanover. At fifteen he left college and entered the Prussian army; fought at Dresden and Leipsic; and at the battle of Waterloo received a ball in his brain, from which unfortunately, only within the month preceding, he lost the use of one eye. Disabled for three years by his wound, on his recovery, with three companions, he sailed for South America, and entered the Peruvian army; married a Hija del Sol, Daughter of the Sun, turned merchant, and came to San José, where he was then living in a style of European hospitality. I shall lose all reputation as a sentimental traveller, but I cannot help mentioning honourably every man who gave me a good dinner; and with this determination I shall offend the reader but once more.

Early the next morning, accompanied by my countryman Mr. Lawrence, and mounted on a noble mule lent me by Mr. Steipel, I set off for Cartago. We left the city by a long, well-paved street, and a little beyond the suburbs passed a neat coffee-plantation, which reminded me of a Continental villa. It was the property of a Frenchman, who died just as he completed it; but his widow had provided another master for his house and father for his children. On both sides were mountains, and in front was the great Volcano of Cartago. The fields were cultivated with corn, plantains, and potatoes. The latter, though indigenous, and now scattered all over Europe, is no longer the food of the natives, and but rarely found in Spanish America. The Cartago potatoes are of good flavour, but not larger than a walnut, doubtless from the want of care in cultivating them.

Entries have been found in the records of Cartago dated in 1598, which show it to be the oldest city in Central America. Coming from San José, its appearance was that of an ancient city. The churches were large and imposing; the houses had yard-walls as high as themselves; and its quiet was extraordinary. We rode up a very long street without seeing a single person, and the cross-streets, extending to a great distance both ways, were desolate. A single horseman crossing at some distance was an object to fix our attention.

The day before we had met at San José Dr. Bridley, the only foreign resident in Cartago, who had promised to procure a guide, and make arrangements for ascending the Volcano of Cartago; and we found that, besides doing all that he had promised, he was himself prepared to go with us. While dinner was preparing, Mr. L. and I visited another countryman, Mr. Lovel, a gentleman whom I had known in New York. After dinner we set out to ascend the volcano.

Passing down the principal street, we crossed in front of the cathedral, and immediately began to ascend. Very soon we reached a height which commanded a view of a river, a village, and an extensive valley not visible from the plain below. The sides of the volcano are particularly favourable for cattle; and while the plains below were unappropriated, all the way up were potreros, or pasture-grounds, and huts occupied by persons who had charge of the cattle.

Our only anxiety was lest we should lose our way. A few months before my companions had attempted to ascend, but, by the ignorance of their guide, got lost; and after wandering the whole night on the sides of the volcano, returned without reaching the top. As we ascended the temperature became colder. I put on my poncha; before we reached our stopping-place my teeth were chattering, and before dismounting I had an ague. The situation was most wild and romantic, hanging on the side of an immense ravine; but I would have exchanged its beauties for a blazing coal fire. The hut was the highest on the mountain, built of mud, with no opening but the door and the cracks in the wall. Opposite the door was a figure of the Virgin, and on each side was a frame for a bed; on one of them my friends spread the bear's skin, and tumbling me upon it, wrapped me up in the poncha. I had promised myself a social evening; but who can be sure of an hour of pleasure? I was entirely unfit for use; but my friends made me some hot tea; the place was perfectly quiet; and, upon the whole, I had as comfortable a chill and fever as I ever experienced.

Before daylight we resumed our journey; the road was rough and precipitous; in one place a tornado had swept the mountain, and the trees lay across the road so thickly as to make it almost impassable; we were obliged to dismount, and climb over some and creep under others. Beyond this we came into an open region, where nothing but cedar and thorns grew; and here I saw whortleberries for the first time in Central America. In that wild region there was a charm in seeing anything that was familiar to me at home, and I should perhaps have become sentimental, but they were hard and tasteless. As we rose we entered a region of clouds; very soon they became so thick that we could see nothing; the figures of our own party were barely distinguishable, and we lost all hope of any view from the top of the volcano. Grass still grew, and we ascended till we reached a belt of barren sand and lava; and here, to our great joy, we emerged from the region of clouds, and saw the top of the volcano, without a vapour upon it, seeming to mingle with the clear blue sky; and at that early hour the sun was not high enough to play upon its top.

Mr. Lawrence, who had exerted himself in walking, lay down to rest, and the doctor and I walked on. The crater was about two miles in circumference, rent and broken by time or some great convulsion; the fragments stood high, bare, and grand as mountains, and within were three or four smaller craters. We ascended on the south side by a ridge running east and west till we reached a high point, at which there was an immense gap in the crater impossible to cross. The lofty point on which we stood was perfectly clear, the atmosphere was of transparent purity, and looking beyond the region of desolation, below us, at a distance of perhaps 2,000 feet, the whole country was covered with clouds, and the city at the foot of the volcano was invisible. By degrees the more distant clouds were lifted, and over the immense bed we saw at the same moment the Atlantic and Pacific Oceans. This was the grand spectacle we had-hoped but scarcely expected to behold. My companions had ascended the volcano several times, but on account of the clouds had only seen the two seas once before. The points at which they were visible were the Gulf of Nicoya and the harbour of San Juan, not directly opposite, but nearly at right angles to each other, so that we saw them without turning the body. In a right line over the tops of the mountains neither was more than twenty miles distant, and from the great height at which we stood they seemed almost at our feet. It is the only point in the world which commands a view of the two seas; and I ranked the sight with those most interesting occasions, when from the top of Mount Sinai I looked out upon the Desert of Arabia, and from Mount Hor I saw the Dead Sea.*

We returned to our horses, and found Mr. Lawrence and the guide asleep. We woke them, kindled a fire, made chocolate, and descended. In an hour we reached the hut at which we had slept, and at two o'clock Cartago.

Toward evening I set out with Mr. Lovel for a stroll. The streets were all alike, long and straight, and there was nobody in them. We fell into one which seemed to have no end, and at some distance were intercepted by a procession coming down a cross street. It was headed by boys playing on violins; and then came a small barrow tastefully decorated, and strewed with flowers. It was a bier carrying the body

* I have understood from several persons who have crossed the isthmus from Chagres to Panama, that there is no point on the road from which the two seas are visible.

of a child to the cemetery. We followed, and passing it at the gate, entered through a chapel, at the door of which sat three or four men selling lottery tickets, one of whom asked us if we wished to see the grave of our countryman. We assented, and he conducted us to the grave of a young American whom I had known by sight, and several members of whose family I knew personally. He died about a year before my visit, and his funeral was attended with mournful circumstances. The vicar refused him burial in consecrated ground. Dr. Bridley, who was the only European resident in Cartago, and at whose house he died, rode over to San José, and, making a strong point of the treaty existing between the United States and Central America, obtained an order from the government for his burial in the cemetery. Still the fanatic vicar, acting, as he said, under a higher power, refused. A messenger was sent to San José, and two companies of soldiers were ordered to the doctor's house to escort the body to the grave. At night men were stationed at its side to watch that it was not dug up and thrown out. The next day the vicar, with the cross and images of saints, and all the emblems of the church, and a large concourse of citizens, moved in solemn procession to the cemetery, and formally reconsecrated the ground which had been polluted by the burial of a heretic. The grave is the third from the corridor.

In the corridor, and in an honoured place among the principal dead of Cartago, lay the body of another stranger, an Englishman named Baillie. The day before his death the alcalde was called in to draw his will, who, according to the customary form, asked him if he was a Christian. Mr. Baillie answered yes; and the alcalde wrote him Catolico Romano Apostolico Christiano Mr. Baillie himself did not contemplate this; he knew the difficulty in the case of my countryman about six months before; and wishing to spare his friends a disagreeable, and, perhaps, unsuccessful controversy, had already indicated a particular tree under which he wished to be buried. Before the will was read to him he died. His answer to the alcalde was considered evidence of his orthodoxy; his friends did not interfere, and he was buried under the special direction of the priests, with all the holiest ceremonies of the Church. It was the greatest day ever known in Cartago. The funeral was attended by all the citizens. The procession started from the door of the church, headed by violins and drums; priests followed, with all the crosses, figures of saints, and banners that had been accumulating from the foundation of the city. At the corners of the plaza and of all the principal streets, the procession stopped to sing hallelujahs, to represent the joy in Heaven over a sinner that repents.

While standing in the corridor we saw pass the man who had accompanied the bier, with the child in his arms. He was its father, and with a smile on his face was carrying it to its grave. He was followed by two boys playing on violins, and others were laughing around. The child was dressed in white, with a wreath of roses around its head; and as it lay in its father's arms it did not seem dead, but sleeping. The grave was not quite ready, and the boys sat on the heap of dirt thrown out, and played the violin till it was finished. The father then laid the child carefully in its final resting-place, with its head to the rising sun; folded its little hands across its breast, and closed its fingers around a small wooden crucifix; and it seemed, as they thought it was, happy at escaping the troubles of an uncertain world. There were no tears shed; on the contrary, all were cheerful; and though it appeared heartless, it was not because the father did not love his child, but because he and all his friends had been taught to believe, and were firm in the conviction, that, taken away so young, it was transferred immediately to a better world. The father sprinkled a handful of dirt over its face, the grave-digger took his shovel, in a few moments the little grave was filled up, and, preceded by the boy playing on his violin, we all went away together.

The next morning, with great regret, I took leave of my kind friends, and returned to San José.

It was my misfortune to be the sport of other men's wives. I lost the best servant I had in Guatimala, because his wife was afraid to trust him with me; and on my return I found 'Hezoos at the convent waiting for me. While putting my things in order, without looking me in the face, he told me of the hardships his wife, "la pobra," had suffered during his absence, and how difficult it was for a married woman to get along without her husband. I saw to what he was tending; and feeling, particularly since the recurrence of my fever and ague, the importance of having a good servant in the long journey I had before me, with the selfishness of a traveller I encouraged his vagabond propensities, by telling him that in a few weeks he would be tired of home, and would not have so good an opportunity of getting away. This seemed so sensible, that he discontinued his hints, and went off contented.

At three o'clock I felt uncertain in regard to my chill, but, determined not to give way, dressed myself, and went to dine with Mr. Steipel. Before sitting down, the blueness of my lips, and a tendency to use superfluous syllables, betrayed me; and my old enemy shook me all the way back to the convent, and into bed Fever followed, and I lay in bed all next day, receiving many visits at the door, and a few inside. One of the latter was from 'Hezoos, who returned stronger than before, and, coming to the point, said that he himself was anxious to go with me, but his wife would not consent. I felt that if she had taken the field against me, it was all over; but told him that he had made a contract, and was already overpaid; and sent her a pair of gold earrings, to keep her quiet.

For four days in succession I had a recurrence of chill and fever. Every kindness was shown me in the convent,—friends visited me, and Dr. Bridley came over from Cartago to attend me; but withal I was desponding. The day fixed for setting out with Alvarado arrived. It was impossible to go; Dr. Bridley told me that it would be unwise, while any tendency to the disease remained, to undertake it. There were six days of desert travelling to the port of San Juan, without a house on the road, but mountains to cross and rivers to ford. The whole party was to go on foot except myself; four extra men would be needed to pass my mule over some difficult places, and there was always more or less rain. San Juan was a collection of miserable huts, and from that place it was necessary to embark in a bungo for ten or fifteen days on an unhealthy river. Besides all this, I had the alternative to return by the Cosmopolita to Zonzonate, or to go to Guatimala by land, a journey of 1,200 miles, through a country destitute of accommodations for travellers, and dangerous from the convulsions of civil war. At night, as I lay alone in the convent, and by the light of a small candle saw the bats flying along the roof, I felt gloomy, and would have been glad to be at home.

Still I could not bear the idea of losing all I came for. The land-route lay along the coast of the Pacific, and for three days was the same as to the port. I determined to go by land, but, by the advice of Dr. Bridley, to start in time for the vessel; and, in the hope that I should not have another chill, I bought two of the best mules in San José, one being that on which I had ascended the Volcano of Cartago, and the other a macho, not more than half broke, but the finest animal I ever mounted.

To return to 'Hezoos. The morning after I gave him the earrings he had not come, but sent word that he had the fever and ague. The next day he had it much worse; and, satisfied that I must lose him, I sent him word that if he would procure me a good substitute, I would release him. This raised him from bed, and in the afternoon he came with his substitute, who had very much the air of being the first man he had picked up in the street. His dress was a pair of cotton trousers, with a shirt outside, and a high, bell-crowned, narrow-brimmed black straw hat; and all that he had in the world was on his back.

His hair was cut very close, except in front, where it hung in long locks over his face; in short, he was the *beau ideal* of a Central American vagabond. I did not like his looks, but I was at the time under the influence of fever, and told him I could give him no answer. He came again the next day, at a moment when I wanted some service; and by degrees, though I never hired him, he quietly engaged me as his master.

The morning before I left, Don Augustin Gutierres called upon me, and, seeing this man at the door, expressed his surprise, telling me that he was the town blackguard, a drunkard, gambler, robber, and assassin; that the first night on the road he would rob, and perhaps murder me. Shortly after, Mr. Lawrence entered, who told me that he had just heard the same thing. I discharged him at once, and apparently not much to his surprise, though he still continued round the convent, as he said, in my employ. It was very important for me to set out in time for the vessel, and I had but that day to look out for another. 'Hezoos was astonished at the changes time had made in the character of his friend. He said that he had known him when a boy, and had not seen him for many years till the day he brought him to me, when he had stumbled upon him in the street. Not feeling perfectly released, after a great deal of running, he brought me another, whose name was Nicolas. In any other country I should have called him a mulatto; but in Central America there are so many different shades that I am at a loss how to designate him. He was by trade a mason. 'Hezoos had encountered him at his work, and talked him into a desire to see Guatimala and Mexico, and come back as rich as himself. He presented himself just as he left his work, with his shirt-sleeves rolled up above his elbows, and his trousers above his knees: a rough diamond for a valet; but he was honest, could take care of mules, and make chocolate. I did not ask more. He was married, too; and, as his wife did not interfere with me, I liked him the better for it.

CHAPTER XVIII.

DEPARTURE FOR GUATIMALA — ESPARZA — TOWN OF COSTA RICA — THE BARRANCA — WILD SCENERY — HACIENDA OF ARANJUEZ — RIVER LAGARTOS — CERROS OF COLLITO — HERDS OF DEER — SANTA ROSA — DON JUAN JOSÉ BONILLA — AN EARTHQUAKE — A CATTLE FARM — BAGASES — GUANACASTE — AN AGREEABLE WELCOME — BELLE OF GUANACASTE — PLEASANT LODGINGS — CORDILLERAS — VOLCANOES OF RINCON AND OROSI — HACIENDA OF SAN TERESA — SUNSET VIEW — THE PACIFIC AGAIN.

On the thirteenth day of February I mounted for my journey to Guatimala. My equipage was reduced to articles of the last necessity: a hammock of striped cotton cloth laid over my pellon, a pair of alforgas, and a poncha strapped on behind. Nicolas had strung across his alvarda a pair of leather cohines, in shape like buckets, with the inner side flat, containing biscuit, chocolate, sausages, and dolces, and in front, on the pommel, my wearing apparel rolled up in an oxhide, after the fashion of the country. During my whole stay at the convent the attentions of the padre were unremitted. Besides the services he actually rendered me, I have no doubt he considers that he saved my life; for during my sickness he entered my room while I was preparing to shave, and made me desist from so dangerous an operation. I washed my face by stealth, but his kindness added another to the list of obligations I was already under to the padres of Central America.

I felt great satisfaction at being able once more to resume my journey, pleased with the lightness of my equipage, the spirit of my mules, and looked my journey of 1,200 miles boldly in the face. All at once I heard a clattering behind, and Nicolas swept by me on a full run. My macho was what was called espantoso, or scary, and started. I had very little strength, and was fairly run away with. If I had bought my beasts for racing I should have had no reason to complain; but, unluckily, my saddle turned, and I came to the ground, fortunately clearing the stirrups, and the beast ran, scattering on the road, pistols, holsters, saddle-cloths, and saddle, and continued on bare-backed toward the town. To my great relief, some muleteers intercepted him, and saved my credit as a horseman in San José. We were more than an hour in recovering scattered articles and repairing broken trappings.

For three days my road was the same that I had travelled in entering Costa Rica. The fourth morning I rose without any recurrence of fever. Mr. Lawrence had kindly borne me company from San José, and was still with me; he had relieved me from all trouble, and had made my journey so easy and comfortable that, instead of being wearied, I was recruited, and abandoned all idea of returning by sea.

At seven o'clock we started, and in half an hour reached Esparza. From this place to Nicaragua, a distance of 300 miles, the road lay through a wilderness; except the frontier town of Costa Rica, there were only a few straggling haciendas, twenty, thirty, and forty miles apart.

In half an hour we crossed the Barranca, a broad, rapid, and beautiful river, but which lost in my eyes all its beauty, for here Mr. Lawrence left me. Since the day of my arrival at San José he had been almost constantly with me, had accompanied me in every excursion, and during my sickness had attended me constantly. We exchanged adieus from the backs of our mules, and, not to be sentimental, lighted our cigars.

I was again setting out alone. I had travelled so long with companions or in ships, that when the moment for plunging into the wilderness came, my courage almost failed me. And it was a moment that required some energy; for we struck off immediately into one of the wildest paths that I met on the whole of that desolate journey. The trees were so close as to darken it, and the branches so low that it was necessary to keep the head constantly bent to avoid hitting them. The noise of the locusts, which had accompanied us since we reached the mountain of Aguacate, here became startling. Very soon families of monkeys, walking heavily on the tops of the trees, disturbed these noisy tenants of the woods, and sent them flying around us in such swarms that we were obliged to beat them off with our hats. My macho snorted and pulled violently on the bit, dragging me against the trees; and I could not help thinking, if this is the outset, what will be the end?

We continued in the woods till about two o'clock, when, turning off by a path to the right, we reached a clearing, on one side of which was the hacienda of Aranjuez. The entrance to the house was by a ladder from the outside, and underneath was a sort of store-house. It was occupied by a major-domo, a Mestitzo, and his wife. Near it was the kitchen, where the wife and another woman were at work. The majo-domo was sitting on the ground doing nothing, and two able-bodied men were helping him.

After dinner I led the mules to a stream, on the banks of which were tufts of young grass, and while I was sitting here two wild turkeys flew over my head and lighted on a tree near by. I sent Nicolas for my gun, and soon had a bird large enough for a household dinner, which I sent immediately to the house to be converted into provender. At sundown I returned, and then discovered a deficiency in my preparations, which I felt during the whole journey, viz. of candles. A light was manufactured by filling a broken clay vessel with grease, and coiling in it some twisted cotton, with one end sticking out about an inch. The workmen on the hacienda took advantage of the light, and brought out a pack of cards. The wife of the major-domo joined them, and seeing no chance of a speedy termination of the game, I undressed myself and went to bed. When they finished, the woman got into a bed directly opposite mine, and before lying down lighted another cigar. The men did the same on the floor, and till the cigars went out, continued discussing the game. The major-domo was already asleep in the hammock. All night the wife of the major-domo smoked, and the men snuffled and snored. At two o'clock I rose and went out of doors. The moon was shining, and the freshness of the morning air was grateful. I woke Nicolas, and paying the major-domo as he lay in his hammock, at three o'clock we resumed our journey. I was charmed with this place when we reached it, and disgusted when we left. The people were kind, and of as good disposition as the expectation of pay could make them, but their habits were intolerable.

The freshness of the morning air restored my equanimity; the moon shed a glorious light over the clearing, and lighted up the darkness of the forest. We heard only the surge of monkeys, as, disturbed by our noise, they moved on the tops of the trees.

At eight o'clock we reached the river Lagartos, breaking rapidly over a bed of white sand and gravel, clear as crystal, and shaded by trees, the branches of which met at the fording-place, and formed a complete arbour. We dismounted, took off the saddles from our mules, and tied them to a tree, kindled a fire on the bank, and breakfasted. Wild scenes had long lost the charm of novelty, but this I would not have exchanged for a déjeûner à la fourchette at the best restaurant of Paris. The wild turkey was not more than enough for my household, which consisted of Nicolas.

Resuming our journey, we travelled all day, and as the sun was getting low, we came out into a large clearing, on one side of which stood the hacienda of Santa Rosa. The house stood on the right, and directly in front, against the side of a hill, was a large cattle-yard, enclosed by a hard clay wall, divided into three parts, and filled with cows and calves. On the left was an almost boundless plain, interspersed with groves of trees; and as we rode up a gentleman in the yard sent a servant to open the gate. Don Juan José Bonilla met me at the porch, and before I had time to present my letter, welcomed me to Santa Rosa.

Don Juan was a native of Cartago, a gentleman by birth and education, and of one of the oldest families in Costa Rica. He had travelled over his own country, and what was very unusual in that region, had visited the United States, and though labouring under the disadvantage of not speaking the language, spoke with great interest of our institutions. He had been an active member of the Liberal party; had laboured to carry out its principles in the administration of the government, and to save his country from the disgrace of falling back into despotism. He had been persecuted, heavy contributions had been laid upon his property, and four years before he had withdrawn from Cartago and retired to this hacienda. But political animosity never dies. A detachment of soldiers was sent to arrest him, and, that no suspicion might be excited, they were sent by sea, and landed at a port on the Pacific within the bounds of his own estate. Don Juan received an intimation of their approach, and sent a servant to reconnoitre, who returned with intelligence that they were within half a day's march. He mounted his horse to escape, but near his own gate was thrown, and his leg badly broken. He was carried back insensible, and when the soldiers arrived they found him in bed; but they made him rise, put him on horseback, hurried him to the frontiers of the state, and left him, communicating to him his sentence of banishment, and death if he returned. The boundary-line of the state of Costa Rica is a river in the midst of a wilderness, and he was obliged to travel on horseback to Nicaragua, a journey of four days. He had never recovered the use of his leg, which was two or three inches shorter than the other. He remained two years in exile; and on the election of Don Manuel de Aguila as chief of the state, returned. On the expulsion of Don Manuel he retired again to his hacienda, and was then busily engaged in making repairs for the reception of his family; but he did not know at what moment another order might come to expel him from his home.

While sitting at the supper-table we heard a noise over our heads, which seemed to me like the opening of the roof. Don Juan raised his eyes to the ceiling, and suddenly started from his chair, threw his arms around the neck of a servant, and with the fearful words "temblor!" "temblor!" "an earthquake!" "an earthquake!" all rushed for the doors. I sprang from my chair, made one bound across the room, and cleared the piazza. The earth rolled like the pitching of a ship in a heavy sea. My step was high, my feet barely touched the ground, and my arms were thrown up involuntarily to save myself from falling. I was the last to start, but, once under way, I was the last to stop. Half way across the yard I stumbled over a man on his knees, and fell. I never felt myself so feeble a thing before. At this moment I heard Don Juan calling to me. He was leaning on the shoulder of his servant, with his face to the door, crying to me to come out of the house. It was pitchy dark; within was the table at which we had sat, with a single candle, the light of which extended far enough to show a few of the kneeling figures, with their faces to the door. We looked anxiously in, and waited for the shock which should prostrate the strong walls, and lay the roof on the ground. There was something awful in our position, with our faces to the door, shunning the place which at all other times offers shelter to man. The shocks were continued perhaps two minutes, during which time it required an effort to stand firm. The return of the earth to steadiness was almost as violent as the shock. We waited a few minutes after the last vibration, when Don Juan said it was over, and, assisted by his servant, entered the house. I had been the last to leave it, but I was the last to return; and my chair lying with its back on the floor, gave an intimation of the haste with which I had decamped. The houses in Costa Rica are the best in the country for resisting these shocks, being, like the others, long and low, and built of adobes, or undried bricks, two feet long and one broad, made of clay mixed with straw to give adhesion, and laid when soft, with upright posts between, so that they are dried by the sun into one mass, which moves with the surface of the earth.

Early in the morning two horses were at the door, and two servants in attendance for a ride. Don Juan mounted the same horse which he had ridden in his exile, and was attended by the same servants. Heretofore I had always heard constant complaints of servants, and, to do them justice, I think they are the worst I ever knew; but Don Juan's were the best in the world, and it was evident that they thought he was the best master.

The estate of Don Juan covered as much ground as a German principality, containing 200,000 acres, and was bounded on one side, for a long distance, by the Pacific Ocean. But a small portion of it was cultivated, not more than enough to raise maize for the workmen, and the rest was a roaming-ground for cattle. More than 10,000 were wandering over it, almost as wild as the deer, and never seen except as they crossed a path in the woods, or at the season of lazoing them, for the purpose of taking an account of the increase.

I had set out on this long journey without any cargo-mule, from the difficulty of procuring one that could keep pace with the riding-beasts; but we had felt the inconvenience of being encumbered with luggage; and, besides Don Juan's kindness to me at his house, he furnished me with one which he had broken expressly for his own use in rapid journeys between Cartago and the hacienda, and which he warranted me, with a light load, would trot and keep up with mine.

Late in the afternoon I left his hospitable dwelling. Don Juan, with his deaf and dumb boy, accompanied me a league on the way, when we dismounted and took-leave of each other. My new mule, like myself, was very reluctant to leave Don Juan, and seemed to have a sentiment that she should never see her old master again. Indeed it was so difficult to get her along, that Nicolas tied her by the halter to his mule's tail, after a manner common in the country, and thus leading her along, I followed at her heels. The deer were more numerous than I have yet seen them, and I now looked at them only as animating a beautiful landscape. At dark we began to have apprehensions about the road. There was a difficult mountain-pass before us, and Nicolas wanted to stop and wait till the moon rose: but as that would derange the journey for the next day, I pushed on for more than an hour through the woods. The mules stumbled along in the dark, and very soon we lost all traces of a path; while trying to find it, we heard the crash of a falling tree, which in the darkness sounded appalling, and made us hesitate to enter the woods. I determined to wait for the moon, and dismounted. Peering into the darkness, I saw a glimmering light on the left. We shouted with all our strength, and were answered by a pack of barking dogs, and moving in that direction, reached a hut where three or four workmen were lying on the ground, who were at first disposed to be merry and impertinent when we asked for a guide to the next hacienda; but one of them recognised my cargo-mule, said that he had known it since he was a child (rather doubtful praise of my new purchase), and was at length induced to make us an offer of his services. A horse was brought, large, wild, and furious, as if never bitted; snorting, rearing, and almost making the ground shake at every tread; and before the rider was fairly on his back he was tearing in the dark across the plain. Making a wide sweep, he returned, and the guide, releasing the cargo-mule from that of Nicolas, tied her to the tail of his horse, and then led the way. Even with the drag of the cargo-mule, it was impossible for him to moderate his pace, and we were obliged to follow at a most unhappy rate. It was the first piece of bad road we had met with, having many sharp turns, and ascents and descents, broken and stony. Fortunately, while we were in the woods, the moon rose, touched with a silvery light the tops of the trees, and when we reached the bank of the river it was almost as light as day. Here my guide left me, and I lost all confidence in the moon, for by her deceitful light I slipped into his hand a gold piece instead of a silver one, without either of us knowing it.

As we ascended the bank after crossing the stream, the hacienda was in full sight. The occupants were in bed, but Don Manuel, to whom I was recommended by Don Juan, rose to receive me.

At daylight the next morning, as the workmen on the hacienda were about going to work, we set off again. In an hour we heard the sound of a horn, giving notice of the approach of a drove of cattle. We drew up into the woods to let them pass, and they came with a cloud of dust, the faces of the drivers covered, and would have trampled to death anything that impeded their progress.

Late in the afternoon we came into a broad avenue and saw marks of wheels. At dusk we reached the river which runs by the suburbs of Guanacaste, the frontier town of Costa Rica. The pass was occupied by an ox cart, with four stubborn oxen, which would not go ahead and could not go back. We were detained half an hour, and it was dark when we entered. We passed through the plaza, before the door of the church, which was lighted up for vespers, and rode to a house at which I had been directed to stop. Nicolas went in to make preliminary inquiries, and returning, told me to dismount, and unloaded the luggage-mule. I went in, took off my spurs, and stetched myself on a bench. Soon it struck me that my host was not particularly glad to see me. Several children came in and stared, and then ran back into another room; and in a few minutes I received the compliments of the lady of the house, and her regret that she could not accommodate me. I was indignant at Nicolas, who had merely asked whether such a person lived there, and without more ado had sent me in. I left the house, and with the halter of my macho in one hand and spurs in the other, and Nicolas following with the mules, sought the house of the commandant. I found him standing on the piazza, with the key in his hand, and all his household stuff packed up outside, only waiting till the moon rose to set out for another post. I believe he regretted that he could not accommodate me, nor could he refer me to any other house; but he sent his servant to look for one, and I waited nearly an hour, up for a bidder.

In the mean time I made inquiries about my road. I did not wish to continue on the direct route to Nicaragua, but to go first to the port of San Juan on the Pacific, the proposed termination of the canal to connect the Atlantic and Pacific Oceans. The commandant regretted that I had not come one day sooner. He mentioned a fact of which I was aware before, that Mr. Bailey, an English gentleman, had been employed by the government to survey the canal route, and had resided some time at the post, and added that since his departure it was perfectly desolate; no one ever visited it, not a person in the place knew the road to it, and, unluckily, a man who had been in Mr. Bailey's employ had left that morning for Nicaragua. Most fortunately, on inquiry, the man was found to be still in the place, and he, too, intended setting out as soon as the moon rose. I had no inducement to remain; nobody seemed very anxious for the honour of my company, and I would have gone on immediately if the mules had been able to continue; but I made an arrangement with him and his son to wait till three in the morning, then to conduct me to the port, and thence to Nicaragua. At length the commandant's servant returned and conducted me to a house with a little shop in front, where I was received by an old lady with a buenos noches that almost surprised me into an idea that I was welcome. I entered through the shop, and passed into a parlour which contained a hammock, an interlaced bedstead, and a very neat catre with a gauze mosquito netting, and pink bows at the corners. I was agreeably disappointed with my posada, and while conversing with the old lady, was dozing over a cup of chocolate, when I heard a lively voice at the door, and a young lady entered, with two or three young men in attendance, who came up to the table in front of me, and throwing back a black mantilla, bade me buenos noches, put out her hand, said that she had heard in church that I was at her house, and was so glad of it; no strangers ever came there; the place was completely out of the world, very dull, &c. &c. I was so surprised that I must have looked very stupid. She was not regularly handsome, but her mouth and eyes were beautiful; and her manner was so different from the cold, awkward and bashful air of her countrywomen, so much like the frank and fascinating welcome which a young lady at home might extend to a friend after a long absence, that if the table had not been between us I could have taken her in my arms and kissed her. I pulled up my shirt collar, and forgot all my troubles and perplexities. Though living in that little remote town, like young ladies in large cities, she had a fancy for strangers, which at that time I regarded as a delightful trait of character in a woman. Her every-day beaux had no chance. At first they were very civil to me, but they became short and crusty, and, very much to my satisfaction, took themselves off. It was so long since I had felt the least interest in a woman, that I gave myself a benefit. The simplest stories of other countries and other people were to her romance, and her eye kindled as she listened; soon the transition came from facts to feelings, and then that highest earthly pleasure, of being lifted above every-day thoughts by the enthusiasm of a high-minded girl.

We sat up till twelve o'clock. The mother, who at first had wearied me, I found exceedingly agreeable; indeed, I had seldom known a more interesting old lady; for she pressed me to remain two or three days and rest; said the place was dull, but that her daughter would try to make it agreeable; and her daughter said nothing, but looked unutterable things.

All pleasure is fleeting. Twelve o'clock came, an unprecedented hour, for that country. My ordinary prudence in looking out for a sleeping-place had not deserted me. Two little boys had taken possession of the leather bed; the old lady had retired; the beautiful little cartaret remained unoccupied, and the young lady withdrew, telling me that this was to be my bed. I do not know why, but I felt uneasy. I opened the mosquito-net. In that country beds are not used, and an oxhide or mat, often not so clean as it might be, is the substitute. This was a mat, very fine, and clean as if perfectly new. At the head was a lovely pillow with a pink muslin covering, and over it a thin white pillow-case with a bewitching ruffle. Whose cheek had rested on that pillow? I pulled off my coat, walked up and down the room, and waked up one of the boys. It was as I supposed. I lay down, but could not sleep, and determined not to continue my journey the next day.

At three o'clock the guide knocked at the door. The mules were already saddled, and Nicolas was putting on the luggage. I had often clung to my pillow, but never as I did to that pink one with its ruffled border. I told Nicolas that the guide must go home and wait another day. The guide refused. It was the young man; his father had already gone, and had ordered him to follow. Very soon I heard a light footstep, and a soft voice expostulating with the guide. Indignant at his obstinacy, I ordered him away; but very soon I reflected that I could not procure another, and might lose the great object I had in view in making this long journey. I called him back, and attempted to bribe him; but his only answer was, that his father had started at the rising of the moon, and ordered him to follow. At length it was arranged that he should go and overtake his father and bring him back; but perhaps his father would not come. I was pertinacious until I carried the point, and then I was more indifferent. After all, why should I wait? Nicolas said we could get our clothes washed in Nicaragua. I walked out of doors, and resolved that it was folly to lose the chance of examining a canal route for the belle of Guanacaste. I hurried through my preparations, and bade her, I may say, an affectionate farewell. There is not the least chance that I shall ever see her again. Living in a secluded town, unknown beyond the borders of its unknown state, between the Andes and Pacific Ocean, probably she is already the happy wife of some worthy townsman, and has forgotten the stranger who owes to her some of the happiest moments he passed in Central America.

It was now broad daylight. It was very rare that I had left a place with so much regret; but I turned my sorrow into anger, and wreaked it upon Nicolas and the guide. The wind was very high, and, sweeping over the great plain, raised such clouds of dust as made riding both disagreeable and difficult. This ought to have had some effect in restoring my equanimity, but it did not. All day we had on our right the grand range of Cordilleras, and crowning it at this point the great volcanoes of Rincon and Orosi. From thence a vast plain, over which the wind swept furiously, extended to the sea. At one o'clock we came in sight of the hacienda of Santa Teresa, standing on a great elevation, and still a long way before us. The hacienda was the property of Don Augustin Gutierres of San José, and, with two others, was under the charge of his son Don Manuel. A letter from his father had informed him of my coming, and he received me as an old acquaintance. The situation of the house was finer than that of any I had seen. It was high, and commanded a view of an immense plain, studded with trees in groups and in forest. The ocean was not visible, but we could see the opposite coast of the Gulf of Nicoya, and the point of the port of Culebra, the finest on the Pacific, only three and a half leagues distant. The hacienda contained 1,000 mares and 400 horses, more than 100 of which were in sight from the door. It was grand enough to give the owner ideas of empire. Toward evening I counted from the door of the house seventeen deer, and Don Manuel told me that he had a contract for furnishing 2,000 skins. In the season a good hunter gets twenty-five a-day. Even the workmen will not eat them, and they are only shot for the hide and horns. He had forty workmen, and an ox was killed every day. Near the house was an artificial lake, more than a mile in circumference, built as a drinking-place for cattle. And yet the proprietors of these haciendas are not rich; the ground is worth absolutely nothing. The whole value is in the stock; and allowing two pounds a head for the horses and mares would probably give the full value of this apparently magnificent estate.

Here, too, I could have passed a week with great satisfaction, but the next morning I resumed my journey. Though early in the dry season, the ground was parched, and the streams were dried up. We carried a large calabash with water, and stopping under the shade of a tree, turned our mules out on the plain and breakfasted. I was riding in advance, with my poncha flying in the wind, when I saw a drove of cattle stop and look wildly at me, and then rush furiously toward me. I attempted to run, but, remembering the bull-fights at Guatimala, I tore off my poncha, and had just time to get behind a high rock as the whole herd darted by at their full speed. We continued our route, from time to time catching glimpses of the Pacific, till we reached a clear, open place, completely protected from the wind, and called the Boca of the Mountain of Nicaragua. A large caravan had already encamped, and among the muleteers Nicolas found acquaintances from San José. Their cargoes consisted of potatoes, sweet bread, and dolces for Nicaragua.

Towards evening we wound for a short distance among the hills that enclosed us, ascended a slight range, and came down directly upon the shore of the sea. I always had a high feeling when I touched the shore of the Pacific, and never more so than at this desolate place. The waves rolled grandly, and broke with a solemn roar. The mules were startled, and my macho shrank from the heaving water. I spurred him into it, and at a moment when I was putting in my pocket some shells which Nicolas had picked up, he ran away. He had attempted it several times before in the woods; and now, having a fair chance, I gave him a full sweep of the coast. We continued nearly an hour on the shore, when we crossed a high, rough headland, and again came down upon the sea. Four times we mounted headlands, and again descended to the shore, and the heat became almost intolerable. The fifth ascent was steep, but we came upon a table covered with a thick forest, through which we proceeded until we came to a small clearing with two huts. We stopped at the first, which was occupied by a black man and his wife. He had plenty of corn; there was a fine pasture-ground near, so hemmed in by the woods that there was no danger of the mules escaping, and I hired the man and woman to sleep out of doors, and give me the hovel to myself.*

* At this place Mr Stephens devoted a few days to examine the ground between the Pacific Ocean and the Lake of Nicaragua, through which the projected Inter-oceanic canal is proposed to be made, and on the 1st of March resumed his journey towards Guatimala.—F. C.

CHAPTER XIX.

VISIT TO THE VOLCANO OF MASAYA—VILLAGE OF MASAYA—LAKE OF MASAYA—NINDIRI—ASCENT OF THE VOLCANO—ACCOUNT OF IT—THE CRATER—DESCENT INTO IT—VOLCANO OF NINDIRI—IGNORANCE OF THE PEOPLE CONCERNING OBJECTS OF INTEREST—RETURN TO MASAYA—ANOTHER COUNTRYMAN—MANAGUA—LAKE OF MANAGUA—FISHING—BEAUTIFUL SCENERY—MATEARES—QUESTA DEL RELOX—NAGAROTIS—CROSSES—A GAMEKEEPER—PUEBLO NUEVO.

March 1.—Anxious as I was to hurry on, I resolved nevertheless to give one day to the Volcano of Masaya. For this purpose I sent a courier ahead to procure me a guide up the volcano, and did not get off till eleven o'clock. At a short distance from the city we met a little negro on horseback, dressed in the black suit that nature had made him, with two large plantain leaves sewed together for a hat, and plantain leaves for a saddle. At the distance of two leagues we came in sight of the volcano, and at four o'clock, after a hot ride, entered the town, one of the oldest and largest in Nicaragua, and though completely inland, containing, with its suburbs, a population of 20,000. We rode to the house of Don Sabino Satroon, who lay, with his mouth open, snoring in a hammock; but his wife, a pretty young half-blood, received me cordially, and with a proper regard for the infirmities of an old husband and for me, did not wake him up. All at once he shut his mouth and opened his eyes, and gave me a cordial welcome. Don Sabino was a Colombian, who had been banished for ten years, as he said, for services rendered his country; and having found his way to Masaya, had married the pretty young half-breed, and set up as a doctor. Inside the door, behind a little stock of sugar, rice, sausages, and chocolate, was a formidable army of jars and bottles, exhibiting as many colours and as puzzling labels as an apothecary's shop at home.

I had time to take a short walk around the town, and turning down the road, at the distance of half a mile came to the brink of a precipice, more than a hundred feet deep, at the foot of which, and a short distance beyond, was the Lake of Masaya. The descent was almost perpendicular, in one place by a rough ladder, and then by steps cut in the rock. I was obliged to stop while fifteen or twenty women, most of them young, passed. Their water-jars were made of the shell of a large gourd, round, with fanciful figures scratched on them, and painted or glazed, supported on the back by a strap across the forehead, and secured by fine net-work. Below they were chattering gaily, but by the time they reached the place where I stood they were silent, their movements very slow, their breathing hard, and faces covered with profuse perspiration. This was a great part of the daily labour of the women of the place, and in this way they procured enough for domestic use; but every horse, mule, or cow was obliged to go by a circuitous road of more than a league for water. Why a large town has grown up and been continued so far from this element of life, I do not know. The Spaniards found it a large Indian village, and as they immediately made the owners of the soil their drawers of water, they did not feel the burden; nor do their descendants now.

In the meantime my guide arrived, who, to my great satisfaction, was no less a personage than the alcalde himself. The arrangements were soon made, and I was to join him the next morning at his house in Nindiri. I gave my mules and Nicolas a day's rest, and started on Don Sabino's horse, with a boy to act as guide and to carry a pair of alforgas with provisions. In half an hour I reached Nindiri, having met more people than on my whole road from San José to Nicaragua. The alcalde was ready, and in company with an assistant, who carried a pair of alforgas with provisions and a calabash of water, all mounted, we set out. At the distance of half a league we left the main road, and turned off on a small path in the woods on the left. We emerged from this into an open field covered with lava, extending to the base of the volcano in front and on each side as far as I could see, black, several feet deep, and in some places lying on high ridges. A faint track was beaten by cattle over this plain of lava. In front were two volcanoes, from both of which streams of lava had run down the sides into the plain. That directly in front my guide said was the Volcano of Masaya. In that on the right, and furthest from us, the crater was broken, and the great chasm inside was visible. This he said was called Ventero, a name I never heard before, and that it was inaccessible. Riding toward that in front, and crossing the field of lava, we reached the foot of the volcano. Here the grass was high, but the ground was rough and uneven, being covered with decomposed lava. We ascended on horseback, until it became too steep for the horses to carry us, and then dismounted, tied them to a bush, and continued on foot. I was already uneasy as to my guides' knowledge of localities, and soon found that they were unwilling or unable to endure much fatigue. Before we were half way up they disencumbered themselves of the water-jar and provisions, and yet they lagged behind. The alcalde was a man about forty, who rode his own horse, and being a man of consequence in the town, I could not order him to go faster; his associate was some ten years older, and physically incapable; and seeing that they did not know any particular path, I left them and went alone.

At eleven o'clock, or three hours from the village of Nindiri, I reached the high point at which we were aiming; and from this point I expected to look down into the crater of the volcano; but there was no crater, and the whole surface was covered with gigantic masses of lava, and overgrown with bushes and scrub trees. I waited till my guides came up, who told me that this was the Volcano of Masaya, and that there was nothing more to see. The alcalde insisted that two years before he had ascended with the cura, since deceased, and a party of villagers, and they all stopped at this place. I was disappointed and dissatisfied. Directly opposite rose a high peak, which I thought, from its position, must command a view of the crater of the other volcano. I attempted to reach it by passing round the circumference of the mountain, but was obstructed by an immense chasm, and returning, struck directly across. I had no idea what I was attempting. The whole was covered with lava lying in ridges and irregular masses, the surface varying at every step, and overgrown with trees and bushes. After an hour of the hardest work I ever had in my life, I reached the point at which I aimed, and, to my astonishment, instead of seeing the crater of the distant volcano, I was on the brink of another.

Among the recorded wonders of the discoveries in America, this mountain was one; and the Spaniards, who in those days never stopped half way in any matter that touched the imagination, called it El Infierno de Masaya, or the Hell of Masaya. The historian, in speaking of Nicaragua, says, "There are burning mountains in this province, the chief of which is Masaya, where the natives at certain times offered up maids, throwing them into it, thinking by their lives to appease the fire, that it might not destroy the country, and they went to it very cheerful;" and in another place he says, "Three leagues from the city of Masaya is a small hill, flat and round, called Masaya, being a burning mountain, the mouth of it being half a league in compass, and the depth within it 250 fathoms. There are no trees nor grass, but birds build without any disturbance from the fire. There is another mouth like that of a well about a bowshot over, the distance from which to the fire is about 150 fathoms, always boiling up, and that mass of fire often rises, and gives a great light, so that it can be seen at a considerable distance. It moves from one side to the other; and sometimes roars so loud that it is dreadful, yet never casts up anything but smoke and flame. The liquor never ceasing at the bottom, nor its boiling, imagining the same to be gold, *F. Blase de*

Yniesta, of the Order of *St. Dominick*, and two other *Spaniards*, were let down into the first mouth in two baskets, with a bucket made of one piece of iron, and a long chain to draw up some of that fiery matter, and know whether it was metal. The chain ran 150 fathoms, and as soon as it came to the fire, the bucket melted, with some links of the chain, in a very short time, and therefore they could not know what was below. They lay there that night without any want of fire or candles, and came out again in their baskets sufficiently frighted."

Either the monk, disappointed in his search for gold, had fibbed, or nature had made one of its most extraordinary changes. The crater was about a mile and a half in circumference, five or six hundred feet deep, with sides slightly sloping, and so regular in its proportions that it seemed an artificial excavation. The bottom was level, both sides and bottom covered with grass, and it seemed an immense conical green basin. There were none of the fearful marks of a volcanic eruption; nothing to terrify, or suggest an idea of an el infierno; but, on the contrary, it was a scene of singular and quiet beauty. I descended to the side of the crater, and walked along the edge, looking down into the area. Toward the other end was a growth of arbolitos or little trees, and in one place no grass grew, and the ground was black and loamy, like mud drying up. This was perhaps the mouth of the mysterious well that sent up the flame, which gave its light a "considerable distance," into which the Indian maidens were thrown, and which melted the monk's iron bucket. Like him, I felt curious to "know what was below;" but the sides of the crater were perpendicular. Entirely alone, and with an hour's very hard work between me and my guides, I hesitated about making any attempt to descend, but I disliked to return without. In one place, and near the black earth, the side was broken, and there were some bushes and scrub trees. I planted my gun against a stone, tied my handkerchief around it as a signal of my whereabout, and very soon was below the level of the ground. Letting myself down by the aid of roots, bushes, and projecting stones, I descended to a scrub tree which grew out of the side about half way from the bottom, and below this it was a naked and perpendicular wall. It was impossible to go any further. I was even obliged to keep on the upper side of the tree, and here I was more anxious than ever to reach the bottom; but it was of no use. Hanging midway, impressed with the solitude and the extraordinary features of a scene upon which so few human eyes have ever rested, and the power of the great Architect who has scattered his wonderful works over the whole face of the earth, I could not but reflect, what a waste of the bounties of Providence in this favoured but miserable land!

At home this volcano would be a fortune; with a good hotel on the top, a railing round to keep children from falling in, a zigzag staircase down the sides, and a glass of iced lemonade at the bottom. Cataracts are good property with people who know how to turn them to account. Niagara and Trenton Falls pay well, and the owners of volcanoes in Central America might make money out of them by furnishing facilities to travellers. This one could probably be bought for ten dollars, and I would have given twice that sum for a rope, and a man to hold it. Meanwhile, though anxious to be at the bottom, I was casting my eyes wistfully at the top. The turning of an ankle, breaking of a branch, rolling of a stone, or a failure of strength, might put me where I should have been as hard to find as the government of Central America. I commenced climbing up, slowly and with care, and in due time hauled myself out in safety.

On my right was a full view of the broken crater of the Volcano of Nindiri. The side toward me was hurled down, and showed the whole interior of the crater. This the alcalde had declared inaccessible; and partly from sheer spite against him, I worked my way to it with extreme labour and difficulty. At length, after five hours of most severe toil among the rugged heaps of lava, I descended to the place where we had left our provisions. Here I seized the calabash of water, and stood for several minutes with my face turned up to the skies, and then I began upon the alcalde and the eatables. Both he and his companion expressed their utter astonishment at what I described, and persisted in saying that they did not know of the existence of such a place.

I was too indignant with the alcalde to have anything further to do with him; and bent upon making another attempt, on my return to the village I rode to the house of the cura, to obtain his assistance in procuring men and making other needful preparations. On the steps of the back piazza I saw a young negro man, in a black gown and cap, sitting by the side of a good-looking, well-dressed white woman, and, if I mistake not, discoursing to her of other things than those connected with his priestly duties. His black reverence was by no means happy to see me. I asked him if I could make an inn of his house, which, though it sounds somewhat free, is the set phrase for a traveller to use; and, without rising from his seat, he said his house was small and incommodious, and that the alcalde had a good one. He was the first black priest I had seen, and the only one in the country who failed in hospitality. I must confess that I felt a strong impulse to lay the butt of a pistol over his head; and spurring my horse so that he sprang almost upon him, I wheeled short and galloped out of the yard. With the alcalde and the cura both against me, I had no chance in the village. It was nearly dark, and I returned to Masaya. My vexation was lost in a sense of overpowering fatigue. It would be impossible to repeat the severe labour of the day, without an interval of rest, and there was so much difficulty in making arrangements, that I determined to mount my macho and push on.

The next morning I resumed my journey. My mules had not been watered. To send them to the lake and back would give them a journey of two leagues; and to save them I bought water, which was measured out in a gourd holding about a quart. At about a league's distance we came in sight of the Lake of Managua, and before us the whole country was a bed of lava from the base of the volcano to the lake.

In about three hours, after a desperately hot ride, we reached Managua, beautifully situated on the banks of the lake. Entering through a collection of thatched huts, we passed a large aristocratic house, with a courtyard occupying a whole square, the mansion of an expatriated family, decayed and going to ruin.

Late in the afternoon I walked down to the lake. It was not so grand as the Lake of Nicaragua, but it was a noble sheet of water, and in full sight was the Volcano of Momotombo. The shore presented the same animated spectacle of women filling their water-jars, men bathing, horses and mules drinking, and in one place was a range of fishermen's huts; on the edge of the water, stakes were set up in a triangular form, and women with small hand-nets were catching fish, which they threw into hollow places dug, or rather scraped, in the sand. The fish were called sardinitos, and at the door of the huts the men were building fires to cook them. The beauty of this scene was enhanced by the reflection that it underwent no change. Here was perpetual summer; no winter ever came to drive the inhabitants shivering to their fires; but still it may be questioned whether, with the same scenery and climate, wants few and easily supplied, luxuriating in the open air, and by the side of this lovely lake, even the descendants of the Anglo-Saxon race would not lose their energy and industry.

At three o'clock the next morning we started. In all the tierras calientes it is the custom to travel at night, or rather very early in the morning. At eight o'clock we entered the village of Mateares, where we procured some eggs, and breakfasted. From this village our road lay directly along the lake, but a few paces from the shore, and shaded by noble trees. Unfortunately, we were obliged to turn off to avoid a large rock which had rolled down several months before, and probably blocks up the road still. This brought us round by the Cuesta del Relox, so called from a venerable sun-dial which stands on one side of the road, of a dark grey stone, with an inscription in Castilian, but the characters so worn and indistinct that I could not make them out. It has no history, except that it was erected by the conquerors; and it stands as an indication of the works with which the Spaniards began the settlement of the country.

At half-past eleven we left the lake for the last time, and entered an open plain. We rode an hour longer, and reached Nagarotis, a miserable village, its houses partly built of mud, with yards in front, trodden bare by mules, and baked white by the sun. I entered one of the houses for shelter, and found in it a young negro priest, on his way to Carthagena, with orders from the Church at Leon. The house was occupied by an old man alone. It had a bedstead, with a mat over it, upon which I lay down, glad to rest awhile, and to escape the scorching heat. Opposite the bed was a rude frame, about six feet high, on the top of which was a sort of baby-house, with the figure of the Virgin sitting on a chair, and dressed in cheap finery.

At three we started again. The sun had lost some of its force, the road was wooded, and I observed more than the usual number of crosses. The people of Nicaragua are said to be the worst in the republic. The inhabitants of the other States always caution a stranger against them, and they are proportionally devout. Everywhere, in the cities and country, on the tops of mountains, and by the side of rivers, these memorials stared me in the face. I noticed one in a cleared place by the roadside, painted black, with a black board suspended to it, containing an inscription in faded white letters; it had been erected to the memory of a padre, who had been murdered and buried at its foot. I stopped to copy the inscription, and while so engaged saw a travelling party approaching, and, knowing the jealousy of the people, shut my note-book and rode on. The party consisted of two men, with their servants, and a woman. The younger man accosted me, and said that he had seen me at Grenada, and regretted that he had not known of my proposed journey. From the style of his dress and equipments, I supposed him to be a gentleman, and was sure of it from the circumstance of his carrying a gamecock under his arm. As we rode on, the conversation turned upon these interesting birds, and I learned that my new acquaintance was going to Leon to fight a match, of which he offered to give me notice. The bird which he carried had won three matches in Grenada; its fame had reached Leon, and drawn forth a challenge from that place. It was rolled up as carefully as a fractured leg, with nothing but the head and tail visible; and, suspended by a string, was as easily carried as a basket. The young man sighed over the miseries of the country, the distress and ruin caused by the wars; and represented the pit at Grenada as being in a deplorable condition; but in Leon he said it was very flourishing, on account of its being the head-quarters of the military. The building, too, did honour to the city: it was only open on Sundays; but he knew the proprietor, and could at any time make an arrangement for a match. He made many inquiries about the state of the science in my country; told me that he had imported two cocks from England, which were game enough, but not sufficiently heavy for theirs; and gave me, besides, much valuable information on this subject, of which I neglected to make any memorandum.

Before dark we reached Pueblo Nuevo, and all went to the same posada. His companion was not so much of a sportsman, though he knew the qualities of a good bird, and showed a familiarity in handling them. It was the first time I had fallen in with travellers for the night. I have avoided details in all places where I was partaking of private hospitality, but this was like a hotel at home, in the main point, that all were expected to pay. We had for supper poached eggs and beans, without plate, knife, fork, or spoon. My companions used their tortillas to take up an egg, and also, by turning up the edges, to scoop out frigoles from the dish; withal, they were courteous and gentlemanly. We had a species of chocolate, made of pounded cocoa, and sweetened, and served in kickories, which, having bottoms like the ends of large eggs, could not stand on the table. My companions twisted their pocket-handkerchiefs, and winding them on the table in circular folds, set the kickories inside the hollow, and one of them did the same with my handkerchief for me. After supper the younger of the two dressed the birds in their *robes de nuit*, a cotton cloth wound tight around the body, compressing the wings, and then, with a string fastened to the back of the cloth, so that the body was balanced, hooked each of them to the hammock. While he was preparing them the woman was showing horn combs, beads, earrings, and rosaries, and entrapped the daughter of the host into the purchase of a comb. The house had an unusual influx of company. The young man, the female merchant, and I do not know how many of the family, slept in a back room. The elder traveller offered me a hammock, but I preferred the long chest, made from the trunk of a tree, which in every house in Nicaragua served as sort of cupboard.

CHAPTER XX.

BEAUTIFUL PLAIN—LEON—STROLL THROUGH THE TOWN—BANEFUL EFFECTS OF PARTY-SPIRIT—SCENES OF HORROR—UNPLEASANT INTELLIGENCE—JOURNEY CONTINUED—A FASTIDIOUS BEGGAR—CHINANDEGA—GULF OF CONCHAGUA—VISIT TO REALEJO—COTTON FACTORY—HARBOUR OF REALEJO—EL VIEJO—PORT OF NAGUISCOLO—IMPORTANCE OF A PASSPORT—EMBARKING MULES—A BUNGO—VOLCANO OF COSEGUINA—ERUPTION OF 1835—LA UNION.

At two o'clock we were awakened by the crowing of the cocks, and at three the cargo-mules were loaded, and we set off. The road was level and wooded, but desperately dusty. For two hours after daylight we had shade, when we came upon an open plain, bounded on the Pacific side by a low ridge, and on the right by a high range of mountains, forming part of the great chain of the Cordilleras. Before us, at a great distance, rising above the level of the plain, we saw the spires of the Cathedral of Leon. This magnificent plain, in richness of soil not surpassed by any land in the world, lay as desolate as when the Spaniards first traversed it. The dry season was near its close; for four months there had been no rain, and the dust hung around us in thick clouds, hot and fine as the sands of Egypt. At nine o'clock we reached Leon, and I parted with my companions, but not without a courteous invitation from the younger to take up my rest at the house of his brother. The suburbs were more miserable than anything I had yet seen. Passing up a long street, across which a sentinel was patrolling, I saw in front of the quartel a group of vagabond soldiers, a match for Carrera's, who cried out insolently, " Quita el sombrero," "Take off your hat." I had to traverse the whole extent of the city before I reached the house to which I had been recommended. I dismounted, and entered it with confidence of a warm reception; but the lady, with considerable expedition, told me that her husband was not at home. I gave her a note with which I had been furnished, addressed to herself; but she said she could not read English, and handed it back. I translated it word for word, being a request that she would give me lodgings. Her brow actually knit with vexation; and she said she had but one spare room, and that was reserved for the English vice-consul from Realejo. I answered that the vice-consul did not intend leaving Realejo for the present. She asked me how long I intended to stay; and when I replied, only that night, she said that if such were the case I might remain. The reader will perhaps wonder at my want of spirit; but the fact is, I was loth to consider any incivility personal. My only alternative was to seek out the young man whose invitation I had declined, and whose name I did not know, or to ask permission from door to door.

It is said that women are governed by appearances, and mine was not very seductive. My dress was the same with which I had left Grenada, soiled by the ascent of the Volcano of Masaya, and now covered with dust. Making the most of my moderate wardrobe, on my reappearance I was more favourably received. At least I had a capital breakfast; and as it was very hot, and I wanted to rest, I remained in doors and played with the children. At dinner I had the seat of honour at the head of the table, and had made such progress, that, if I had desired it, I could have ventured to broach the subject of remaining another day; and I owe it to the lady to say, that, having assented to my remaining, she treated me with great civility and attention, and particularly used great exertions in procuring me a guide to enable me to set out the next day.

After dinner Nicolas came to my room, and with uplifted hands cried out against the people of Leon, " Gente indecente, sin verguenza;" literally, "Indecent people, without shame." He had been hooted in the streets, and had heard such stories of the state of the country before us that he wanted to return home. I was extremely loth to make another change, and particularly for any of the assassin-looking scoundrels whom I had seen on my entry; but I did not like the responsibility of taking him against his will, and told him that if he would procure me two honest men he might leave me. I had advanced him more than was due, but I had a security against his deserting me in his apprehension of being taken for a soldier.

This over, I walked out to take a view of the town. It had an appearance of old and aristocratic respectability, which no other city in Central America possessed. The houses were large, and many of the fronts were covered with stucco ornaments; the plaza was spacious, and the squares of the churches and the churches themselves magnificent. It was the seat of a bishopric, and distinguished for the costliness of its churches and convents, its seats of learning, and its men of science, down to the time of its revolution against Spain; but in walking through its streets I saw palaces in which nobles had lived dismantled and roofless, and occupied by half-starved wretches, pictures of misery and want; and on one side an immense field of ruins, covering half the city.

I must confess that I felt a degree of uneasiness in walking the streets of Leon that I never felt in any city in the East. My change of dress did not make my presence more acceptable, and the eagle on my hat attracted particular attention. At every corner was a group of scoundrels, who stared at me as if disposed to pick a quarrel. With some my official character made me an object of suspicion; for in their disgraceful fights they thought that the eyes of the whole world were upon them, and that England, France, and the United States were secretly contending for the possession of their interesting country. I intended to pay a visit to the chief of the state; but, afraid of being insulted or getting into some difficulty that might detain me, I returned to the house.

By means of the servants, Nicolas had found two men who were willing to accompany me, but I did not like their looks, or even to let them know when I intended to set out. I had hardly disposed of them before my guide came to advise me not to set out the next day, as 500 soldiers, who had been making preparations for several days, were to march the next morning against San Salvador. This was most unpleasant intelligence. I did not wish to travel with them, or to fall in with them on the road; and calculating that their march would be slower than mine, told the guide to ascertain their time for starting, and we would set out two hours before them. Nicolas went out with him to take the mules to water; but they returned in great haste, with intelligence that piquets were scouring the city for men and mules, and had entered the yard of a padre near by and taken three of his animals. The lady of the house ordered all the doors to be locked and the keys brought to her, and an hour before dark we were all shut in, and my poor mules went without water.

At about eight o'clock we heard the tramp of cavalry in the streets, and gathering inside the doorway, saw about 600 men taking up their line of march. There was no music, no shouting, no waving of handkerchiefs, to cheer them as defenders of their country or as adventurers in the road to glory; but in the dark, and barefooted, their tread seemed stealthy; people looked at them with fear; and it seemed rather the sally of a band of conspirators than a march by the soldiers of a republic.

My muleteer did not return till daylight the next morning. Fortunately for us, he had learned that the troops were destined on another, but even a more inglorious expedition. Expenses had been incurred in sending troops into Honduras, of which Grenada refused to pay its portion, on the ground that, by the constitution, it was not liable except for expenses incurred in defending the borders of its own state. This was admitted; but the expense had been incurred; Leon had fought the battle, and had the same materials with which she gained it to enforce the contribution. In order that Grenada might be taken unawares, it was given out that the troops were destined for San Salvador, and they were actually marched out on the San Salvador road; but at midnight made a circuit, and took the route for Grenada. War between different states was bad enough, but here the flame which had before laid the capital in ruins was lighted again within its own borders. What the result of this expedition was I never heard; but probably, taken unawares and without arms, Grenada was compelled by bayonets to pay what, by the constitution, she was not bound to pay.

Outside of Leon, and once more on the back of my macho, I breathed more freely. Nicolas was induced to continue by hearing that there was a vessel at Realejo for Costa Rica, and I hoped to find one for Zonzonate The great plain of Leon was even more beautiful than before; too beautiful for the thankless people to whom the bounty of Providence had given it. On the left was the same low ridge separating it from the Pacific Ocean, and on the right the great range of Cordilleras, terminated by the volcano of the Viejo.

I had passed through the village of Chichuapa when I heard a cry of "caballero" behind me, and turning, saw divers people waving their hands, and a woman running, almost out of breath, with a pocket-handkerchief which I had left at the house where I breakfasted. I was going on, when a respectable-looking gentleman stopped me, with many apologies for the liberty, and asked for a medio, sixpence. I gave him one, which he examined, and handed back, saying, "No corre," "it does not pass." It was always, in paying money, a matter of course to have two or three pieces returned, and this I sometimes resisted; but as in this land everything was al reverso, it seemed regular for beggars to be choosers, and I gave him another.

My stopping-place was at the house of Mr. Bridges, an Englishman from one of the West India islands; and, as usual, my first business was to make arrangements for continuing my journey. My whole road was along the coast of the Pacific, but beyond this the Gulf of Conchagua made a large indentation in the land, which it was customary to cross in a bungo, sending the mules around the head of the gulf. I was informed that the latter was hazardous, as the Honduras troops were marching upon San Salvador, and would seize them. I might save them by going myself; but it was a journey of six days, through a country so desolate that it was necessary to carry food for the mules, and as I had still a long road beyond, I felt it necessary to economise my strength. I was loth to run the risk of losing my mules, and sent a courier to El Viejo, where the owners of the bungoes lived, to hire the largest, determined to run the risk of taking them with me. The next morning the courier returned, having procured a bungo, to be ready the next evening, and with a message from the owner that the embarcation must be at my risk.

Early the next morning I sent on an ox wagon with the luggage, and a stock of corn and grass for the mules during the voyage, and, after a pleasant ride of a league, reached the Viejo, one of the most respectable-looking towns in Nicaragua. The house of the owner of the bungo was one of the largest in the place, and furnished with two mahogany sofas made by a Yankee cabinet-maker in Lima, two looking-glasses with gilt frames, a French clock, gilt chairs with cane bottoms, and two Boston rocking-chairs, which had made the passage round Cape Horn. Don Francisco went over to the commandant. He, unluckily, had received his orders direct from the government, and dared not let me pass. I went over myself with Mr. Foster, the English vice-consul. The order was positive, and I was in agony. Here I made a push with my official character, and after an hour's torment, by the warm help of Mr. Foster, and upon his undertaking to save the commandant harmless, and to send an express immediately to Leon for a passport from the chief of the state, it was agreed that in the meantime I might go on.

I did not wait long, but, taking leave of Mr. Foster and Don Francisco, set out for the port. It was seven leagues, through an unbroken forest. On the way I overtook my bungo men, nearly naked, moving in single file, with the pilot at their head, and each carrying on his back an open network containing tortillas and provisions for the voyage. At half past two we reached the port of Naguiscolo. There was a single hut, at which a woman was washing corn, with a naked child near her on the ground, its face, arms, and body one running sore, a picture of squalid poverty. In front was a large muddy plain, through the centre of which ran a straight cut called a canal, with an embankment on one side dry, the mud baked hard, and bleached by the sun. In this ditch lay several bungoes high and dry, adding to the ugliness of the picture. I had a feeling of great satisfaction that I was not obliged to remain there long; but the miserable woman, with a tone of voice that seemed to rejoice in the chance of making others as miserable as herself, desisted from washing her maize, and screeched in my ears that a guarda had been sent direct from the capital, with orders to let no one embark without a passport. The guarda had gone down the river in a canoe, in search of a bungo which had attempted to go away without a passport; and I walked down the bank of the canal in hope to catch him alone when he returned. The sun was scorching hot, and as I passed the bungoes, the boatmen asked me if I had a passport. At the end of the canal, under the shade of a large tree, were two women; and they had been in that place three days, waiting for one of their party who had gone to Leon to procure a passport.

It was more than an hour before the guarda appeared. He was taken by the eagle on my hat, and while I told him my story, said, "Si, señor," to everything; but when I talked of embarking, said, "Señor, you have no passport." I will not inflict upon the reader the details of all my vexations and anxiety that afternoon. I was most eager to hurry on. To send a courier to Leon would keep me in suspense insufferable. Some difficulty might happen, and the only way for peace of mind was to return myself. I had already made a longer journey than is ever made in the country without an interval of rest. The road before me led through the seat of war, and four days' detention might throw me into the midst of it. (In fact, the result proved that one day would have done so.) I walked with the guarda to the hut, and in greater anxiety than I had felt since my departure from home, showed him my papers—a larger bundle, perhaps, than he had ever seen before, and with bigger seals, particularly my original passport from my own government—jumbling together his government and my government, the amicable relations existing between them, and trying to give him an overwhelming idea of my importance; but he knew no more what it meant than if I had repeated to him in English the fifth problem in Euclid. The poor man was almost in as great perplexity as I was. Several times he assented and retracted; and at length, upon my giving him a letter promising him the protection of Mr. Foster and the commandant at Viejo, he agreed to let the bungo go.

It was about an hour before dark when we went down to embark the mules. My bungo was at the extreme end of the canal, and the tide had risen so that she was afloat. We began with the grey, by casting a noose around her legs, drawing them together, and throwing her down. The men then attempted to lift her up bodily over the side of the bungo; but failing in this, took off the rudder, and leaning it against the side, hauled the mule up it, then tilted the rudder, and dropped her into the boat. In the meantime the macho stood under a tree, looking on very suspiciously, and with fearful forebodings. The noose was put round his legs, with a rope before and behind to pull on, and struggling desperately, he was thrown down, but hardly touched the ground before, with a desperate effort, he broke the ropes and rose upon his feet. A second attempt was more successful; but the two abreast made a close fit, and I was obliged to leave behind the luggage mule. I paid the guarda to take her to Mr. Foster, but whether she reached him or not I have never heard.

We were assisted by the boatmen of another bungo, and I ordered supper and agua ardiente for the whole. This was furnished at the hut by the guarda, and when it was over, the men, all in good spirits, commenced taking the luggage on board. At this time some who were detained were grumbling, and a new man entered the hut, as he said, direct from the Pueblo, who croaked in my ears the odious order, and the guard again made objections. I was excessively vexed by this last interruption; and fairly bullying the new comer out of the hut, told the guard that the thing was settled, and that I would not be trifled with, took up my gun, and told the men to follow me. I saw beforehand that they were elevated by their good cheer, and that I could rely upon them. The guard, and all those compelled to wait, followed; but we got on board, and my crew were so tipsy that they defied all opposition. One push cleared the bungo from the canal, and as she was passing out a stranger unexpectedly stepped on board, and in the dark slipped down under the awning with the mules. I was surprised and a little indignant that he had not asked leave, and it occurred to me that he was a partisan who might compromise me; but to return might lead to new difficulty, and, besides, he was probably some poor fellow escaping for his life, and it was better that I should know nothing about it. In the midst of my doubts a man on the bank cried out that fifty soldiers had arrived from Leon. It was pitchy dark; we could see nothing, and my men answered with a shout of defiance.

In the meantime we were descending rapidly, whirling around and hitting against the branches of trees; the mules were thrown down, the awning carried away, and in the midst of darkness and confusion we struck with a violent crash against another bungo, which knocked us all into a heap, and I thought would send us to the bottom. The men rose with roars of laughter. It was a bad beginning. Still I was overjoyed at being clear of the port, and there was a wild excitement in the scene itself. At length the men sat down to the oars, and pulled for a few minutes as if they would tear the old bungo out of the water, shouting all the time like spirits of darkness let loose. The pilot sat quietly at the helm without speaking, and dark as it was, at times I saw a smile steal over his face at the wild sallies of the boatmen. Again they began rowing furiously as before, and suddenly one of the sweeps broke and the oarsman fell backward. The bungo was run up among the trees, and the men climbed ashore by the branches. The blows of machetes, mingled with shouts and laughter, rang through the woods; they were the noisiest party I met in Central America. In the dark they cut down a dozen saplings before they found what they wanted, and in about an hour returned, and the shattered awning was refitted. By this time they were more sobered; and taking their sweeps, we moved silently down the dark river until one o'clock, when we came to anchor.

The bungo was about forty feet long, dug out of the trunk of a Guanacaste tree, about five feet wide and nearly as deep, with the bottom round, and a toldo, or awning, round like the top of a market-wagon, made of matting and bulls' hides, covered ten feet of the stern. Beyond were six seats across the sides of the bungo for the oarsmen. The whole front was necessary for the men, and in reality I had only the part occupied by the awning, where, with the mules as tenants in common, there were too many of us. They stood abreast, with their halters tied to the first bench. The bottom was rounding, and gave them an unsteady foothold; and when the boat heaved they had a scramble to preserve their centre of gravity. The space between their heels and the end of the log, or stern of the bungo, was my sleeping-room. Nicolas was afraid to pass between the mules to get a place among the men, and he could not climb over the awning. I had their heads tethered close up to the bench, and putting him outside to catch the first kick, drew up against the stern of the bungo and went to sleep.

At half past seven we weighed anchor, or hauled up a large stone, and started with oars. My boatmen were peculiar in their way of wearing pantaloons First they pulled them off, folded them about a foot wide and two feet long, and then suspended them over the belts of their machetes like little aprons. At nine o'clock we reached the mouth of the river. Here we hoisted sail, and while the wind was fair, did very well. The sun was scorching, and under the awning the heat was insufferable. Following the coast, at eleven o'clock we were opposite the volcano of Coseguina, a long dark mountain range, with another ridge running below it, and then an extensive plain covered with lava to the sea. The wind headed us, and in order to weather the point of headland from which we could lay our course, the boatmen got into the water to tow the bungo. I followed them, and with a broad-brimmed straw hat to protect me from the sun, I found the water was delightful. During this time one of the men brought sand from the shore to break the roundness of the bottom of the boat, and give the mules a foothold. Unable to weather the point, at half past one we came to anchor, and very soon every man on board was asleep.

I woke with the pilot's legs resting on my shoulder. It was rather an undignified position, but no one saw it. Before me was the volcano of Coseguina, with its field of lava and its desolate shore, and not a living being was in sight except my sleeping boatmen. Five years before, on the shores of the Mediterranean, and at the foot of Mount Etna, I read in a newspaper an account of the eruption of this volcano; little did I then ever expect to see it; the most awful in the history of volcanic eruptions, the noise of which startled the people of Guatimala 400 miles off; and at Kingston, Jamaica, *eight hundred miles* distant, was supposed to be signal guns of distress from some vessel at sea. The face of nature was changed; the cone of the volcano was gone; a mountain and field of lava ran down to the sea; a forest, old as creation, had entirely disappeared, and two islands were formed in the sea; shoals were discovered, in one of which a large tree was fixed upside down; one river was completely choked up, and another formed running in an opposite direction; seven men in the employ of my bungo proprietor ran down to the water, pushed off in a bungo, and were never heard of more; wild beasts, howling, left their caves in the mountains, and ounces, leopards, and snakes fled for shelter to the abodes of men.

This eruption took place on the 20th of January, 1835. Mr. Savage was on that day on the side of the volcano of San Miguel, distant 120 miles, looking for cattle. At eight o'clock he saw a dense cloud rising in the south in a pyramidal form, and heard a noise which sounded like the roaring of the sea. Very soon the thick clouds were lighted up by vivid flashes, rose-coloured and forked, shooting and disappearing, which he supposed to be some electrical phenomenon. These appearances increased so fast that his men became frightened, and said it was a ruina, and that the end of the world was nigh. Very soon he himself was satisfied that it was the eruption of a volcano; and as Coseguina was at that time a quiet mountain, not suspected to contain subterraneous fires, he supposed it to proceed from the volcano of Tigris. He returned to the town of San Miguel, and in riding a short distance, felt three severe shocks of earthquake. The inhabitants were distracted with terror. Birds flew wildly through the streets, and, blinded by the dust, fell dead on the ground. At four o'clock it was so dark that, as Mr. S. says, he held up his hand before his eyes, and could not see it. Nobody moved without a candle, which gave a dim and misty light, extending only a few feet. At this time the church was full, and could not contain half who wished to enter. The figure of the Virgin was brought out into the plaza and borne through the streets, followed by the inhabitants, with candles and torches, in penitential procession, crying upon the Lord to pardon their sins. Bells tolled, and during the procession there was another earthquake, so violent and long that it threw to the ground many people walking in the procession. The darkness continued till eleven o'clock the next day, when the sun was partially visible, but dim and hazy, and without any brightness. The dust on the ground was four inches thick; the branches of trees broke with its weight, and people were so disfigured by it that they could not be recognised.

Towards evening my men all woke; the wind was fair, but they took things quietly, and after supper hoisted sail. About twelve o'clock, by an amicable arrangement, I stretched myself on the pilot's bench under the tiller, and when I woke we had passed the volcano of Tigris, and were in an archipelago of islands more beautiful than the islands of Greece. The wind died away, and the boatmen, after playing for a little while with the oars, again let fall the big stone and went to sleep. Outside the awning the heat of the sun was withering, under it the closeness was suffocating, and my poor mules had had no water since their embarkation. In the confusion of getting away I had forgotten it till the moment of departure, and then there was no vessel in which to carry it. After giving them a short nap I roused the men, and with the promise of a reward induced them to take to their oars. Fortunately, before they got tired we had a breeze, and at about four o'clock in the afternoon the big stone was dropped in the harbour of La Union, in front of the town. One ship was lying at anchor, a whaler from Chili, which had put in in distress and been condemned.

The commandant was Don Manuel Romero, one of Morazan's veterans, who was anxious to retire altogether from public life, but remained in office because, in his present straits, he could be useful to his benefactor and friend. He had heard of me, and his attentions reminded me of, what I sometimes forgot, but which others very rarely did, my official character; he invited me to his house while I remained in La Union, but gave me intelligence which made me more anxious than ever to hurry on. General Morazan had left the port but a few days before, having accompanied his family thither on their way to Chili. On his return to San Salvador he intended to march directly against Guatimala. By forced marches I might overtake him, and go up under the escort of his army, trusting to chance to avoid being on the spot in case of a battle, or from my acquaintance with Carrera get passed across the lines. Fortunately, the captain of the condemned ship wished to go to San Salvador, and agreed to accompany me the next day.

CHAPTER XXI.

JOURNEY TO SAN SALVADOR—A NEW COMPANION—SAN ALEJO—WAR ALARMS—STATE OF SAN SALVADOR—RIVER LEMPA—SAN VICENTE—VOLCANO OF SAN VICENTE—THERMAL SPRINGS—COJUTEPEQUE—ARRIVAL AT SAN SALVADOR—PREJUDICE AGAINST FOREIGNERS—CONTRIBUTIONS—PRESS-GANGS—VICE-PRESIDENT VIGIL—TAKING OF SAN MIGUEL AND SAN VICENTE—RUMOURS OF A MARCH UPON SAN SALVADOR—DEPARTURE FROM SAN SALVADOR—LA BARRANCA DE GUARAMAL—VOLCANO OF IZALCO—DEPREDATIONS OF RASCON—ZONZONATE—NEWS FROM GUATIMALA—JOURNEY CONTINUED—AGUISALCO—APENECA—MOUNTAIN OF AGUACHAPA—SUBTERRANEAN FIRES—AGUACHAPA—DEFEAT OF MORAZAN—CONFUSION AND TERROR.

AT five o'clock the next afternoon we set out for San Salvador. Don Manuel Romero furnished me with letters of introduction to all the Gefes Politicos, and the captain's name was inserted in my passport.

I must introduce the reader to my new friend. Captain Antonio V. F., a little over thirty, when six months out on a whaling voyage, with a leaky ship and a mutinous crew, steered across the Pacific for the Continent of America, and reached the port of La Union with seven or eight feet water in the hold and half his crew in irons. He knew nothing of Central America until necessity threw him upon its shore. While waiting the slow process of a regular condemnation and order for the sale of his ship, General Morazan, with an escort of officers, came to the port to embark his wife and family for Chili. Captain F. had become acquainted with them, and through them with their side of the politics of the country; and in the evening, while we were riding along the ridge of a high mountain, he told me that he had been offered a lieutenant-colonel's commission, and was then on his way to join Morazan in his march against Guatimala. His ship was advertised for sale, he had written an account of his misadventures to his owners and his wife, was tired of remaining at the port, and a campaign with Morazan was the only thing that offered. He liked General Morazan, and he liked the country, and thought his wife would; if Morazan succeeded there would be vacant offices and estates without owners, and some of them worth having. He went from whaling to campaigning as coolly as a Yankee would from cutting down trees to editing a newspaper. It was no affair of mine, but I suggested that there was no honour to be gained; that he would get his full share of hard knocks, bullets, and sword-cuts; that if Morazan succeeded he would have a desperate struggle for his share of the spoils, and if Morazan failed he would certainly be shot. All this was matter he had thought on, and before committing himself he intended to make his observations at San Salvador.

At ten o'clock we reached the village of San Alejo, and stopped at a very comfortable house, where all were in a state of excitement from the report of an invasion from Honduras.

The captain had great difficulty in procuring mules; he had two enormous trunks, containing, among other things, Peruvian chains and other gold trinkets to a large amount; in fact, all he was worth. In the evening we walked to the plaza; groups of men, wrapped in their ponchas, were discussing in low tones the movements of the enemy, how far they had marched that day, how long they would require for rest, and the moment when it would be necessary to fly. We returned to the house, placed two naked wooden-bottomed bedsteads in one, and having ascertained by calculation that we were not likely to be disturbed during the night, forgot the troubles of the flying inhabitants, and slept soundly.

On account of the difficulty of procuring mules, we did not set out till ten o'clock. The climate is the hottest in Central America, and insalubrious under exposure to the sun; but we would not wait. Every moment there were new rumours of the approach of the Honduras army, and it was all important for us to keep in advance of them. I shall hasten over our hurried journey through the state of San Salvador, the richest in Central America, extending 180 miles along the shores of the Pacific, producing tobacco, the best indigo, and richest balsam in the world.

In the afternoon of the second day we came in sight of the Lempa, now a gigantic river rolling on to the Pacific. Three months before I had seen it a little stream among the mountains of Esquipulas. Here we were overtaken by Don Carlos Rivas, a leading Liberal from Honduras, flying for life before partisan soldiers of his own state. We descended to the bank of the river, and followed it through a wild forest, which had been swept by a tornado, the trees still lying as they fell. At the crossing-place, the valley of the river was half-a-mile wide; but being the dry season, on this side there was a broad beach of sand and stones. We rode to the water's edge, and shouted for the boatman on the opposite side. Other parties arrived, all fugitives, among them the wife and family of Don Carlos, and we formed a crowd upon the shore. At length the boat came, took on board sixteen mules, saddles and luggage, and as many men, women and children as could stow themselves away, leaving a multitude behind. We crossed in the dark, and on the opposite side found every hut and shed filled with fugitives; families in dark masses were under the trees, and men and women crawled out to congratulate friends who had put the Lempa between them and the enemy. We slept upon our luggage on the bank of the river, and before daylight were again in the saddle.

That night we slept at San Vicente, and the next morning the captain, in company with an invalid officer of Morazan's, who had been prevented by sickness from accompanying the general in his march against Guatimala, rode on with the luggage, while I, with Colonel Hoyas, made a circuit to visit El Infierno of the volcano of San Vicente. Crossing a beautiful plain running to the base of the volcano, we left our animals at a hut, and walked some distance to a stream in a deep ravine, which we followed upward to its source, coming from the very base of the volcano. The water was warm, and had a taste of vitriol, and the banks were incrusted with white vitriol and flour of sulphur. At a distance of 100 or 200 yards it formed a basin, where the water was hotter than the highest grade of my Réaumur's thermometer. In several places we heard subterranean noises, and toward the end of the ravine, on the slope of one side, was an orifice about 30 feet in diameter, from which, with a terrific noise, boiling water was spouted into the air. This is called El Infiernillo, or the "little infernal regions." The inhabitants say that the noise is increased by the slightest agitation of the air, even by the human voice. Approaching to within range of the falling water, we shouted several times, and as we listened and gazed into the fearful cavity, I imagined that the noise was louder and more angry, and that the boiling water spouted higher at our call. Colonel Hoyas conducted me to a path, from which I saw my road, like a white line, over a high verdant mountain. He told me that many of the inhabitants of San Miguel had fled to San Vicente, and at that place the Honduras arms would be repelled; we parted, little expecting to see each other again so soon, and under such unpleasant circumstances for him.

I overtook the captain at a village where he had breakfast prepared, and in the afternoon we arrived at Cojutepeque, until within two days the temporary capital, beautifully situated at the foot of a small extinct volcano, its green and verdant sides broken only by a winding path, and on the top a fortress, which Morazan had built as his last rallying-place, to die under the flag of the Republic.

The next day at one o'clock we reached San Salvador. Entering by a fine gate, and through suburbs teeming with fruit and flower trees, the meanness of the houses was hardly noticed. Advancing, we saw heaps of rubbish, and large houses with their fronts cracked and falling, marks of the earthquakes which had broken it up as the seat of government, and almost depopulated the city. This series of earthquakes commenced on the third of the preceding October, and for twenty days the earth was tremulous, sometimes suffering fifteen or twenty shocks in twenty-four hours, and one so severe that, as Mr. Chatfield told me, a bottle standing in his sleeping-room was thrown down. Most of the inhabitants abandoned the city, and those who remained slept under matting in the courtyards of their houses. Every house was more or less injured; some were rendered untenantable, and many were thrown down. Two days before, the vice-president and officers of the Federal and State Governments, impelled by the crisis of the times, had returned to their shattered capital. It was about one o'clock, intensely hot, and there was no shade; the streets were solitary, the doors and windows of the houses closed, the shops around the plaza shut, the little matted tents of the market-women deserted, and the inhabitants, forgetting earthquakes, and that a hostile army was marching upon them, were taking their noonday siesta. In a corner of the plaza was a barricado, constructed with trunks of trees, rude as an Indian fortress, and fortified with cannon, intended as the scene of the last effort for the preservation of the city. A few soldiers were asleep under the corridor of the quartel, and a sentinel was pacing before the door. Inquiring our way of him, we turned the corner of the plaza, and stopped at the house of Don Pedro Negrete, at that time acting as vice-consul both of England and France, and the only representative at the capital of any foreign power.

In the evening I called upon the vice-president. Great changes had taken place since I saw him at Zonzonate. The troops of the Federal government had been routed in Honduras; Carrera had conquered Quezaltenango, garrisoned it with his own soldiers, destroyed its existence as a separate state, and annexed it to Guatimala. San Salvador stood alone in support of the Federal Government. But Señor Vigil had risen with the emergency. The chief of the state, a bold-looking mulatto, and other officers of the government, were with him. They knew that the Honduras troops were marching upon the city, had reason to fear they would be joined by those of Nicaragua, but they were not dismayed; on the contrary, all showed a resolution and energy I had not seen before. General Morazan, they said, was on his march against Guatimala. Tired as they were of war, the people of San Salvador, Señor Vigil said, had risen with new enthusiasm. Volunteers were flocking in from all quarters; and with a determination that was imposing, though called out by civil war, he added that they were resolved to sustain the Federation, or die under the ruins of San Salvador. It was the first time my feelings had been at all roused. In all the convulsions of the time I had seen no flush of heroism, no high love of country. Self-preservation and self-aggrandisement were the ruling passions. It was a bloody scramble for power and place; and sometimes, as I rode through the beautiful country, and saw what Providence had done for them, and how unthankful they were, I thought it would be a good riddance if they would play out the game of the Kilkenny cats.

In the excitement and alarm of the place, it was very difficult to procure mules. As to procuring them direct for Guatimala, it was impossible. No one would move on that road until the result of Morazan's expedition was known; and even to get them for Zonzonate it was necessary to wait a day. That day I intended to abstract myself from the tumult of the city and ascend the volcano of San Salvador; but the next morning a woman came to inform us that one of our men had been taken by a pressgang of soldiers, and was in the carcel. We followed her to the place, and, being invited in by the officer to pick out our man, found ourselves surrounded by 100 of Vigil's volunteers, of every grade in appearance and character, from the frightened servant-boy torn from his master's door to the worst of desperadoes; some asleep on the ground, some smoking stumps of cigars, some sullen, and others perfectly reckless. Two of the supreme worst did me the honour to say they liked my looks, called me captain, and asked me to take them into my company. Our man was not ambitious, and could do better than be shot at for a shilling a day; but we could not take him out without an order from the chief of the state, and went immediately to the office of the government, where I was sorry to meet Señor Vigil, as the subject of my visit and the secrets of the prison were an unfortunate comment upon his boasts of the enthusiasm of the people in taking up arms. With his usual courtesy, however, he directed the proper order to be made out, and the names of all in my service to be sent to the captains of the different pressgangs, with orders not to touch them. All day men were caught and brought in, and petty officers were stationed along the street drilling them. In the afternoon intelligence was received that General Morazan's advanced guard had defeated a detachment of Carrera's troops, and that he was marching with an accession of forces upon Guatimala. A feu-de-joie was fired in the plaza, and all the church bells rang peals of victory.

In the evening I saw Señor Vigil again and alone. He was confident of the result. The Honduras troops would be repulsed at San Vicente; Morazan would take Guatimala. He urged me to wait; he had his preparations all made, his horses ready, and, on the first notice of Morazan's entry, intended to go up to Guatimala, and establish that city once more as the capital. But I was afraid of delay, and we parted to meet in Guatimala; but we never met again. A few days afterwards he was flying for his life, and is now in exile, under sentence of death if he returns; the party that rules Guatimala is heaping opprobrium upon his name; but in the recollection of my hurried tour I never forget him who had the unhappy distinction of being vice-president of the Republic.

I did not receive my passport till late in the evening, and though I had given directions to the contrary, the captain's name was inserted. We had already had a difference of opinion in regard to our movements. He was not so bent as I was upon pushing on to Guatimala, and besides, I did not consider it right, in an official passport, to have the name of a partisan. Accordingly, early in the morning I went to the Government House to have it altered. The separate passports were just handed to me when I heard a clatter in the streets, and fifteen or twenty horsemen galloped into the courtyard, covered with sweat and dust, among whom I recognised Colonel Hoyas, with his noble horse, so broken that I did not know him. They had ridden all night. The Honduras troops had taken San Miguel and San Vicente, and were then marching upon San Salvador. If not repulsed at Cojutepeque, that day they would be upon the capital. For four days I had been running before these troops, and now, by a strange caprice, at the prospect of actual collision, I regretted that my arrangements were so far advanced, and that I had no necessity for remaining. I had a strong curiosity to see a city taken by assault, but, unfortunately, I had not the least possible excuse. I had my passport in my hand and my mules were ready. Nevertheless, before I reached Don Pedro's house I determined to remain. The captain had his sword and spurs on, and was only waiting for me. I told him the news, and he uttered an exclamation of thankfulness that we were all ready, and mounted immediately. I added that I intended to remain. He refused; said that he knew the sanguinary character of the people better than I did, and did not wish to see an affair without having a hand in it. I replied, and after a short controversy, the result was as usual between two obstinate men: I would not go and he would not stay. I sent my luggage-mules and servants under his charge, and he rode off, to stop for me at a hacienda on the road, while I unsaddled my horse and gave him another mess of corn.

In the meantime the news had spread, and great excitement prevailed in the city. Here there was no thought of flight; the spirit of resistance was general. The impressed soldiers were brought out from the prisons and furnished with arms, and drums beat through the streets for volunteers. On my return from the Government House I noticed a tailor on his board at work; when I passed again his horse was at the door, his sobbing wife was putting pistols in his holsters, and he was fastening on his spurs. Afterward I saw him mounted before the quartel, receiving a lance with a red flag, and then galloping off to take his place in the line. In two hours all that the impoverished city could do was done. Vigil, the chief of the state, clerks, and household servants, were preparing for the last struggle. At twelve o'clock the city was as still as death. I lounged on the shady side of the plaza, and the quiet was fearful. At two o'clock intelligence was received that the troops of San Vicente had fallen back upon Cojutepeque, and that the Honduras troops had not yet come up. An order was immediately issued to make this the rallying-place, and to send thither the mustering of the city. About 200 lancers set off from the plaza with a feeble shout, under a burning sun, and I returned to the house. The commotion subsided; my excitement died away, and I regretted that I had not set out with the captain, when, to my surprise, he rode into the courtyard. On the road he thought that he had left me in the lurch, and that, as a travelling companion, he ought to have remained with me. I had no such idea, but I was glad of his return, and mounted, and left my capital to its fate, even yet uncertain whether I had any government.

The captain had given me a hint in a led horse which he kept for emergencies, and I had bought one of an officer of General Morazan, who sold him because he would not stand fire, and recommended him for a way he had of carrying his rider out of the reach of bullets. At the distance of two leagues we reached a hacienda where our men where waiting for us with the luggage. It was occupied by a miserable old man alone, with a large swelling under his throat, very common all through this country, the same as is seen among the mountains of Switzerland. While the men were reloading, we heard the tramp of horses, and fifteen or twenty lancers galloped up to the fence; and the leader, a dark, stern, but respectable-looking man about forty, in a deep voice, called to the old man to get ready and mount; the time had come, he said, when every man must fight for his country; if they had done so before, their own ships would be floating on the Atlantic and the Pacific, and they would not now be at the mercy of strangers and enemies. Altogether the speech was a good one, but made from the back of a horse by a powerful man, well armed, and with twenty lancers at his heels, it was not pleasant in the ears of the "strangers" for whom it was intended. Really I respected the man's energy, but his expression and manner precluded all courtesies; and though he looked at us for an answer, we said nothing The old man answered that he was too old to fight, and the officer told him then to help others to do so, and to contribute his horses or mules. This touched us again; and taking ours apart, we left exposed and alone an object more miserable as a beast than his owner was as a man. The old man said this was his all. The officer, looking as if he would like a pretext for seizing ours, told him to give her up; and the old man, slowly untying her, without a word led her to the fence, and handed the halter across to one of the lancers. They laughed as they received the old man's all, and pricking the mule with their lances, galloped off in search of more " contributions."

Some time after dark we reached the hacienda of Guaramal, and before day-light the next morning we were in the saddle. In the evening we arrived at Izalco, and I again heard the deep rumbling noise of the volcano, sounding like distant thunder.

Early in the morning we started, arrived at Zonzonate before breakfast, and rode to the house of my friend M. de Nouvelle. It was exactly two months since I left it, and, with the exception of my voyage on the Pacific and sickness at Costa Rica, I had not had a day of repose.

I was now within four days of Guatimala, but the difficulty of going on was greater than ever. The captain could procure no mules. No, intelligence had been received of Morazan's movements; intercourse was entirely broken off, business at a stand, and the people anxiously waiting for news from Guatimala. Nobody would set out on that road. I was very much distressed. The rainy season was coming on, and by the loss of a month, the journey to Palenque would be prevented. I considered it actually safer to pass through while all was in this state of suspense, than after the floodgates of war were opened. Rascon's band had prevented my passing the road before, and other Rascons might spring up. The captain had not the same inducement to push ahead that I had. I had no idea of incurring any unnecessary risk, and on the road would have no hesitation at any time in putting spurs to my horse; and on deliberate consideration, my mind was so fully made up that I determined to procure a guide at any price, and set out alone.

In the midst of my perplexity, a tall thin, gaunt-looking Spaniard, whose name was Don Saturnino Tinocha, came to see me. He was a merchant from Costa Rica, so far on his way to Guatimala, and, by the advice of his friends rather than his own judgment, had been already waiting a week at Zonzonate. He was exactly in the humour.

to suit me, very anxious to reach Guatimala; and his views and opinions were just the same as mine. The captain was indifferent, and, at all events, could not go unless he could procure mules. I told Don Saturnino that I would go at all events, and he undertook to provide for the captain. In the evening he returned, with intelligence that he had scoured the town and could not procure a single mule, but he offered to leave two of his own cargoes and take the captain's, or to sell him two of his mules. I offered to lend him my horse or macho, and the matter was arranged.

In the evening we were again in the midst of tumult. Two of Captain D'Yriarte's passengers for Guayaquil, whom he had given up, arrived that evening direct from Guatimala, and reported that Carrera, with 2,000 men, had left the city at the same time with them to march upon San Salvador. Carrera knew nothing of Morazan's approach; his troops were a disorderly and tumultuous mass; and three leagues from the city, when they halted, the horses were already tired. Here our informants slipped away, and three hours afterward met Morazan's army, in good order, marching single file, with Morazan himself at their head, he and all his cavalry dismounted, and leading their horses, which were fresh and ready for immediate action. Morazan stopped them, and made them show their passports and letters, and they told him of the sally of Carrera's army, and its condition; and we all formed the conclusion that Morazan had attacked them the same day, defeated them, and was then in possession of Guatimala. Upon the whole, we considered the news favourable to us, as his first business would be to make the roads secure.

At three o'clock the next morning we were again in the saddle. A stream of fire was rolling down the volcano of Izalco, bright, but paler by the moonlight. The road was good for two leagues, when we reached the Indian village of Aguisalco. Our mules were overloaded, and one of Don Saturnino's gave out entirely. We tried to procure others or Indian carriers, but no one would move from home. Don Saturnino loaded his saddle-mule, and walked; and if it had not been for his indefatigable perseverance, we should have been compelled to stop.

At one o'clock we reached Apeneco, and rode up to one of the best houses, where an old man and his wife undertook to give us breakfast. Our mules presented a piteous spectacle. Mine, which had carried my light luggage like a feather all the way from La Union, had gone on with admirable steadiness up hill and down dale, but when we stopped she trembled in every limb, and before the cargo was removed I expected to see her fall. Nicolas and the muleteer said she would certainly die, and the faithful brute seemed to look at me reproachfully for having suffered so heavy a load to be put upon her back. I tried to buy or hire another, but all were removed one or two days' journey out of the line of march of the soldiers.

It was agreed that I should go on to Aguachapa and endeavour to have other mules ready early the next morning; but in the meantime the captain conceived some suspicions of the old man and woman, and resolved not to remain that night in the village. Fortunately, my mule revived and began to eat. Don Saturnino repeated his "'sta bueno," with which he had cheered us through all the perplexities of the day, and we determined to set out again. Neither of us had any luggage he was willing to leave, for in all probability he would never see it again. We loaded our saddle-beasts, and walked. Immediately on leaving the village we commenced ascending the mountain of Aguachapa, the longest and worst in the whole road, in the wet season requiring two days to cross it. A steep pitch at the beginning made me tremble for the result. The ascent was about three miles, and on the very crest, embowered among the trees, was a blacksmith's shop, commanding a view of the whole country back to the village, and on the other side, of the slope of the mountain to the plain of Aguachapa. The clink of the hammer and the sight of a smith's grimed face seemed a profanation of the beauties of the scene. Here our difficulties were over; the rest of our road was down hill. The road lay along the ridge of the mountain. On our right we looked down the perpendicular side to a plain 2,000 feet below us: and in front, on another part of the same plain, were the lake and town of Aguachapa. Instead of going direct to the town, we turned round the foot of the mountain, and came into a field smoking with hot springs. The ground was incrusted with sulphur, and dried and baked by subterranean fires. In some places were large orifices, from which steam rushed out violently and with noise, and in others large pools or lakes, one of them 150 feet in circumference, of dark brown water, boiling with monstrous bubbles three or four feet high, which Homer might have made the head-waters of Acheron. All around, for a great extent, the earth was in a state of combustion, burning our boots and frightening the horses, and we were obliged to be careful to keep the horses from falling through. At some distance was a stream of sulphur-water, which we followed up to a broad basin, made a dam with stones and bushes, and had a most refreshing warm bath.

It was nearly dark when we entered the town, the frontier of the State and the outpost of danger. All were on the tiptoe of expectation for news from Guatimala. Riding through the plaza, we saw a new corps of about 200 "patriot soldiers," uniformed and equipped, at evening drill, which was a guarantee against the turbulence we had seen in Izalco. Colonel Angoula, the commandant, was the same who had broken up the band of Rascon. Every one we met was astonished at our purpose of going on to Guatimala, and it was vexatious and discouraging to have ominous cautions perpetually dinned into our ears. We rode to the house of the widow Padilla, a friend of Don Saturnino, whom we found in great affliction. Her eldest son, on a visit to Guatimala on business, with a regular passport, had been thrown into prison by Carrera, and had then been a month in confinement; and she had just learned, what had been concealed from her, that the other son, a young man just twenty-one, had joined Morazan's expedition. Our purpose of going to Guatimala opened the fountain of her sorrows. She mourned for her sons, but the case of the younger seemed to give her most distress. She mourned that he had become a soldier; she had seen so much of the horrors of war; and, as if speaking of a truant boy, begged us to urge General Morazan to send him home. She was still in mourning for their father, who was a personal friend of General Morazan, and had, besides, three daughters, all young women, the eldest not more than twenty-three, married to Colonel Molina, the second in command; all were celebrated in that country for their beauty; and though the circumstances of the night prevented my seeing much of them, I looked upon this as one of the most lady-like and interesting family groups I had seen in the country.

Our first inquiry was for mules. Colonel Molina, the son-in-law, after endeavouring to dissuade us from continuing, sent out to make inquiries, and the result was that there were none to hire, but there was a man who had two to sell, and who promised to bring them early in the morning. We had vexations enough without adding any between ourselves; but, unfortunately, the captain and Don Saturnino had an angry quarrel, growing out of the breaking down of the mules. I was appealed to by both, and, in trying to keep the peace, came near having both upon me. The dispute was so violent that none of the female part of the family appeared in the sala, and while it was pending Colonel Molina was called off by a message from the commandant. In half an hour he returned, and told us that two soldiers had just entered the town, who reported that Morazan had been defeated in his attack on Guatimala, and his whole army routed and cut to pieces; that he himself, with fifteen dragoons, was escaping by the way of the coast, and the whole of Carrera's army was in full pursuit. The soldiers were at first supposed to be deserters, but they were recognised by some of the townspeople; and after a careful examination and calculation of the lapse of time since the last intelligence, the news was believed to be true. The consternation it created in our little household cannot be described. Morazan's defeat was the death-knell of sons and brothers It was not a moment for strangers to offer idle consolation, and we withdrew.

Our own plans were unsettled; the very dangers I feared had happened; the soldiers, who had been kept together in masses, were disbanded, to sweep every road in the country with the ferocity of partisan war. But for the night we could do nothing. Our men were already asleep, and, not without apprehensions, the captain and I retired to a room opening upon the courtyard. Don Saturnino wrapped himself in his poncha, and lay down under the corridor.

None of us undressed, but the fatigue of the day had been so great that I soon fell into a profound sleep. At one o'clock we were roused by Colonel Molina shouting in the doorway, " La gente viene ! " "The people are coming !" His sword glittered, his spurs rattled, and by the moonlight I saw men saddling horses in the courtyard. We sprang up in a moment, and he told us to save ourselves; "la gente", were coming, and within two hours' march of the town. My first question was, What had become of the soldiers ? They were already marching out; everybody was preparing to fly; he intended to escort the ladies to a hiding-place in the mountains, and then to overtake the soldiers. I must confess that my first thought was " devil take the hindmost;" and I ordered Nicolas, who was fairly blubbering with fright, to saddle for a start. The captain, however, objected, insisting that to fly would be to identify ourselves with the fugitives; and if we were overtaken with them we should certainly be massacred. Don Saturnino proposed to set out on our journey, and go straight on to a hacienda two leagues beyond; if we met them on the road we should appear as travellers; in their hurry they would let us pass; and, at all events, we should avoid the dangers of a general sacking and plunder of the town. I approved of this suggestion; the fact is, I was for anything that put us on horseback; but the captain again opposed it violently. Unluckily, he had four large, heavy trunks, containing jewellery and other valuables, and no mules to carry them. I made a hurried but feeling comment upon the comparative value of life and property; but the captain said that all he was worth in the world was in those trunks; he would not leave them; he would not risk them on the road; he would defend them as long as he had life; and, taking them up one by one from the corridor, he piled them inside of our little sleeping-room, shut the door, and swore that nobody should get into them without passing over his dead body. Now I, for my own part, would have taken a quiet stripping, and by no means approved this desperate purpose of the captain's. The fact is, I was very differently situated from him. My property was chiefly in horse-flesh and mule-flesh, at the moment the most desirable thing in which money could be invested; and with two hours' start I would have defied all the Cachurecos in Guatimala to catch me. But the captain's determination put an end to all thoughts of testing the soundness of my investment; and perhaps, at all events, it was best to remain.

I entered the house, where the old lady and her daughters were packing up their valuables, and passed through to the street. The church bells were tolling with a frightful sound, and a horseman, with a red banneret on the point of his lance, was riding through the streets, warning the inhabitants to fly. Horses were standing before the doors saddled and bridled, and all along men were issuing from the doors with loads on their backs, and women with packages and bundles in their hands, and hurrying children before them. The moon was beaming with unrivalled splendour: the women did not scream, the children did not cry; terror was in every face and movement, but too deep for utterance. I walked down to the church; the cura was at the altar, receiving hurried confessions and administering the sacrament; and as the wretched inhabitants left the altar they fled from the town. I saw a poor mother searching for a missing child; but her friends, in hoarse whispers, said, "La gente viene!" and hurried her away. A long line of fugitives, with loaded mules interspersed, was moving from the door of the church, and disappearing beneath the brow of the hill. It was the first time I ever saw terror operating upon masses, and I hope never to see it again. I went back to the house. The family of Padilla had not left, and the poor widow was still packing up. We urged Colonel Molina to hasten; as commandant, he would be the first victim. He knew his danger, but in a tone of voice that told the horrors of this partisan war, said he could not leave behind him the young women. In a few moments all was ready; the old lady gave us the key of the house, we exchanged the Spanish farewell with a mutual recommendation to God, and sadly and silently they left the town. Colonel Molina remained a moment behind. Again he urged us to fly, saying that the enemy were robbers, murderers, and assassins, who would pay no respect to person or character, and disappointment at finding the town deserted would make them outrageous with us. He drove his spurs into his horse, and we never saw him again. On the steps of the church were sick and infirm old men and children, and the cura's house was thronged with the same helpless beings. Except these, we were left in sole possession of the town.

It was not yet an hour since we had been roused from sleep. We had not been able to procure any definite information as to the character of the approaching force. The alarm was, "La gente viene;" no one knew or thought of more,—no one paid any attention to us,— and we did not know whether the whole army of Carrera was approaching, or merely a roving detachment. If the former, my hope was that Carrera was with them, and that he had not forgotten my diplomatic coat. I felt rejoiced that the soldiers had marched out, and that the inhabitants had fled; there could be no resistance, no bloodshed, nothing to excite a lawless soldiery. Again we walked down to the church; old women and little boys gathered around us, and wondered that we did not fly. We went to the door of the cura's house; the room was small, and full of old women. We tried to cheer them, but old age had lost its garrulity; they waited their fate in silence. We returned to the house, smoked, and waited in anxious expectation. The enemy did not come, the bell ceased its frightful tolling, and after a while we began to wish they would come, and let us have the thing over. We went out, and looked, and listened; but there was neither sound nor motion. We became positively tired of waiting: there were still two hours to daylight; we lay down, and, strange to say, again fell asleep.

CHAPTER XXII.

APPROACH OF CARRERA'S FORCES—TERROR OF THE INHABITANTS—THEIR FLIGHT—SURRENDER OF THE TOWN—FEROCITY OF THE SOLDIERY—A BULLETIN—DIPLOMACY—A PASSPORT—A BREAKFAST—AN ALARM—THE WIDOW PADILLA—AN ATTACK—DEFEAT OF CARRERA'S FORCES—THE TOWN TAKEN BY GENERAL MORAZAN—HIS ENTRY—THE WIDOW'S SON—VISIT TO GENERAL MORAZAN—HIS APPEARANCE, CHARACTER, ETC.—PLANS DERANGED.

IT was broad daylight when we woke, without any machete cuts, and still in undisturbed possession of the town. My first thought was for the mules; they had eaten up their sacate, and had but a poor chance for more, but I sent them immediately to the river for water. They had hardly gone when a little boy ran in from the church, and told us that "la gente" were in sight. We hurried back with him, and the miserable beings on the steps, with new terrors, supposing that we were friends of the invaders, begged us to save them. Followed by three or four trembling boys, we ascended to the steeple, and saw the Cachurecos at a distance, descending the brow of a hill in single file, their muskets glittering in the sunbeams. We saw that it was not the whole of Carrera's army, but apparently only a pioneer company; but they were too many for us, and the smallness of their numbers gave them the appearance of a lawless predatory band. They had still to cross a long plain and ascend the hill on which the town was built. The bell-rope was in reach of my hand; I gave it one strong pull, and telling the boys to sound loud the alarm, hurried down. As we passed out of the church, we heard loud cries from the old women in the house of the cura; and the old men and children on the steps asked us whether they would be murdered.

The mules had not returned, and, afraid of their being intercepted in the street, I ran down a steep hill toward the river, and meeting them, hurried back to the house. While doing so I saw at the extreme end of the street a single soldier moving cautiously; and watching carefully every house, as if suspecting treachery, he advanced with a letter directed to Colonel Angoula. The captain told him that he must seek Angoula among the mountains. We inquired the name of his commanding officer, how many men he had, said that there was no one to oppose him, and forthwith surrendered the town. The man could hardly believe that it was deserted. General Figoroa did not know it; he had halted at a short distance, afraid to make the attack at night, and was then expecting immediate battle. The General himself could not have been much better pleased at avoiding it than we were. The envoy returned, and in a short time we saw at the extreme end of the street the neck of a horse protruding from the cross-street on the left. A party of cavalry armed with lances followed, formed at the head of the street, looking about them carefully as if still suspecting an ambush. In a few moments General Figoroa, mounted on a fierce little horse, without uniform, but with dark wool saddle-cloth, pistols, and basket-hilted sword, making a warlike appearance, came up, leading the van. We took off our hats as he approached our door, and he returned the salute. About 100 lancers followed him, two abreast, with red flags on the ends of their lances, and pistols in their holsters. In passing, one ferocious-looking fellow looked fiercely at us, and grasping his lance, cried "Viva Carrera!" We did not answer it immediately, and he repeated it in a tone that brought forth the response louder and more satisfactory, from the spite with which it was given; the next man repeated it, and the next; and before we were aware of our position, every lancer that passed, in a tone of voice regulated by the gentleness or the ferocity of his disposition, and sometimes with a most threatening scowl, put to us as a touchstone, "Viva Carrera."

The infantry were worse than the lancers in appearance, being mostly Indians, ragged, half-naked, with old straw hats, and barefooted; armed with muskets and machetes, and many with old-fashioned Spanish blunderbusses They vied with each other in sharpness and ferocity, and sometimes actually levelling their pieces, cried at us, "Viva Carrera." We were taken completely unawares; there was no escape; and I believe they would have shot us down on the spot if we had refused to echo the cry. I compromised with my dignity by answering no louder than the urgency of the case required, but I never passed through a more trying ordeal. Don Saturnino had had the prudence to keep out of sight; but the captain, who had intended to campaign against these fellows, never flinched, and when the last man passed added an extra "Viva Carrera." I again felt rejoiced that the soldiers had left the town and that there had been no fight. It would have been a fearful thing to fall into the hands of such men, with their passions roused by resistance and bloodshed. Reaching the plaza, they gave a general shout of "Viva Carrera," and stacked their arms. In a few minutes a party of them came down to our house, and asked for breakfast; and when we could not give them that, they begged a medio or sixpence. By degrees others came in, until the room was full. They were really no great gainers by taking the town. They had had no breakfast, and the town was completely stripped of eatables. We inquired the news from Guatimala, and bought from them several copies of the "Parté Official" of the Supreme Government, headed "Viva la Patria! Viva el General Carrera! The enemy has been completely exterminated in his attack upon the city, which he intended to devastate. The tyrant Morazan flies terrified, leaving the plaza and streets strewed with corpses sacrificed to his criminal ambition. The principal officers associated in his staff have perished, &c. *Eternal glory to the Invincible Chief* GENERAL CARRERA, and the valiant troops under his command." They told us that Carrera, with 3,000 men, was in full pursuit. In a little while the demand for sixpences became so frequent, that, afraid of being supposed to have mucha plata, we walked to the plaza to present ourselves to General Figoroa, and settle the terms of our surrender, or, at all events, to "define our position." We found him at the cabildo, quite at home, with a parcel of officers, white men, Mestitzoes, and mulattoes, smoking, and interrogating some old men from the church as to the movements of Colonel Angoula and the soldiers, the time of their setting out, and the direction they took. He was a young man—all the men in that country were young—about thirty-two or three, dressed in a snuff-coloured cloth roundabout jacket, and pantaloons of the same colour; and off his war-horse, and away from his assassin-like band, had very much the air of an honest man.

It was one of the worst evils of this civil war that no respect was paid to the passports of opposite parties. The captain had only his San Salvador passport, which was here worse than worthless. Don Saturnino had a variety from partisan commandants, and upon this occasion made use of one from a colonel under Ferrera. The captain introduced me by the title of Señor Ministro del Norte America, and I made myself acceptable by saying that I had been to San Salvador in search of a government, and had not been able to find any. The fact is, although I was not able to get into regular business, I was practising diplomacy on my own account all the time; and in order to define at once and clearly our relative positions, I undertook to do the honours of the town, and invited General Figoroa and all his officers to breakfast. This was a bold stroke, but Talleyrand could not have touched a nicer chord. They had not eaten anything since noon the day before, and I believe they would have evacuated their empty conquest for a good breakfast all round. They accepted my invitation with a promptness that put an end to my small stock of provisions for the road. General Figoroa confirmed the intelligence of Morazan's defeat and flight, and Carrera's pursuit, and the "invincible chief" would perhaps have been somewhat surprised at the pleasure I promised myself in meeting him.

With a very few moments' interchange of opinion, we made up our minds to get out of this frontier town as soon as possible, and again to go forward. I had almost abandoned ulterior projects, and looked only to personal safety. To go back, we reasoned, would carry us into the very focus of war and danger. The San Salvador people were furious against strangers, and the Honduras troops were invading them on one side, and Carrera's hordes on the other. To remain where we were was certain exposure to attacks from both parties. By going on we should meet Carrera's troops, and if we passed them we left war behind us. We had but one risk, and that would be tested in a day. Under this belief, I told the general that we designed proceeding to Guatimala, and that it would add to our security to have his passport. It was the general's first campaign. He was then only a few days in service, having set off in a hurry to get possession of this town, and cut off Morazan's retreat. He was flattered by the request, and said that his passport would be indispensable. His aid and secretary had been clerk in an apothecary's shop in Guatimala, and therefore understood the respect due to a ministro, and said that he would make it out himself. I was all eagerness to get possession of this passport. The captain, in courtesy, said we were in no hurry. I dismissed courtesy, and said that we were in a hurry; that we must set out immediately after breakfast. I was afraid of postponements, delays, and accidents, and in spite of impediments and inconveniences, I persisted till I got the secretary down at the table, who, without any trouble, and by a mere flourish of the pen, made me " ministro plenipotentiario." The captain's name was inserted in the passport, General Figoroa signed it, and I put it in my pocket, after which I breathed more freely.

We returned to the house, and in a few minutes the general, his secretary, and two mulatto officers came over to breakfast. It was very considerate in them that they did not bring more. Our guests cared more for quantity than quality, and this was the particular in which we were most deficient. We had plenty of chocolate, a stock of bread for the road, and some eggs that were found in the house. We put on the table all that we had, and gave the general the seat of honour at the head. One of the officers preferred sitting away on a bench, and eating his eggs with his fingers. It is unpleasant for a host to be obliged to mark the quantity that his guests eat, but I must say I was agreeably disappointed. If I had been breakfasting with them instead of *vice versa*, I could have astonished them as much as their voracious ancestors did the Indians. The breakfast was a neat fit; there was none over, and I believe nothing short.

There was but one unpleasant circumstance attending upon it, viz.

General Figoroa requested us to wait an hour, until he could prepare despatches to Carrera, advising him of his occupation of Aguachapa. I was extremely anxious to get away while the game was good. Of General Figoroa and his secretary we thought favourably; but we saw that he had no control over his men, and as long as we were in the town we should be subject to their visits, inquiries, and importunities, and some difficulties might arise. At the same time, despatches to Carrera would be a great security on the road. Don Saturnino undertook to set off with the luggage, and we, glad of the opportunity of travelling without any encumbrance, charged him to push on as fast as he could, not to stop for us, and we would overtake him.

In about an hour we walked over to the plaza for the despatches, but unluckily found ourselves in a new scene of confusion. Figoroa was already in the saddle, the lancers were mounting in haste, and all running to arms. A scout had brought in word that Colonel Angoula, with the soldiers of the town, was hovering on the skirts of the mountain, and our friends were hurrying to attack them. In a moment the lancers were off on a gallop, and the ragged infantry snatched up their guns and ran after them, keeping up with the horses. The letter to Carrera was partly written, and the aide-de-camp asked us to wait, telling us that the affair would soon be over. He was left in command of about seventy or eighty men, and we sat down with him under the corridor of the quartel. He was several years younger than Figoroa, more intelligent, and seemed very amiable except on political matters, and there he was savage against the Morazan party. He was gentlemanly in his manners, but his coat was out at the elbows, and his pantaloons were torn. He said he had a new frock-coat, for which he had paid sixteen dollars, but which did not fit him, and he wished to sell it. I afterwards spoke of him to one of Morazan's officers, whom I would believe implicitly except in regard to political opponents, who told me that this same secretary stole a pair of pantaloons from him, and he had no doubt the coat was stolen from somebody else.

There was no order or discipline among the men; the soldiers lay about the quartel, joined in the conversation, or strolled through the town, as they pleased. The inhabitants had fortunately carried away everything portable: two or three times a foraging party returned with a horse or mule; and once they were all roused by an alarm that Angoula was returning upon the town in another direction. Immediately all snatched up their arms, and at least one half, without a moment's warning, took to their heels. We had a fair chance of having the town again upon our hands, but the alarm proved groundless. We could not, however, but feel uncomfortable at the facility with which our friends abandoned us, and the risk we ran of being identified with them. There were three brothers, the only lancers who did not go out with Figoroa, white men, young and athletic, the best dressed and best armed in the company, swaggering in their manner, and disposed to cultivate an acquaintance with us. They told us that they purposed going to Guatimala; but I shrank from them instinctively, eluded their questions as to when we intended to set out, and I afterwards heard that they were natives of the town, and had been compelled to leave it on account of their notorious characters as assassins. One of them, as we thought, in a mere spirit of bravado, provoked a quarrel with the aide-de-camp, strutted before the quartel, and, in the hearing of all, said that they were under no man's orders; they only joined General Figoroa to please themselves, and would do as they thought proper. In the meantime, a few of the townsmen who had nothing to lose, among them an alguazil, finding there was no massacreing, had returned or emerged from their hiding-places; and we procured a guide to be ready the moment General Figoroa should return, went back to the house, and to our surprise found the widow Padilla there She had been secreted somewhere in the neighbourhood, and had heard, by means of an old woman-servant, of the general's breakfasting with us, and our intimacy with him. We inquired for her daughters' safety, but not where they were, for we had already found that we could answer inquiries better when we knew nothing.

We waited till four o'clock, and hearing nothing of General Figoroa, made up our minds that we should not get off till evening. We therefore strolled up to the extreme end of the street, where Figoroa had entered, and where stood the ruins of an old church. We sat on the foundation walls, and looked through the long and desolate street to the plaza, where were a few stacks of muskets and some soldiers. All around were mountains, and among them rose the beautiful and verdant volcano of Chingo. While sitting there, two women ran past, and, telling us that the soldiers were returning in that direction, hid themselves among the ruins. We turned down a road, and were intercepted on a little eminence, where we were obliged to stop and look down upon them as they passed. We saw that they were irritated by an unsuccessful day's work, and that they had found agua ardiente; for many of them were drunk. A drummer on horseback, and so tipsy that he could hardly sit, stopped the line to glorify General Carrera. Very soon they commenced the old touchstone, "Viva Carrera!" and one fellow, with the strap of his knapsack across his naked shoulders, again stopped the whole line, and turning round, with a ferocious expression, said, "You are counting us, are you?"

We disappeared, and by another street got back to the house. We waited a moment, and, determined to get out of the town and sleep at the first hacienda on the road, left the house to go again to General Figoroa for his despatches; but before reaching it we saw new confusion in the plaza, a general remounting and rushing to arms. As soon as General Figoroa saw us, he spurred his horse down the street to meet us, and told us, in great haste, that General Morazan was approaching, and almost upon the town. He had that moment received the news, and was going out to attack him. He had no time to sign the despatches, and while he was speaking the lancers galloped past. He shook hands, bade us good-bye, hasta luego (until presently), asked us to call upon Carrera in case we did not see him again, and dashing down the line, put himself at the head of the lancers. The foot-soldiers followed in single file on a run, carrying their arms as was most convenient. In the hurry and excitement we forgot ourselves till we heard some flattering epithets, and saw two fellows shaking their muskets at us with the expression of fiends; but, hurried on by those behind, they cried out ferociously, "Estos picaros otro vez," "Those rascals again." The last of the line had hardly disappeared before we heard a volley of musketry, and in a moment fifty or sixty men left in the plaza snatched up their arms, and ran down a street opening from the plaza. Very soon a horse without a rider came clattering down the street at full speed; three others followed, and in five minutes we saw thirty or forty horsemen, with our friend Figoroa at their head, dash across the street, all running for their lives; but in a few moments they rallied and returned. We walked toward the church, to ascend the steeple, when a sharp volley of musketry rolled up the street on that side, and before we got back into the house there was firing along the whole length of the street. We knew that a chance shot might kill a non combatant, and secured the doors and windows; but finally, as the firing was sharp, and the balls went beyond us, and struck the houses on the opposite side, with an old servant-woman (what had become of the widow I do not know), we retired into a small room on the courtyard, with delightful walls, and a door three inches thick, and bullet-proof, shutting which, and in utter darkness, we listened valiantly. Here we considered ourselves out of harm's way, but we had serious apprehensions for the result. The spirit on both sides was to kill; giving quarter was not thought of. Morazan's party was probably small, but they would not be taken without a desperate fight; and from the sharpness of the firing, and the time occupied, there was probably a sanguinary affair. Our quondam friends, roused by bloodshed, wounds, and loss of companions, without any one to control them, would be very likely to connect "those rascals" with the arrival of Morazan. I will not say that we wished they might all be killed, but we did wish that their bad blood might be let out, and that was almost the same thing. In fact, I did most earnestly hope never to see their faces again. I preferred being taken by any roving band in the country rather than by them, and never felt more relieved than when we heard the sound of a bugle. It was the Morazan blast of victory; and, though sounding fiercely the well-known notes of "degollar, degollar," "cut-throat, cut-throat," it was music to our ears. Very soon we heard the tramp of cavalry, and leaving our hiding-place, returned to the sala, and heard a cry of "Viva la Federacion!" This was a cheering sound. It was now dark. We opened the door an inch or two, but a lancer riding by struck it open with his lance, and asked for water. We gave him a large calabash, which another took from his hands. We threw open the door, and kept two large calabashes on the sill; and the soldiers, as they passed, took a hasty draught. Asking a question of each, we learned that it was General Morazan himself, with the survivors of his expedition against Guatimala. Our house was well known; many of the officers inquired for the family, and an aid-de-camp gave notice to the servant-woman that Morazan himself intended stopping there. The soldiers marched into the plaza, stacked their arms, and shouted "Viva Morazan!" In the morning the shout was, "Viva Carrera!" None cried "Viva la Patria!"

There was no end to our troubles. In the morning we surrendered to one party, and in the evening were captured out of their hands by another; probably before daylight Carrera would be upon us. There was only one comfort: the fellows who had broken our rest the night before, and scared the inhabitants from their homes, were now looking out for lodgings in the mountains themselves. I felt sorry for Figoroa and his aid, and on abstract principles, for the killed. As for the rest, I cared but little what became of them.

In a few moments a party of officers came down to our house. For six days they had been in constant flight through an enemy's country, changing their direction to avoid pursuit, and only stopping to rest their horses. Entering under the excitement of a successful skirmish, they struck me as the finest set of men I had seen in the country. Figoroa had come upon them so suddenly, that General Morazan, who rode at the head of his men, had two bullets pass by his head before he could draw his pistol, and he had a narrower escape than in the whole of his bloody battle in Guatimala. Colonel Cabañas, a small, quiet, gentlemanly man, the commander of the troops massacred in Honduras, struck the first blow, broke his sword over a lancer, and, wresting the lance out of its owner's hands, ran it through his body, but was wounded himself in the hand. A tall, gay, rattling young man, who was wiping warm blood from off his sword, and drying it on his pocket-handkerchief, mourned that he had failed in cutting off their retreat; and a quiet middle-aged man, wiping his forehead, drawled out that if their horses had not been so tired they would have killed every man. Even they talked only of killing; taking prisoners was never thought of. The verb *matar*, to kill, with its inflexions, was so continually ringing in my ears that it made me nervous. In a few minutes the widow Padilla, who, I am inclined to believe, was secreted somewhere in the neighbourhood, knowing of General Morazan's approach, rushed in, crying wildly for her sons. All answered that the eldest was with them; all knew her, and one after another put his right arm respectfully over her shoulder and embraced her; but the young man who was wiping his sword drove it into its scabbard, and, catching her up in his arms, lifted her off the floor and whirled her about the room. The poor old lady, half laughing and half crying, told him he was as bad as ever, and continued asking for her sons. At this moment a man about forty, whom I had noticed before as the only one without arms, with a long beard, pale and haggard, entered from the court-yard. The old lady screamed, rushed toward him, and fell on his neck, and for some moments rested her head upon his shoulder. This was the one who had been imprisoned by Carrera. General Morazan had forced his way into the plaza, broken open the prisons, and liberated the inmates; and when he was driven out, this son made his escape. But where was her younger and dearer son? The young man answered that he had escaped and was safe. The old lady looked at him with distrust, and, calling him by his Christian name, told him he was deceiving her; but he persisted and swore that he had escaped; he himself had given him a fresh horse; he was seen outside the barrier, was probably concealed somewhere, and would soon make his appearance. The other officers had no positive knowledge. One had seen him at such a time, and another at such a time during the battle; and all agreed that the young man ought to know best, for their posts were near each other; and he, young, ardent, and reckless, the dearest friend of her son, and loving her as a mother, told me afterward that she should have one night's comfort, and that she would know the truth soon enough; but the brother, narrowly escaped from death himself, and who looked as if smiles had been for ever driven from his face, told me he had no doubt his mother's darling was killed.*

* I have lately learned that he escaped, and is now safe with his mother in Aguachapa.

During these scenes the captain and I were not unnoticed. The captain found among the officers several whom he had become acquainted with at the port, and he learned that others had made their last campaign. In the first excitement of meeting them, he determined to turn back and follow their broken fortunes; but, luckily for me, those trunks had gone on. He felt that he had a narrow escape. Among those who had accompanied General Morazan were the former secretary of state and war, and all the principal officers, civil and military, of the shattered general government. They had heard of my arrival in the country. I had been expected at San Salvador, was known to them all by reputation, and very soon personally; particularly I became acquainted with Colonel Saravia, a young man about twenty-eight, handsome, brave, and accomplished in mind and manners, with an enthusiastic attachment for General Morazan, from whom, in referring to one affair in the attack on Guatimala, with tears almost starting from his eyes, he said, Providence seemed to turn the bullets away. I had often heard of this gentleman in Guatimala, and his case shows the unhappy rending of private and social ties produced by these civil wars. His father was banished by the Liberal party eight years before, and was then a general in the Carlist service in Spain. His mother and three sisters lived in Guatimala, and I had visited at their house perhaps oftener than at any other in that city. They lived near the plaza, and while Morazan had possession of it, the colonel had run home to see them; and in the midst of a distracted meeting, rendered more poignant by the circumstance of his being joined in an attack upon his native city, he was called away to go into action; his horse was shot under him, he was wounded, and escaped with the wreck of the army. His mother and sisters knew nothing of his fate. He said, what I was sure was but too true, that they would have dreadful apprehensions about him, and begged me, immediately on my arrival at Guatimala, to visit them and inform them of his safety.

In the meantime, General Morazan, apprehensive of a surprise from Carrera during the night, sent word that he should sleep in the plaza; and escorted by Colonel Saravia, I went to pay my respects to him. From the time of his entry I felt perfectly secure, and never had a moment of apprehension from unruly soldiers. For the first time I saw something like discipline. A sentinel was pacing the street leading from the plaza, to prevent the soldiers straggling into the town; but the poor fellows seemed to have no disposition for straggling. The town was stripped of everything; even the poor horses had no food. Some were gathered at the window of the cabildo, each in his turn holding up his hat for a portion of hard corn bread; some were sitting around fires, eating this miserable fare; but most were stretched on the ground, already asleep. It was the first night they had lain down except in an enemy's country.

General Morazan, with several officers, was standing in the corridor of the cabildo; a large fire was burning before the door, and a table stood against the wall, with a candle and chocolate-cups upon it. He was about forty-five years old, five feet ten inches high, thin, with a black moustache and week's beard, and wore a military frock-coat, buttoned up to the throat, and sword. His hat was off, and the expression of his face mild and intelligent. Though still young, for ten years he had been the first man in the country, and eight, President of the Republic. He had risen and had sustained himself by military skill and personal bravery; always led his forces himself; had been in innumerable battles, and often wounded, but never beaten. A year before, the people of Guatimala, of both parties, had implored him to come to their relief, as the only man who could save them from Carrera and destruction. At that moment he added another to the countless instances of the fickleness of popular favour. After the expiration of his term he had been elected chief of the state of San Salvador, which office he had resigned, and then acted as commander-in-chief under the Federal Government. Denounced personally, and the Federation under which he served disavowed, he had marched against Guatimala with 1,400 men, and forced his way into the plaza; forty of his oldest officers and his eldest son were shot down by his side; and cutting his way through masses of human flesh, with about 450 men then in the plaza, made his escape. I was presented to him by Colonel Saravia. From the best information I could acquire, and from the enthusiasm with which I had heard him spoken of by his officers, and, in fact, by every one else in his own State, I had conceived almost a feeling of admiration for General Morazan, and my interest in him was increased by his misfortunes. I was really at a loss how to address him; and while my mind was full of his ill-fated expedition, his first question was if his family had arrived in Costa Rica, or if I had heard anything of them. I did not tell him, what I then thought, that his calamities would follow all who were connected with him, and probably that his wife and daughters would not be permitted an asylum in that state; but it spoke volumes that, at such a moment, with the wreck of his followers before him, and the memory of his murdered companions fresh in his mind, in the overthrow of all his hopes and fortunes, his heart turned to his domestic relations. He expressed his sorrow for the condition in which I saw his unhappy country; regretted that my

T

visit was at such a most unfortunate moment; spoke of Mr. De Witt, and the relations of that country with ours, and his regret that our treaty had not been renewed, and that it could not be done now; but these things were not in my mind. Feeling that he must have more important business, I remained but a short time, and returned to the house.

The moon had risen, and I was now extremely anxious to set out, but our plans were entirely deranged. The guide whom we had engaged to conduct us to the Rio Paz was missing, and no other could be found; in fact not a man could be induced, either by promises or threats, to leave the town that night from fear of falling in with the routed troops. Several of the officers took chocolate with us, and at the head of the table sat a priest with a sword by his side. I had breakfasted men who would have been happy to cut their throats, and they were now hiding among the mountains or riding for life. If Carrera came, my new friends would be scattered. They all withdrew early, to sleep under arms in the plaza, and we were left with the widow and her son. A distressing scene followed, of inquiries and forebodings by the widow for her younger son, which the elder could only get rid of by pleading excessive fatigue, and begging to be permitted to go to sleep. It was rather singular, but it had not occurred to us before to inquire about the dead and wounded in the skirmish. There were none of the latter; all who fell were lanced, and the dead were left on the ground. He was in the rear of the Morazan party; the fire was scattering; but on the line by which he entered the town he counted eighteen bodies.

CHAPTER XXIII.

VISIT FROM GENERAL MORAZAN—END OF HIS CAREER—PROCURING A GUIDE—DEPARTURE FOR GUATIMALA—FRIGHT OF THE PEOPLE—THE RIO PAZ—HACIENDA OF PAMITA—A FORTUNATE ESCAPE—HACIENDA OF SAN JOSÉ—AN AWKWARD PREDICAMENT—A KIND HOST—RANCHO OF HOCTILLA—ORATORIO AND LEON—RIO DE LOS ESCLAVOS—THE VILLAGE—APPROACH TO GUATIMALA—ARRIVAL AT GUATIMALA—A SKETCH OF THE WARS—DEFEAT OF MORAZAN—SCENE OF MASSACRE.

In the morning, to our surprise, we found several shops open, and people in the street, who had been concealed somewhere in the neighbourhood, and returned as soon as they knew of Morazan's entry. The alcalde reappeared, and our guide was found, but he would not go with us, and told the alcalde that he might kill him on the spot; that he would rather die there than by the hands of the Cachurecos.

While I was taking chocolate, General Morazan called upon me. Our conversation was longer and more general. I did not ask him his plans or purposes, but neither he nor his officers exhibited despondency. Once reference was made to the occupation of Santa Anna by General Cascara, and with a spirit that reminded me of Claverhouse in "Old Mortality," he said, "We shall visit that gentleman soon." He spoke without malice or bitterness of the leaders of the Central party, and of Carrera as an ignorant and lawless Indian, from whom the party that was now using him would one day be glad to be protected. He referred, with a smile, to a charge current among the Cachurecos of an effort made by him to have Carrera assassinated, of which a great parade had been made, with details of time and place, and which was generally believed. He had supposed the whole story a fabrication; but accidentally, in retreating from Guatimala, he found himself in the very house where the attempt was said to have been made; and the man of the house told him that Carrera, having offered outrage to a member of his family, he himself had stabbed him, as was supposed mortally; and in order to account for his wounds, and turn away inquiries from the cause, it was fastened upon Morazan, and so flew all through the country. One of his officers accompanied the story with details of the outrage; and I felt very sure that, if Carrera ever fell into his hands, he would shoot him on the spot.

With the opinion that he entertained of Carrera and his soldiers, he of course considered it unsafe for us to go on to Guatimala. But I was exceedingly anxious to set out; and the flush of excitement over, as the captain's trunks had gone on, he was equally so. Carrera might arrive at any moment, in which case we might again change owners, or, at all events, be the witnesses of a sanguinary battle, for Morazan would defend the frontier town of his own State to the death.

I told General Morazan my wish and purpose, and the difficulty of procuring a guide. He said that an escort of soldiers would expose us to certain danger; even a single soldier, without his musket and cartridge-box (these being the only distinguishing marks of a soldier), might be recognised; but he would send for the alcalde, and procure us some trusty person from the town. I bade him farewell with an interest greater than I had felt for any man in the country. Little did we then know the calamities that were still in store for him; that very night most of his soldiers deserted, having been kept together only by the danger to which they were exposed while in an enemy's country. With the rest he marched to Zonzonate, seized a vessel at the port, manning her with his own men, and sent her to Libertad, the port of San Salvador. He then marched to the capital, where the people, who had for years idolized him in power, turned their backs upon him in misfortune, and received him with open insults in the streets. With many of his officers, who were too deeply compromised to remain, he embarked for Chili. Suffering from confinement on board a small vessel, he stopped in Costa Rica, and asked permission for some of them to land. He did not ask it for himself, for he knew it would be refused. Leaving some of them behind, he went on to join his family in Chili. Amid the fierceness of party spirit it was impossible for a stranger to form a true estimate of the character of a public man. The great outcry against General Morazan was hostility to the church, and forced loans. For his hostility to the church there is the justification, that it is at this day a pall upon the spirit of free institutions, degrading and debasing instead of elevating the Christian character; and for forced loans constant wars may plead. His worst enemies admit that he was exemplary in his private relations, and, what they consider no small praise, that he was not sanguinary. He is now fallen and in exile, probably for ever, under sentence of death if he returns; all the truckling worshippers of a rising sun are blasting his name and memory; but I verily believe—and I know I shall bring down upon me the indignation of the whole Central party by the assertion—I verily believe they have driven from their shores the best man in Central America.*

The population of the town was devoted to General Morazan, and

* General Morazan returned about a year after these occurrences to Costa Rica, was captured, tied to a tree, and shot.—F. C.

an old man brought to us his son, a young man about twenty-two, as a guide; but when he learned that we wanted him to go with us all the way to Rio Paz, he left us, as he said, to procure a horse. We waited nearly an hour, when the old man reappeared with a little boy about ten years old, dressed in a staw hat and shirt, and mounted on a bare-backed horse. The young man had disappeared, and could not be found; in fact, he was afraid to go, and it was thought this little boy would run less risk. I was never much disturbed by general reports of robbers or assassins, but there was palpable danger in meeting any of the routed troops. Desperate by defeat, and assassin-like in disposition; not very amiable to us before; and now, from having seen us lounging about the town at that inauspicious moment, likely to connect us with the movements of Morazan, I believed that if we fell in with them we should be murdered. But, on the other hand, they had not let the grass grow under their feet; had probably been flying all night, in apprehension of pursuit; shunning the main road, had perhaps crossed the Rio Paz, and, once in Guatimala, had dispersed to their own villages; besides which, the rout had been so total that they were probably escaping three or four together, and would be as likely to run from us as we from them. At all events, it was better to go than wait till Carrera came upon the town.

With these calculations and really uncomfortable feelings, we bade farewell to some of the officers who were waiting to see us off, and at nine o'clock set out. Descending from the table-land on which the town is built, we entered an open plain, over which we could see to a great distance, and which would furnish, if necessary, a good field for the evolutions of our cavalry. We passed the Lake of Aguachapa, the beauty of which, under other circumstances, would have attracted our admiration; and as our little guide seemed at fault, we stopped at a hut to inquire the road. The people were afraid to answer any questions. Figoroa's soldiers and Morazan's had passed by, but they did not know it; they could not tell whether any fugitive soldiers had passed, and only knew the road to the Rio Paz. It was easy to see that they thought of nothing else; but they said they were poor people, and at work all the time, and did not know what was going on. In half an hour we met three Indians, with loads of pottery on their backs. The poor fellows pulled off their hats, and trembled when we inquired if there were any routed soldiers on before. It occurred to us that this inquiry would expose us to the suspicion of being officers of Morazan in pursuit, and that if we met any one, we had better ask no questions. Beyond this there were many roads, all of which, the boy said, led to the Rio Paz; but he had never been there before, and did not know the right one. We followed one which took us into the woods, and soon commenced descending. The road was broken, stony, and very steep; we descended rapidly, and soon it was manifest no horses had passed on this road for a long time before. Trees lay across it so low that we dismounted, and were obliged to slip our high-peaked saddles to pass under them. It was evidently an old cattle-path, now disused even by cattle. We descended some distance farther, and I proposed to return. My only argument was, that it was safer; we knew we were wrong, and might get down so low that our physical strength would not carry us back. The captain said that I had chosen this path; if we had followed his advice, we should have been safe, and now that it was impossible to return. We had an angry quarrel, and, fortunately, in consideration of my having led into the difficulty, I gave way, and very soon we were cheered by hearing below us the rushing of the river. After a most difficult descent, we reached the bank; but here there was no fording-place, and no path on the opposite side

The river itself was beautiful. The side which we had descended was a high and almost perpendicular mountain, and on both sides trees spread their branches over the water. It was called the River of Peace, but was now the dividing-line of deadly war, the boundary between Guatimala and San Salvador. The inhabitants of the opposite side were in an enemy's country, and the routed troops, both of Morazan and Figoroa, had fled to it for refuge. Riding some distance up the stream, we worked our way across, and on the opposite side found a guacal, or drinking-shell, which had probably been left there by some flying soldier. We drank from it, as if it had been intended for our use, and left it on the bank for the benefit of the next comer.

We were now in the State of Guatimala, on the banks of a wild river, without any visible path; and our situation was rather more precarious than before, for here the routed soldiers would consider themselves safe, and probably many, after a day and night of toil and fighting, would lie down to rest. We were fortunate in regard to a path; for, riding a short distance through the woods, along the bank of the river, we struck one which turned off to the left, and terminated in the camino real, leading from the regular fording-place. Here we dismissed our little guide, and set out on the main road. The face of the country was entirely changed, broken and stony, and we saw no one till we reached the hacienda of Palmita. This, too, seemed desolate. We entered the yard, and did not see a single person till we pushed open the door of the house. The proprietor was an old gentleman, opposed to Morazan, who sat in the sala with his wife's saddle and his own, and two bundles of bed and bedding packed up on the floor, ready for a start. He seemed to feel that it was too late, and with an air of submission answered our questions, and then asked us how many men we had with us. It was amusing that, while half frightened to death ourselves, we carried terror wherever we went. We relieved him by inquiring about Don Saturnino and our luggage, remounted, and rode on. In an hour we reached the hacienda del Cacao, where Don Saturnino was to sleep. Owing to the position of the ground, we came suddenly upon the front of the house, and saw under the piazza three Cachureco soldiers, eating tortillas. They saw us at the same moment, snatched up their muskets, and ran; but suddenly one stopped, and levelled at us a blunderbuss. The barrel looked as big as a church door, and seemed to cover both the captain and me. We were in awful danger of being shot by mistake, when one of them rushed back, knocked up the blunderbuss, and, crying out, "Amigos, los Ingleses!" gave us a chance to reach them. This amiable and sensible young Cachureco vagabond was one of those who had paid us a visit to beg a breakfast and a medio. Probably there never was a sixpence put out at better interest. He had seen us intimate with Figoroa, and, taught by his betters to believe that General Morazan was a cut-throat and murderer, and not conceiving that we could be safe with him, considered us sharers of the same danger, and inquired how we had escaped. As it turned out, we were extremely happy to meet with these; another party might have received us very differently; and they relieved us in an important point, for they told us that most of the routed soldiers had fled on the Santa Anna road. Don Saturnino had passed the night at this hacienda, and set out very early in the morning. The soldiers returned to finish their meal, and, giving their thanks in payment, set out again with us. They had a good horse which they had stolen on the road, and which they said paid them very well for the expedition, and rode by turns bare-backed. Passing El Cacao, their appearance created a sensation, for they brought the first intelligence of the rout of Figoroa. This was ominous news, for all had considered Morazan completely crushed by his defeat at Guatimala. In his retreat, he had avoided the villages, and they did not know that he had escaped with so strong a force. We endeavoured to procure a guide, but not a man could be induced to leave the village, and we rode on. In a short time it began to rain: the road was very stony; and we crossed a high, bleak volcanic mountain. Late in the afternoon, the captain conceived suspicions of the soldiers, and we rode on very unceremoniously, leaving them behind. About five o'clock, we avoided the road that led to a village, and taking el Camino de los Partidos, which was very rough and stony, soon came to a place where there were branches, and we were at a loss which to take; but the course lay through a broad valley, bounded by two ranges of mountains. We felt sure that our road did not cross either of these ranges, and these were our only guides. A little before dark, we passed beyond the range of mountains, and on our right saw a road leading into the woods, and presently heard the sound of a bell, and saw through the trees a hacienda, to arrive at which we had to go on some distance, and then turn back by a private road. It was situated in a large clearing, with cocina and sheds, and a large sugar-mill. Twenty or thirty workmen, principally Indians, were assembled to give an account of their day's work, and receive orders for the next. Our appearance created a sensation. The proprietors of the hacienda, two brothers, stood in the door while we were talking with the men, and we rode up and asked permission to stop there for the night. The elder assented, but with an embarrassment that showed the state of alarm and suspicion existing in the country. The gentlemen wore the common hacienda dress, and the interior was miserably poor, but had a hammock, and two rude frames with matting over them for beds. There was a small room adjoining, in which was the wife of one of them with a child. The proprietors were men of education and intelligence, thoroughly acquainted with the condition of the country; and we told them what had happened at Aguachapa, and that we were hurrying on to Guatimala. We had supper at a small table, placed between the hammock and one of the beds, consisting of fried eggs, frigoles, and tortillas, as usual without knife, fork, or spoon.

After supper our elder host was called out, but in a few minutes returned, and, closing the door, told us that there was a great excitement among the workmen on our account. They did not believe our story of going to Guatimala, for a woman had seen us come in from the Guatimala road, and they believed that we were officers of Morazan retreating from the attack on Guatimala, and endeavouring to escape into San Salvador. Here was a ground of suspicion we had not anticipated. The gentleman was much agitated; he regretted that he was obliged to violate the laws of hospitality, but said we knew the distracted state of the country, and the frenzy of party spirit. He himself was against Morazan, his men were violent Cachurecos, and at this moment capable of committing any outrage. He had incurred great peril by receiving us for a moment under his roof, and begged us, both for our own sake and his, to leave his house; adding that, even if we were of those unfortunate men, our horses should be brought up and we should go away unharmed; more he could not promise. Now if we had really been the fugitives he supposed us, we should no doubt have been very thankful for his kindness; but to be turned out by mistake in a dark night, an unknown country, and without any guide, was almost as bad as coming at us with a blunderbuss. Fortunately, he was not a suspicious man; if he had been another Don Gregorio we should have "walked Spanish;" and, more fortunately still, my pertinacity had secured Figoroa's passport; it was the only thing that could have cleared our character. I showed it to him, pointing to the extra flourish which the secretary had made of plenipotentiario, and I believe he was not more astonished at finding who had honoured him by taking possession of his house, than pleased that we were not Morazan's officers. Though an intelligent man, he had passed a retired life on his hacienda. He had heard of such a thing as "a ministro plenipotentiario," but had never seen one. My accoutrements and the eagle on my hat sustained the character, and he called in the major-domo and two leading men on the hacienda, read to them the passport, and explained to them the character of a ministro plenipotentiario, while I sat upon the bed with my coat off and hat on to show the eagle, and the captain suppressed all partialities for Morazan, and talked of my intimacy with Carrera. The people are so suspicious that, having once formed an idea, they do not willingly abandon it, and it was uncertain whether all this would satisfy them; but our host was warm in his efforts, the major-domo was flattered by being made the medium of communicating with the men, and his influence was at stake in satisfying them. It was one of Talleyrand's maxims, never to do to-day what you can put off till to-morrow. On this occasion at least of my diplomatic career I felt the benefit of the old opposite rule. From the moment I saw Figoroa I had an eye only to getting his passport, and did not rest until I had it in my pocket. If we had waited to receive this with his letters, we should now have been in a bad position. If we escaped immediate violence, we should have been taken to the village, shut up in the cabildo, and exposed to all the dangers of an ignorant populace, at that moment excited by learning the success of Morazan and the defeat of Figoroa. In setting out, our idea was that, if taken by the Cachurecos, we should be carried up to Guatimala; but we found that there was no accountability to Guatimala; the people were in a state to act entirely from impulses, and nothing could induce any party of men to set out for Guatimala, or under any circumstances to go farther than from village to village.

This difficulty over, the major-domo promised us a guide before daylight for the next village. At three o'clock we were awakened by the creaking of the sugar-mill. We waited till daylight for a guide, but as none came we bade farewell to our kind host, and set out alone. The name of the hacienda is San José, but in the hurry of my movements I never learned the name of the proprietor. In the constant revolutions of Central America, it may happen that he will one day be flying for his life; in his hour of need, may he meet a heart as noble as his own!

At a distance of five leagues we reached the rancho of Hocotilla, where Don Saturnino and our men had slept. The road lay in a magnificent ravine, with a fine bottom land and noble mountain sides. We passed through the straggling settlements of Oratorio and Leon, mostly single huts, where several times we saw women snatch up their children and run into the woods at sight of us. Bury the war-knife, and this valley would be equal to the most beautiful in Switzerland. At twelve o'clock we came upon four posts with a thatched roof, occupied by a scouting-party of Cachureco soldiers. We should have been glad to avoid them, but they could not have judged so from the way in which we shouted "Amigos!" We inquired for Carrera; expected to meet him on the road; Figoroa had told us he was coming; Figoroa had entered Aguachapa; and, taking special good care not to tell them that Figoroa had been driven out, we bade them good-bye and hurried on.

At twelve o'clock we reached the Rio de los Esclavos, a wild and noble river, the bridge across which is the greatest structure in Central America, a memorial of the Spanish dominion. We crossed it and entered the village, a mere collection of huts, standing in a magnificent situation on the bank of the river, looking up to a range of giant mountains on the other side, covered to the top with noble pines. The miserable inhabitants were insensible to its beauties, but there were reasons to make them so. Every hostile expedition between Guatimala and San Salvador passed through their village. Twice within one week Morazan's party had done so; the inhabitants carried off what they could, and, locking their doors, fled to the mountains. The last time, Morazan's soldiers were so straitened for provisions, and pressed by fear of pursuit, that huts were torn down for firewood, and bullocks slain and eaten half raw in the street, without bread or tortillas.

At two we set off again, and from the village entered a country covered with lava. At four we reached the hacienda of Coral de Piedra, situated on the crest of a stony country, looking like a castle, very large, with a church and village, where, although it rained, we did not stop, for the whole village seemed to be intoxicated. Opposite one house we were hailed by a Cachureco officer, so tipsy that he could hardly sit on his horse, who came to us and told us how many of Morazan's men he had killed. A little before dark, riding through a forest, in the apprehension that we were lost, we emerged suddenly from the woods, and saw towering before us the great volcanoes of Agua and Fuego, and at the same moment were hailed by the joyful shouts of Don Saturnino and our men. They had encamped in a small hut on the borders of a large plain, and the mules were turned out to pasture. Don Saturnino had been alarmed about us, but he had followed our parting injunction to go on, as, if any accident had happened, he could be of more service in Guatimala. They had not met Morazan's troops, having been at a hacienda off the road when they passed, and hurrying on, had not heard of the rout of Figoroa.

The rancho contained a single small room, barely large enough for the man and woman who occupied it, but there was plenty of room out of doors. After a rough ride of more than fifty miles, with the most comfortable reflection of being but one day from Guatimala, I soon fell asleep.

The next morning one of the mules was missing, and we did not get off till eight o'clock. Toward evening we descended a long hill, and entered the plain of Guatimala. It looked beautiful, and I never thought I should be so happy to see it again. I had finished a journey of 1,200 miles, and the gold of Peru could not have tempted me to undertake it again. At the gate the first man I saw was my friend Don Manuel Pavon. I could but think, if Morazan had taken the city, where would he be now? Carrera was not in the city; he had set out in pursuit of Morazan, but on the road received intelligence which induced him to turn off for Quezaltenango. I learned with deep satisfaction that not one of my acquaintance was killed, but, as I afterwards found, not one of them had been in the battle.

I gave Don Manuel the first intelligence of General Morazan. Not a word had been heard of him since he left the Antigua. Nobody had come up from that direction; the people were still too frightened to travel, and the city had not recovered from its spasm of terror. As we advanced I met acquaintances who welcomed me back to Guatimala. I was considered as having run the gauntlet for life, and escape from dangers created a bond between us. I could hardly persuade myself that the people who received me so cordially, and whom I was really glad to meet again, were the same whose expulsion by Morazan I had considered probable. If he had succeeded, not one of them would have been there to welcome me. Repeatedly I was obliged to stop and tell over the affair of Aguachapa; how many men Morazan had; what officers; whether I spoke to him; how he looked, and what he said. I introduced the captain; each had his circle of listeners; and the captain, as a slight indemnification for his forced "Viva Carreras!" on the road, feeling, on his arrival once more among civilized and well-dressed people, a comparative security for liberty of speech, said that if Morazan's horses had not been so tired, every man of Figoroa's would have been killed. Unhappily, I could not but see that our news would have been more acceptable if we could have reported Morazan completely prostrated, wounded, or even dead. As we advanced I could perceive that the sides of the houses were marked by musket-balls, and the fronts on the plaza were fearfully scarified. My house was near the plaza, and three musket-balls, picked out of the woodwork, were saved for my inspection, as a sample of the battle. In an hour after my arrival I had seen nearly all my old friends. Engrossed by my own troubles, I had not imagined the full extent of theirs. I cannot describe the satisfaction with which I found myself once more among them, and for a little while, at least, at rest. I still had anxieties; I had no letters from home, and Mr. Catherwood had not arrived; but I had no uneasiness about him, for he was not in the line of danger; and when I lay down I had the comfortable sensation that there was nothing to drive me forward the next day. The captain took up his abode with me. It was an odd finale to his expedition against Guatimala, but, after all, it was better than remaining at the port.

Great changes had taken place in Guatimala since I left, and it may not be amiss here to give a brief account of what had occurred in my absence. The reader will remember the treaty between Carrera and Guzman, the general of the state of Los Altos, by which the former surrendered to the latter 400 old muskets. Since that time Guatimala had adopted Carrera (or had been adopted by him, I hardly know which), and, on the ground that the distrust formerly entertained of him no longer existed, demanded a restitution of the muskets to him. The State of Los Altos refused. This State was at that time the focus of Liberal principles, and Quezaltenango, the capital, was the asylum of Liberals banished from Guatimala. Apprehending, or pretending to apprehend, an invasion from that State, and using the restitution of the 400 worthless muskets as a pretext, Carrera marched against Quezaltenango with 1,000 men. The Indians, believing that he came to destroy the whites, assisted him. Guzman's troops deserted him, and Carrera with his own hands took him prisoner, sick and encumbered with a great coat, in the act of dashing his horse down a deep ravine to escape: he sent to Guatimala Guzman's military coat, with the names of Omoa, Truxillos, and other places where Guzman had distinguished himself in the service of the republic, labelled on it, and a letter to the government, stating that he had sent the coat as a proof that he had taken Guzman. A gentleman told me that he saw this coat on its way, stuck on a pole, and paraded by an insulting rabble around the plaza of the Antigua. After the battle Carrera marched to the capital, deposed the chief of the State and other officers, garrisoned it with his own soldiers, and, not understanding the technical distinctions of state lines, destroyed its existence as a separate State, and annexed it to Guatimala, or, rather, to his own command.

In honour of his distinguished services, public notice was given that on Monday the 17th he would make his triumphal entry into Guatimala; and on that day he did enter, under arches erected across the streets, amid the firing of cannon, waving of flags, and music, with General Guzman, personally known to all the principal inhabitants, who but a year before had hastened at their piteous call to save them from the hands of this same Carrera, placed sideways on a mule, with his feet tied under him, his face so bruised, swollen, and disfigured by stones and blows of machetes that he could not be recognised, and the prisoners tied together with ropes; and the chief of the state, secretary of state, and secretary of the Constituent Assembly rode by Carrera's side in this disgraceful triumph.

General Guzman was one of those who had been liberated from prison by General Morazan. He had escaped from the plaza with the remnant of his forces, but, unable to endure the fatigues of the journey, he was left behind, secreted on the road; and General Morazan told me that, in consequence of the cruelties exercised upon him, and the horrible state of anxiety in which he was kept, reason had deserted its throne, and his once strong mind was gone.

From this time the city settled into a volcanic calm, quivering with apprehensions of an attack by General Morazan, a rising of the Indians and a war of castes, and startled by occasional rumours that Carrera intended to bring Guzman and the prisoners out into the plaza and shoot them. On the 14th of March intelligence was received from Figoroa that General Morazan had crossed the Rio Paz and was marching against Guatimala. This swallowed up all other apprehensions. Carrera was the only man who could protect the city. On the 15th he marched out with 900 men, toward Arazola, leaving the plaza occupied by 500 men. Great gloom hung over the city. The same day Morazan arrived at the Coral de Piedra, eleven leagues from Guatimala. On the 16th the soldiers commenced erecting parapets at the corners of the plaza; many

Indians came in from the villages to assist, and Carrera took up his position at the Aceytuna, a league and a half from the city. On the 17th Carrera rode into the city, and with the chief of the state and others, went around to visit the fortifications and rouse the people to arms. At noon he returned to the Aceytuna, and at four o'clock intelligence was received that Morazan's army was descending the Questa de Pinula, the last range before reaching the plain of Guatimala. The bells tolled the alarm, and great consternation prevailed in the city. Morazan's army slept that night on the plain.

Before daylight he marched upon the city, and entered the gate of Buena Vista, leaving all his cavalry and part of his infantry at the Plaza de Toros and on the heights of Calvario, under Colonel Cabanes, to watch the movements of Carrera, and with 700 men occupied the Plaza of Guadaloupe, depositing his parque, equipage, a hundred women (more or less of whom always accompany an expedition in that country), and all his train, in the Hospital of San Juan de Dios. Hence he sent Perez and Rivas, with 400 or 500 men, to attack the plaza. These passed up a street descending from the centre of the city, and, while covered by the brow of the hill, climbed over the yard-wall of the church of Escuela de Cristo, and passed through the church into the street opposite the mint, in the rear of one side of the plaza. Twenty-seven Indians were engaged in making a redoubt at the door, and twenty-six bodies were found on the ground, nine killed and seventeen wounded. When I saw it the ground was still red with blood. Entering the mint, the invaders were received with a murderous fire along the corridor; but, forcing their way through, they broke open the front portal, and rushed into the plaza. The plaza was occupied by the 500 men left by Carrera, and 200 or 300 Indians, who fell back, closed up near the porch of the cathedral, and in a few moments all fled, leaving the plaza, with all their ammunition, in the possession of the assailants. Rivera Paz and Don Luis Bartres, the chief and secretary of the state, were in the plaza at the time, and but few other white citizens. Carrera did not want white soldiers, and would not permit white men to be officers. Many young men had presented themselves in the plaza, and were told that there were no arms.

In the meantime, Carrera, strengthened by masses of Indians from the villages around, attacked the division on the heights of Calvario. Morazan, with the small force left at San Juan de Dios, went to the assistance of Cabanes. The battle lasted an hour and a half, fierce and bloody, and fought hand to hand. Morazan lost some of his best officers. Sanches was killed by Sotero Carrera, a brother of the general. Carrera and Morazan met, and Carrera says that he cut

Morazan's saddle nearly in two. Morazan was routed, pursued so closely that he could not take up his equipage, and hurried on to the plaza, having lost 300 muskets, 400 men killed, wounded, and prisoners, and all his baggage. At ten o'clock his whole force was penned up in the plaza, surrounded by an immense mass of Indian soldiers, and fired upon from all the corners. Manning the parapets and stationing pickets on the roofs of the houses, he kept up a galling fire in return.

Pent up in this fearful position, Morazan had time to reflect. But a year before he was received with ringing of bells, firing of cannon, joyful acclamations, and deputations of grateful citizens, as the only man who could save them from Carrera and destruction. Among the few white citizens in the plaza at the time of the entry of the soldiers was a young man, who was taken prisoner and brought before General Morazan. The latter knew him personally, and inquired for several of his old partisans by name, asking whether they were not coming to join him. The young man answered that they were not, and Morazan and his officers seemed disappointed. No doubt he had expected a rising of citizens in his favour, and again to be hailed as a deliverer from Carrera. In San Salvador I had heard that he had received urgent solicitations to come up; but, whatever had been contemplated, there was no manifestation of any such intention; on the contrary, the hoarse cry was ringing in his ears, "Muera el tyranno! Muera el General Morazan!" Popular feeling had undergone an entire revolution, or else it was kept down by the masses of Indians who came in from the villages around to defend the city against him.

In the meantime the fire slackened, and at twelve o'clock it died away entirely; but the plaza was strewed with dead, dense masses choked up the streets, and at the corners of the plaza the soldiers, with gross ribaldry and jests, insulted and jeered at Morazan and his men. The firing ceased only from want of ammunition, Carrera's stock having been left in Morazan's possession. Carrera, in his eagerness to renew the attack, sat down to make cartridges with his own hands.

The house of Mr. Hall, the British vice-consul, was on one of the sides of the plaza. Mr. Chatfield, the consul-general, was at Escuintla, about twelve leagues distant, when intelligence was received of Morazan's invasion. He mounted his horse, rode up to the city, and hoisted the English flag on Mr. Hall's house, to Morazan's soldiers the most conspicuous object on the plaza. Carrera himself was hardly more obnoxious to them than Mr. Chatfield. A picket of soldiers was stationed on the roof of the house, commanding the plaza on the one side, and the courtyard on the other. Orellana, the former minister of war, was on the roof, and cut into the staff with his sword, but desisted on a remonstrance from the courtyard that it was the house of the vice-consul. At sundown the immense mass of Indians who now crowded the city fell on their knees, and set up the Salve or hymn to the Virgin. Orellana and others of Morazan's officers had let themselves down in the courtyard, and were at the moment taking chocolate in Mr. Hall's house. Mrs. Hall, a Spanish lady of the city, asked Orellana why he did not fall on his knees; and he answered, in jest, that he was afraid his own soldiers on the roof would take him for a Cachureco and shoot him; but it is said that to Morazan the noise of this immense chorus of voices was appalling, bringing home to him a consciousness of the immense force assembled to crush him, and for the first time he expressed his sense of the danger they were in. The prayer was followed by a tremendous burst of "Viva la Religion! Viva Carrera! y muera el General Morazan!" and the firing commenced more sharply than before. It was returned from the plaza, and for several hours continued without intermission. At two o'clock in the morning Morazan made a desperate effort to cut his way out of the plaza, but was driven back behind the parapets. The plaza was strewed with dead. Forty of his oldest officers and his eldest son were killed; and at three o'clock he stationed 300 men at three corners of the plaza, directed them to open a brisk fire, threw all the powder into the fountain, and while attention was directed to these points, sallied by the other, and left them to their fate. I state this on the authority of the Guatimala official account of the battle —of course I heard nothing of it at Aguachapa—and if true, it is a blot on Morazan's character as a soldier and as a man. He escaped from the city with 500 men, and strewing the road with wounded and dead, at twelve o'clock arrived at the Antigua. Here he was urged to proclaim martial law, and make another attack on the city; but he answered, No; blood enough had been shed. He entered the cabildo, and, it is said, wrote a letter to Carrera recommending the prisoners to mercy; and Baron Mahelin, the French consul-general, related to me an anecdote, which does not, however, seem probable; that he laid his glove on the table, and requested the alcalde to give it to Carrera as a challenge, and explain its meaning. From that place he continued his retreat by the coast until I met him at Aguachapa.

In the meantime Carrera's soldiers poured into the plaza with a tremendous feu-de-joie, and kept up a terrible firing in the air till daylight. Then they commenced searching for fugitives, and a general massacre took place. Colonel Arias, lying on the ground with one of his eyes out, was bayoneted to death. Perez was shot. Marescal, concealed under the Cathedral, was dragged out and shot. Padilla, the son of the widow at Aguachapa, found on the ground, while begging a Centralist whom he knew to save him, was killed with bayonets. The unhappy fugitives were brought into the plaza two, three, five, and ten at a time. Carrera stood pointing with his finger to this man and that, and every one that he indicated was removed a few paces from him and shot. Major José Viera, and several of the soldiers on the roof of Mr. Hall's house, let themselves down into the court-yard, and Carrera sent for all who had taken refuge there. Viera was taking chocolate with the family, and gave Mrs Hall a purse of doubloons and a pistol to take care of for him. They were delivered up, with a recommendation to mercy, particularly in behalf of Viera; but a few moments after Mr. Skinner entered the house, and said that he saw Viera's body in the plaza. Mr. Hall could not believe it, and walked round the corner, but a few paces from his own door, and saw him lying on his back, dead. In this scene of massacre the Padre Zezena, a poor and humble priest, exposed his own life to save his fellow-beings. Throwing himself on his knees before Carrera, he implored him to spare the unhappy prisoners, exclaiming, they are Christians like ourselves; and by his importunities and prayers induced Carrera to desist from murder, and send the wretched captives to prison.

Carrera and his Indians had the whole danger and the whole glory of defending the city. The citizens, who had most at stake, took no part in it. The members of the government most deeply compromised fled, or remained shut up in their houses. It would be hard to analyse the feelings with which they straggled out to gaze upon the scene of horror in the streets and in the plaza, and saw on the ground the well-known faces and mangled bodies of the leaders of the Liberal party. There was one overpowering sense of escape from immense danger, and the feeling of the Central Government burst out in its official bulletin: "Eternal glory to the invincible chief, General Carrera, and the valiant troops under his command!"

In the morning, as at the moment of our arrival, this subject was uppermost in every one's mind; no one could talk of anything else, and each one had something new to communicate. In our first walk through the streets our attention was directed to the localities, and everywhere we saw marks of the battle. Vagabond soldiers accosted us, begging medios, pointing their muskets at our heads to show how they shot the enemy, and boasting how many they had killed. These fellows made me feel uncomfortable, and I was not singular; but if there was a man who had a mixture of uncomfortable and comfortable feelings, it was my friend the captain. He was for Morazan; had left

La Union to join his expedition, left San Salvador to pay him a visit at Guatimala, and partake of the festivities of his triumph, and left Aguachapa because his trunks had gone on before. Ever since his arrival in the country he had been accustomed to hear Carrera spoken of as a robber and assassin, and the noblesse of Guatimala ridiculed, and all at once he found himself in a hornet's nest. He now heard Morazan denounced as a tyrant, his officers as a set of cut-throats, banded together to assassinate personal enemies, rob churches, and kill priests; they had met the fate they deserved, and the universal sentiment was,—So perish the enemies of Guatimala! The captain had received a timely caution. His story, that Morazan would have killed every man of Figoroa's if the horses had not been so tired, had circulated; it was considered very partial, and special inquiries were made as to who that captain was. He was compelled to listen and assent, or say nothing. On the road he was an excessively loud talker, spoke the language perfectly, with his admirable arms and horse equipments always made a dashing entrée into a village, and was called "muy valiente," "very brave;" but here he was a subdued man, attracting a great deal of attention, but without any of the éclat which had attended him on the road, and feeling that he was an object of suspicion and distrust. But he had one consolation that nothing could take away: he had not been in the battle, or, to use his own expression, he might now be lying on the ground with his face upward.

In the afternoon, unexpectedly, Mr. Catherwood arrived. He had passed a month at the Antigua, and had just returned from a second visit to Copan, and had also explored other ruins, of which mention will be made hereafter. In our joy at meeting we tumbled into each other's arms, and in the very first moment resolved not to separate again while in that distracted country.

CHAPTER XXIV.

RUINS OF QUIRIGUA—VISIT TO THEM—LOS AMATES—PYRAMIDAL STRUCTURE—A COLOSSAL HEAD—AN ALTAR—A COLLECTION OF MONUMENTS—STATUES—CHARACTER OF THE RUINS—A LOST CITY—PURCHASING A RUINED CITY.

To recur to Mr. Catherwood's operations, who, during my absence, had not been idle. On reaching Guatimala the first time from Copan, I made it my business to inquire particularly for ruins. I did not meet a single person who had ever visited those of Copan, and but few who took any interest whatever in the antiquities of the country; but, fortunately, a few days after my arrival, Don Carlos Meany, an Englishman from Trinidad, long resident in the country, proprietor of a large hacienda, and extensively engaged in mining operations, made one of his regular business visits to the capital. Besides a thorough acquaintance with all that concerned his own immediate pursuits, this gentleman possessed much general information respecting the country, and a curiosity which circumstances had never permitted him to gratify in regard to antiquities; and he told me of the ruins of Quirigua, on the Motagua River, near Encuentros, the place at which we slept the second night after crossing the Mico Mountain. He had never seen them, and I hardly believed it possible they could exist, for at that place we had made special inquiries for the ruins of Copan, and were not informed of any others. I became satisfied, however, that Don Carlos was a man who did not speak at random. They were on the estate of Señor Payes, a gentleman of Guatimala lately deceased. He had heard of them from Señor Payes, and had taken such interest in the subject as to inquire for and obtain the details of particular monuments. Three sons of Señor Payes had succeeded to his estate, and at my request Don Carlos called with me upon them. Neither of the sons had ever seen the ruins, or even visited the estate. It was an immense tract of wild land, which had come into their father's hands many years before for a mere trifle. He had visited it once; and they too had heard him speak of these ruins. Lately the spirit of speculation had reached that country; and from its fertility and position on the bank of a navigable river contiguous to the ocean, the tract had been made the subject of a prospectus, to be sold on shares in England. The prospectus set forth the great natural advantages of the location, and the inducements held out to emigrants, in terms and phrases that might have issued from a laboratory in New York before the crash. The Señores Payes were in the first stage of anticipated wealth, and talked in the familiar strains of city builders at home. They were roused by the prospect of any indirect addition to the value of their real estate; told me that two of them were then making arrangements to visit the tract, and immediately proposed that I should accompany them. Mr. Catherwood, on his road from Copan, had fallen in with a person at Chiquimula who told him of such ruins, with the addition that Colonel Galindo was then at work among them. Being in the neighbourhood, he had some idea of going to visit them; but being much worn with his labours at Copan, and knowing that the story was untrue as regarded Colonel Galindo, whom he knew to be in a different section of the country, he was incredulous as to the whole. We had some doubt whether they would repay the labour; but as there was no occasion for him to accompany me to San Salvador, it was agreed that during my absence he should, with the Señores Payes, go to Quirigua, which he accordingly did.

The reader must go back to Encuentros, the place at which we slept the second night of our arrival in the country. From this place they embarked in a canoe about twenty-five feet long and four broad, dug out of the trunk of a mahogany-tree, and descending two hours, disembarked at Los Amates, near El Poso, on the main road from Yzabal to Guatimala, the place at which we breakfasted the second morning of our arrival in the country, and where the Señores Payes were obliged to wait two or three days. The place was a miserable collection of huts, scant of provisions, and the people drank a muddy water at their doors, rather than take the trouble of going to the river.

On a fine morning, after a heavy rain, they set off for the ruins. After a ride of about half an hour, over an execrable road, they again reached the Amates. The village was pleasantly situated on the bank of the river, and elevated about thirty feet. The river was here about 200 feet wide, and fordable in every part except a few deep holes. Generally it did not exceed three feet in depth, and in many places was not so deep; but below it was said to be navigable to the sea for boats not drawing more than three feet water. They embarked in two canoes dug out of cedar-trees, and proceeded down the river for a couple of miles, where they took on board a negro man named Juan Lima, and his two wives. This black scoundrel, as Mr. C. marks him down in his note-book, was to be their guide. They then proceeded two or three miles farther, and stopped at a rancho on the left side of the river, and passing through two corn-fields, entered a forest of large

25. IDOL AT QUIRIGUA.

cedar and mahogany-trees. The path was exceedingly soft and wet, and covered with decayed leaves, and the heat very great. Continuing through the forest toward the north-east, in three quarters of an hour they reached the foot of a pyramidal structure like those at Copan with the steps in some places perfect. They ascended to the top about 25 feet, and descending by steps on the other side, at a short distance beyond came to a colossal head two yards in diameter, almost buried by an enormous tree, and covered with moss. Near it was a large altar, so covered with moss that it was impossible to make anything out of it. The two are within an enclosure.

Retracing their steps across the pyramidal structure, and proceeding to the north about 300 or 400 yards, they reached a collection of monuments of the same general character with those at Copan, but twice or three times as high

The first is about 20 feet high, 5 feet 6 inches on two sides, and 2 feet 8 on the other two. The front represents the figure of a man, well preserved; the back that of a woman, much defaced. The sides are covered with hieroglyphics in good preservation, but in low relief, and of exactly the same style as those at Copan.

Another, represented in the engraving, No. 36, is 23 feet out of the ground, with figures of men on the front and back, and hieroglyphics in low relief on the sides, and surrounded by a base projecting 15 or 16 feet from it.

At a short distance, standing in the same position as regards the points of the compass, is an obelisk or carved stone, 26 feet out of the ground, and probably 6 or 8 feet under, which is represented in the engraving No. 37. It is leaning 12 feet 2 inches out of the perpendicular, and seems ready to fall, which is probably prevented only by a tree that has grown up against it, and the large stones around the base. The side toward the ground represents the figure of a man very perfect and finely sculptured. The upper side seemed the same, but was so hidden by vegetation as to make it somewhat uncertain. The other two contain hieroglyphics in low relief. In size and sculpture this is the finest of the whole.

A statue 10 feet in length is lying on the ground, covered with moss and herbage, and another about the same size lies with its face upward.

There are four others erect, about 12 feet high, but not in a very good state of preservation, and several altars so covered with herbage that it was difficult to ascertain their exact form. One of them is round, and situated on a small elevation within a circle formed by a wall of stones. In the centre of the circle, reached by

27. IDOL AT QUIRIGUA.

descending very narrow steps, is a large round stone, with the sides sculptured in hieroglyphics, covered with vegetation, and supported on what seemed to be two colossal heads.

These are all at the foot of a pyramidal wall, near each other, and in the vicinity of a creek which empties into the Motagua. Besides these they counted thirteen fragments, and doubtless many others may yet be discovered.

At some distance from them is another monument, 9 feet out of ground, and probably 2 or 3 under, with the figure of a woman on the front and back, and the two sides richly ornamented, but without hieroglyphics.

The next day the negro promised to show Mr. C. eleven square columns higher than any he had seen, standing in a row at the foot of a mountain; but after dragging him three hours through the mud, Mr. C. found by the compass that he was constantly changing his direction; and as the man was armed with pistols, notoriously a bad fellow, and indignant at the owners of the land for coming down to look after their squatters, Mr. C. became suspicious of him, and insisted upon returning. The Payes were engaged with their own affairs, and having no one to assist him, Mr. Catherwood was unable to make any thorough exploration or any complete drawings.

The general character of these ruins is the same as at Copan. The monuments are much larger, but they are sculptured in lower relief, less rich in design, and more faded and worn, probably being of a much older date.

Of one thing there is no doubt: a large city once stood there; its name is lost, its history unknown; and, except for a notice taken from Mr. C.'s notes, and inserted by the Señores Payes in a Guatimala paper after the visit, which found its way to this country and Europe, no account of its existence has ever before been published. For centuries it has lain as completely buried as if covered with the lava of Vesuvius. Every traveller from Yzabal to Guatimala has passed within three hours of it; we ourselves had done the same; and yet there it lay, like the rock-built city of Edom, unvisited, unsought, and utterly unknown.

The morning after Mr. C. returned I called upon Señor Payes, the only one of the brothers then in Guatimala, and opened a negotiation for the purchase of these ruins. Besides their entire newness and immense interest as an unexplored field of antiquarian research, the monuments were but about a mile from the river, the ground was level to the bank, and the river from that place was navigable; the city might be transported bodily, and set up in New York. I expressly stated (and my reason for doing so will be obvious) that I was acting in this matter on my own account, that it was entirely a personal affair; but Señor Payes would consider me as acting for my government, and said, what I am sure he meant, that if his family was as it had been once, they would be proud to present the whole to the United States; in that country they were not appreciated, and he would be happy to contribute to the cause of science in ours; but they were impoverished by the convulsions of the country; and, at all events, he could give me no answer till his brothers returned, who were expected in two or three days. Unfortunately, as I believe for both of us, Señor Payes consulted with the French consul general, who put an exaggerated value upon the ruins, referring him to the expenditure of several hundred thousand dollars by the French government in transporting one of the obelisks of Luxor from Thebes to Paris. Probably, before the speculating scheme referred to, the owners would have been glad to sell the whole tract, consisting of more than 50,000 acres, with everything on it, known and unknown, for a few thousand dollars. I was anxious to visit them myself, and learn with more certainty the possibility of their removal, but was afraid of increasing the extravagance of his notions. His brothers did not arrive, and one of them unfortunately died on the road. I had not the government for paymaster; it might be necessary to throw up the purchase on account of the cost of removal; I left an offer with Mr. Savage, which was not accepted, and the monuments remain where first discovered.

CHAPTER XXV.

RECEPTION AT THE GOVERNMENT HOUSE—THE CAPTAIN IN TROUBLE—A CHANGE OF CHARACTER—ARRANGEMENTS FOR JOURNEY TO PALENQUE—ARREST OF THE CAPTAIN—HIS RELEASE—DANGERS IN PROSPECT—FEARFUL STATE OF THE COUNTRY—LAST INTERVIEW WITH CARRERA—DEPARTURE FROM GUATIMALA—A DON QUIXOTE—CIUDAD VIEJA—PLAIN OF EL VIEJA—VOLCANOES, PLAINS, AND VILLAGES—SAN ANDRES ISAPA—DANGEROUS ROAD —A MOLINO—JOURNEY CONTINUED—BARRANCAS—TECPAN GUATIMALA—A NOBLE CHURCH— A SACRED STONE—THE ANCIENT CITY—DESCRIPTION OF THE RUINS—A MOLINO—ANOTHER EARTHQUAKE—PATZUN—A RAVINE—FORTIFICATIONS—LOS ALTOS—GODINES—LOSING A GOOD FRIEND—MAGNIFICENT SCENERY—SAN ANTONIO—LAKE OF ATITLAN.

The next day I called upon the chief of the state. At this time there was no question of presenting credentials, and I was received by him and all gentlemen connected with him without any distrust or suspicion, and more as one identified with them in feelings and interests than as a foreign agent. I had seen more of their country than any one present, and spoke of its extraordinary beauty and fertility, its volcanoes and mountains, the great canal which might make it known to all the civilized world, and its immense resources, if they would let the sword rest and be at peace among themselves. Some of the remarks in these pages will perhaps be considered harsh, and a poor return for the kindness shown to me. My predilections were in favour of the Liberal party, as well because they sustained the Federation as because they gave me a chance for a government; but I have a warm feeling toward many of the leading members of the Central party. If I speak harshly, it is of their public and political character only; and if I have given offence, I regret it.

As I was leaving the Government House a gentleman followed me, and asked me who that captain was that had accompanied me, adding, what surprised me not a little, that the government had advices of his travelling up with me from La Union, his intention to join Morazan's expedition, and his change of purpose in consequence of meeting Morazan defeated on the road; that as yet he was not molested only because he was staying at my house. I was disturbed by this communication. I was open to the imputation of taking advantage of my official character to harbour a partisan. I was the only friend the captain had, and of course determined to stand by him; but he was not only an object of suspicion, but actually known; for much less cause men were imprisoned and shot; in case of any outbreak, my house would not be a protection; it was best to avoid any excitement, and to have an understanding at once. With this view I returned to the chief of the state, and mentioned the circumstances under which we had travelled together, with the addition that, as to myself, I would have taken a much more questionable companion rather than travel alone; and as to the captain, if he had happened to be thrown ashore on their coast, he would very likely have taken a campaign on their side; that he was not on his way to join the expedition when we met Morazan, and assured him most earnestly that now he understood better the other side of the question, and I would answer for his keeping quiet. Don Rivera Paz, as I felt well assured, was desirous to allay rather than create excitement in the city, received my communication in the best spirit possible, and said the captain had better present himself to the government. I returned to my house, and found the captain alone, already by no means pleased with the turn of his fortunes. My communication did not relieve him, but he accompanied me to the Government House. I could hardly persuade myself that he was the same man whose dashing appearance on the road, had often made the women whisper "muy valiente," and whose answer to all intimations of danger was, that a man can only die once. To be sure, the soldiers in the corridor seemed to intimate that they had found him out; the gentlemen in the room surveyed him from head to foot, as if taking notes for an advertisement of his person, and their looks appeared to say they would know him when they met him again. On horseback and with a fair field, the captain would have defied the whole noblesse of Guatimala; but he was completely cowed, spoke only when he was spoken to, and walked out with less effrontery than I supposed possible.

And now I would fain let the reader sit down and enjoy himself quietly in Guatimala, but I cannot. The place did not admit of it. I could not conceal from myself that the Federal Government was broken up; there was not the least prospect of its ever being restored; nor, for a long time to come, of any other being organized in its stead. Under these circumstances I did not consider myself justified in remaining any longer in the country. I was perfectly useless for all the purposes of my mission, and made a formal return to the authorities of Washington, in effect, "after diligent search, no government found."

I was once more my own master, at liberty to go where I pleased, at my own expense, and immediately we commenced making arrangements for our journey to Palenque. We had no time to lose; it was 1,000 miles distant, and the rainy season was approaching, during which part of the road was impassable. There was no one in the city who had ever made the journey. The archbishop, on his exit from Guatimala eight years before, had fled by that road, and since his time it had not been travelled by any resident of Guatimala; but we learned enough to satisfy us that it would be less difficult to reach Palenque from New York than from where we were. We had many preparations to make, and, from the impossibility of getting servants upon whom we could rely, were obliged to attend to all the details ourselves. The captain was uncertain what to do with himself, and talked of going with us. The next afternoon, as we were returning to the house, we noticed a line of soldiers at the corner of the street. As usual, we gave them the sidewalk, and in crossing I remarked to the captain that they eyed us sharply and spoke to each other. The line extended past my door and up to the corner of the next street. Supposing that they were searching for General Guzman or other officers of General Morazan who were thought to be secreted in the city, and that they would not spare my house, I determined to make no difficulty, and let them search. We went in, and the porter, with great agitation, told us that the soldiers were in pursuit of the captain He hardly finished when an officer entered to summon the captain before the corregidor. The captain turned as pale as death. I do not mean it as an imputation upon his courage; any other man would have done the same. I was as much alarmed as he, and told him that if he said so I would fasten the doors; but he answered it was of no use; they would break them down; and it was better for him to go with the officers. I followed him to the door, telling him not to make any confessions, not to commit himself, and that I would be with him in a few minutes. I saw at once that the affair was out of the hands of the chief of the state, and had got before an inferior tribunal. Mr. Catherwood and Mr. Savage entered in time to see the captain moving down the street with his escort. Mr. S., who had charge of my house during my absence, and had hoisted the American flag during the attack upon the city, had lived so long in that country, and had beheld so many scenes of horror, that he was not easily disturbed, and knew exactly what to do. He accompanied me to the cabildo, where we found the captain sitting bolt upright within the railing, and the corregidor and his clerk, with pen, ink, and paper, and ominous formality, examining him. His face brightened at sight of the only man in Guatimala who took the least interest in his fate. Fortunately, the corregidor was an acquaintance, who had been pleased with the interest I took in the sword of Alvarado, an interesting relic in his custody, and was one of the many whom I found in that country proud of showing attentions to a foreign agent. I claimed the captain as my travelling companion, said that we had had a rough journey together, and I did not like to lose sight of him. He welcomed me back to Guatimala, and appreciated the peril I must have encountered in meeting on the road the tyrant Morazan. The captain took advantage of the opportunity to detach himself, without any compunctions, from such dangerous fellowship, and we conversed till it was too dark to write, when I suggested that, as it was dangerous to be out at night, I wished to take the captain home with me, and would be responsible for his forthcoming. He assented with great courtesy, and told the captain to return at nine o'clock the next morning. The captain was immensely relieved; but he had already made up his mind that he had come to Guatimala on a trading expedition, and to make great use of his gold chains.

The next day the examination was resumed. The captain certainly did not commit himself by any confessions; indeed, the revolution in his sentiments was most extraordinary. The Guatimala air was fatal to partialities for Morazan. The examination, by favour of the corregidor, was satisfactory; but the captain was advised to leave the city. In case of any excitement he would be in danger. Carrera was expected from Quezaltenango in a few days, and if he took it up, which he was not unlikely to do, it might be a bad business. The captain did not need any urging. A council was held to determine which way he should go, and the road to the port was the only one open. On a bright morning he pulled off his frockcoat, put on his travelling dress, mounted, and set off for Balize. I watched him as he rode down the street till he was out of sight. Poor captain, where is he now? The next time I saw him was at my own house in New York. He was taken sick at Balize, and got on board a brig bound for Boston, was there at the time of my arrival, and came on to see me; and the last that I saw of him, afraid to return across the country to get the account sales of his ship, he was about to embark for the Isthmus of Panama, cross over, and go up the Pacific. I was knocked about myself in that country, but I think the captain will not soon forget his campaign with Morazan.

In my race from Nicaragua I had cheered myself with the idea that, on reaching Guatimala, all difficulty was over, and that our journey to Palenque would be attended only by the hardships of travelling in a country destitute of accommodations; but, unfortunately, the horizon in that direction was lowering. The whole mass of the Indian population of Los Altos was in a state of excitement, and there were whispers of a general rising and massacre of the whites. General Prem, to whom I have before referred, and his wife, while travelling toward Mexico, had been attacked by a band of assassins; he himself was left on the ground for dead, and his wife murdered, her fingers cut off, and the rings torn from them. Lieutenant Nichols, the aide-de-camp of

Colonel M'Donald, arrived from the Balize with a report that Captain Caddy and Mr. Walker, who had set out for Palenque by the Balize River, had been speared by the Indians; and there was a rumour of some dreadful atrocity committed by Carrera in Quezaltenango, and that he was hurrying back from that place infuriate, with the intention of bringing all the prisoners out into the plaza and shooting them. Every friend in Guatimala, and Mr. Chatfield particularly, urged us not to undertake the journey. We felt that it was a most inauspicious moment, and almost shrunk; I have no hesitation in saying that it was a matter of most serious consideration whether we should not abandon it altogether and return by the way we came; but we had set out with the purpose of going to Palenque, and could not return without seeing it.

Among the petty difficulties of fitting ourselves out I may mention that we wanted four iron chains for trunks, but could only get two, for every blacksmith in the place was making chains for the prisoners. In a week from the time of my arrival everything was ready for our departure. We provided ourselves with all the facilities and safeguards that could be procured. Besides passports, the government furnished us special letters of recommendation to all the corregidors; a flattering notice appeared in the government paper, *El Tiempo*, mentioning my travels through the provinces and my intended route, and recommending me to hospitality; and, upon the strength of the letter of the Archbishop of Baltimore, the venerable Provisor gave me a letter of recommendation to all the curas under his charge. But these were not enough; Carrera's name was worth more than them all, and we waited two days for his return from Quezaltenango. On the 6th of April, early in the morning, he entered the city. At about nine o'clock I called at his house, and was informed that he was in bed, had ridden all night, and would not rise till the afternoon.

I have mentioned that there were rumours in the city of some horrible outrage committed by Carrera at Quezaltenango. He had set out from Guatimala in pursuit of Morazan. Near the Antigua he met one of his own soldiers from Quezaltenango, who reported that there had been a rising in that town, and the garrison were compelled to lay down their arms. Enraged at this intelligence, he abandoned his pursuit of Morazan, and, without even advising the government of his change of plan, marched to Quezaltenango, and among other minor outrages seized eighteen of the municipality, the first men of the state, and without the slightest form of trial shot them in the plaza; and, to heighten the gloom which this news cast over the city, a rumour preceded him that, immediately on his arrival, he intended to order out all the prisoners and shoot them also. At this time the repressed excitement in the city was fearful. An immense relief was experienced on the repulse of Morazan, but there had been no rejoicing; and again the sword seemed suspended by a single hair.

And here I would remark, as at a place where it has no immediate connexion with what precedes or what follows, and consequently, where no application of it can be made, that some matters of deep personal interest, which illustrate, more than volumes, the dreadful state of the country, I am obliged to withhold altogether, lest, perchance, these pages should find their way to Guatimala and compromise individuals. In my long journey I had had intercourse with men of all parties, and was spoken to freely, and sometimes confidentially. Heretofore, in all the wars and revolutions the whites had the controlling influence, but at this time the Indians were the dominant power. Roused from the sloth of ages, and with muskets in their hands, their gentleness was changed into ferocity; and even among the adherents of the Carrera party there was a fearful apprehension of a war of castes, and a strong desire, on the part of those who could get away, to leave the country. I was consulted by men having houses and large landed estates, but who could only command 2,000 or 3,000 dollars in money, as to their ability to live on that sum in the United States; and individuals holding high offices under the Central party told me that they had their passports from Mexico, and were ready at any moment to fly. There seemed ground for the apprehension that the hour of retributive justice was nigh, and that a spirit was awakened among the Indians to make a bloody offering to the spirits of their fathers, and recover their inheritance. Carrera was the pivot on which this turned. He was talked of as El Rey de los Indios, The King of the Indians. He had relieved them from all taxes, and, as they said, supported his army by levying contributions upon the whites. His power by a word to cause the massacre of every white inhabitant, no one doubted. Their security was, as I conceived, that, in the constant action of his short career, he had not had time to form any plans for extended dominion, and knew nothing of the immense country from Texas to Cape Horn, occupied by a race sympathising in hostility to the whites. He was a fanatic, and, to a certain extent, under the dominion of the priests; and his own acuteness told him that he was more powerful with the Indians themselves while supported by the priests and the aristocracy than at the head of the Indians only; but all knew that, in the moment of passion, he forgot entirely the little of plan or policy that ever governed him; and when he returned from Quezaltenango, his hands red with blood, and preceded by the fearful rumour that he intended to bring out 200 or 300 prisoners and shoot them, the citizens of Guatimala felt that they stood on the brink of a fearful gulf. A leading member of the government, whom I wished to call with me upon him and ask him for his passport, declined doing so, lest, as he said, Carrera should think the government was trying to lead him. Others paid him formal visits of ceremony and congratulation upon his return, and compared notes with each other as to the manner in which they were received. Carrera made no report, official or verbal, of what he had done; and though all were full of it, no one of them dared ask him any questions, or refer to it. They will perhaps pronounce me a calumniator, but even at the hazard of wounding their feelings, I cannot withhold what I believe to be a true picture of the state of the country as it was at that time.

Unable to induce any of the persons I wished, to call with me upon Carrera; afraid, after such a long interval and such exciting scenes as he had been engaged in, that he might not recognise me; and feeling that it was all important not to fail in my application to him, I remembered that in my first interview he had spoken warmly of a doctor who had extracted a ball from his side. This doctor I did not know, but I called upon him, and asked him to accompany me, to which, with great civility, he immediately assented.

It was under these circumstances that I made my last visit to Carrera. He had removed into a much larger house, and his guard was more regular and formal. When I entered, he was standing behind a table on one side of the room, with his wife, and Rivera Paz, and one or two others, examining some large Costa Rica chains; and at the moment he had one in his hands, which had formed part of the contents of those trunks of my friend the captain, and which had often adorned his neck. I think it would have given the captain a spasm if he had known that anything once around his neck was between Carrera's fingers. His wife was a pretty, delicate-looking Mestitzo, not more than twenty, and seemed to have a woman's fondness for chains and gold. Carrera himself looked at them with indifference. My idea at the time was, that these jewels were sent in by the government as a present to his wife, and, through her, to propitiate him; but perhaps I was wrong. The face of Rivera Paz seemed anxious. Carrera had passed through so many terrible scenes since I saw him, that I feared he had forgotten me; but he recognised me in a moment, and made room for me behind the table next to himself. His military coat lay on the table, and he wore the same roundabout jacket,—his face had the same youthfulness, quickness, and intelligence, his voice and manners the same gentleness and seriousness,—and he had again been wounded. I regretted to meet Rivera Paz there; for I thought it must be mortifying to him, as the head of the government, to see that his passport was not considered a protection without Carrera's indorsement: but I could not stand upon ceremony, and took advantage of Carrera's leaving the table to say to him that I was setting out on a dangerous road, and considered it indispensable to fortify myself with all the security I could get. When Carrera returned, I told him my purpose,—that I had waited only for his return,—showed him the passport of the government, and asked him to put his stamp upon it. Carrera had no delicacy in the matter; and taking the passport out of my hand, threw it on the table, saying he would make me out a new one, and sign it himself. This was more than I expected; but in a quiet way, telling me to "be seated," he sent his wife into another room for the secretary, and told him to make out a passport for the "Consul of the North." He had an indefinite idea that I was a great man in my own country, but he had a very indefinite idea as to where that country was. I was not particular about my title, so that it was big enough; but the North was rather a broad range, and, to prevent mistakes, I gave the secretary my other passport. He took it into another room, and Carrera sat down at the table beside me. He had heard of my having met Morazan on his retreat, and inquired about him, though less anxiously than others; but he spoke more to the purpose,—said that he was making preparations, and in a week he intended to march upon San Salvador with 3,000 men,—adding that if he had had cannon he would have driven Morazan from the plaza very soon. I asked him whether it was true that he and Morazan met personally on the heights of Calvary; and he said that they did—that it was towards the last of the battle, when the latter was retreating. One of Morazan's dismounted troopers tore off his holsters; Morazan fired a pistol at him, and he struck at Morazan with his sword, and cut his saddle. Morazan, he said, had very handsome pistols; and it struck me that he thought if he had killed Morazan, he would have got the pistols. I could not but think of the strange positions into which I was thrown—shaking hands and sitting side by side with men who were thirsting for each other's blood, well received by all, hearing what they said of each other, and in many cases their plans and purposes, as unreservedly as if I was a travelling member of both cabinets. In a few minutes the secretary called him, and he went out and brought back the passport himself, signed with his own hand, the ink still wet. It had taken him longer than it would have done to cut off a head, and he seemed more proud of it. Indeed, it was the only occasion in which I saw him in the slightest elevation of feeling. I made a comment upon the excellence of the handwriting; and with his good wishes for my safe arrival in the North, and speedy return to Guatimala, I took my leave. Now, I do not believe, if he knew what I say of him, that he would give me a very cordial welcome; but I believe him honest, and if he knew how, and could curb his passions, he would do more good for Central America than any other man in it.

I was now fortified with the best security we could have for our journey. We passed the evening in writing letters and packing up things to be sent home (among which was my diplomatic coat), and on the 7th of April we rose to set out. The first movement was to take down our beds. Every man in that country has a small cot called a catre, made to double with a hinge, which may be taken down and wrapped up, with pillows and bedclothes, in an oxhide, to carry on a journey. Our great object was to travel lightly. Every additional mule and servant gave additional trouble, but we could not do with less than a cargo-mule apiece. Each of us had two petacas, trunks made of oxhide lined with thin straw matting, having a top like that of a box, secured by a clumsy iron chain with large padlocks, containing, besides other things, a hammock, blanket, one pair of sheets, and pillow, which, with alforgas of provisions, made one load apiece. We carried one catre, in case of sickness. We had one spare cargo-mule; the grey mule with which I had ascended the volcano of Cartago and my macho for Mr. Catherwood and myself, and a horse for relief, in all six animals; and two mozos, or men of all work, untried. While in the act of mounting, Don Saturnino Tinoca, my companion from Zonzonate, rode into the yard, to accompany us two days on our journey. We bade farewell to Mr. Savage, my first, last, and best friend, and in a few minutes, with a mingled feeling of regret and satisfaction, left for the last time the barrier of Guatimala.

Don Saturnino was most welcome to our party. His purpose was to visit two brothers of his wife, curas, whom he had never seen, and who lived at Santiago Atitan, two or three days' journey distant. His father was the last governor of Nicaragua under the royal rule, with a large estate, which was confiscated at the time of the revolution; he still had a large hacienda there, had brought up a stock of mules to sell at San Salvador, and intended to lay out the proceeds in goods in Guatimala. He was about forty, tall, and as thin as a man could be to have activity and vigour, wore a roundabout jacket and trousers of dark olive cloth, large pistols in his holsters, and a long sword with a leather scabbard, worn at the point, leaving about an inch of the steel naked. He sat his mule as stiff as if he had swallowed his own sword, holding the reins in his right hand, with his left arm crooked from the elbow, standing out like a pump-handle, the hand dropping from the wrist, and shaking with the movement of the mule. He rode on a Mexican saddle plated with silver, and carried behind a pair of alforgas with bread and cheese, and atole, a composition of pounded parched corn, cocoa, and sugar, which, mixed with water, was almost his living. His mozo was as fat as he was lean, and wore a bell-crowned straw hat, cotton shirt, and drawers reaching down to his knees. Excepting that instead of Rosinaute and the ass, the master rode a mule and the servant went afoot, they were a genuine Don Quixote and Sancho Panza, the former of which appellations, very early in our acquaintance, we gave to Don Saturnino.

We set out for Quezaltenango, but intended to turn aside and visit ruins, and that day we went three leagues out of our road to say farewell to our friend Padre Alcantara at Ciudad Vieja.

At five o'clock in the afternoon we reached the convent, where I had the pleasure of meeting again Padre Alcantara, Señor Vidaurre, and Don Pepé, the same party with whom I had passed the day with so much satisfaction before. Mr. Catherwood had in the meantime passed a month at the convent. Padre Alcantara had fled at the approach of the *tyrant* Morazan; Don Pepé had had a shot at him as he was retreating from the Antigua, and the padre had a musket left at night by a flying soldier against the wall of the convent.

The morning opened with troubles. The grey mule was sick. Don Saturnino bled her on both sides of her neck, but the poor animal was not in a condition to be ridden. Shortly afterwards Mr. Catherwood had one of the mozos by the throat, but Padre Alcantara patched up a peace. Don Saturnino said that the grey mule would be better for exercise, and for the last time we bade farewell to our kind host.

Don Pepé escorted us, and crossing the plain of El Vieja in the direction in which Alvarado entered it, we ascended a high hill, and turning the summit, through a narrow opening looked down upon a beautiful plain, cultivated like a garden, which opened to the left as we advanced, and ran off to the lake of Duenos, between the two great volcanoes of Fire and Water. Descending to the plain, we entered the village of San Antonio, occupied entirely by Indians. The cura's house stood on an open plaza, with a fine fountain in front, and the huts of the Indians were built with stalks of sugarcane. Early in the occupation of Guatimala, the lands around the capital were partitioned out among certain canonigos, and Indians were allotted to cultivate them. Each village was called by the canonigo's own name. A church was built, and a fine house for himself, and by judicious management the Indians became settled and the artisans for the capital. In the stillness and quiet of the village, it seemed as if the mountains and volcanoes around had shielded it from the devastation and alarm of war. Passing through it, on the other side of the plain we commenced ascending a mountain. About half way up, looking back over the village and plain, we saw a single white line over the mountain we had crossed to the Ciudad Vieja, and the range of the eye embraced the plain and lake at our feet, the great plain of Escuintla, the two volcanoes of Agua and Fuego, extending to the Pacific Ocean. The road was very steep, and our mules laboured. On the other side of the mountain the road lay for some distance between shrubs and small trees, emerging from which we saw an immense plain, broken by the track of the direct road from Guatimala, and afar off the spires of the town of Chimaltenango. At the foot of the mountain we reached the village of Paramos. We had been three hours and a half making six miles. Don Pepé summoned the alcalde, showed him Carrera's passport, and demanded a guide to the next village. The alcalde called his alguazils, and in a very few minutes a guide was ready. Don Pepé told us that he left us in Europa, and with many thanks we bade him farewell.

We were now entering upon a region of country which, at the time of the conquest, was the most populous, the most civilized, and best cultivated in Guatimala. The people who occupied it were the descendants of those found there by Alvarado, and perhaps four-fifths were Indians of untainted blood. For three centuries they had submitted quietly to the dominion of the whites, but the rising of Carrera had waked them up to a recollection of their fathers, and it was rumoured that their eyes rolled strangely upon the white men as the enemies of their race. For the first time we saw fields of wheat and peach-trees. The country was poetically called Europa; and though the volcano de Agua still reared in full sight its stupendous head, it resembled the finest part of England on a magnificent scale.

But it was not like travelling in England. The young man with whose throat Mr. Catherwood had been so familiar loitered behind with the sick mule and a gun. He had started from Ciudad Vieja with a drawn knife in his hand, the blade about a foot and a half long, and we made up our minds to get rid of him; but we feared that he had anticipated us, and had gone off with the mule and gun. We waited till he came up, relieved him from the gun, and made him go forward, while we drove the mule. At the distance of two leagues we reached the Indian village of San Andres Isapa. Don Saturnino flourished Carrera's passport, introduced me as El Ministro de Neuva-York, demanded a guide, and in a few minutes an alguazil was trotting before us for the next village. At this village, on the same requisition, the alcalde ran out to look for an alguazil, but could not find one immediately, and ventured to beg Don Saturnino to wait a moment. Don Saturnino told him he must go himself; Carrera would cut off his head if he did not; " the minister of New York" could not be kept waiting. Don Saturnino, like many others of my friends in that country, had no very definite notions in regard to titles or places A man happened to be passing, whom the alcalde pressed into service, and he trotted on before with the halter of the led horse. Don Saturnino hurried him along; as we approached the next village Carrera's soldiers were in sight, returning on the direct road to Guatimala, fresh from the slaughter at Quezaltenango. Don Saturnino told the guide that he must avoid the plaza and go on to the next village. The guide begged, and Don Saturnino rode up, drew his sword, and threatened to cut his head off. The poor fellow trotted on, with his eye fixed on the uplifted sword; and when Don Saturnino turned to me with an Uncle Toby expression of face, he threw down the halter, leaped over a hedge fence, and ran toward the town. Don Saturnino, not disconcerted, caught up the halter, and, spurring his mule, pushed on. The road lay on a magnificent table-land, in some places having trees on each side for a great distance. Beyond this we had a heavy rain-storm, and late in the afternoon reached the brink of an immense precipice, in which, at a great distance, we saw the molino or wheat-mill, looking like a New-England cotton factory. The descent was very steep and muddy, winding in places close along the precipitous side of the ravine. Great care was necessary with the mules; their tendency was to descend sidewise, which was very dangerous; but in the steepest places, by keeping their heads straight, they would slip in the mud several paces, bracing their feet and without falling.

At dark, wet and muddy, and in the midst of a heavy rain, we reached the molino. The major-domo was a Costa Rican, a countryman of Don Saturnino, and, fortunately, we had a room to ourselves, though it was damp and chilly. Here we learned that Tecpan Guatimala, one of the ruined cities we wished to visit, was but three leagues distant, and the major-domo offered to go with us in the morning.

In the morning the major-domo furnished us with fine horses, and we started early. Almost immediately we commenced ascending the other side of the ravine which we had descended the night before, and on the top entered on a continuation of the same beautiful and extensive table-land. On one side, for some distance, were high hedge fences, in which aloes were growing, and in one place were four in full bloom. In an hour we arrived at Patzum, a large Indian village. Here we turned off to the right from the high road to Mexico by a sort of by-path; but the country was beautiful, and in parts well cultivated. The morning was bracing, and the climate like a spring morning in May. The immense table-land was elevated some 5,000 or 6,000 feet, but none of these heights have ever been taken. We passed on the right two mounds, such as are seen in many parts of the United States, and on the left an immense barranca. The table-land was level to the very edge, where the earth seemed to have broken off and sunk, and we looked down into a frightful abyss 2,000 or 3,000 feet deep. Gigantic trees at the bottom of the immense cavity looked like shrubs. At some distance beyond we passed a second of these immense barrancas, and in an hour and a half reached the Indian village of Tecpan Guatimala. For some distance before reaching it the road was shaded by trees and shrubs, among which were aloes thirty feet high. The long street by which we entered was paved with stones from the ruins of the old city, and filled with drunken Indians; and rushing across it was one with his arms around a woman's neck. At the head of this street was a fine plaza, with a large cabildo, and twenty or thirty Indian alguazils under the corridor, with wands of office in their hands, silent, in full suits of blue cloth, the trousers open at the knees, and cloak with a hood like the Arab burnouse. Adjoining this was the large courtyard of the church, paved with stone, and the church itself was one of the most magnificent in the country. It was the second built after the conquest. The façade was 200 feet wide, very lofty, with turrets and spires gorgeously ornamented with stuccoed figures, and a high platform, on which were Indians, the first we had seen in picturesque costume; and with the widely-extended view of the country around, it was a scene of wild magnificence in nature and in art. We stopped involuntarily; and while the Indians, in mute astonishment, gazed at us, we were lost in surprise and admiration. As usual, Don Saturnino was the pioneer, and we rode up to the house of the padre, where we were shown into a small room, in which the padre was dozing in a large chair, with the window closed and a ray of light admitted from the door. Before he had fairly opened his eyes, Don Saturnino told him that we had come to visit the ruins of the old city, and wanted a guide, and thrust into his hands Carrera's passport and the letter of the Provisor. The padre was old, fat, rich, and infirm, had been 35 years cura of Tecpan Guatimala, and was not used to doing things in a hurry; but our friend, knowing the particular objects of our visit, with great earnestness and haste told the padre that the minister of

New York had heard in his country of a remarkable stone, and the Provisor and Carrera were anxious for him to see it. The padre said that it was in the church, and lay on the top of the grand altar; the cup of the sacrament stood upon it; it was covered up, and very sacred; he had never seen it, and he was evidently unwilling to let us see it, but said he would endeavour to do so when we returned from the ruins. He sent for a guide, and we went out to the courtyard of the church; and while Mr. Catherwood was attempting a sketch, I walked up the steps. The interior was lofty, spacious, richly ornamented with stuccoed figures and paintings, dark and solemn, and in the distance was the grand altar, with long wax candles burning upon it, and Indians kneeling before it. At the door a man stopped me, and said that I must not enter with sword and spurs, and even that I must take off my boots. I would have done so, but saw that the Indians did not like a stranger going into *their* church. They were evidently entirely unaccustomed to the sight of strangers, and Mr. Catherwood was so annoyed by their gathering round him that he gave up his drawing; and fearing it would be worse on our return, I told Don Saturnino that we must make an effort to see the stone now. Don Saturnino had a great respect for the priests and the Church. He was not a fanatic, but he thought a powerful religious influence good for the Indians. Nevertheless, he said we ought to see it; and we went back in a body to the padre, and Don Saturnino told him that we were anxious to see the stone now, to prevent delay on our return. The good padre's heavy body was troubled. He asked for the Provisor's letter again, read it over, went out on the corridor and consulted with a brother about as old and round as himself, and at length told us to wait in that room and he would bring it. As he went out he ordered all the Indians in the courtyard, about forty or fifty, to go to the cabildo and tell the alcalde to send the guide. In a few minutes he returned, and opening with some trepidation the folds of his large gown, produced the stone.

Fuentes, in speaking of the old city, says—" To the westward of the city there is a little mount that commands it, on which stands a small round building about six feet in height, in the middle of which there is a pedestal formed of a shining substance resembling glass, but the precise quality of which has not been ascertained. Seated around this building, the judges heard and decided the causes brought before them, and their sentences were executed upon the spot. Previous to executing them, however, it was necessary to have them confirmed by the oracle, for which purpose three of the judges left their seats and proceeded to a deep ravine, where there was a place of worship containing a black transparent stone, on the surface of which the Deity was supposed to indicate the fate of the criminal. If the decision was approved, the sentence was executed immediately; if nothing appeared on the stone, the accused was set at liberty. This oracle was also consulted in the affairs of war. The Bishop Francisco Marroquin, having obtained intelligence of this slab, ordered it to be cut square, and consecrated it for the top of the grand altar in the Church of Tecpan Guatimala. It is a stone of singular beauty, about a yard and a half each way." The "Modern Traveller" refers to it as an " interesting specimen of ancient art;" and, in 1824, concludes—" we may hope, before long, to receive some more distinct account of this oracular stone."

The world—meaning thereby the two classes into which an author once divided it, of subscribers and non-subscribers to his work—the world that reads these pages is indebted to Don Saturnino for some additional information. The stone was sewed up in a piece of cotton cloth drawn tight, which looked certainly as old as the thirty-five years it had been under the cura's charge, and probably was the same covering in which it was enveloped when first laid on the top of the altar. One or two stitches were cut in the middle, and this was perhaps all we should have seen; but Don Saturnino, with a hurried jargon of "strange, curious, sacred, incomprehensible, the Provisor's letter, minister of New York," &c., whipped out his penknife, and the good old padre, heavy with agitation and his own weight, sunk into his chair, still holding on with both hands. Don Saturnino ripped till he almost cut the good old man's fingers, slipped out the sacred tablet, and left the sack in the padre's hands. The padre sat a picture of self-abandonment, helplessness, distress, and self-reproach. We moved toward the light, and Don Saturnino, with a twinkle of his eyes and a ludicrous earnestness, consummated the padre's fear and horror by scratching the sacred stone with his knife. This oracular slab is a piece of common slate, fourteen inches by ten, and about as thick as those used by boys at school, without characters of any kind upon it. With a strong predilection for the marvellous, and scratching it most irreverently, we could make nothing more out of it. Don Saturnino handed it back to the padre, and told him he had better sew it up and put it back; and probably it is now in its place on the top of the grand altar, with the sacramental cup upon it, an object of veneration to the fanatic Indians.

But the agitation of the padre destroyed whatever there was of comic in the scene. Recovering from the shock, he told us not to go back through the town; that there was a road direct to the old city; and concealing the tablet under his gown, he walked out with a firm step, and in a strong, unbroken voice, rapidly, in their own unintelligible dialect, called to the Indians to bring up our horses, and directed the guide to put us in the road which led direct to the molino. He feared that the Indians might discover our sacrilegious act; and as we looked in their stupid faces, we were well satisfied to get away before any such discovery was made, rejoicing more than the padre that we could get back to the molino without returning though the town.

We had but to mount and ride. At the distance of a mile and a half we reached the bank of an immense ravine. We descended it, Don Saturnino leading the way; and at the foot, on the other side, he stopped at a narrow passage, barely wide enough for the mule to pass. This was the entrance to the old city. It was a winding passage cut in the side of the ravine, twenty or thirty feet deep, and not wide enough for two horsemen to ride abreast; and this continued to the high table-land on which stood the ancient city of Patinamit.

When we rose upon the table-land for some distance it bore no marks of ever having been a city. Very soon we came upon an Indian burning down trees, and preparing a piece of ground for planting corn. Don Saturnino asked him to go with us and show us the ruins, but he refused. Soon after we reached a hut, outside of which a woman was washing. We asked her to accompany us, but she ran into the hut. Beyond this we reached a wall of stones, but broken and confused. We tied our horses in the shade of trees, and commenced exploring on foot. The ground was covered with mounds of ruins. In one place we saw the foundations of two houses, one of them about 100 feet long by 50 feet broad. It was 140 years since Fuentes published the account of his visit; during that time the Indians had carried away on their backs stones to build up the modern village of Tecpan Guatimala, and the hand of ruin had been busily at work. We inquired particularly for sculptured figures; our guide knew of two, and after considerable search brought us to them. They were lying on the ground, about three feet long, so worn that we could not make them out, though on one the eyes and nose of an animal were distinguishable. The position commanded an almost boundless view, and it is surrounded by an immense ravine, which warrants the description given of it by Fuentes. In some places it was frightful to look down into its depths. On every side it was inaccessible, and the only way of reaching it was by the narrow passage through which we entered, its desolation and ruin adding another page to the burdened record of human contentions, and proving that, as in the world whose history we know, so in this of whose history we are ignorant, man's hand has been against his fellow. The solitary Indian hut is all that now occupies the site of the ancient city; but on Good Friday of every year a solemn procession of the whole Indian population is made to it from the village of Tecpan Guatimala, and, as our guide told us, on that day bells are heard sounding under the earth.

Descending by the same narrow passage, we traversed the ravine, and ascended on the other side. Our guide put us into the road that avoided the town, and we set off on a gallop.

Don Saturnino possessed the extremes of good temper, simplicity, uprightness, intelligence, and perseverance. Ever since I fell in with him he had been most useful, but this day he surpassed himself; and he was so well satisfied with us as to declare that if it were not for his wife in Costa Rica, he would bear us company to Palenque. He had an engagement in Guatimala on a particular day; every day that he lost with us was so much deducted from his visit to his relatives; and at his earnest request we had consented to pass a day with them, though a little out of our road. We reached the molino in time to walk over the mill. On the side of the hill above was a large building to receive grain, and below it an immense reservoir for water in the dry season, but which did not answer the purpose intended. The mill had seven sets of grindstones, and working night and day, ground from seventy to ninety negases of wheat in the twenty-four hours, each negas being six arobas of twenty-five pounds. The Indians bring the wheat, and each one takes a stone and does his own grinding, paying a rial (sixpence halfpenny) per negas for the use of the mill. Flour is worth about from fourteen to sixteen shillings the barrel.

Don Saturnino was one of the best men that ever lived, but in undress there was a lankness about him that was ludicrous. In the evening, as he sat on the bed with his thin arms wound around his thin legs, and we reproved him for his sacrilegious act in cutting open the cotton cloth, his little eyes twinkled, and Mr. C. and I laughed as we had not before laughed in Central America.

But in that country one extreme followed close upon another. At midnight we were roused from sleep by that movement which, once felt, can never be mistaken. The building rocked, our men in the corridor cried out, "temblor," and Mr. C. and I at the same moment exclaimed, "an earthquake!" Our catres stood transversely. By the undulating movement of the earth he was rolled from side to side, and I from head to foot. The sinking of my head induced an awful faintness of heart. I sprang upon my feet, and rushed to the door. In a moment the earth was still. We sat on the sides of the bed, compared movements and sensations, lay down again, and slept till morning.

Early in the morning we resumed our journey. Unfortunately, the grey mule was no better. Perhaps she would recover in a few days, but we had no time to wait. My first mule, too, purchased at the price of seeing Don Clementino's sister, which had been a most faithful animal, was drooping. Don Saturnino offered me his own, a strong, hardy animal, in exchange for the latter, and the former I left behind, to be sent back and turned out on the pasture-grounds of Padre Alcantara. There were few trials greater in that country than that of being obliged to leave on the road these tried and faithful companions.

To Patzum our road was the same as the day before. Before reaching it we had difficulty with the luggage, and left at a hut on the road, our only catre. Leaving Patzum on the left, our road lay on the high, level table-land, and at ten o'clock we came to the brink of a ravine, 3,000 feet deep, saw an immense abyss at our feet, and opposite, the high, precipitous wall of the ravine. Our road lay across it. At the very commencement the descent was steep. As we advanced the path wound fearfully along the edge of the precipice, and we met a caravan of mules at a narrow place, where there was no room to turn out, and we were obliged to go back, taking care to give them the outside. All the way down we were meeting them; perhaps more than 500 passed us, loaded with wheat for the mills, and cloths for Guatimala. In meeting so many mules laden with merchandise, we lost the vague and indefinite apprehensions with which we had set out on this road. We were kept back by them more than half an hour, and with great labour reached the bottom of the ravine. A stream ran through it; for some distance our road lay in the stream, and we crossed it thirty or forty times. The sides of the ravine were of an immense height. In one place we rode along a perpendicular wall of limestone rock smoking with spontaneous combustion.

At twelve o'clock we commenced ascending the opposite side. About half way up we met another caravan of mules, with heavy boxes on their sides, tumbling down the steep descent. They came upon us so suddenly that our cargo-mules got entangled among them, turned around, and were hurried down the mountain. Our men got them disengaged, and we drew up against the side. As we ascended, toward the summit, far above us, were rude fortifications, commanding the road up which we were toiling. This was the frontier post of Los Altos, and the position taken by General Guzman to repel the invasion of Carrera. It seemed certain death for any body of men to advance against it; but Carrera sent a detachment of Indians, who clambered up the ravine at another place, and attacked it in the rear. The fortifications were pulled down and burned, the boundary lines demolished, and Los Altos annexed to Guatimala. Here we met an Indian, who confirmed what the muleteers had told us, that the road to Santiago Atitlan, the place of residence of Don Saturnino's relatives, was five leagues, and exceedingly bad, and, in order to save our luggage-mules, we resolved to leave them at the village of Godines, about a mile further on. The village consisted of but three or four huts, entirely desolate; there was not a person in sight. We were afraid to trust our mozos alone; they might be robbed, or they might rob us themselves; besides, they had nothing to eat. We were about at the head of the lake of Atitlan. It was impossible, with the cargo-mules, to reach Santiago Atitlan that day; it lay on the left border of the lake; our road was on the right, and it was agreed for Don Saturnino to go on alone, and for us to continue on our direct road to Panajachel, a village on the right border opposite Atitlan, and cross the lake to pay our visit to him. We were told that there were canoes for this purpose, and bade farewell to Don Saturnino with the confident expectation of seeing him the next day at the house of his relatives; but we never met again.

At two o'clock we came out upon the lofty table-land bordering the lake of Atitlan. In general I have forborne attempting to give any idea of the magnificent scenery amid which we were travelling, but here forbearance would be a sin. From a height of 3,000 or 4,000 feet we looked down upon a surface shining like a sheet of molten silver, enclosed by rocks and mountains of every form, some barren, and some covered with verdure, rising from 500 to 5,000 feet in height. Opposite, down on the borders of the lake, and apparently inaccessible by land, was the town of Santiago Atitlan, to which our friend was wending his way, situated between two immense volcanoes 8,000 or 10,000 feet high. Farther on was another volcano, and farther still another, more lofty than all, with its summit buried in clouds. There were no associations connected with this lake; until lately we did not know it even by name; but we both agreed that it was the most magnificent spectacle we ever saw. We stopped and watched the fleecy clouds of vapour rising from the bottom, moving up the mountains and the sides of the volcanoes. We descended at first by a steep pitch, and then gently for about three miles along the precipitous border of the lake, leaving on our right the camino real and the village of San Andres, and suddenly reached the brink of the table-land, 2,000 feet high. At the foot was a rich plain running down to the water; and on the opposite side another immense perpendicular mountain-side, rising to the same height with that on which we stood. In the middle of the plain, buried in foliage, with the spire of the church barely visible, was the town of Panajachel. Our first view of the lake was the most beautiful we had ever seen, but this surpassed it. All the requisites of the grand and beautiful were there; gigantic mountains, a valley of poetic softness, lake, and volcanoes, and from the height on which we stood a waterfall marked a silver line down its sides. A party of Indian men and women were moving in single file from the foot of the mountain toward the village, and looked like children. The descent was steep and perpendicular, and, reaching the plain, the view of the mountain-walls was sublime. As we advanced, the plain formed a triangle with its base on the lake, the two mountain ranges converged to a point, and communicated by a narrow defile beyond with the village of San Andres.

Riding through a thick forest of fruit and flower trees, we entered the village, and at three o'clock rode up to the convent. The padre was a young man, cura of four or five villages, rich, formal, and polite; but all over the world women are better than men; his mother and sister received us cordially. They were in great distress on account of the outrage at Quezaltenango. Carrera's troops had passed through on their return to Guatimala, and they feared that the same bloody scenes were to be enacted all through the country. Part of his outrages were against the person of a cura, and this seemed to break the only chain that was supposed to keep him in subjection. Unfortunately, we learned that there was little or no communication with Santiago Atitlan, and no canoe on this side of the lake. Our only chance of seeing Don Saturnino again was that he would learn this fact at Atitlan, and if there was a canoe there, send it for us. After dinner, with a servant of the house as guide, we walked down to the lake. The path lay through a tropical garden. The climate was entirely different from the table-land above, and productions which would not grow there flourished here. Sapotes, jocotes, aguacates, manzanas, pine-apples, oranges, and lemons, the best fruits of Central America, grew in profusion, and aloes grew 30 to 35 feet high, and 12 or 14 inches thick, cultivated in rows, to be used for thatching miserable Indian huts. We came down to the lake at some hot springs, so near the edge that the waves ran over the spring, the former being very hot, and the latter very cold.

According to Juarros, "the Lake of Atitlan is one of the most remarkable in the kingdom. It is about twenty-four miles from east to west, and ten from north to south, entirely surrounded by rocks and mountains. There is no gradation of depth from its shores, and the bottom has not been found with a line of 300 fathoms. It receives several rivers, and all the waters that descend from the mountains, but there is no known channel by which this great body is carried off. The only fish caught in it are crabs, and a species of small fish about the size of the little finger. These are in such countless myriads that the inhabitants of the surrounding ten villages carry on a considerable fishing for them."

At that hour of the day, as we understood to be the case always at that season of the year, heavy clouds were hanging over the mountains and volcanoes, and the lake was violently agitated by a strong southwest wind; as our guide said, " la laguna es muy brava." Santiago Atitlan was nearly opposite, at a distance of seven or eight leagues, and in following the irregular and mountainous border of the lake, from the point where Don Saturnino left us, we doubted whether he could reach it that night. It was much farther off than we supposed, and with the lake in such a state of agitation, and subject, as our guide told us, at all times to violent gusts of wind, we had but little inclination to cross it in a canoe. It would have been magnificent to see there a tropical storm, to hear the thunder roll among the mountains, and see the lightnings flash down into the lake. We sat on the shore till the sun disappeared behind the mountains at the head of the lake. Mingled with our contemplations of it were thoughts of other and far distant scenes, and at dark we returned to the convent.

CHAPTER XXVI.

LAKE OF ATITLAN—CONJECTURES AS TO ITS ORIGIN, ETC.—A SAIL ON THE LAKE—A DANGEROUS SITUATION—A LOFTY MOUNTAIN RANGE—ASCENT OF THE MOUNTAINS—COMMANDING VIEW—BEAUTIFUL PLAIN—AN ELEVATED VILLAGE—RIDE ALONG THE LAKE—SOLOLA—VISIT TO SANTA CRUZ DEL QUICHÉ—SCENERY ON THE ROAD—BARRANCAS—SAN THOMAS—WHIPPING POSTS—PLAIN OF QUICHÉ—THE VILLAGE—RUINS OF QUICHÉ—ITS HISTORY—DESOLATE SCENE—A FACETIOUS CURA—DESCRIPTION OF THE RUINS—PLAN—THE ROYAL PALACE—THE PLACE OF SACRIFICE—AN IMAGE—TWO HEADS, ETC.—DESTRUCTION OF THE PALACE RECENT—AN ARCH.

EARLY in the morning we again went down to the lake. Not a vapour was on the water, and the top of every volcano was clear of clouds. We looked over to Santiago Atitlan, but there was no indication of a canoe coming for us. We whiled away the time in shooting wild ducks, but could only get two ashore, which we afterward found of excellent flavour. According to the account given by Juarros, the water of this lake is so cold that in a few minutes it benumbs and swells the limbs of all who bathe in it. But it looked so inviting that we determined to risk it, and were not benumbed, nor were our limbs swollen. The inhabitants, we were told, bathed in it constantly; and Mr. C. remained a long time in the water, supported by his life-preserver, and without taking any exercise, and was not conscious of extreme coldness. In the utter ignorance that exists in regard to the geography and geology of that country, it may be that the account of its fathomless depth, and the absence of any visible outlet, is as unfounded as that of the coldness of its waters.

While we were dressing, Juan, one of our mozos, found a canoe along the shore. It was an oblong "dug-out," awkward and rickety, and intended for only one person; but the lake was so smooth that a plank seemed sufficient. We got in, and Juan pushed off, and paddled out. As we moved away the mountainous borders of the lake rose grandly before us; and I had just called Mr. C.'s attention to a cascade opening upon us from the great height of perhaps 3,000 or 4,000 feet, when we were struck by a flaw, which turned the canoe, and drove us out into the lake. The canoe was overloaded, and Juan was an unskilful paddler. For several minutes he pulled, with every sinew stretched, but could barely keep her head straight. Mr. C. was in the stern, I on my knees in the bottom of the canoe. The loss of a stroke, or a tottering movement in changing places might swamp her; and if we let her go she would be driven out into the lake, and cast ashore, if at all, twenty or thirty miles distant, whence we should have to scramble back over mountains; and there was a worse danger than this, for in the afternoon the wind always came from the other side, and might drive us back again into the middle of the lake. We saw the people on the shore looking at us, and growing smaller every moment, but they could not help us. In all our difficulties we had none that came upon us so suddenly and unexpectedly, or that seemed more threatening. It was hardly ten minutes since we were standing quietly on the beach, and if the wind had continued five minutes longer, I do not know what would have become of us; but, most fortunately, it lulled. Juan's strength revived; with a great effort he brought us under cover of the high headland beyond which the wind first struck us, and in a few minutes we reached the shore.

We had had enough of the lake; time was precious, and we determined to set out after dinner and ride four leagues to Solola. We took another mozo, whom the padre recommended as a bobon, or great fool. The first two were at swords' points, and with such a trio there was not much danger of combination. In loading the mules they fell to quarrelling, Bobon taking his share. Ever since we left, Don Saturnino had superintended this operation, and without him everything went wrong. One mule slipped part of its load in the courtyard, and we made but a sorry party for the long journey we had before us. From the village our road lay toward the lake, to the point of the opposite mountain, which shut in the plain of Panajachel. Here we began to ascend. For a while the path commanded a view of the village and plain; but by degrees we diverged from it, and after an hour's ascent came out upon the lake, rode a short distance upon the brink, with another immense mountain range before us, and breaking over the top the cataract which I had seen from the canoe. Very soon we commenced ascending; the path ran zig-zag, commanding alternately a view of the plain and of the lake. The ascent was terrible for loaded mules, being in some places steps cut in the stone like a regular staircase. Every time we came upon the lake there was a different view. At 4 o'clock, looking back over the high ranges of mountains we had crossed, we saw the great volcanoes of Agua and Fuego. Six volcanoes were in sight at once, four of them above 10,000, and two nearly 15,000 feet high. Looking down upon the lake we saw a canoe, so small as to present a mere speck on the water, and, as we supposed, it was sent for us by our friend Don Saturnino. Four days afterwards, after diverging and returning to the main road, I found a letter from him, directed to "El Ministro de Nueva York," stating that he found the road so terrible that night overtook him, and he was obliged to stop three leagues short of Atitlan. On arriving at that place he learned that *the* canoe was on his side of the lake, but the boatmen would not cross till the afternoon wind sprang up. The letter was written after the return of the canoe, and sent by courier two days' journey, begging us to return, and offering as a bribe a noble mule, which, in our bantering on the road, he affirmed was better than my macho. Twice the mule-track led us almost within the fall of cataracts, and the last time we came upon the lake we looked down upon a plain even more beautiful than that of Panajachel. Directly under us, at an immense distance below, but itself elevated 1,500 or 2,000 feet, was a village, with its church conspicuous, and it seemed as if we could throw a stone down upon its roof. From the moment this lake first opened upon us until we left it, our ride along it presented a greater combination of beauties than any locality I ever saw. The last ascent occupied an hour and three-quarters. As old travellers, we would have avoided it if there had been any other road; but, once over, we would not have missed it for the world. Very soon we saw Solola. In the suburbs drunken Indians stood in a line, and took off their old petates (straw hats) with both hands. It was Sunday, and the bells of the church were ringing for vespers, rockets were firing, and a procession, headed by violins, was parading round the plaza the figure of a saint on horseback, dressed like a harlequin. Opposite the cabildo the alcalde, with a crowd of Mestitzoes, was fighting cocks.

It was our purpose at this place to send our luggage on by the main road to Totonicapan, one day's journey beyond, while we struck off at an angle and visited the ruins of Santa Cruz del Quiché. The Indians of that place, even in the most quiet times, bore a very bad name, and we were afraid of hearing such an account of them as would make it impossible to go there. Carrera had left a garrison of soldiers in Solola, and we called upon the commandant, a gentlemanly man, suspected of disaffection to Carrera's government, and therefore particularly desirous to pay respect to his passport, who told me that there had been less excitement at that place than in some of the other villages, and promised to send the luggage on under safe escort to the corregidor of Totonicapan, and give us a letter to his commissionado in Santa Cruz del Quiché.

On our return we learned that a lady had sent for us. Her house was on the corner of the plaza. She was a chapetone from Old Spain, which country she had left with her husband thirty years before, on account of wars. At the time of Carrera's last invasion her son was alcalde-mayor, and fled. If he had been taken he would have been shot. The wife of her son was with her. They had not heard from him, but he had fled toward Mexico, and they supposed him to be in the frontier town, and wished us to carry letters to him, and to inform him of their condition. Their house had been plundered, and they were in great distress. It was another of the instances we were constantly meeting of the effects of civil war. They insisted on our remaining at the house all night, which, besides that they were interesting, we were not loth to do on our own account. The place was several thousand feet higher than where we slept the night before, and the temperature cold and wintry by comparison. Hammocks, our only beds, were not used at all. There were not even supporters in the cabildo to hang them on. The next morning the mules were all drawn up by the cold, their coats were rough, and my poor horse was so chilled that he could hardly move. In coming in he had attracted attention, and the alcalde wanted to buy him In the morning he told me that, being used to a hot climate, the horse could not bear the journey across the Cordilleras, which was confirmed by several disinterested persons to whom he appealed. I almost suspected him of having done the horse some injury, so as to make me leave him behind. However, by moving him in the sun his limbs relaxed, and we sent him off with the men and luggage, and the promised escort, to Totonicapan, recommended to the corregidor.

At a quarter before nine we left Solola, and at twelve o'clock met some Indians, who told us that Santo Thomas was three leagues distant, and five minutes afterwards we saw the town apparently not more than a mile off; but we were arrested by another immense ravine. The descent was by a winding zigzag path, part of the way with high walls on either side, so steep that we were obliged to dismount and walk all the way, hurried on by our own impetus and the mules crowding upon us from behind. At the foot of the ravine was a beautiful stream, at which, choked with dust and perspiration, we stopped to drink. We mounted to ford the stream, and almost immediately dismounted again to ascend the opposite side of the ravine. This was even more difficult than the descent, and when we reached the top it seemed a good three.leagues. We passed on the right another awful barranca, broken off from the table-land, and riding close along its edge, looked down into an abyss of 2,000 or 3,000 feet, and very soon reached Santo Thomas. A crowd of Indians was gathered in the plaza, well dressed in brown cloth, and with long black hair, without hats. The entire population was Indian. There was not a single white man in the place, no one who could speak Spanish, except an old Mestitzo, who was the secretary of the alcalde. We rode up to the cabildo, and tied our mules before the prison door.

Groups of villanous faces were fixed in the bars of the windows. We called for the alcalde, presented Carrera's passport, and demanded sacate, eggs, and frigoles, for ourselves, and a guide to Quiché. While these were got, the alcalde, and as many alguazils as could find a place, seated themselves silently on a bench occupied by us. In front was a new whipping-post. There was not a word spoken; but a man was brought up before it, his feet and wrists tied together, and he was drawn up by a rope which passed through a groove at the top of the post. His back was naked, and an alguazil stood on his left with a heavy cowhide whip. Every stroke made a blue streak, rising into a ridge, from which the blood started and trickled down his back. The poor fellow screamed in agony. After him a boy was stretched up in the same way. At the first lash, with a dreadful scream, he jerked his feet out of the ropes, and seemed to fly up to the top of the post. He was brought back and secured, and whipped till the alcalde was satisfied. This was one of the reforms instituted by the Central government of Guatimala. The Liberal party had abolished this remnant of barbarity; but within the last month, at the wish of the Indians themselves, and in pursuance of the general plan to restore old usages and customs, new whipping posts had been erected in all the villages. Not one of the brutal beings around seemed to have the least feeling for the victims. Among the amateurs were several criminals, whom we had noticed walking in chains about the plaza, and among them a man and woman in rags, bareheaded, with long hair streaming over their eyes, chained together by the hand and foot, with strong bars between them to keep them out of each other's reach. They were husband and wife, who had shocked the moral sense of the community by not living together. The punishment seemed the very refinement of cruelty, but while it lasted it was an effectual way of preventing a repetition of the offence.

At half-past three, with an alguazil running before us and Bobon trotting behind, we set out again, and crossed a gently-rolling plain, with a distant side-hill on the left, handsomely wooded, and reminding us of scenes at home, except that on the left was another immense barranca, with large trees, whose tops were 2,000 feet below us. Leaving a village on the right, we passed a small lake, crossed a ravine, and rose to the plain of Quiché. At a distance on the left were the ruins of the old city, the once large and opulent capital of Utatlan, the court of the native kings of Quiché, and the most sumptuous discovered by the Spaniards in this part of America. It was a site worthy to be the abode of a race of kings. We passed between two small lakes, rode into the village, passed on, as usual, to the convent, which stood beside the church, and stopped at the foot of a high flight of stone steps. An old Indian on the platform told us to walk in, and we spurred our mules up the steps, rode through the corridor into a large apartment, and sent the mules down another flight of steps into a yard enclosed by a high stone fence. The convent was the first erected in the country by the Dominican friars, and dated from the time of Alvarado. It was built entirely of stone, with massive walls, and corridors, pavements, and courtyard strong enough for a fortress; but most of the apartments were desolate or filled with rubbish; one was used for sacate, another for corn, and another fitted up as a roosting-place for fowls. The padre had gone to another village, his own apartments were locked, and we were shown into one adjoining, about thirty feet square, and nearly as high, with stone floor and walls, and without a single article in it except a shattered and weather-beaten soldier in one corner, returning from campaigns in Mexico. As we had brought with us nothing but our ponchas, and the nights in that region were very cold, we were unwilling to risk sleeping on the stone floor, and with the padre's Indian servant went to the alcalde, who, on the strength of Carrera's passport, gave us the audience-room of the cabildo, which had at one end a raised platform with a railing, a table, and two long benches with high backs. Adjoining was the prison, being merely an enclosure of four high stone walls, without any roof, and filled with more than the usual number of criminals, some of whom, as we looked through the gratings, we saw lying on the ground with only a few rags of covering, shivering in the cold. The alcalde provided us with supper, and promised to procure us a guide to the ruins.

Early in the morning, with a Mestitzo armed with a long baskethilted sword, who advised us to carry our weapons, as the people were not to be trusted, we set out for the ruins. At a short distance we passed another immense barranca, down which, but a few nights before, an Indian, chased by alguazils, either fell or threw himself off into the abyss, 1,500 feet deep, and was dashed to pieces. At about a mile from the village we came to a range of elevations, extending to a great distance, and connected by a ditch, which had evidently formed the line of fortifications of the ruined city. They consisted of the remains of stone buildings, probably towers, the stones well cut and laid together, and the mass of rubbish around abounded in flint arrow-heads. Within this line was an elevation, which grew more imposing as we approached, square, with terraces, and having in the centre a tower, in all 120 feet high. We ascended by steps to three ranges of terrace, and on the top entered an area enclosed by stone

Distant view of the Ruins.

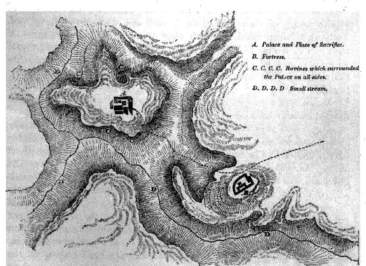

A. *Palace and Place of Sacrifice.*
B. *Fortress.*
C. C. C. C. *Ravines which surrounded the Palace on all sides.*
D. D. D. D *Small stream.*

F. Catherwood

38. SANTA CRUZ DEL QUICHÉ.

walls, and covered with hard cement, in many places still perfect. Thence we ascended by stone steps to the top of the tower, the whole of which was formerly covered with stucco, and stood as a fortress at the entrance of the great city of Utatlan, the capital of the kingdom of the Quiché Indians.

According to Fuentes, the chronicler of the kingdom of Guatimala, the kings of Quiché and Kachiquel were descended from the Toltecan Indians, who, when they came into this country, found it already inhabited by people of different nations. According to the manuscript of Don Juan Torres, the grandson of the last king of the Quichés, which was in the possession of the lieutenant-general appointed by Pedro de Alvarado, and which Fuentes says he obtained by means of Father Francis Vasques, the historian of the order of San Francis, the Toltecas themselves descended from the house of Israel, who were released by Moses from the tyranny of Pharaoh, and after crossing the Red Sea, fell into idolatry. To avoid the reproofs of Moses, or from fear of his inflicting upon them some chastisement, they separated from him and his brethren, and under the guidance of Tanub, their chief, passed from one continent to the other, to a place which they called the seven caverns, a part of the kingdom of Mexico, where they founded the celebrated city of Tula. From Tanub sprang the families of the kings of Tula and Quiché, and the first monarch of the Toltecas. Nimaquiché, the fifth king of that line, and more beloved than any of his predecessors, was directed by an oracle to leave Tula, with his people, who had by this time multiplied greatly, and conduct them from the kingdom of Mexico to that of Guatimala. In performing this journey they consumed many years, suffered extraordinary hardships, and wandered over an immense tract of country, until they discovered the lake of Atitlan, and resolved to settle near it in a country which they called Quiché.

Nimaquiché was accompanied by his three brothers, and it was agreed to divide the new country between them. Nimaquiché died; his son Axcopil became chief of the Quichés, Kachiquels, and Zutugiles, and was at the head of his nation when they settled in Quiché, and the first monarch who reigned in Utatlan. Under him the monarchy rose to a high degree of splendour. To relieve himself from some of the fatigues of administration, he appointed thirteen captains or governors, and at a very advanced age divided his empire into three kingdoms, viz the Quiché, the Kachiquel, and the Zutugil, retaining the first for himself, and giving the second to his eldest son, Jintemal, and the third to his youngest son, Acxigual. This division was made on a day when three suns were visible at the same time, which extraordinary circumstance, says the manuscript, has induced some persons to believe that it was made on the day of our Saviour's birth. There were seventeen Toltecan kings who reigned in Utatlan, the capital of Quiché, whose names have come down to posterity, but they are so hard to write out that I will take it for granted the reader is familiar with them.

Their history, like that of man in other parts of the world, is one of war and bloodshed. Before the death of Axcopil his sons were at war, which, however, was settled by his mediation, and for two reigns peace existed. In the reign of Balam Acan, the next king of Quiché, while living on terms of great intimacy and friendship with his cousin Zutugilebpop, king of the Zutugiles, the latter abused his generosity, and ran away with his daughter Ixconsocil; and at the same time Iloacab, his relative and favourite, ran away with Ecselixpua, the niece of the king. The rape of Helen did not produce more wars and bloodshed than the carrying off of these two young ladies with unpronounceable names. Balam Acan was naturally a mild man, but the abduction of his daughter was an affront not to be pardoned. With 80,000 veterans, himself in the centre squadron, adorned with three diadems and other regal ornaments, carried in a rich chair of state, splendidly ornamented with gold, emeralds, and other precious stones, upon the shoulders of the nobles of his court, he marched against Zutugilebpop, who met him with 60,000 men, commanded by Iloacab, his chief general and accomplice. The most bloody battle ever fought in the country took place; the field was so deeply inundated with blood that not a blade of grass could be seen. Victory long remained undecided, and at length Iloacab was killed, and Balam Acan remained master of the field. But the campaign did not terminate here. Balam Acan, with 30,000 veterans under his personal command, and two other bodies of 30,000 each, again met Zutugilebpop with 40,000 of his own warriors, and 40,000 auxiliaries. The latter was defeated, and escaped at night. Balam Acan pursued and overtook him; but while his bearers were hastening with him to the thickest of the fight, they lost their footing, and precipitated him to the earth. At this moment Zutugilebpop was advancing with a chosen body of 10,000 lancers. Balam Acan was slain, and 14,000 Indians were left dead on the field.

The war was prosecuted by the successor of Balam, and Zutugilebpop sustained such severe reverses that he fell into a despondency and died. The war was continued down to the time of Kicah Tanub, who, after a sanguinary struggle, reduced the Zutugiles and Kachiquels to subjection to the kings of Quiché. At this time the kingdom of the

Quichés had attained its greatest splendour, and this was contemporaneous with that eventful era in American history, the reign of Montezuma and the invasion of the Spaniards. The kings of Mexico and Quiché acknowledged the ties of relationship, and in a manuscript of sixteen quarto leaves, preserved by the Indians of San Andres Xecul, it is related that when Montezuma was made prisoner, he sent a private ambassador to Kicah Tanub, to inform him that some white men had arrived in his state, and made war upon him with such impetuosity that the whole strength of his people was unable to resist them; that he was himself a prisoner, surrounded by guards; and hearing it was the intention of his invaders to pass on to the kingdom of Quiché, he sent notice of the design, in order that Kicah Tanub might be prepared to oppose them. On receiving this intelligence, the king of Quiché sent for four young diviners, whom he ordered to tell him what would be the result of this invasion. They requested time to give their answers; and, taking their bows, discharged some arrows against a rock; but, seeing that no impression was made upon it, returned very sorrowfully, and told the king there was no way of avoiding the disaster; the white men would certainly conquer them. Kicah, dissatisfied, sent for the priests, desiring to have their opinions on this important subject; and they, from the ominous circumstance of a certain stone, brought by their forefathers from Egypt, having suddenly split into two, predicted the inevitable ruin of the kingdom. At this time he received intelligence of the arrival of the Spaniards on the borders of Soconusco to invade his territory; but, undismayed by the auguries of diviners or priests, he prepared for war. Messages were sent by him to the conquered kings and chiefs under his command, urging them to co-operate for the common defence; but, glad of an opportunity to rebel, Sinacam, the king of Guatimala, declared openly that he was a friend to the Teules, or Gods, as the Spaniards were called by the Indians; and the king of the Zutugiles answered haughtily that he was able to defend his kingdom alone against a more numerous and less famished army than that which was approaching Quiché. Irritation, wounded pride, anxiety, and fatigue, brought on a sickness which carried Tanub off in a few days.

His son Tecum Umam succeeded to his honours and troubles. In a short time intelligence was received that the captain (Alvarado) and his Teules had marched to besiege Xelahuh (now Quezaltenango), next to the capital the largest city of Quiché. At that time it had within its walls 80,000 men; but such was the fame of the Spaniards that Tecum Umam determined to go to its assistance. He left the capital, at the threshold of which we stood, borne in his litter on the shoulders of the principal men of his kingdom, and preceded by the music of flutes, cornets, and drums, and 70,000 men, commanded by his general Ahzob, his lieutenant Ahzumanche, the grand shield-bearer Ahpocob, other officers of dignity with still harder names, and numerous attendants bearing parasols and fans of feathers for the comfort of the royal person. An immense number of Indian carriers followed with baggage and provisions. At the populous city of Totonicapan the army was increased to 90,000 fighting men. At Quezaltenango he was joined by ten more chiefs, well armed and supplied with provisions, displaying all the gorgeous insignia of their rank, and attended by 24,000 soldiers. At the same place he was reinforced by 46,000 more, adorned with plumes of different colours, and with arms of every description, the chiefs decorated with the skins of lions, tigers, and bears, as distinguishing marks of their bravery and warlike prowess. Tecum Umam marshalled under his banners on the plain of Tzaccapa 230,000 warriors, and fortified his camp with a wall of loose stones, enclosing within its circuit several mountains. In the camp were several military machines, formed of beams on rollers, to be moved from place to place. After a series of desperate and bloody battles, the Spaniards routed this immense army, and entered the city of Xelahuh. The fugitives rallied outside, and made a last effort to surround and crush the Spaniards. Tecum Umam commanded in person, singled out Alvarado, attacked him three times hand to hand, and wounded his horse; but the last time Alvarado pierced him with a lance, and killed him on the spot. The fury of the Indians increased to madness; in immense masses they rushed upon the Spaniards; and, seizing the tails of the horses, endeavoured by main force to bring horse and rider to the ground; but, at a critical moment, the Spaniards attacked in close column, broke the solid masses of the Quichés, routed the whole army, and slaying an immense number, became completely masters of the field. But few of the 70,000 who marched out from the capital with Tecum Umam ever returned; and, hopeless of being able to resist any longer by force, they had recourse to treachery. At a council of war called at Utatlan by the king, Chinanivalut, son and successor of Tecum Umam, it was determined to send an embassy to Alvarado, with a valuable present of gold, suing for pardon, promising submission, and inviting the Spaniards to the capital. In a few days Alvarado, with his army, in high spirits at the prospect of a termination of this bloody war, encamped upon the plain.

This was the first appearance of strangers at Utatlan, the capital of the great Indian kingdom, the ruins of which were now under our eyes, once the most populous and opulent city, not only of Quiché, but of the whole kingdom of Guatimala. According to Fuentes, who visited it for the purpose of collecting information, and who gathered his facts partly from the remains and partly from manuscripts, it was surrounded by a deep ravine that formed a natural fossé, leaving only two very narrow roads as entrances, both of which were so well defended by the castle of Resguardo, as to render it impregnable. The centre of the city was occupied by the royal palace, which was surrounded by the houses of the nobility; the extremities were inhabited by the plebeians; and some idea may be formed of its vast population from the fact, before mentioned, that the king drew from it no less than 72,000 fighting men to oppose the Spaniards. It contained many very sumptuous edifices, the most superb of which was a seminary, where between 5,000 and 6,000 children were educated at the charge of the royal treasury. The castle of the Atalaya was a remarkable structure, four stories high, and capable of furnishing quarters for a very strong garrison. The castle of Resguardo was five stories high, extending 180 paces in front, and 230 in depth. The grand alcazar, or palace of the kings of Quiché, surpassed every other edifice, and in the opinion of Torquemada, it could compete in opulence with that of Montezuma in Mexico, or that of the Incas in Cuzco. The front extended 376 geometrical paces from east to west, and it was 728 paces in depth. It was constructed of hewn stones of various colours There were six principal divisions. The first contained lodgings for a numerous troop of lancers, archers, and other troops, constituting the royal body-guard. The second was assigned to the princes and relations of the king; the third to the monarch himself, containing distinct suites of apartments for the mornings, evenings, and nights In one of the saloons stood the throne, under four canopies of feathers; and in this portion of the palace were the treasury, tribunals of the judges, armory, aviaries, and menageries. The fourth and fifth divisions were occupied by the queen and royal concubines, with gardens, baths, and places for breeding geese, which were kept to supply feathers for ornaments. The sixth and last division was the residence of the daughters and other females of the blood royal

Such is the account as derived by the Spanish historians from manuscripts composed by some of the caciques who first acquired the art of writing; and it is related that from Tanub, who conducted them from the old to the new continent, down to Tecum Umam, was a line of twenty monarchs.

Alvarado, on the invitation of the king, entered this city with his army; but, observing the strength of the place; that it was well walled, and surrounded by a deep ravine, having but two approaches to it, the one by an ascent of twenty-five steps, and the other by a causeway, and both extremely narrow; that the streets were but of trifling breadth, and the houses very lofty; that there were neither women nor children to be seen, and that the Indians seemed agitated, the soldiers began to suspect some deceit. Their apprehensions were soon confirmed by Indian allies of Quezaltenango, who discovered that the people intended that night to fire their capital, and while the flames were rising, to burst upon the Spaniards with large bodies of men concealed in the neighbourhood, and put every one to death. These tidings were found to be in accordance with the movements of the Utatlans; and on examining the houses, the Spaniards discovered that there were no preparations of provisions to regale them, as had been promised, but everywhere was a quantity of light, dry fuel, and other combustibles. Alvarado called his officers together, and laid before them their perilous situation, and the immediate necessity of withdrawing from the place; and pretending to the king and his caciques that their horses were better in the open fields, the troops were collected, and without any appearance of alarm, marched in good order to the plain. The king, with pretended courtesy, accompanied them, and Alvarado, taking advantage of the opportunity, made him prisoner, and after trial and proof of his treachery, hung him on the spot. But neither the death of Tecum nor the ignominious execution of his son could quell the fierce spirit of the Quichés. A new ebullition of animosity and rage broke forth. A general attack was made upon the Spaniards; but Spanish bravery and discipline increased with danger; and after a dreadful havoc by the artillery and horses, the Indians abandoned a field covered with their dead, and Utatlan, the capital, with the whole kingdom of Quiché, fell into the hands of Alvarado and the Spaniards.

As we stood on the ruined fortress of Resguardo, the great plain, consecrated by the last struggle of a brave people, lay before us grand and beautiful, its bloodstains all washed out, and smiling with fertility, but perfectly desolate. Our guide leaning on his sword in the area beneath was the only person in sight. But very soon Bobon introduced a stranger, who came stumbling along under a red silk umbrella, talking to Bobon, and looking up at us. We recognised him as the cura, and descended to meet him. He laughed to see us grope our way down; by degrees his laugh became infectious, and when we met we all laughed together. All at once he stopped, looked very solemn, pulled off his neckcloth, and wiped the perspiration from his face, took out a paper of cigars, laughed, thrust them back, pulled out another, as he said, of Habaneras, and asked what was the news from Spain.

Our friend's dress was as unclerical as his manner, viz. a broad-brimmed black glazed hat, an old black coat reaching to his heels, glossy from long use, and pantaloons to match; a striped roundabout, a waistcoat, flannel shirt, and under it a cotton one, perhaps washed when he shaved last, some weeks before. He laughed at our coming to see the ruins, and said that he laughed prodigiously himself when he first saw them. He was from Old Spain; had seen the battle of Trafalgar, looking on from the heights on shore, and laughed whenever he thought of it; the French fleet was blown sky high, and the Spanish went with it; Lord Nelson was killed—all for glory—he could not help laughing. He had left Spain to get rid of wars and revolutions: here we all laughed; sailed with twenty Dominican friars; was fired upon, and chased into Jamaica by a French cruiser: here we laughed again; got an English convoy to Omoa, where he arrived at the breaking out of a revolution; had been all his life in the midst of revolutions, and it was now better than ever. Here we all laughed incontinently. His own laugh was so rich and catching that it was perfectly irresistible In fact, we were not disposed to resist, and in half an hour we were as intimate as if acquainted for years. The world was our butt, and we laughed at it outrageously. Except the Church, there were few things which the cura did not laugh at; but politics was his favourite subject. He was in favour of Morazan, or Carrera, or el Demonio: "vamos adelante," "go ahead," was his motto; he laugh at them all. If we had parted with him then, we should always have remembered him as the laughing padre; but, on farther acquaintance, we found in him such a vein of strong sense and knowledge, and, retired as he lived, he was so intimately acquainted with the country and all the public men, as a mere looker on his views were so correct and his satire so keen, yet without malice, that we improved his title by calling him the laughing philosopher.

Having finished our observations at this place, stopping to laugh as some new greatness or folly of the world, past, present, or to come, occurred to us, we descended by a narrow path, crossed a ravine, and entered upon the table-land, on which stood the palace and principal part of the city. Mr. Catherwood and I began examining and measuring the ruins, and the padre followed us, talking and laughing all the time; and when we were on some high place, out of his reach, he seated Bobon at the foot, discoursing to him of Alvarado, and Montezuma, and the daughter of the king of Tecpan Guatimala, and books and manuscripts in the convent; to all which Bobon listened without comprehending a word or moving a muscle, looking him directly in the face, and answering his long low laugh with a respectful "Si, señor."

The plan in the division of the last engraving marked A, represents the topography of the ground in the heart of the city which was occupied by the palace and other buildings of the royal house of Quiché. It is surrounded by an immense barranca or ravine, and the only entrance is through that part of the ravine by which we reached it, and which is defended by the fortress before referred to, marked B in the plate. The cura pointed out to us one part of the ravine which, he said, according to old manuscripts formerly existing in the convent, but now carried away, was artificial, and upon which 40,000 men had been employed at one time.

The whole area was once occupied by the palace, seminary, and other buildings of the royal house of Quiché, which now lie for the most part in confused and shapeless masses of ruins. The palace, as the cura told us, with its courts and corridors, once covering the whole diameter, is completely destroyed, and the materials have been carried away to build the present village. In part, however, the floor remains entire, with fragments of the partition walls, so that the plan of the apartments can be distinctly made out. This floor is of a hard cement, which, though year after year washed by the floods of the rainy season, is hard and durable as stone. The inner walls were covered with plaster of a finer description, and in corners where there had been less exposure were the remains of colours; no doubt the whole interior had been ornamented with paintings. It gave a strange sensation to walk the floor of that roofless palace, and think of that king who left it at the head of 70,000 men to repel the invaders of his empire. Corn was now growing among the ruins. The ground was used by an Indian family which claimed to be descended from the royal house. In one place was a desolate hut, occupied by them at the time of planting and gathering the corn. Adjoining the palace was a large plaza or courtyard, also covered with hard cement, in the centre of which were the relics of a fountain.

The most important part remaining of these ruins is that which appears in the engraving, No. 39, and which is called El Sacrificatorio, or the place of sacrifice. It is a quadrangular stone structure, 66 feet on each side at the base, and rising in a pyramidal form to the height, in its present condition, of 33 feet. On three sides there is a range of steps in the middle, each step 17 inches high, and but 8 inches on the upper surface, which makes the range so steep that in descending some

39. VIEW OF THE PLACE OF SACRIFICE IN RUINS AT SANTA CRUZ DEL QUICHÉ.

caution is necessary. At the corners are four buttresses of cut stone, diminishing in size from the line of the square, and apparently intended to support the structure. On the side facing the west there are no steps, but the surface is smooth and covered with stucco, grey from long exposure. By breaking a little at the corners we saw that there were different layers of stucco, doubtless put on at different times, and all had been ornamented with painted figures. In one place we made out part of the body of a leopard, well drawn and coloured.

The top of the Sacrificatorio is broken and ruined, but there is no doubt that it once supported an altar for those sacrifices of human victims which struck even the Spaniards with horror. It was barely large enough for the altar and officiating priests, and the idol to whom the sacrifice was offered. The whole was in full view of the people at the foot.

The barbarous ministers carried up the victim entirely naked, pointed out the idol to which the sacrifice was made, that the people might pay their adorations, and then extended him upon the altar. This had a convex surface, and the body of the victim lay arched, with the trunk elevated and the head and feet depressed. Four priests held the legs and arms, and another kept his head firm with a wooden instrument made in the form of a coiled serpent, so that he was prevented from making the least movement. The head priest then approached, and with a knife made of flint cut an aperture in the breast, and tore out the heart, which, yet palpitating, he offered to the sun, and then threw it at the feet of the idol. If the idol was gigantic and hollow, it was usual to introduce the heart of the victim into its mouth with a golden spoon. If the victim was a prisoner of war, as soon as he was sacrificed they cut off the head to preserve the skull, and threw the body down the steps, when it was taken up by the officer or soldier to whom the prisoner had belonged, and carried to his house to be dressed and served up as an entertainment for his friends. If he was not a prisoner of war, but a slave purchased for the sacrifice, the proprietor carried off the body for the same purpose. In recurring to the barbarous scenes of which the spot had been the theatre, it seemed a righteous award that the bloody altar was hurled down, and the race of its ministers destroyed.

It was fortunate for us, in the excited state of the country, that it was not necessary to devote much time to an examination of these ruins. In 1834 a thorough exploration had been made under a commission from the government of Guatimala. Don Miguel Rivera y Maestre, a gentleman distinguished for his scientific and antiquarian

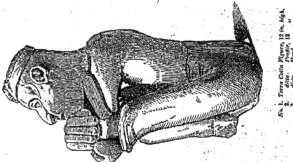
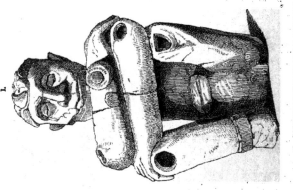
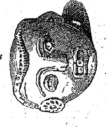

40. FIGURES FOUND AT SANTA CRUZ DEL QUICHE.

No. 1. Terra Cotta Figure, 12 in. high.
2. ditto Profile, 12 „
3. ditto Head „
4. ditto Mask.

F. Catherwood.

tastes, was the commissioner, and kindly furnished me with a copy of his manuscript report to the government, written out by himself. This report is full and elaborate, and I have no doubt is the result of a thorough examination, but it does not refer to any objects of interest except those I have mentioned. He procured, however, the image, of which a front and side view appear in the engraving No. 41, and which, without my venturing to express a wish for it, he kindly gave to me. It is made of baked clay, very hard, and the surface as smooth as if coated with enamel. It is twelve inches high, and the interior is hollow, including the arms and legs. In his report to the government, Don Miguel calls it Cabuahuil, or one of the deities of the ancient inhabitants of Quiché. I do not know upon what authority he has given it this name, but to me it does not seem improbable that his supposition is true, and that to this earthen vessel human victims have been offered in sacrifice.

The heads in the engraving were given me by the cura. They are of terra cotta; the lower one is hollow and the upper is solid, with a polished surface. They are hard as stone, and in workmanship will compare with images in the same material by artists of the present day.

In our investigation of antiquities we considered this place important from the fact that its history is known and its date fixed. It was in its greatest splendour when Alvarado conquered it. It proves the character of the buildings which the Indians of that day constructed, and in its ruins confirms the glowing accounts given by Cortez and his companions of the splendour displayed in the edifices of Mexico. The point to which we directed our attention was to discover some resemblance to the ruins of Copan and Quirigua; but we did not find statues, or carved figures, or hieroglyphics, nor could we learn that any had ever been found there. If there had been such evidences we should have considered these remains the works of the same race of people, but in the absence of such evidences we believed that Copan and Quirigua were cities of another race and of a much older date.

The padre told us that thirty years before, when he first saw it, the palace was entire to the garden. He was then fresh from the palaces of Spain, and it seemed as if he was again among them. Shortly after his arrival a small gold image was found and sent to Seravia, the president of Guatimala, who ordered a commission from the capital to search for hidden treasure. In this search the palace was destroyed; the Indians, roused by the destruction of their ancient capital, rose, and threatened to kill the workmen unless they left the country; and but for this, the cura said, every stone would have been razed to the ground. The Indians of Quiché have at all times a bad name; at Guatimala it was always spoken of as an unsafe place to visit; and the padre told us that they looked with distrust upon any stranger coming to the ruins. At that moment they were in a state of universal excitement; and coming close to us, he said that in the village they stood at swords' points with the Mestitzoes, ready to cut their throats, and with all his exertions he could barely keep down a general rising and massacre. Even this information he gave us with a laugh. We asked him if he had no fears for himself. He said no; that he was beloved by the Indians; he had passed the great part of his life among them; and as yet the padres were safe: the Indians considered them almost as saints. Here he laughed. Carrera was on their side; but if he turned against them it would be time to fly. This was communicated and received with peals of laughter, and the more serious the subject, the louder was our cachinnation. And all the time the padre made continual reference to books and manuscripts, showing antiquarian studies and profound knowledge.

Under one of the buildings was an opening which the Indians called a cave, and by which they said one could reach Mexico in an hour. I crawled under, and found a pointed-arch roof formed by stones lapping over each other, but was prevented exploring it by want of light, and the padre's crying to me that it was the season of earthquakes; and he laughed more than usual at the hurry with which I came out; but all at once he stopped, and grasping his pantaloons, hopped about, crying, "A snake, a snake!" The guide and Bobon hurried to his relief; and by a simple process, but with great respect, one at work on each side, were in a fair way of securing the intruder; but the padre could not stand still, and with his agitation and restlessness tore loose from their hold, and brought to light a large grasshopper. While Bobon and the guide, without a smile, restored him, and put each button in its place, we finished with a laugh, outrageous to the memory of the departed inhabitants, and to all sentiment connected with the ruins of a great city.

As we returned to the village the padre pointed out on the plain the direction of four roads, which led, and which, according to him, are still open to Mexico, Tecpan Guatimala, Los Altos, and Vera Paz.

CHAPTER XXVII.

INTERIOR OF A CONVENT—ROYAL BIRD OF QUICHÉ—INDIAN LANGUAGES—THE LORD'S PRAYER IN THE QUICHÉ LANGUAGE—NUMERALS IN THE SAME—CHURCH OF QUICHÉ—INDIAN SUPERSTITIONS—ANOTHER LOST CITY—TIERRA DE GUERRA—THE ABORIGINES—THEIR CONVERSION TO CHRISTIANITY—THEY WERE NEVER CONQUERED—A LIVING CITY—INDIAN TRADITION RESPECTING THIS CITY—PROBABLY HAS NEVER BEEN VISITED BY THE WHITES—PRESENTS A NOBLE FIELD FOR FUTURE ENTERPRISE—DEPARTURE—SAN PEDRO—VIRTUE OF A PASSPORT—A DIFFICULT ASCENT—MOUNTAIN SCENERY—TOTONICAPAN—AN EXCELLENT DINNER—A COUNTRY OF ALOES—"RIVER OF BLOOD"—ARRIVAL AT QUEZALTENANGO.

It was late in the afternoon when we returned to the convent. The good padre regretted not being at home when we arrived, and said that he always locked his room to prevent the women throwing things into confusion. When we entered it was in what he called order, but this order was of a class that beggars description. The room contained a table, chairs, and two settees, but there was not a vacant place even on the table to sit down or to lay a hat upon. Every spot was encumbered with articles, of which four bottles, a cruet of mustard and another of oil, bones, cups, plates, sauce-boat, a large lump of sugar, a paper of salt, minerals and large stones, shells, pieces of pottery, skulls, bones, cheese, books, and manuscripts formed part. On a shelf over his bed were two stuffed *quezales*, the royal bird of Quiché, the most beautiful that flies, so proud of its tail that it builds its nest with two openings, to pass in and out without turning, and whose plumes were not permitted to be used except by the royal family.

Amid this confusion a corner was cleared on the table for dinner. The conversation continued in the same unbroken stream of knowledge, research, sagacity, and satire on his part. Political matters were spoken of in whispers when any servants were in the rooms. A laugh was the comment upon everything, and in the evening we were deep in the mysteries of Indian history.

Besides the Mexican or Aztec language, spoken by the Pipil Indians along the coast of the Pacific, there are twenty-four dialects peculiar to Guatimala. Though sometimes bearing such a strong resemblance in some of their idioms, that the Indians of one tribe can understand each other, in general the padres, after years of residence, can only speak the language of the tribe among which they live. This diversity of languages had seemed to me an insuperable impediment in the way of any thorough investigation and study of Indian history and traditions; but the cura, profound in everything that related to the Indians, told us that the Quiché was the parent tongue, and that, by one familiar with it, the others are easily acquired. If this be true, a new and most interesting field of research is opened. During my whole journey, even at Guatimala, I had not been able to procure any grammar of an Indian language, nor any manuscripts. I made several vocabularies, which I have not thought it worth while to publish; but the padre had a book prepared by some of the early fathers for the church service, which he promised to have copied for me and sent to a friend at Guatimala, and from which I copied the Lord's prayer in the Quiché language. It is as follows:—

"Cacahan chicah lae coni Vtzah. Vcahaxtizaxie mayih Bila Chipa ta pa Cani ahauremla Chibantah. Ahuamla Uaxale Chiyala Chiqueeh hauta Vleus quehexi Caban Chicah. Uacamic Chiyala. Chiqueeh hauta. Eihil Caua. Zachala Camac quehexi Cacazachbep qui. Mac Xemocum Chiqueeh: moho Estachcula maxa Copahic Chupamtah Chibal mac xanare Cohcolta la ha Vonohel itgel quehe Chucoe. Amen."

I will add the following numerals, as taken from the same book:—

Hun, *one.*
Quieb, *two.*
Dxib, *three.*
Quicheb, *four.*
Hoob, *five.*
Uacacguil, *six.*
Veuib, *seven.*
Uahxalquib, *eight.*
Beleheb, *nine.*
Lahuh, *ten,*
Hulahuh, *eleven.*
Cablahuh, *twelve.*
Dxlahuh, *thirteen.*
Cahlahuh, *fourteen.*
Hoolahuh, *fifteen.*
Uaelahuh, *sixteen.*
Vclahuh, *seventeen.*
Uapxaelahuh, *eighteen.*
Belchalahuh, *nineteen.*
Huuinac, *twenty.*
Huuinachun, *twenty-one.*
Huuinachlahuh, *thirty.*
Cauinac, *forty.*
Lahuh Raxcal, *fifty.*
Oxcal, *sixty.*
Lahuh Vhumuch, *seventy.*
Humuch, *eighty.*
Lahuh Rocal, *ninety.*
Ocal, *a hundred.*
Otuc Rox Ocob, *a thousand.*

Whether there is any analogy between this language and that of any of the North American tribes, I am not able to say.

For a man who has not reached that period when a few years tell upon his teeth and hair, I know of no place where (if the country becomes quiet) they might be passed with greater interest than at Santa Cruz del Quiché, in studying, by means of their language, the character and traditionary history of the Indians; for here they still exist, in many respects, an unchanged people, cherishing the usages and customs of their ancestors; and though the grandeur and magnificence of the churches, the pomp and show of religious ceremonies, affect their rude imaginations, the padre told us that in their hearts they were full of superstitions, and still idolaters; had their idols in the mountains and ravines, and in silence and secrecy practised the rites received from their fathers. He was compelled to wink at them; and there was one proof which he saw every day. The church of Quiché stands east and west. On entering it for vespers the Indians always bowed to the west, in reverence to the setting sun. He told us, too, what requires confirmation, and what we were very curious to judge of for ourselves, that in a cave near a neighbouring village were skulls much larger than the natural size, and regarded with superstitious reverence by the Indians. He had seen them, and vouched for their gigantic dimensions. Once he placed a piece of money in the mouth of the cave, and a year afterwards found the money still lying in the same place, while, he said, if it had been left on his table, it would have disappeared with the first Indian who entered.

The padre's whole manner was now changed; his keen satire and his laugh were gone. There was interest enough about the Indians to occupy the mind and excite the imagination of one who laughed at everything else in the world; and his enthusiasm, like his laugh, was infectious. Notwithstanding our haste to reach Palenque, we felt a strong desire to track them in the solitude of their mountains and deep ravines, and watch them in the observance of their idolatrous rites; but the padre did not give us any encouragement. In fact, he opposed our remaining another day, even to visit the cave of skulls. He made no apology for hurrying us away. He lived in unbroken solitude, in a monotonous routine of occupations, and the visit of a stranger was to him an event most welcome; but there was danger in our remaining. The Indians were in an inflammable state; they were already inquiring what we came there for, and he could not answer for our safety. In a few months, perhaps, the excitement might pass away, and then we could return. He loved the subjects we took interest in, and would join us in all our expeditions, and aid us with all his influence.

And the padre's knowledge was not confined to his own immediate neighbourhood. His first curacy was at Coban, in the province of Vera Paz; and he told us that four leagues from that place was another ancient city, as large as Santa Cruz del Quiché, deserted and desolate, and almost as perfect as when abandoned by its inhabitants. He had wandered through its silent streets and over its gigantic buildings, and its palace was as entire as that of Quiché when he first saw it. This is within 200 miles of Guatimala, and in a district of country not disturbed by war; yet, with all our inquiries, we had heard nothing of it. And now, the information really grieved us. Going to the place would add 800 miles to our journey. Our plans were fixed, our time already limited; and in that wild country and its unsettled state, we had superstitious apprehensions that it was ominous to return. My impression, however, of the existence of such a city is most strong. I do most earnestly hope that some future traveller will visit it. He will not hear of it even at Guatimala, and perhaps will be told that it does not exist. Nevertheless, let him seek for it; and if he do find it, experience sensations which seldom fall to the lot of man.

But the padre told us more; something that increased our excitement to the highest pitch. On the other side of the great traversing range of Cordilleras lies the district of Vera Paz, once called Tierra de Guerra, or land of war, from the warlike character of its aboriginal inhabitants. Three times the Spaniards were driven back in their attempts to conquer it. Las Casas, vicar of the convent of the Dominican order in the city of Guatimala, mourning over the bloodshed caused by what was called converting the Indians to Christianity, wrote a treatise to prove that Divine Providence had instituted the preaching of the Gospel as the only means of conversion to the Christian faith; that war could not with justice be made upon those who had never committed any aggressions against Christians; and that to harass and destroy the Indians was to prevent the accomplishing of this desired object. This doctrine he preached from the pulpit, and enforced in private assemblies. He was laughed at, ridiculed, and sneeringly advised to put his theory in practice. Undisturbed by this mockery, he accepted the proposal, choosing as the field of his operations the unconquerable district called Tierra de Guerra, and made an arrangement that no Spaniards should be permitted to reside in that country for five years. This agreed upon, the Dominicans composed some hymns in the Quiché language, describing the creation of the world, the fall of Adam, the redemption of mankind, and the principal mysteries of the life, passion, and death of our Saviour. These were learned by some Indians who traded with the Quichés, and a principal cacique of the country, afterward called Don Juan, having heard them sung, asked those who had repeated them to explain in detail the meaning of things so new to him. The Indians excused themselves, saying that they could only be explained by the fathers who had taught them. The cacique sent one of his brothers with many presents, to entreat that they would come and make him acquainted with what was contained in the songs of the Indian merchants. A single Dominican friar returned with the ambassador, and the cacique, having been made to comprehend the mysteries of the new faith, burned his idols and preached Christianity to his own subjects. Las Casas and another associate followed, and, like the apostles of old, without scrip or staff, effected what Spanish arms could not, bringing a portion of the Land of War to the Christian faith. The rest of the Tierra de Guerra never was conquered; and at this day the northeastern section, bounded by the range of the Cordilleras and the state of Chiapas, is occupied by Candones or unbaptized Indians, who live as their fathers did, acknowledging no submission to the Spaniards, and the government of Central America does not pretend to exercise any control over them. But the thing that roused us was the assertion by the padre that, four days on the road to Mexico, on the other side of the great sierra, was a living city, large and populous, occupied by Indians, precisely in the same state as before the discovery of America. He had heard of it many years before at the village of Chajul, and was told by the villagers that from the topmost ridge of the sierra this city was distinctly visible. He was then young, and with much labour climbed to the naked summit of the sierra, from which, at a height of 10,000 or 12,000 feet, he looked over an immense plain extending toward Yucatan and the Gulf of Mexico, and saw at a great distance a large city spread over a great space, and with turrets white and glittering in the sun. The traditionary account of the Indians of Chajul is, that no white man has every reached this city; that the inhabitants speak the Maya language, are aware that a race of strangers has conquered the whole country around, and murder any white man who attempts to enter their territory. They have no coin or other circulating medium; no horses, cattle, mules, or other domestic animals except fowls, and the cocks they keep under ground to prevent their crowing being heard.

There was a wild novelty—something that touched the imagination—in every step of our journey in that country; the old padre, in the deep stillness of the dimly-lighted convent, with his long black coat like a robe, and his flashing eye, called up an image of the bold and resolute priests who accompanied the armies of the conquerors; and as he drew a map on the table, and pointed out the sierra to the top of which he had climbed, and the position of the mysterious city, the interest awakened in us was the most thrilling I ever experienced. One look at that city was worth ten years of an every-day life. If he be right, a place is left where Indians and an Indian city exist as Cortez and Alvarado found them; there are living men who can solve the mystery that hangs over the ruined cities of America; perhaps who can go to Copan and read the inscriptions on its monuments. No subject more exciting and attractive presents itself to my mind, and the deep impression of that night will never be effaced.

Can it be true? Being now in my sober senses, I do verily believe there is much ground to suppose that what the padre told us is authentic. That the region referred to does not acknowledge the government of Guatimala, has never been explored, and that no white man ever pretends to enter it, I am satisfied. From other sources we heard that from that sierra a large *ruined* city was visible, and we were told of another person who had climbed to the top of the sierra, but, on account of the dense cloud resting upon it, had been unable to see anything. At all events, the belief at the village of Chajul is general, and a curiosity is roused that burns to be satisfied. We had a craving desire to reach the mysterious city. No man, even if willing to peril his life, could undertake the enterprise with any hope of success, without hovering for one or two years on the borders of the country, studying the language and character of the adjoining Indians, and making acquaintance with some of the natives. Five hundred men could probably march directly to the city, and the invasion would be more justifiable than any ever made by the Spaniards; but the government is too much occupied with its own wars, and the knowledge could not be procured except at the price of blood. Two young men of good constitution, and who could afford to spare five years, might succeed. If the object of search prove a phantom, in the wild scenes of a new and unexplored country there are other objects of interest; but if real, besides the glorious excitement of such a novelty, they will have something to look back upon through life. As to dangers, these are always magnified, and, in general, peril is discovered soon enough for escape. But in all probability, if any discovery is ever made it will be by the padres. As for ourselves, to attempt it alone, ignorant of the language, and with mozos who were a constant annoyance to us, was out of the question. The most we thought of was a climb to the top of the sierra, thence to look down upon the mysterious city; but we had difficulties enough in the road before us; it would add ten days to a journey already most appalling in prospective; for days the sierra might be covered with clouds; in attempting too much we might lose all; Palenque was our great point, and we determined not to be diverted from the course we had marked out.

The next morning we had one painful moment with the cura, and that was the moment of parting. He was then calm and kind, his irresistible laugh and his enthusiasm all gone. We had one village to pass at which he told us the Indians were bad, for which reason he gave us a letter to the juez; and in the kindness of his heart insisted on my accepting one of his beautiful quezales.

As this was Holy Week, we had great difficulty in procuring a guide. None of the Indians wished to leave the village, and the alcalde told an alguazil to take a man out of prison. After a parley with the inmates through the grating, one was selected, but kept in confinement till the moment of starting, when the alguazil opened the door and let him out, our roll of luggage was put on his back, and he set off. The battered soldier accompanied us a short distance, and Bobon went before, carrying on a stick the royal bird of Quiché. Crossing the plain and the ravine on which the city stood, we ascended a mountain in the rear, commanding a magnificent view of the plain of Quiché, and descending on the other side, at the distance of two leagues reached the village of San Pedro. A thatched church, with a cross before it, stood near the road, and the huts of the village were a little in the rear. The padre had told us that the Indians of this place were "muy malos," very bad; and as our guide, when he returned, had to be locked up in prison, to avoid the necessity of stopping we tried to induce him to continue; but he dropped his load at the foot of the cross, and ran back in such haste that he left behind his ragged chamar. The juez was a Mestitzo, who sent for the alcalde, and presently that worthy trotted down with six alguazils, marching in single file, all with wands in their hands, and dressed in handsome cloth cloaks, the holiday costume for the Holy Week. We told them that we wanted a guide, and the whole six set off to look for one. In about ten minutes they returned single file, exactly on the same trot as before, and said they could not find any; the whole week was holiday, and no one wanted to leave home. I showed Carrera's passport, and told the juez he must go himself, or send one of his alguazils, and they set off again in pursuit. After waiting a little while, I walked to the top of a hill near by, and saw them all seated below, apparently waiting for us to go. As soon as they saw me they ran back in a body to repeat that they could not find a guide. I offered them double price, but they were immovable; and feeling rather uncertain what turn things might take, I talked largely of Carrera's vengeance, not contenting myself with turning them out of office, but taking off their heads at once. After a few moments' consultation they all rose quietly; one doffed his dignity and dress, the rest rolled up the cargo, and throwing it on his bare back, placed the band across his forehead, and set him off on a run. We followed, the secretary begging me to write to Carrera that it was not through his fault we were kept waiting, and that he would have been my guide himself if I had not found another.

At a short distance another alguazil, by a cross cut, intercepted and relieved the first, and they ran so fast that on the rough road we could not keep up with them.

The road was indeed rough and wild beyond all description; and very soon we reached another immense ravine, descended it, and commenced an ascent on the opposite side, which occupied three hours. Through openings in the woods we looked down precipices 1,000 or 2,000 feet deep, while the mountain side was still higher above us. The whole mountain was clothed with luxuriant vegetation, and though wanting the rocky, savage grandeur of Alpine scenery, at every turn the view was sublime. As we climbed up we met a few Indians who could speak no language but their own, and reaching the top, saw a wretched spectacle of the beings made in God's image. A drunken Indian was lying on the ground, his face cut with a machete, and weltering in his blood; and a drunken woman was crying over him. Our Indians stopped and spoke to them, but we could not understand what they said. At about three o'clock we emerged from the woods, and very soon saw Totonicapan, at a great distance and far below us, on a magnificent plain, with a high table-land behind it, a range of mountains springing from the table, and rising above them the volcano of Quezaltenango. The town was spread over a large space, and the flat roofs of the houses seemed one huge covering, broken only by the steeple of the church. We descended the mountain to the banks of a beautiful stream, along which, Indian women were washing; and following it, entered the town, and rode up to the house of the corregidor, Don José Azmitia. Our luggage had arrived safely, and in a few minutes our men presented themselves to receive us.

Much might be said of Totonicapan as the head of a department, and surrounded by mountains visible on all sides from the plaza; but I stop only to record an event. All along, with the letters to corregidors, the passport of Carrera, and the letter of the archbishop, our road had been a sort of triumphal march; but at this place we dined, *i. e.* we had a dinner. The reader may remember that in Costa Rica I promised to offend but once more by referring to such a circumstance. That time has come, and I should consider myself an ingrate if I omitted to mention it. We were kept waiting perhaps two hours, and we had not eaten anything in more than twelve. We had clambered over terrible mountains; and at six o'clock, on invitation, with hands and faces washed, and in dress-coats, sat down with the corregidor. Courses came regularly and in right succession. Servants were well trained, and our host did the honours as if he was used to the same thing every day. But it was not so with us. Like Rittmaster Dugald

Dalgetty, we ate very fast and very long, on his principle deeming it the duty of every commander of a fortress, on all occasions which offer, to secure as much munition and viveres as their magazines can possibly hold.

We were again on the line of Carrera's operations; the place was alive with apprehensions; white men were trembling for their lives; and I advised our host to leave the country and come to the United States.

The next morning we breakfasted with him, and at eleven o'clock, while a procession was forming in the plaza, we started for Quezaltenango, descended a ravine commanding at every point a beautiful view, ascended a mountain, from which we looked back upon the plain and town of Totonicapan, and on the top entered a magnificent plain, cultivated with corn-fields and dotted with numerous flocks of sheep, the first we had seen in the country; on both sides of the road were hedges of gigantic aloes.* In one place we counted upward of 200 in full bloom. In the middle of the plain, at the distance of two and a half leagues, we crossed on a rude bridge of logs a broad river, memorable for the killed and wounded thrown into it in Alvarado's battle with the Quiché Indians, and called the "River of Blood." Two leagues beyond we came in sight of Quezaltenango, standing at the foot of a great range of mountains, surmounted by a rent volcano constantly emitting smoke, and before it a mountain ridge of lava, which, if it had taken its course toward the city, would have buried it like Herculaneum and Pompeii.

* Agave Americana.

CHAPTER XXVIII.

QUEZALTENANGO—ACCOUNT OF IT—CONVERSION OF THE INHABITANTS TO CHRISTIANITY—APPEARANCE OF THE CITY—THE CONVENT—INSURRECTION—CARRERA'S MARCH UPON QUEZALTENANGO—HIS TREATMENT OF THE INHABITANTS—PREPARATIONS FOR HOLY WEEK—THE CHURCH—A PROCESSION—GOOD FRIDAY—CELEBRATION OF THE RESURRECTION—OPENING CEREMONY—THE CRUCIFIXION—A SERMON—DESCENT FROM THE CROSS—GRAND PROCESSION—CHURCH OF CALVARIO—THE CASE OF THE CURA—WARM SPRINGS OF ALMOLONGA.

WE were again on classic soil. The reader perhaps requires to be reminded that the city stands on the site of the ancient Xelahuh, next to Utatlan the largest city in Quiché, the word Xelahuh meaning "under the government of ten;" that is, it was governed by ten principal captains, each captain presiding over 8,000 dwellings, in all 80,000, and containing according to Fuentes more than 300,000 inhabitants; that on the defeat of Tecum Umam by Alvarado, the inhabitants abandoned the city, and fled to their ancient fortresses, Excansel, the volcano, and Cekxak, another mountain adjoining; that the Spaniards entered the deserted city, and according to a manuscript found in the village of San Andres Xecul, their videttes captured the four celebrated caciques, whose names, the reader doubtless remembers, were Calel Kalek, Ahpopgueham, Calelahan, and Calelaboy; the Spanish records say that they fell on their knees before Pedro Alvarado, while a priest explained to them the nature of the Christian faith, and they declared themselves ready to embrace it. Two of them were retained as hostages, and the others sent back to the fortresses, who returned with such multitudes of Indians ready to be baptized, that the priests, from sheer fatigue, could no longer lift their arms to perform the ceremony.

As we approached, seven towering churches showed that the religion so hastily adopted had not died away. In a few minutes we entered the city. The streets were handsomely paved, and the houses picturesque in architecture; the cabildo had two stories and a corridor. The Cathedral, with its façade richly decorated, was grand and imposing. The plaza was paved with stone, having a fine fountain in the centre, and commanding a magnificent view of the volcano and mountains around. It was the day before Good Friday; the streets and plaza were crowded with people in their best attire, the Indians wearing large black cloaks, with broad-brimmed felt sombreros, and the women a white frock, covering the head, except an oblong opening for the face; some wore a sort of turban of red cord plaited with the hair. The bells were hushed, and wooden clappers sounded in their stead. As we rode through, armed to the teeth, the crowd made way in silence. We passed the door of the church, and entered the great gate of the convent. The cura was absent at the moment, but a respectable-looking servant-woman received us in a manner that assured us of a welcome from her master. There was, however, an air of excitement and trepidation in the whole household, and it was not long before the good woman unburdened herself of matters fearfully impressed upon her mind.

After chocolate, we went to the corregidor, to whom we presented our letters from the government and Carrera's passport. He was one of Morazan's expulsados, a fine, military-looking man, but, as he told us, not a soldier by profession; he was in office by accident, and exceedingly anxious to lay down his command; indeed, his brief service had been no sinecure. He introduced us to Don Juan Lavanigno, an Italian from Genoa, banished on account of a revolution. How the signor found his way to this place I did not learn, but he had not found peace; and, if I am not deceived, he was as anxious to get out of it as ever he was to leave Genoa.

On our return to the convent we found the cura, who gave us personally the welcome assured to us by his housekeeper. With him was a respectable-looking Indian, bearing the imposing title of Gobernador, being the Indian alcalde; and it was rather singular that, in an hour after our arrival at Quezaltenango, we had become acquainted with the four surviving victims of Carrera's wrath, all of whom had narrowly escaped death at the time of the outrage, the rumour of which reached us at Guatimala. The place was still quivering under the shock of that event. We had heard many of the particulars on the road, and in Quezaltenango, except the parties concerned, no one could speak of anything else.

On the first entry of Morazan's soldiers into the plaza at Guatimala, in an unfortunate moment, a courier was sent to Quezaltenango to announce the capture of the city. The effect there was immediate and decided; the people rose upon the garrison left by Carrera, and required them to lay down their arms. The corregidor, not wishing to fire upon the townsmen, and finding it would be impossible with his small force to repress the insurrection, by the advice of the cura and Don Juan Lavanigno, to prevent bloodshed and a general massacre, induced the soldiers to lay down their arms and leave the town. The same night the municipality, without his knowledge, nominated Don Juan Lavanigno as commandant. He refused to serve; but the town was in a

41. PLAZA AT QUEZALTENANGO.
F. Catherwood.

violent state of excitement, and they urged him to accept for that night only, representing that if he did not, the fury of the populace would be directed against him. The same night they made a pronunciamento in favour of Morazan, and addressed a letter of congratulation to him, which they despatched immediately by an Indian courier. It will be remembered, however, that in the meantime Morazan had been driven out of Guatimala, and that Carrera had pursued him in his flight. At the Antigua the latter met a disarmed sergeant, who informed him of the proceedings at Quezaltenango, whereupon, abandoning his pursuit of Morazan, he marched directly thither. Early intelligence was received of his approach, and the corregidor, the cura, and Don Juan Lavanigno were sent as a deputation to receive him. They met him at Totonicapan. Carrera had heard on the road of their agency in inducing the soldiers to surrender their arms, and his first greeting was a furious declaration that their heads should lie at that place; laying aside his fanaticism and respect for the priests, he broke out against the cura in particular, who, he said, was a relative of Morazan. The cura said he was not a relative, but only a countryman (which in that region means a townsman), and could not help the place of his birth; but Carrera forthwith ordered four soldiers to remove him a few paces and shoot him on the spot. The gobernador, the old Indian referred to, threw himself on his knees and begged the cura's life; but Carrera drew his sword and struck the Indian twice across the shoulder, and the wounds were still unhealed when we saw him; but he desisted from his immediate purpose of shooting the cura, and delivered him over to the soldiers. Don Juan Lavanigno was saved by Carrera's secretary, who exhibited in El Tiempo, the government paper of Guatimala, an extract from a letter written by Don Juan to a friend in Guatimala, praising Carrera's deportment on his previous entry into Quezaltenango, and the discipline and good behaviour of his troops.

Early the next morning, Carrera marched into Quezaltenango, with the cura and Don Juan as prisoners. The municipality waited upon him in the plaza; but, unhappily, the Indian entrusted with the letter to Morazan had loitered in the town, and at this unfortunate moment presented it to Carrera. Before his secretary had finished reading it, Carrera, in a transport of fury, drew his sword to kill them on the spot with his own hand, wounded Molina, the alcalde-mayor, and two other members of the municipality, but checked himself, and ordered the soldiers to seize them. He then rode to the corregidor, where he again broke out into fury, and drew his sword upon him. A woman in the room threw herself before the corregidor, and Carrera struck around her several times, but finally checked himself again, and ordered the corregidor to be shot unless he raised 5,000 dollars by contributions upon the town. Don Juan and the cura he had locked up in a room with the threat to shoot them at five o'clock that afternoon unless they paid him 1,000 dollars each, and the former 200, and the latter 100 to his secretary. Don Juan was the principal merchant in the town, but even for him it was difficult to raise that sum. The poor cura told Carrera that he was not worth a cent in the world except his furniture and books. No one was allowed to visit him except the old housekeeper who first told us the story. Many of his friends had fled or hidden themselves away, and the old housekeeper ran from place to place with notes written by him, begging five dollars, ten dollars, anything she could get. One old lady sent him 100 dollars. At four o'clock, with all his efforts, he had raised but 700 dollars; but after undergoing all the mental agonies of death, when the cura had given up all hope, Don Juan, who had been two hours at liberty, made up the deficiency, and he was released.

The next morning Carrera sent to Don Juan to borrow his shaving apparatus, and Don Juan took them over himself. He had always been on good terms with Carrera, and the latter asked him if he had got over his fright, talking with him as familiarly as if nothing had happened. Shortly afterwards he was seen at the window playing on a guitar; and in an hour thereafter, eighteen members of the municipality, without the slightest form of trial, not even a drum-head court-martial, were taken out into the plaza and shot. They were all the very first men in Quezaltenango; and Molina, the alcalde-mayor, in family, position, and character was second to no other in the republic. His wife was clinging to Carrera's knees, and begging for his life when he passed with a file of soldiers She screamed "Robertito;" he looked at her, but did not speak. She shrieked and fainted, and before she recovered, her husband was dead. He was taken round the corner of the house, seated on a stone, and dispatched at once. The others were seated in the same place, one at a time; the stone and the wall of the house were still red with their blood. I was told that Carrera shed tears for the death of the first two, but for the rest he said he did not care. Heretofore, in all their revolutions, there had been some show of regard for the tribunals of justice, and the horror of the citizens at this lawless murder of their best men, cannot be conceived. The facts were notorious to everybody in Quezaltenango. We heard them, with but little variation of detail, from more than a dozen different persons.

Having consummated this enormity, Carrera returned to Guatimala, and the place had not yet recovered from its consternation. It was considered a blow at the whites, and all feared the horrors of a war of castes. I have avoided speaking harshly of Carrera when I could. I consider myself under personal obligations to him, and without his protection we never could have travelled through the country; but it is difficult to suppress the feelings of indignation excited against the government, which, conscious of the enormity of his conduct and of his utter contempt for them, never dared call him to account, and now cajoles and courts him, sustaining itself in power by his favour alone.

To return to the cura: he was about forty-five, tall, stout, and remarkably fine-looking; he had several curacies under his charge, and next to a canonigo's, his position was the highest in the country; but it had its labours. He was at that time engrossed with the ceremonies of the Holy Week, and in the evening we accompanied him to the church. At the door the *coup-d'œil* of the interior was most striking. The church was 250 feet in length, spacious and lofty, richly decorated with pictures and sculptured ornaments, blazing with lights, and crowded with Indians. On each side of the door was a grating, behind which stood an Indian to receive offerings. The floor was strewed with pine-leaves. On the left was the figure of a dead Christ on a bier, upon which every woman who entered threw a handful of roses, and near it stood an Indian to receive money. Opposite, behind an iron grating, was the figure of Christ bearing the cross, the eyes bandaged, and large silver chains attached to the arms and other parts of the body, and fastened to the iron bars. Here, too, stood an Indian to receive contributions. The altar was beautiful in design and decorations, consisting of two rows of Ionic columns, one above another, gilded, surmounted by a golden glory, and lighted by candles ten feet high. Under the pulpit was a piano. After a stroll around the church, the cura led us to seats under the pulpit. He asked us to give them some of the airs of our country, and then himself sat down at the piano. On Mr. C.'s suggesting that the tune was from one of Rossini's operas, he said that this was hardly proper for the occasion, and changed it.

At about ten o'clock the crowd in the church formed into a procession, and Mr. C. and I went out and took a position at the corner of a street to see it pass. It was headed by Indians, two abreast, each carrying in his hand a long lighted wax candle; and then, borne aloft on the shoulders of four men, came the figure of Judith, with a bloody sword in one hand, and in the other the gory head of Holofernes. Next, also on the shoulders of four men, the archangel Gabriel, dressed in red silk, with large wings puffed out. The next were men in grotesque armour, made of black and silver paper, to resemble Moors, with shield and spear like ancient cavaliers; and then four little girls, dressed in white silk and gauze, and looking like little spiritualities, with men on each side bearing lighted candles. Then came a large figure of Christ bearing the cross, supported by four Indians; on each side were young Indian lads, carrying long poles horizontally, to keep the crowd from pressing upon it, and followed by a procession of townsmen. In turning the corner of the street at which we stood, a dark Mestitzo, with a scowl of fanaticism on his face, said to Mr. Catherwood, "Take off your spectacles and follow the cross." Next followed a procession of women with children in their arms, half of them asleep, fancifully dressed with silver caps and headdresses, and finally a large statue of the Virgin, in a sitting posture, magnificently attired, with Indian lads on each side, as before, supporting poles with candles. The whole was accompanied with the music of drums and violins; and, as the long train of light passed down the street, we returned to the convent.

The night was very cold, and the next morning was like one in December at home. It was the morning of Good Friday; and throughout Guatimala, in every village, preparations were making to celebrate, with the most solemn ceremonies of the Church, the resurrection of the Saviour. In Quezaltenango, at that early hour, the plaza was thronged with Indians from the country around; but the whites, terrified and grieving at the murder of their best men, avoided, to a great extent, taking part in the celebration.

At nine o'clock the corregidor called for us, and we accompanied him to the opening ceremony. On one side of the nave of the church, near the grand altar, and opposite the pulpit, were high cushioned chairs for the corregidor and members of the municipality, and we had seats with them. The church was thronged with Indians, estimated at more than 3,000. Formerly, at this ceremony no women or children were admitted; but now the floor of the church was filled with Indian women on their knees, with red cords plaited in their hair, and perhaps one-third of them had children on their backs, their heads and arms only visible. Except ourselves and the padre, there were no white people in the church; and, with all eyes turned upon us, and a lively recollection of the fate of those who but a few days before had occupied our seats, we felt that the post of honour was a private station.

At the steps of the grand altar stood a large cross, apparently of solid silver, richly carved and ornamented, and over it a high arbour of pine and cypress branches. At the foot of the cross stood a figure of Mary Magdalen weeping, with her hair in a profusion of ringlets, her frock low in the neck, and altogether rather immodest. On the right was the figure of the Virgin gorgeously dressed, and in the nave of the church stood St. John the Baptist, placed there, as it seemed, only because they had the figure on hand. Very soon strains of wild

Indian music rose from the other end of the church, and a procession advanced, headed by Indians with broad-brimmed felt hats, dark cloaks, and lighted wax candles, preceding the body of the Saviour on a bier borne by the cura and attendant padres, and followed by Indians with long wax candles. The bier advanced to the foot of the cross; ladders were placed behind against it; the gobernador, with his long black cloak and broad-brimmed felt hat, mounted on the right, and leaned over, holding in his hands a silver hammer and a long silver spike; another Indian dignitary mounted on the other side, while the priests raised the figure up in front; the face was ghastly, blood trickled down the cheeks, the arms and legs were movable, and in the side was a gaping wound, with a stream of blood oozing from it. The back was affixed to the cross, the arms extended, spikes driven through the hands and feet, the ladders taken away, and thus the figure of Christ was nailed to the cross.

This over, we left the church, and passed two or three hours in visiting. The white population was small, but equal in character to any in the republic; and there was hardly a respectable family that was not afflicted by the outrage of Carrera. We knew nothing of the effect of this enormity until we entered domestic circles. The distress of women whose nearest connexions had been murdered or obliged to fly for their lives, and then wandering they knew not where, those only can realize who can appreciate woman's affection.

I was urged to visit the widow of Molina. Her husband was but thirty-five, and his death under any circumstances would have been lamented, even by political enemies. I felt a painful interest in one who had lived through such a scene, but at the door of her house I stopped. I felt that a visit from a stranger must be an intrusion upon her sorrows.

In the afternoon we were again seated with the municipality in the church, to behold the descent from the cross. The spacious building was thronged to suffocation, and the floor was covered by a dense mass of kneeling women, with turbaned headdresses, and crying children on their backs, their imaginations excited by gazing at the bleeding figure on the cross; but among them all I did not see a single interesting face. A priest ascended the pulpit, thin and ghastly pale, who, in a voice that rang through every part of the building, preached emphatically a passion sermon. Few of the Indians understood even the language, and at times the cries of children made his words inaudible; but the thrilling tones of his voice played upon every chord in their hearts; and mothers, regardless of their infants' cries, sat motionless, their countenances fixed in high and stern enthusiasm. It was the same church, and we could imagine them to be the same women who, in a frenzy and fury of fanaticism, had dragged the unhappy vice-president by the hair, and murdered him with their hands. Every moment the excitement grew stronger. The priest tore off his black cap, and leaning over the pulpit, stretched forward both his arms, and poured out a frantic apostrophe to the bleeding figure on the cross. A dreadful groan, almost curdling the blood, ran through the church. At this moment, at a signal from the cura, the Indians sprang upon the arbour of pine branches, tore it asunder, and with a noise like the crackling of a great conflagration, struggling and scuffling around the altar, broke into bits the consecrated branches to save as holy relics. Two Indians in broad-brimmed hats mounted the ladders on each side of the cross, and with embroidered cloth over their hands, and large silver pincers, drew out the spikes from the hands. The feelings of the women burst forth in tears, sobs, groans, and shrieks of lamentation, so loud and deep, that, coming upon us unexpectedly, our feelings were disturbed, and even with sane men the empire of reason tottered. Such screams of anguish I never heard called out by mortal suffering; and as the body, smeared with blood, was held aloft under the pulpit, while the priest leaned down and apostrophized it with frantic fervour, and the mass of women, wild with excitement, heaved to and fro like the surges of a troubled sea, the whole scene was so thrilling, so dreadfully mournful, that, without knowing why, tears started from our eyes. Four years before, at Jerusalem, on Mount Calvary itself, and in presence of the scoffing Mussulman, I had beheld the same representation of the descent from the cross; but the enthusiasm of Greek pilgrims in the Church of the Holy Sepulchre was nothing compared with this whirlwind of fanaticism and frenzy. By degrees the excitement died away; the cracking of the pine branches ceased, the whole arbour was broken up and distributed, and very soon commenced preparations for the grand procession.

We went out with the corregidor and officers of the municipality, and took our place in the balcony of the cabildo. The procession opened upon us in a manner so extraordinary, that, screening myself from observation below, I endeavoured to make a note of it on the spot. The leader was a man on horseback, called the centurion, wearing a helmet and cuirass of pasteboard covered with silver leaf, a black crape mask, black velvet shorts and white stockings, a red sash, and blue and red ribands on his arms, a silver-hilted sword, and a lance, with which, from time to time turning round, he beckoned and waved the procession on. Then came a led horse, having on its back an old Mexican saddle richly plated with silver. Then two men wearing long blue gowns, with round hoods covering their heads, and having only holes for the eyes, leading two mules abreast, covered with black cloth dresses enveloping their whole bodies to their feet, the long trains of which were supported by men attired like the other two. Then followed the large silver cross of the crucifixion, with a richly ornamented silver pedestal, and ornaments dangling from each arm of the cross that looked like lanterns, supported by four men in long black dresses. Next came a procession of Indians, two abreast, wearing long black cloaks, with black felt hats, the brims six or eight inches wide, all with lighted candles in their hands, and then four Indians in the same costume, but with crowns of thorns on their heads, dragging a long low carriage or bier filled with pine-leaves, and having a naked scull laid on the top at one end.

Next, and in striking contrast with this emblem of mortality, advanced an angel in the attitude of an opera-dancer, borne on the shoulders of six men, dressed in flounced purple satin, with lace at the bottom, gauze wings, and a cloud of gauze over her head, holding in her right hand a pair of silver pincers, and in her left a small wooden cross, and having a train of white muslin ten yards long, supported by a pretty little girl fancifully dressed. Then another procession of Indians with lighted candles; then a group of devils in horrible masquerade. Then another angel, still more like an opera-dancer, dressed in azure blue satin, with rich lace wings, and clouds, and fluttering ribands, holding in her right hand a ladder, and in her left a silver hammer; her train supported as before; and we could not help seeing that she wore black velvet smallclothes. Then another angel, dressed in yellow, holding in her right hand a small wooden cross, and in the other I could not tell what.

The next in order was a beautiful little girl about ten years old, armed cap-a-pie, with breastplate and helmet of silver, also called the centurion, who moved along in a slow and graceful dance, keeping time to the music, turning round, stopping, resting on her sword, and waving on a party worthy of such a chief, being twelve beautiful children fancifully dressed, intended to represent the twelve apostles; one of them carrying in his arms a silver cock, to signify that he was the representative of St. Peter. The next was the great object of veneration, the figure of the Christ crucified, on a bier, in a full length case of plate glass, strewed with roses inside and out, and protected by a mourning canopy of black cloth, supported by men in long black gowns, with hoods covering all but the eyes. This was followed by the cura and priests in their richest robes and bareheaded, the muffled drum, and soldiers with arms reversed; the Virgin Mary, in a long black mourning dress, closed the procession. It passed on to make the tour of the city; twice we intercepted it, and then went to the church of El Calvario. It stands on an elevation at the extreme end of a long street, and the steps were already crowded with women dressed in white from the head to the feet, with barely an oval opening for the face. It was dark when the procession made its appearance at the foot of the street, but by the blaze of innumerable lighted candles every object was exhibited with more striking wildness, and fanaticism seemed written in letters of fire on the faces of the Indians. The centurion cleared a way up the steps; the procession, with a loud chant, entered the church, and we went away.

In the evening we made several visits, and late at night we were called to a conference by some friends of the cura, and on his behalf. His troubles were not yet over. On the day of our arrival he had received a peremptory order from the provisor to repair to Guatimala, with notice that "some proper person" would be appointed in his place. We knew that the terms of the order afflicted the cura, for they implied that he was not a proper person. All Quezaltenango, he said, could answer for his acts, and he could answer to God that his motives were only to prevent the effusion of blood. His house was all in confusion; he was packing up his books and furniture, and preparing to obey the provisor's order. But his friends considered that it was dangerous for him to go to Guatimala. At that place, they said, he would be under the eyes of Carrera, who, meeting him in an angry moment, might cut him down in the street. If he did not go, the provisor would send soldiers after him, such was the rigour of church discipline. They wished him to fly the country, to go with us into Mexico; but he could not leave without a passport from Guatimala, and this would be refused. The reason of their unburdening themselves to us showed the helplessness of his condition. They supposed that I might have influence with the provisor, and begged me to write to Guatimala, and state the facts as they were known to all Quezaltenango. I had determined to take no part in the public or personal affairs of this unhappy revolution, but here I would not have hesitated to incur any trouble or risk to serve the cura could it have done him any good; but I knew the sensitiveness of the men in power, and believed that the provisor and the government would resent my interference. I proposed, however, to write to a friend who I knew stood well with the provisor, and request him to call upon that dignitary and state the facts as from me; and I suggested that he should send some friend to Guatimala expressly to see the provisor in person. Returned to a land of government and laws, I can hardly realize that so short a time since, I was called in to counsel for the safety of a man of the cura's character and station. Relatively, the most respectable clergyman in our country does not stand higher than he did.

The next morning we were invited to breakfast with another friend and counsellor, and about as strange a one as myself, being the old lady who had sent the cura 100 dollars, before mentioned. The plan was discussed and settled, and in the course of the day two friends undertook to visit Guatimala on the cura's behalf. We intended that day to ascend the volcano of Quezaltenango, but were disappointed in our guide. In the morning we made purchases and provisions for continuing our journey, and as one of our mules' backs was badly galled, we requested the gobernador to procure us Indian carriers.

In the afternoon, in company with the corregidor, we rode to the warm springs of Almolonga. The road crosses a spur of the volcano, and descends precipitously into a deep valley, in which, about a league distant, stand the village and hot springs. There is a good bathing-house, at which we were not allowed to pay, being considered the guests of the city. Outside, in a beautiful natural reservoir, Indian men, women, and children were bathing together.

We returned by another road, passing up a valley of extraordinary beauty, and the theme of conversation was the happiness the country might enjoy but for wars and revolutions. Beautiful as it was, all wished to leave it, and seek a land where life was safe—*Mexico* or El Norte. Toward evening, descending the spur of the volcano, we met several hundred Indians returning from the ceremonies of the Holy Week, and exceeding in drunkenness all the specimens we had yet encountered. In one place a man and woman, the latter with a child on her back, were staggering so near the brink of a precipice, that the corregidor dismounted and took the child from them, and made them go before us into the town.

There was no place we had visited, except ruined cities, so unique and interesting, and which deserved to be so thoroughly explored, as Quezaltenango. A month, at least, might be satisfactorily and profitably employed in examining the many curious objects in the country around. For botanical researches it is the richest region in Central America. But we had no time even for rest.

I passed the evening in writing, packing things to be sent to Guatimala, among others my quezal, which, however, never arrived, and in writing letters, one of which was on account of the cura, and in which, intending, even if it fell into wrong hands, to be out of the country myself, I spoke in no measured terms of the atrocity committed by Carrera.

CHAPTER XXIX.

JOURNEY CONTINUED — A MOUNTAIN PLAIN — LOST GUIDES — A TRYING MOMENT — AGUAS CALIENTES — A MAGNIFICENT VIEW — GOLD ORE — SAN SEBASTIANO — GUEGUETENANGO — SIERRA MADRE — A HUGE SKELETON — THE RUINS — PYRAMIDAL STRUCTURES — A VAULT — MOUNDS — A WELCOME ADDITION — INTERIOR OF A MOUND — VASES — ASCENT OF THE SIERRA MADRE — BUENA VISTA — THE DESCENT — TODOS SANTOS — SAN MARTIN — SAN ANDRES PETAPAN — A FOREST ON FIRE — SUFFERING OF THE MULES FROM SWARMS OF FLIES — SAN ANTONIO GUISTA.

EARLY in the morning our mules were saddled for the journey. The gobernador and another friend of the cura came to receive parting instructions, and set off for Guatimala. The Indians engaged for us did not make their appearance; and, desirous to save the day, we loaded the mules, and sent Juan and Bobon forward with the luggage. In a little while two women came and told us that our Indians were in prison. I accompanied them to two or three officials, and with much difficulty and loss of time found the man having charge of them, who said that, finding we had paid them part of their hire in advance, and afraid they would buy agua ardiente and be missing, he had shut them up the night before to have them ready, and had left word to that effect with one of the servants of the cura. I went with him to the prison, paid sixpence a-piece for their lodging, and took them over to the convent. The poor fellows had not eaten since they were shut up, and, as usual, wanted to go home for tortillas for the journey. We refused to let them go, but gave them money to buy some in the plaza, and kept the woman and their chamars as hostages for their return. But we became tired of waiting. Mr. Catherwood picked up their chamars and threw them across his saddle as a guarantee for their following, and we set off.

We had added to our equipments armas de agua, being undressed goatskins embroidered with red leather, which hung down from the saddlebow, to protect the legs against rain, and were now fully accoutred in Central American style.

It was cold and wintry. We ascended and crossed a high plain, and at the distance of a league descended to a village, where we learned that Juan and Bobon had passed on some time before. Beyond this we ascended a high and rugged mountain, and on the top reached a magnificent plain. We rode at a brisk pace, and it was one o'clock before our "jail-birds" overtook us. By this time we were surprised at not overtaking our men with the luggage. We could not have passed them, for there was but one road. Since leaving the village we had not seen a single person, and at two o'clock we met a man with a loaded mule coming from Aguas Calientes, the end of our day's journey, who had not met them. Mr. Catherwood became alarmed, fearing that they had robbed us, and run away. I was always careless with luggage, but never lost any, and was slow in coming to this belief. In half an hour we met another man, who told us that he had not seen them, and that there was no other road than the one by which he came. Since our apprehensions began, we had not been able to discover any tracks, but went on to within two leagues of our halting-place, when we stopped, and held one of the most anxious consultations that occurred in our whole journey. We knew but little of the men. Juan cheated us every day in the little purchases for the road, and we had detected him in the atrocity of keeping back part of the money we gave him to buy corn and sacate, and starving the mules. After a most unhappy deliberation, we concluded that they had broken open the trunks, taken out the money, thrown the rest of the contents down some ravine, mounted the mules, and made off. Besides money, beds, and bedding, these trunks contained all Mr. Catherwood's drawings, and the precious notebooks to which the reader is indebted for these pages. The fruits of all our labour were gone. In all our difficulties and perplexities we never had a more trying moment. We were two leagues from Aguas Calientes. To go on, rouse the village, get fresh horses, and return in pursuit, was our first idea; but this would widen the distance between us, and probably we should not be able to get horses.

With hearts so heavy that nothing but the feeble hope of catching them while dividing the money kept us from sinking, we turned back. It was four o'clock in the afternoon; neither our mules nor we had eaten anything since early in the morning. Night would be upon us, and it was doubtful whether our mules could hold out. Our prisoners told us we had been very imprudent to let the men set out alone, and took it for granted that they had not let slip the opportunity of robbing us. As we rode back, both Mr. C. and I brooded over an apprehension which for some time neither mentioned to the other. It was the letter I had written on behalf of the cura. We should again be within reach of Carrera. If the letter by accident fell into his hands, he would be indignant at what he considered my ingratitude, and he could very easily take his revenge. Our plans, however, were made up at once. We determined, at all events, not to go back to Guatimala, nor, broken as we were in fortune and spirit, to give up Palenque, but, if possible, to borrow money for the road, even if we set out on foot; but, O GLORIA ETERNAL! as the official bulletin said of

Carrera's victory; on reaching the top of a mountain we saw the men climbing up a deep ravine on the other side. We did not tell them our agony, but had not gone far before the Indians told all; and they were not surprised or hurt. How we passed them neither of us know; but another such a spasm would have put a period to our journey of life; and from that time, however tedious, or whatever might be the inducements, we resolved to keep by our luggage. At dusk we reached the top of a high mountain, and by one of those long, steep, and difficult descents, of which it is impossible to give the reader any idea, entered the village of Aguas Calientes.

It was occupied entirely by Indians, who gathered round us in the plaza, and, by the light of pine sticks, looked at Carrera's passport. Not one of them could read it, but it was enough to pronounce the name; and the whole village was put in requisition to provide us with something to eat. The alcalde distributed the money we gave him, and one brought sixpence worth of eggs; another of beans, another of tortillas, another of lard, another of candles, and a dozen or more received sixpence a-piece for sacate; not one of them would bring anything until he had the money in hand. A fire was kindled in the square, and in process of time we had supper. Our usual supper of fried eggs, beans, tortillas, and chocolate—any one of them enough to disturb digestion in a state of repose—with the excitement and vexation of our supposed loss, made me ill. The cabildo was a wretched shed, full of fleas, with a coat of dust an inch thick to soften the hard earthen floor. It was too cold to sleep out of doors, and there were no pins to hang hammocks on, for in this region hammocks were not used at all. We made inquiries with the view of hiring for the night the bedsteads of the principal inhabitants, but there was not one in the village; all slept on the bosom of mother earth, and we had part of the family bed. Fortunately, however, and most important for us, our mules fared well.

Early in the morning we resumed our journey. There are warm springs in this neighbourhood; but we did not go out of our way to visit them. A short distance from the village we crossed a river and commenced ascending a mountain. On the top we came upon a narrow neck of land, with a magnificent forest on both sides far below us. The wind swept over the lofty height, so that with our ponchas, which were necessary on account of the cold, it was difficult to keep the saddle. The road was broken and stony, and the track scarcely perceptible. At about ten o'clock the whole surface of the mountain was a bare ridge of limestone, from which the sun was reflected with scorching heat, and the whiteness was dazzling and painful to the eyes. Below us, on each side, continued an immense forest of gigantic pines. The road was perfectly desolate; we met no travellers. In four hours we saw on our left, at a great distance below, a single hacienda, with a clearing around it, seemingly selected for a magnificent seclusion from the convulsions of a distracted country. The ridge was broken by gullies and deep ravines; and we came to one across which, by way of bridge, lay the trunks of two gigantic pines. My macho always pulled back when I attempted to lead him, and I remained on his back, and was carried steadily over; but at the other end we started at a noise behind us. Our best cargo-mule had fallen, rolled over, and hung on the brink of the precipice, with her feet kicking in the air, kept from falling to the bottom only by being entangled among bushes. In a moment we scrambled down to her, got her head turned up the bank, and by means of strong halters heaved her out; but she was bruised and crippled, and barely able to stagger under her load. Continuing along the ridge, swept by fierce blasts of wind, we descended again to a river, rode some distance along its bank, and passed a track up the side of a mountain on the right, so steep that I had no idea it could be our road, and passed it, but was called back. It was the steepest ascent we had yet had in the country. It was cruel to push my brave macho, but I had been tormented all day with a violent headache, and could not walk; so I beat up, making the best tacks I could, and stopping every time I put about. On the top broke upon us one of those grand and magnificent views which, when we had wiped off perspiration and recovered breath, always indemnified us for our toil. It was the highest ground on which we had yet stood. Around us was a sea of mountains, and peeping above them, but so little as to give full effect to our own great height, were the conical tops of two new volcanoes. The surface was of limestone rock, in immense strata, with quartz, in one piece of which we discovered a speck of gold. Here again, in this vast wilderness of mountains, deep in the bowels of the earth, are those repositories of the precious ores for which millions upon millions all over the world are toiling, bargaining, craving, and cheating every day.

Continuing on this ridge, we came out upon a spur commanding a view, far below us, of a cultivated valley, and the village of San Sebastiano. We descended to the valley, left the village on our right, crossed the spur, and saw the end of our day's journey, the town of Gueguetenango, situated on an extensive plain, with a mild climate, luxuriant with tropical productions, surrounded by immense mountains, and before us the great Sierra Madre, the natural bulwark of Central America, the grandeur and magnificence of the view disturbed only by the distressing reflection that we had to cross it. My macho, brought up on the plains of Costa Rica, had long seemed puzzled to know what mountains were made for; if he could have spoken, he would have cried out in anguish,

"Hills peep o'er hills, and Alps on Alps arise."

Our day's journey was but twenty-seven miles, but it was harder for man and beast than any sixty since we left Guatimala. We rode into the town, the chief place of the last district of Central America and of the ancient kingdom of Quiché. It was well built, with a large church or plaza; and again a crowd of Mestitzoes were engaged in the favourite occupation of fighting cocks. As we rode through the plaza, the bell sounded for the oracion, or vesper prayers: the people fell on their knees, and we took off our hats. We stopped at the house of Don Joaquin Mon, an old Spaniard of high consideration, by whom we were hospitably received; and who, though a Centralist, on account of some affair of his sons, had had his house at Chiantla plundered by Carrera's soldiers. His daughters were compelled to take refuge in the church, and forty or fifty mules were driven from his hacienda. In a short time we had a visit from the corregidor, who had seen our proposed journey announced in the Government paper, and treated us with the consideration due to persons specially recommended by the Government.

We reached Gueguetenango in a shattered condition. Our cargo-mules had their backs so galled that it was distressing to use them; and the saddle-horse was no better off. Bobon, in walking barefooted over the stony road, had bruised the ball of one of his feet, so that he was disabled; and that night Juan's enormous supper gave him an indigestion. He was a tremendous feeder; on the road nothing eatable was safe. We owed him a spite for pilfering our bread, and bringing us down to tortillas, and were not sorry to see him on his back; but he rolled over the floor of the corridor, crying out uproariously, so as to disturb the whole household, "Voy morir!—Voy morir!" ("I am going to die!—I am going to die!") He was a hard subject to work upon, but we took him in hand strongly, and unloaded him.

Besides our immediate difficulties, we heard of others in prospect. In consequence of the throng of emigrants from Guatimala towards Mexico, no one was admitted into that territory without a passport from Ciudad Real, the capital of Chiapas, four or five days' journey from the frontier. The frontier was a long line of river in the midst of a wilderness; and there were two roads, a lower one but little travelled, on account of the difficulty of crossing the rivers, but at that time passable. As we intended, however, at all events, to stop at this place for the purpose of visiting the ruins, we postponed our decision till the next day.

The next morning Don Joaquin told us of the skeleton of a colossal animal, supposed to be a mastodon, which had been found in the neighbourhood. Some of the bones had been collected, and were then in the town; and, having seen them, we took a guide and walked to the place where they had been discovered, on the borders of the Rio Chinaca, about half a mile distant. At this time the river was low, but the year before, swelled by the immense floods of the rainy season, it had burst its bounds, carried away its right bank, and laid bare one side of the skeleton. The bank was perpendicular, about thirty feet high, and the animal had been buried in an upright position. Besides the bones in the town, some had been carried away by the flood, others remained imbedded in the earth; but the impression of the whole animal, from twenty-five to thirty feet long, was distinctly visible. We were told that about eight leagues above, on the bank of the same river, the skeleton of a much larger animal had been discovered.

In the afternoon we rode to the ruins, which in the town were called *las cuevas*, the caves. They lie about half a league distant, on a magnificent plain, bounded in the distance by lofty mountains, among which is the great Sierra Madre.

The site of the ancient city, as at Patinamit and Santa Cruz del Quiché, was chosen for its security against enemies. It was surrounded by a ravine, and the general character of the ruins is the same as at Quiché, but the hand of destruction has fallen upon it more heavily: the whole is a confused heap of grass-grown fragments. The principal remains are two pyramidal structures of this form:—

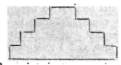

One of them measures at the base 102 feet; the steps are 4 feet high, and 7 feet deep, making the whole height 28 feet. They are not of cut stone, as at Copan, but of rough pieces cemented with lime; and the whole exterior was formerly coated with stucco, and painted. On the top is a small square platform, and at the base lies a long slab of rough stone, apparently hurled down from the top; perhaps the altar on which human victims were extended for sacrifice.

The owner of the ground, a Mestitzo, whose house was near by, and who accompanied us to the ruins, told us that he had bought the land from Indians, and that for some time after his purchase, he was annoyed by their periodical visits to celebrate some of their ancient rites on the top of this structure. This annoyance continued until he whipped two or three of the principal men, and drove them away.

At the foot of the structure was a vault, faced with cut stone, in which were found a collection of bones and a terra cotta vase, then in his possession. The vault was not long enough for the body of a man extended, and the bones must have been separated before they were placed there.

The owner believed that these structures contained interior apartments, with hidden treasures; and there were several mounds, supposed to be sepulchres of the ancient inhabitants, which also, he had no doubt, contained treasure. The situation of the place was magnificent. We had never before enjoyed so good an opportunity for working, and agreed with him to come the next day and make excavations, promising to give him all the treasure, and taking for our share only the sculls, vases, and other curiosities.

The next morning, before we were up, the door was thrown open, and to our surprise we received a salutation in English. The costume of the stranger was of the country; his beard long: and he looked as if already he had made a hard morning's ride. To my great surprise and pleasure, I recognised Pawling, whom I had known as superintendent of a cochineal hacienda at Amatitan. He had heard of our setting out for Mexico, and, disgusted with his occupation and the country, had mounted his horse, and with all he was worth tied on behind his saddle, pushed on to overtake us. On the way he had bought a fine mule, and by hard riding, and changing from one animal to the other, had reached us in four days. He was in difficulty about a passport, and was anxious to have the benefit of mine, in order to get out of the country, offering to attach himself to me in any capacity necessary for that purpose. Fortunately, my passport was broad enough to cover him, and I immediately constituted him the general manager of the expedition, the material of which was now reduced to Juan sick, and but one cargo-mule sound.

At nine o'clock, attended by three men and a boy with machetes, being all we could procure at so short a notice, we were again among the ruins. We were not strong enough to pull down a pyramid, and lost the morning in endeavouring to make a breach in one of the sides, but did not accomplish anything.

In the afternoon we opened one of the mounds. The interior was a rough coat of stones and lime, and after an hour's digging we came to fragments of bones and the two lower vases in the plate No. 42. The first of the two was entire when we discovered it, but, unfor-

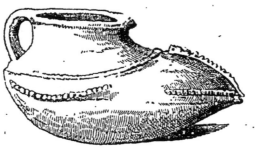

42. VASES FOUND AT GUEGUETENAGO.

tunately, was broken in getting it out, though we obtained all the pieces. It is graceful in design, the surface is polished, and the workmanship very good. The last was already broken, and though more complicated, the surface is not polished. The tripod at the top of the engraving is a copy of the vase before referred to, found in the tomb, which I procured from the owner of the land. It is twelve inches in diameter, and the surface is polished. We discovered no treasure, but our day's work was most interesting, and we only regretted that we had not time to explore more thoroughly.

In the meantime Don Joaquin had made arrangements for us, and the next morning we resumed our journey. We left behind a mule, a horse, and Bobon, and were reinforced by Pawling, well-mounted, and armed with a pair of pistols, and a short double-barrelled gun slung to his saddle-bow, and Santiago, a Mexican fugitive soldier. Juan was an interesting invalid mounted on a mule, and the whole was under escort of a respectable old muleteer, who was setting out with empty mules to bring back a load of sugar.

At a short distance from the village we commenced ascending the Sierra Madre. The first range was stony, and on the top of it we came upon a cultivated plain, beyond which rose a second range, covered with a thick forest of oak. On the top of this range stood a cross. The spot was called Buena Vista, or Fine View, and commanded a magnificent expanse of mountains and plains, five lakes and two volcanoes, one of which, called Tujamulco, our guide said was a water volcano. Beyond this rose a third range. At some distance up was an Indian rancho, at which a fine little boy thrust his face through a bush fence and said "adios" at every one that passed. Beyond was another boy, to whom we all in succession said "adios," but the surly little fellow would not answer one of us. On the summit of this range we were almost on a level with the tops of the volcanoes. As we ascended the temperature grew colder, and we were compelled to put on our ponchas. At half-past two we reached the top of the Sierra Madre, the dividing line of the waters, being twelve miles from Gueguetenango, and in our devious course making the second time that we had crossed the sierra. The ridge of the mountain was a long level table about half a mile wide, with rugged sides rising on the right to a terrific peak. Riding about half an hour on this table, by the side of a stream of clear and cold water, which passed on, carrying its tribute to the *Pacific Ocean*, we reached a miserable rancho, in front of which the arriero proposed to encamp, as he said it would be impossible to reach the next village. At a distance it was a glorious idea, that of sleeping on the top of the Sierra Madre, and the scene was wild enough for the most romantic imagination; but, being poorly provided against cold, we would have gladly exchanged it for an Indian village.

The occupants of the hut were a man and woman, who lived there rent free. Like the eagle, they had fixed their habitation where they were not likely to be disturbed. While the men were unloading, Juan, as an invalid, asked permission to stretch his huge body before the fire, but the woman told him there was more room out of doors. I succeeded, however, in securing him a place inside. We had an hour to wander over the top of the sierra. It belonged to our friend Don Joaquin Mon, and was what would be called at home a pretty substantial piece of fast property. At every step there was some fresh opening, which presented a new view of the grand and magnificent in nature. In many places, between cliffs and under certain exposures, were fine pieces of ground, and about half a mile distant a potrero or pasture-ground for brood mares, which we visited to buy some corn for our mules. A vicious jack reigned lord of the sierra.

Adjoining the occupied hut was another about ten feet square, made of small upright poles, thatched with branches of cypress, and open on all sides to the wind. We collected a quantity of wood, made a fire in the centre, had supper, and passed a social evening. The muleteers had a large fire outside, and with their pack-saddles and cargoes built a breastwork to shelter themselves against the wind. Fancy called up a picture of far-distant scenes: a small circle of friends, possibly at that moment thinking of us. Perhaps, to tell the truth, we wished to be with them; and, above all, as we looked to our sleeping places, thought of the comforts of home. Nevertheless, we soon fell asleep. Towards morning, however, we were reminded of our elevated region. The ground was covered with a hoar frost, and water was frozen a quarter of an inch thick. Our guide said that this happened regularly every night in the year when the atmosphere was clear. It was the first ice we had seen in the country. The men were shivering around a large fire, and, as soon as they could see, went out to look for the mules. One of them had strayed; and while the men were looking for her, we had breakfast, and did not get off till a quarter before eight. Our road traversed the ridge of the sierra, which for two leagues was a level table, a great part composed of immense beds of red slate and blue limestone or chalk rock, lying in vertical strata. At ten o'clock we began to descend, the cold being still severe. The descent surpassed in grandeur and magnificence all that we had yet encountered. It was by a broad passage with perpendicular mountain walls, rising in rugged and terrific peaks, higher and higher as we descended, out of which gigantic cypress-trees were growing, their trunks and all their branches dead. Before us, between these immense walls, was a vista reaching beyond the village of San Andres, twenty-four miles distant. A stream of water was dashing down over rocks and stones, hurrying on to the Atlantic; we crossed it perhaps fifty times on bridges wild and rude as the stream itself and the mountains between which it rolled. As we descended, the temperature became milder. At twelve o'clock the immense ravine opened into a rich valley a mile in width, and in half an hour we reached the village of Todos Santos. On the right, far below us, was a magnificent table-land cultivated with corn, and bounded by the side of the great sierra; and in the suburbs of the village were apple and peach-trees covered with blossoms and young fruit. We had again reached the tierras templadas, and in Europe or North America the beauty of this miserable unknown village would be a theme for poetry.

As we rode through it, at the head of the street we were stopped by a drunken Indian, supported by two men hardly able to stand themselves, who, we thought, were taking him to prison; but, staggering before us, they blocked up the passage, and shouted, "Pasaporte!" Pawling, in anticipation, and to assume his new character, had tied his jacket around his waist by the sleeves, and was dragging one of the mules by its halter. Not one of the three could read the passport, and they sent for the secretary, a bare-headed Indian, habited in nothing but a ragged cotton shirt, who examined it very carefully, and read aloud the name of Rafael Carrera, which, I think, was all that he attempted to make out. We were neither sentimental, nor philosophical, nor moralizing travellers, but it gave us pangs to think that such a magnificent country was in the possession of such men.

Passing the church and convent, we ascended a ridge, then descended an immense ravine, crossed another magnificent valley, and at length reached the Indian village of San Martin, which, with loveliness and grandeur all around us, might have been selected for its surpassing beauty of position. We rode to the cabildo, and then to the hut of the alcalde. The people were all Indians; the secretary was a bare-legged boy, who spelled out every word in the passport except our names; but his reading sufficed to procure supper for us, and provender for the mules, and early in the morning we pushed on again.

For some distance we rode on a lofty ridge, with a precipitous ravine on each side, in one place so narrow that, as our arriero told us, when the wind is high there is danger of being blown off. We continued descending, and at a quarter-past twelve reached San Andres Petapan, fifteen miles distant, blooming with oranges, sapotes, and other fruit-trees. Passing through the village, at a short distance beyond we were stopped by a fire in the woods. We turned back, and attempted to pass by another road, but were unable. Before we returned the fire had reached the place we left, and increased so fast that we had apprehensions for the luggage-mules, and hurried them back with the men toward the village. The flames came creeping and crackling toward us, shooting up and whirled by currents of wind, and occasionally, when fed with dry and combustible materials, flashing and darting along like a train of gunpowder. We fell back, keeping as near as we could to the line of fire, the road lying along the side of a mountain; while the fire came from the ravine below, crossing the road, and moving upward. The clouds of smoke and ashes, the rushing of currents of wind and flames, the crackling of burning branches, and trees wrapped in flames, and the rapid progress of the destroying element, made such a wild and fearful scene that we could not tear ourselves away. At length we saw the flames rush up the side of the ravine, intercepting the path before us. We spurred our horses, shot by, and in a moment the whole was a sheet of flame. The fire was now spreading so rapidly that we became alarmed, and hurried back to the church, which, on an elevation strongly defined against the immense mountain in the background, stood before us as a place of refuge. By this time the villagers had become alarmed, and men and women were hurrying to the height to watch the progress of the flames. The village was in danger of conflagration; it would be impossible to urge the loaded mules up the hill we had descended, and we resolved to deposit the luggage in the church, and save the mules by driving them up unburdened. It was another of those wild scenes to which no effect can be given in words. We stopped on the brow of the hill before the square of the church, and while we were watching the fire, the black clouds and sheets of flame rolled up the side of the mountain, and spared the village. Relieved from apprehension, we sat down under a tree in front of the church to the calm enjoyment of the terrific spectacle and a cold fowl. The cinders and ashes fell around, and the destructive element rushed on, sparing the village before us, perhaps to lay some other in ruins.

We were obliged to wait two hours. From the foot of the hill on which the village stood, the ground was hot, and covered with a light coat of ashes; the brush and underwood were burned away; in some places were lying trees, reduced to masses of live coal, and others were standing with their trunks and branches all on fire. In one place we passed a square of white ashes, the remains of some miserable Indian hut. Our faces and hands were scorched, and our whole bodies heated when we emerged from the fiery forest. For a few moments the open air was delightful; but we were hardly out of one trouble before we had another. Swarms of enormous flies, perhaps driven out by the fire, and hovering on the borders of the burned district, fell upon the mules. Every bite drew blood, and the tormentors clung to the suffering animals until brushed off by a stick. For an hour we laboured hard, but could not keep their heads and necks free. The poor beasts were almost frantic, and, in spite of all we could do, their necks, the inside of their legs, mouths, ears, nostrils, and every tender part of their skin, were trickling with blood. Hurrying on, in three hours we saw the Church of San Antonio Güista, and in a few minutes entered the village, beautifully situated on a table-land projecting from the slope of a mountain, looking upon an immense opening, and commanding on all sides a magnificent view. At this time we were beyond the reach of war, and free from all apprehensions. With the addition of Pawling's pistols and double-barrelled gun, a faithful muleteer, Santiago, and Juan on his legs again, we could have stormed an Indian village, and locked up a refractory alcalde in his own cabildo. We took possession of San Antonio Güista, dividing ourselves between the cabildo and the convent, sent for the alcalde (even on the borders of Central America the name of Carrera was omnipotent), and told him to stay there and wait upon us, or send an alguazil.

The alcalde and his major had roused the village. In a few moments, instead of the mortifying answer "no hay," there is none, the provision made for us was almost equal to the offers of the Turkish paradise. Twenty or thirty women were in the convent at one time, with baskets of corn, tortillas, dolces, plantains, hocotes, sapotes, and a variety of other fruits, each one's stock in trade being of the value of three halfpence; and among them was a species of tortillas, thin and baked hard, about 12 inches in diameter, 120 for three pence, of which, as they were not expensive, we laid in a large supply.

At this place our muleteer was to leave us. We had but one cargo-mule fit for service, and applied to the alcalde for two carriers to go with us across the frontier to Comitan. He went out, as he said, to consult with the mozos, and told us that they asked six dollars apiece. We spoke to him of our friend Carrera, and on a second consultation the demand was reduced by two-thirds. We were obliged to make provisions for three days, and even to carry corn for the mules; and Juan and Santiago had a busy night, boiling fowls and eggs.

CHAPTER XXX.

COMFORTABLE LODGINGS—JOURNEY CONTINUED—STONY ROAD—BEAUTIFUL RIVER—SUSPENSION BRIDGE—THE DOLORES—RIO LAGERTERO—ENTHUSIASM BROUGHT DOWN—ANOTHER BRIDGE—ENTRY INTO MEXICO—A BATH—A SOLITARY CHURCH—A SCENE OF BARRENNESS—ZAPOLOUTA—COMITAN—ANOTHER COUNTRYMAN—MORE PERPLEXITIES—OFFICIAL COURTESY—TRADE OF COMITAN—SMUGGLING—SCARCITY OF SOAP.

The next morning we found the convent was so comfortable, we were so abundantly served, the alcalde or his major, staff in hand, being in constant attendance, and the situation so beautiful, that we were in no hurry to go; but the alcalde told us that all was ready. We did not see our carriers, and found that he and his major were the mozos whom he had consulted. They could not let slip two dollars a-piece, and laying down their staves and dignity, bared their backs, placed the straps across their foreheads, took up the loads, and trotted off.

We started at five minutes before eight. The weather was fine, but hazy. From the village we descended a hill to an extensive stony plain, and at about a league's distance reached the brink of a precipice, from which we looked down into a rich oblong valley, 2,000 or 3,000 feet deep, shut in all around by a mountain wall, and seeming an immense excavation. Toward the other end of the valley was a village with a ruined church, and the road led up a precipitous ascent to a plain on the same level with that on which we stood, undulating and boundless as the sea. Below us it seemed as if we could drop a stone to the bottom. We descended by one of the steepest and most stony paths we had yet encountered in the country, crossing and recrossing in a zigzag course along the side of the height, perhaps making the descent a mile and a half long. Very soon we reached the bank of a beautiful river, running lengthwise through the valley, bordered on each side by immense trees, throwing their branches clear across, and their roots washed by the stream; and while the plain beyond was dry and parched, they were green and luxuriant. Riding along it, we reached a suspension bridge of most primitive appearance and construction, called by the natives La Hammaca, which had existed there from time immemorial. It was made of oziers twisted into cords, about three feet apart, and stretched across the river with a hanging network of vines, the ends fastened to the trunks of two opposite trees. It hung about twenty-five feet above the river, which was here some eighty feet wide, and was supported in different places by vines tied to the branches. The access was by a rude ladder to a platform in the crotch of the tree. In the bottom of the hammaca were two or three poles to walk on. It waved with the wind, and was an unsteady and rather insecure means of transportation. From the centre the vista of the river both ways under the arches of the trees was beautiful, and in every direction the hammaca was a most picturesque-looking object. We continued on to the village, and after a short halt and a smoke with the alcalde, rode on to the extreme end of the valley, and by a steep and stony ascent, at twenty minutes past twelve reached the level ground above. Here we dismounted, slipped the bridles of our mules, and seated ourselves to wait for our Indians, looking down into the deep embosomed valley, and back at the great range of Cordilleras, crowned by the Sierra Madre, seeming a barrier fit to separate worlds.

Free from all apprehensions, we were now in the full enjoyment of the wild country and wild mode of travelling. But our poor Indians, perhaps, did not enjoy it so much. The usual load was from three to four arrobas, seventy-five to one hundred pounds; ours were not more than fifty; but the sweat rolled in streams down their naked bodies, and every limb trembled. After a short rest they started again. The day was hot and sultry, the ground dry, parched, and stony. We had two sharp descents, and reached the River Dolores. On both sides were large trees, furnishing a beautiful shade, which, after our scorching ride, we found delightful. The river was about 300 feet broad. In the rainy season it is impassable, but in the dry season not more than three or four feet deep, very clear, and the colour a greyish green, probably from the reflection of the trees. We had had no water since we left the suspension bridge, and both our mules and we were intemperate.

We remained here half an hour; and now apprehensions, which had been operating more or less all the time, made us feel very uncomfortable. We were approaching, and very near, the frontier of Mexico. This road was so little travelled, that, as we were told, there was no regular guard; but piquets of soldiers were scouring the whole line of frontier to prevent smuggling, who might consider us contraband. Our passports were good for going out of Central America; but to go into Mexico, the passport of the Mexican authorities at Ciudad Real, four days' journey, was necessary. Turning back was not in our vocabulary; perhaps we should be obliged to wait in the wilderness till we could send for one.

In half an hour we reached the Rio Lagertero, the boundary line between Guatimala and Mexico, a scene of wild and surpassing beauty, with banks shaded by some of the noblest trees of the tropical forests, water as clear as crystal, and fish a foot long playing in it as gently as if there were no such things as fish-hooks. No soldiers were visible; all was as desolate as if no human being had ever crossed the boundary before. We had a moment's consultation on which side to encamp, and determined to make a lodgment in Mexico. I was riding Pawling's horse, and spurred him into the water, to be the first to touch the soil. With one plunge his fore-feet were off the bottom, and my legs under water. For an instant I hesitated; but as the water rose to my holsters my enthusiasm gave way, and I wheeled back into Central America. As we afterward found, the water was ten or twelve feet deep.

We waited for the Indians, in some doubt whether it would be possible to cross at all with the luggage. At a short distance above was a ledge of rocks, forming rapids, over which there had been a bridge with a wooden arch and stone abutments, the latter of which were still standing, the bridge having been carried away by the rising of the waters seven years before. It was the last of the dry season; the rocks were in some places dry, the body of the river running in channels on each side, and a log was laid to them from the abutments of the bridge. We took off the saddles and bridles of the mules, and cautiously, with the water breaking rapidly up to the knees, carried everything across by hand; an operation in which an hour was consumed. One night's rain on the mountains would have made it impassable. The mules were then swum across, and we were all landed safely in Mexico.

On the bank opposite the place where I attempted to cross was a semicircular clearing, from which the only opening was the path leading into the Mexican provinces. We closed this up, and turned the mules loose, hung our traps on the trees, and bivouacked in the centre. The men built a fire, and while they were preparing supper we went down to the river to bathe. The rapids were breaking above us. The wildness of the scene, its seclusion and remoteness, the clearness of the water, the sense of having accomplished an important part of our journey, all revived our physical and moral being. Clean apparel consummated the glory of the bath. For several days our digestive organs had been out of order; but when we sat down to supper they could have undertaken the bridles of the mules; and my brave macho —it was a pleasure to hear him craunch his corn. We were out of Central America, safe from the dangers of revolution, and stood on the wild borders of Mexico, in good health, with good appetites, and something to eat. We had still a tremendous journey before us, but it seemed nothing. We strode the little clearing as proudly as the conquerors of Mexico, and in our extravagance resolved to have a fish for breakfast. We had no hooks, and there was not even a pin in our travelling equipage; but we had needles and thread. Pawling, with the experience of seven years' "roughing," had expedients, and put a needle in the fire, which softened its temper, so that he bent it into a hook. A pole was on every tree, and we could see the fish in the water; all that we wanted was for them to open their mouths and hook themselves to the needle; but this they would not do, and for this reason alone we had none for breakfast. We returned. Our men cut some poles, and resting them in the crotch of a tree, covered them with branches. We spread our mats under, and our roof and beds were ready. The men piled logs of wood on the fire, and our sleep was sound and glorious.

At daylight the next morning we were again in the water. Our bath was even better than that of the night before, and when I mounted I felt able to ride through Mexico and Texas to my own door in New York. Returned once more to steamboats and railroads, how flat, tame, and insipid all their comforts seem.

We started at half-past seven. At a very short distance three wild boars crossed our path, all within gunshot; but our men carried the guns, and in an instant it was too late. Very soon we emerged from woods that bordered the river, and came out into an open plain. At half-past eight we crossed a low stony hill, and came to the dry bed of a river. The bottom was flat and baked hard, and the sides smooth and regular as those of a canal. At the distance of half a league water appeared, and at half-past nine it became a considerable stream. We again entered a forest, and riding by a narrow path, saw directly before us, closing the passage, the side of a large church. We came out, and saw the whole gigantic building, without a single habitation, or the vestige of one, in sight. The path led across the broken wall of the courtyard. We dismounted in the deep shade of the front. The façade was rich and perfect. It was 60 feet front and 250 feet deep, but roofless, with trees growing out of the area above the walls. Nothing could exceed the quiet and desolation of the scene; but there was something strangely interesting in these roofless churches, standing in places entirely unknown. Santiago told us that this was called Conata, and the tradition is, that it was once so rich that the inhabitants carried their water-jars by silken cords. Giving our mules to Santiago, we entered the open doorway of the church. The altar was thrown down, the roof lay in broken masses on the ground, and the whole area was a forest of trees. At the foot of the church, and connected with it, was a convent. There was no roof, but the apartments were entire as when a good padre stood to welcome a traveller. In front of the church, on each side, was a staircase leading up to a belfry in the centre of the façade. We ascended to the top. The bells which had called to matin and vesper prayers were gone; the crosspiece was broken from the cross. The stone of the belfry was solid masses of petrified shells, worms, leaves, and insects. On one side we looked down into the roofless area, and on the other over a region of waste. One man had written his name there:

Joaquin Rodriques,
Conata, Mayo 1º, 1836.

We wrote our names under his and descended, mounted, rode over a stony and desolate country; crossed a river, and saw before us a range of hills, and beyond a range of mountains. Then we came upon a bleak stony table-land, and after riding four hours and a half, saw the road leading across a barren mountain on our right, and, afraid we had missed our way, halted under a low spreading tree to wait for our men. We turned the mules loose, and, after waiting some time, sent Santiago back to look for them. The wind was sweeping over the plain, and while Mr. Catherwood was cutting wood, Pawling and I descended to a ravine to look for water. The bed was entirely dry, and one took his course up and the other down. Pawling found a muddy hole in a rock, which, even to thirsty men, was not tempting. We returned, and found Mr. Catherwood warming himself by the blaze of three or four young trees, which he had piled one upon another. The wind was at this time sweeping furiously over the plain. Night was approaching; we had not eaten anything since morning; our small stock of provisions was in unsafe hands, and we began to fear that none would be forthcoming. Our mules were as badly off. The pasture was so poor that they required a wide range, and we let all go loose except my poor macho, which, from certain roving propensities acquired before he came into my possession, we were obliged to fasten to a tree. It was some time after dark when Santiago appeared with the alforgas of provisions on his back. He had gone back six miles when he found the track of Juan's foot, one of the squarest ever planted, and followed it to a wretched hut in the woods, at which we had expected to stop. We had lost nothing by not stopping; all they could get to bring away was four eggs. We supped, piled up our trunks to windward, spread our mats, lay down, gazed for a few moments at the stars, and fell asleep. During the night the wind changed, and we were almost blown away.

The next morning, preparatory to entering once more upon habitable regions, we made our toilet; *i. e.* we hung a looking-glass on the branch of a tree, and shaved the upper lip and a small part of the chin. At a quarter past seven we started, having eaten up our last fragment. Since we left Güista we had not seen a human being; the country was still desolate and dreary; there was not a breath of air; hills, mountains, and plains were all barren and stony; but, as the sun peeped above the horizon, its beams gladdened this scene of barrenness. For two hours we ascended a barren stony mountain. Even before this the desolate frontier had seemed almost an impregnable barrier; but Alvarado had crossed it to penetrate an unknown country teeming with enemies, and twice a Mexican army has invaded Central America.

At half-past ten we reached the top of the mountain, and on a line before us saw the church of Zapolouta, the first village in Mexico. Here our apprehensions revived from want of a passport. Our great object was to reach Comitan, and there bide the brunt. Approaching the village, we avoided the road that led through the plaza, and leaving the luggage to get along as it could, hurried through the suburbs, startled some women and children, and before our entry was known at the cabildo we were beyond the village. We rode briskly for about a mile, and then stopped to breathe. An immense weight was removed from our minds, and we welcomed each other to Mexico. Coming in from the desolate frontier, it opened upon us like an old, long-settled, civilized, quiet, and well-governed country.

Four hours' ride over an arid and sandy plain brought us to Comitan. Santiago, being a deserter from the Mexican army, afraid of being caught, left us in the suburbs to return alone across the desert we had passed, and we rode into the plaza. In one of the largest houses fronting it lived an American. Part of the front was occupied as a shop, and behind the counter was a man whose face called up the memory of home. I asked him in English if his name was M'Kinney, and he answered "Si, señor." I put several other questions in English, which he answered in Spanish. The sounds were familiar to him, yet it was some time before he could fully comprehend that he was listening to his native tongue; but when he did, and understood that I was a countryman, it awakened feelings to which he had long been a stranger, and he received us as one in whom absence had only strengthened the links that bound him to his country.

Dr. James M'Kinney, whose unpretending name is in Comitan transformed to the imposing one of Don Santiago Maquene, was a native of Westmoreland county, Virginia, and went out to Tobasco to pass a winter for the benefit of his health and the practice of his profession. Circumstances induced him to make a journey into the interior, and he established himself at Ciudad Real. At the time of the cholera in Central America, he went to Quezaltenango, where he was employed by the government, and lived two years on intimate terms with the unfortunate General Guzman, whom he described as one of the most gentlemanly, amiable, intelligent, and best men in the country. He afterwards returned to Comitan, and married a lady of a once rich and powerful family, but stripped of a portion of its wealth by a revolution only two years before. In the division of what was left, the house on the plaza fell to his share; and disliking the practice of his profession, he abandoned it, and took to selling goods. Like every other stranger in the country, by reason of constant wars and revolutions, he had become nervous. He had none of this feeling when he first arrived, and at the time of the first revolution in Ciudad Real he stood in the plaza looking on, when two men were shot down by his side. Fortunately, he took them into a house to dress their wounds, and during this time the attacking party forced their way into the plaza, and cut down every man in it.

Up to this place we had travelled on the road to Mexico; here Pawling was to leave us, and go on to the capital; Palenque lay on our right, toward the coast of the Atlantic. The road Dr. M'Kinney described as more frightful than any we had yet travelled; and there were other difficulties. War was again in our way; and, while all the rest of Mexico was quiet, Tobasco and Yucatan, the two points in our journey, were in a state of revolution. This might not have disturbed us greatly but for another difficulty. It was necessary to present ourselves at Ciudad Real, three days' journey directly out of our road, to procure a passport, without which we could not travel in any part of the Mexican republic. And, serious as these things were, they merged in a third; viz. the government of Mexico had issued a peremptory order to prevent all strangers visiting the ruins of Palenque. Dr. M'Kinney told us of his own knowledge that three Belgians, sent out on a scientific expedition by the Belgian government, had gone to Ciudad Real expressly to ask permission to visit them, and had been refused. These communications damped somewhat the satisfaction of our arrival in Comitan.

By Dr. M'Kinney's advice we presented ourselves immediately to the commandant, who had a small garrison of about thirty men, well uniformed and equipped, and, compared with the soldiers of Central America, giving me a high opinion of the Mexican army. I showed him my passport, and a copy of the government paper of Guatimala, which fortunately stated that I intended going to Campeachy to embark for the United States. With great courtesy he immediately undertook to relieve us from the necessity of presenting ourselves in person at Ciudad Réal, and offered to send a courier to the governor for a passport. This was a great point, but still there would be detention; and by his advice we called upon the Prefeto, who received us with courtesy, regretted the necessity of embarrassing our movements, showed us a copy of the order of the government, which was imperative, and made no exceptions in favour of Special Confidential Agents. He was really anxious, however, to serve us, said he was willing to incur some responsibility, and would consult with the commandant. We left him with a warm appreciation of the civility and good feeling of the Mexican officials, and satisfied that, whatever might be the result, they were disposed to pay great respect to their neighbours of the North. The next morning the Prefeto sent back the passport, with a courteous message that they considered me in the same light as if I had come accredited to their own government, would be happy to render me every facility in their power, and that Mexico was open to me to travel which way I pleased. Thus one great difficulty was removed. I recommend all who wish to travel to get an appointment from Washington.

As to the revolutions, after having gone through the crash of a Central American, we were not to be put back by a Mexican. But the preventive order against visiting the ruins of Palenque was not so easily disposed of. If we made an application for permission, we felt sure of the good disposition of the local authorities; but if they had no discretion, were bound by imperative orders, and obliged to refuse, it would be uncourteous and improper to make the attempt. At the same time it was discouraging, in the teeth of Dr. M'Kinney's information, to undertake the journey without. To be obliged to retrace our steps, and make the long journey to the capital to ask permission, would be terrible; but we learned that the ruins were removed some distance from any habitation; we did not believe that, in the midst of a formidable revolution, the government had any spare soldiers to station there as a guard. From what we knew of other ruins, we had reason to believe that the place was entirely desolate; we might be on the ground before any one knew we were in the neighbourhood, and then make terms either to remain or evacuate, as the case might require; and it was worth the risk if we got one day's quiet possession. With this uncertain prospect we immediately commenced repairing and making preparations for our journey.

The comfort of finding ourselves at this distant place in the house of a countryman can hardly be appreciated. In dress, manner, appearance, habits, and feelings, the doctor was as natural as if we had met him at home. The only difference was his language, which he could not speak connectedly, but interlarded it with Spanish expressions. He moved among the people, but he was not of them; and the only tie that bound him was a dark-eyed Spanish beauty, one of the few that I saw in that country for whom a man might forget kindred and home. He was anxious to leave the country, but trammelled by a promise made his mother-in-law not to do so during her life. He lived, however, in such constant anxiety, that he hoped she would release him.

Comitan, the frontier town of Chiapas, contains a population of about 10,000. It has a suburb church, and well-filled convent of Dominican Friars. It is a place of considerable trade, and has become so by the effect of bad laws; for, in consequence of the heavy duties on regular importations at the Mexican ports of entry, most of the European goods consumed in this region are smuggled in from Balize and Guatimala. The proceeds of confiscations and the perquisites of officers are such an important item of revenue that the officers are vigilant, and the day before we arrived twenty or thirty mule-loads that had been seized were brought into Comitan; but the profits are so large that smuggling is a regular business, the risk of seizure being considered one of the expenses of carrying it on. The markets, however, are but poorly supplied, as we found. We sent for a washerwoman, but there was no soap in the town. We wanted our mules shod, but there was only iron enough to shoe one. Buttons for pantaloons, in size, made up for other deficiencies. The want of soap was a deplorable circumstance. For several days we had indulged in the pleasing expectation of having our sheets washed. The reader may perhaps consider us fastidious, as it was only three weeks since we left Guatimala, but we had slept in wretched cabildoes, and on the ground, and they had become of a very doubtful colour. In time of trouble, however, commend me to the sympathy of a countryman. Don Santiago, alias Doctor M'Kinney, stood by us in our hour of need, provided us with soap, and our sheets were purified.

Pawling's difficulties were now over. I procured for him a separate passport, and he had before him a clear road to Mexico; but his interest had been awakened; he was loth to leave us, and after a long consultation and deliberation resolved that he would go with us to Palenque.

CHAPTER XXXI,

PARTING—SOTANÁ—A MILLIONAIRE—OCOSINGO—RUINS—BEGINNING OF THE RAINY SEASON—A FEMALE GUIDE—ARRIVAL AT THE RUINS—STONE FIGURES—PYRAMIDAL STRUCTURES—AN ARCH—A STUCCO ORNAMENT—A *wooden* LINTEL—A CURIOUS CAVE—BUILDINGS, ETC—A CAUSEWAY—MORE RUINS—JOURNEY TO PALENQUE—RIO GRANDE—CASCADES—SUCCESSION OF VILLAGES—A MANIAC—THE YAHALON—TUMBALA—A WILD PLACE—A SCENE OF GRANDEUR AND SUBLIMITY—INDIAN CARRIERS—A STEEP MOUNTAIN—SAN PEDRO.

ON the first of May, with much bustle and confusion, we moved out of Don Santiago's house, mounted, and bade him farewell.

I must pass over the next stage of our journey, which was through a region less mountainous, but not less solitary than that we had already traversed. The first afternoon we stopped at the hacienda of Sotaná, belonging to a brother-in-law of Don Santiago, in a soft and lovely valley, with a chapel attached, and bell that at evening called the Indian workmen, women and children to vesper prayers. The next day, at the abode of Padre Solis, a rich old cura, short and broad, living on a fine hacienda, we dined off solid silver dishes, drank out of silver cups, and washed in a silver basin. He had lived at Palenque, talked of Candones or unbaptized Indians, and wanted to buy my macho, promising to keep him till he died; and the only thing that relieves me from self-reproach in not securing him such pasture-grounds is the recollection of the padre's weight.

At four o'clock on the third day we reached Ocosingo, likewise in a beautiful situation, surrounded by mountains, with a large church; and in the wall of the yard we noticed two sculptured figures from the ruins we proposed to visit, somewhat in the same style as those at Copan. In the centre of the square was a magnificent Ceiba tree. We rode up to the house of Don Manuel Pasada, the prefet, which, with an old woman-servant, we had entirely to ourselves, the family being at his hacienda. The house was a long enclosure, with a shed in front, and furnished with bedsteads made of reeds split into two, and supported on sticks resting in the ground.

The alcalde was a Mestitzo, very civil, and glad to see us, and spoke of the neighbouring ruins in the most extravagant terms, but said they were so completely buried in El Monte that it would require a party of men for two or three days to cut a way to them; and he laid great stress upon a cave, the mouth of which was completely choked up with stones, and which communicated by a subterraneous passage with the old city of Palenque, about 150 miles distant. He added that if we would wait a few days to make preparations, he and all the village would go with us, and make a thorough exploration. We told him that first we wished to make preliminary observations, and he promised us a guide for the next morning. That night broke upon us the opening storm of the rainy season. Peals of crashing thunder reverberated from the mountains, lightning illuminated with fearful flashes the darkness of night, rain poured like a deluge upon our thatched roof, and the worst mountains in the whole road were yet to be crossed. All our efforts to anticipate the rainy season had been fruitless.

In the morning dark clouds still obscured the sky, but they fell back and hid themselves before the beams of the rising sun. The grass and trees, parched by six months' drought, started into a deeper green, and the hills and mountains seemed glad. The alcalde, I believe vexed at our not being willing to make an immediate affair of exploring the ruins, had gone away for the day without sending us a guide, and leaving word that all the men were engaged in repairing the church. We endeavoured to entice one of them away, but unsuccessfully. Returning, we found that our piazza was the schoolhouse of the village. Half a dozen children were sitting on a bench, and the schoolmaster, half tipsy, was educating them, *i.e.* teaching them to repeat by rote the formal parts of the church service. We asked him to help us, but he advised us to wait a day or two; in that country nothing could be done *violenter*. We were excessively vexed at the prospect of losing the day; and at the moment when we thought we had nothing left but to submit, a little girl came to tell us that a woman, on whose hacienda the ruins were, was then about going to visit it, and offered to escort us. Her horse was already standing before the door, and before our mules were ready she rode over for us. We paid our respects, gave her a good cigar, and, lighting all around, set out. She was a pleasant Mestitza, and had a son with her, a fine lad about fifteen. We started at half-past nine, and, after a hot and sultry ride, at twenty minutes past eleven reached her rancho. It was a mere hut, made of poles and plastered with mud, but the situation was one of those that warmed us to country life. Our kind guide sent with us her son and an Indian with his machete, and in half an hour we were at the ruins.

Soon after leaving the rancho, and at nearly a mile distant, we saw, on a high elevation, through openings in trees growing around it, one of the buildings of Tonila, the Indian name in this region for stone houses. Approaching it, we passed on the plain in front, two stone figures lying on the ground, with the faces upward; they were well

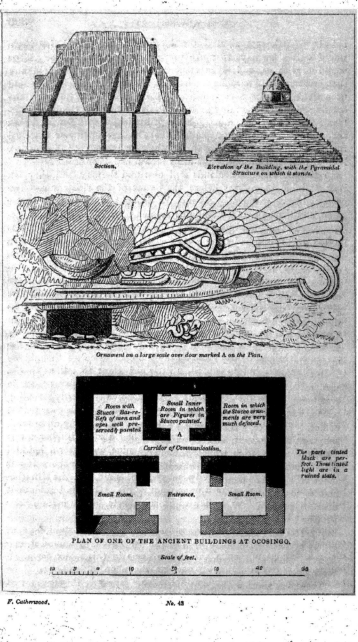

carved, but the characters were somewhat faded by long exposure to the elements, although still distinct. Leaving them we rode on to the foot of a high structure, probably a fortress, rising in a pyramidal form with five spacious terraces. These terraces had all been faced with stone and stuccoed, but in many places they were broken and overgrown with grass and shrubs. Taking advantage of one of the broken parts, we rode up the first pitch, and, following the platform of the terrace, ascended by another breach to the second, and in the same way to the third. There we tied our horses, and climbed up on foot. On the top was a pyramidal structure overgrown with trees, supporting the building which we had seen from the plain below. Among the trees were several wild lemons, loaded with fruit, and of very fine flavour, which, if not brought there by the Spaniards, must be indigenous. The building is 50 feet front and 35 feet deep; it is constructed of stone and lime, and the whole front was once covered with stucco, of which part of the cornice and mouldings still remain. The entrance is by a doorway 10 feet wide, which leads into a sort of antechamber, on each side of which is a small doorway leading into an apartment 10 feet square. The walls of these apartments were once covered with stucco, which had fallen down; part of the roof had given way, and the floor was covered with ruins. In one of them was the same pitchy substance we had noticed in the sepulchre at Copan. The roof was formed of stones, lapping over in the usual style, and forming as near an approach to the arch as was made by the architects of the Old World. (See engraving, No. 43.)

In the back wall of the centre chamber was a doorway of the same size with that in front, which led to an apartment without any partitions, but in the centre was an oblong enclosure 18 feet by 11, which was manifestly intended as the most important part of the edifice. The door was choked up with ruins to within a few feet of the top, but over it, and extending along the whole front of the structure, was a large stucco ornament, which at first impressed us most forcibly by its striking resemblance to the winged globe over the doors of Egyptian temples. Part of this ornament had fallen down, and, striking the heap of rubbish underneath, had rolled beyond the door of entrance. We endeavoured to roll it back and restore it to its place, but it proved too heavy for the strength of four men and a boy. The part which remains is represented in the engraving, and differs in detail from the winged globe. The wings are reversed; there is a fragment of a circular ornament which may have been intended for a globe, but there are no remains of serpents entwining it.

There was another surprising feature in this door. The lintel was *a beam of wood;* of what species we did not know, but our guide said it was of the sapote-tree. It was so hard that, on being struck, it rang like metal, and perfectly sound, without a worm-hole or other symptom of decay. The surface was smooth and even, and from a very close examination we were of the opinion that it must have been trimmed with an instrument of metal.

The opening under this doorway was what the alcalde had intended as the mouth of the cave that led to Palenque, and which, by-the-way, he had told us was so completely buried in El Monte that it would require two days digging and clearing to reach it. Our guide laughed at the ignorance prevailing in the village in regard to the difficulty of reaching it, but stoutly maintained the story that it led to Palenque. We could not prevail on him to enter it. A short cut to Palenque was exactly what we wanted. I took off my coat, and, lying down on my breast, began to crawl under. When I had advanced about half the length of my body, I heard a hideous hissing noise, and starting back, saw a pair of small eyes, which in the darkness shone like balls of fire. The precise portion of time that I employed in backing out is not worth mentioning. My companions had heard the noise, and the guide said it was "un tigre." I thought it was a wild-cat; but, whatever it was, we determined to have a shot at it. We took it for granted that the animal would dash past us, and in a few moments our guns and pistols, swords and machetes, were ready; taking our positions, Pawling, standing close against the wall, thrust under a long pole, and with a horrible noise out fluttered a huge turkey-buzzard, which flapped itself through the building and took refuge in another chamber.

This peril over, I renewed the attempt, and holding a candle before me, quickly discovered the whole extent of the cave that led to Palenque. It was a chamber corresponding with the dimensions given of the outer walls. The floor was encumbered with rubbish two or three feet deep, the walls were covered with stuccoed figures, among which that of a monkey was conspicuous, and against the back wall, among curious and interesting ornaments, were two figures of men in profile, with their faces toward each other, well drawn and as large as life, but the feet concealed by the rubbish on the floor. Mr. Cather-wood crawled in to make a drawing of them, but, on account of the smoke from the candles, the closeness, and excessive heat, it was impossible to remain long enough. In general appearance and character they were the same as we afterward saw carved on stone at Palenque.

By means of a tree growing close against the wall of this building, I climbed to the top, and saw another edifice very near and on the top of a still higher structure. We climbed up to this, and found it of the same general plan, but more dilapidated. Descending, we passed between two other buildings on pyramidal elevations, and came out upon an open space of ground, which had probably once been the site of the city. It was protected on all sides by the same high terraces, overlooking for a great distance the whole country around, and rendering it impossible for an enemy to approach from any quarter without being discovered. Across the space was a high and narrow causeway, which seemed partly natural and partly artificial, and at some distance on which was a mound, with the foundations of a building that had probably been a tower. Beyond this the causeway extended till it joined a range of mountains. From the few Spanish books within my reach I have not been able to learn anything whatever of the history of this place, whether it existed at the time of the conquest or not. I am inclined to think, however, that it did, and that mention is made of it in some Spanish authors. At all events, there was no place we had seen which gave us such an idea of the vastness of the works erected by the aboriginal inhabitants. Pressed as we were, we determined to remain and make a thorough exploration.

It was nearly dark when we returned to the village. Immediately we called upon the alcalde, but found on the very threshold detention and delay. He repeated the schoolmaster's warning that nothing could be done *violentar*. It would take two days to get together men and implements, and these last of the kind necessary could not be had at all. There was not a crowbar in the place; but the alcalde said one could be made, and in the same breath that there was no iron; there was half a blacksmith, but no iron nearer than Tobasco, about eight or ten days' journey. While we were with him another terrible storm came on. We hurried back in the midst of it, and determined forthwith to push on to Palenque. I am strongly of opinion that there is at this place much to reward the future traveller. We were told that there were other ruins about ten leagues distant, along the same range of mountains; and it has additional interest in our eyes, from the circumstance that this would be the best point from which to attempt the discovery of the mysterious city seen from the top of the Cordilleras.

At Ocosingo we were on the line of travel of Captain Dupaix, whose great work on Mexican Antiquities, published in Paris in 1834-5, awakened the attention of the learned in Europe. His expedition to Palenque was made in 1807. He reached this place from the city of Mexico, under a commission from the government, attended by a draughtsman and secretary, and part of a regiment of dragoons.

"Palenque," he says, " is eight days' march from Ocosingo. The journey is very fatiguing. The roads, if they can be so called, are only narrow and difficult paths, which wind across mountains and precipices, and which it is necessary to follow sometimes on mules, sometimes on foot, sometimes on the shoulders of Indians, and sometimes in hammocks. In some places it is necessary to pass on bridges, or, rather, trunks of trees badly secured, and over lands covered with wood, desert and dispeopled, and to sleep in the open air, excepting a very few villages and huts.

" We had with us thirty or forty vigorous Indians to carry our luggage and hammocks. After having experienced in this long and painful journey every kind of fatigue and discomfort, we arrived, thank God, at the village of Palenque."

This was now the journey before us; and, according to the stages we had arranged, to avoid sleeping out at night, it was to be made in five instead of eight days. The terrible rains of the two preceding nights had infected us with a sort of terror, and Pawling was completely shaken in his purpose of continuing with us. The people of the village told him that after the rains had fairly set in, it would be impossible to return, and in the morning, though reluctantly, he determined abruptly to leave us and go back. We were very unwilling to part with him, but, under the circumstances, could not urge him to continue. Our luggage and little traps, which we had used in common, were separated; Mr. Catherwood bade him good-by and rode on; but while mounted, and in the act of shaking hands to pursue our opposite roads, I made him a proposition which induced him again to change his determination, at the risk of remaining on the other side of the mountains until the rainy season was over. In a few minutes we overtook Mr. Catherwood.

The fact is, we had some apprehensions from the badness of the roads. Our route lay through an Indian country, in parts of which the Indians bore a notoriously bad character. We had no dragoons, our party of attendants was very small, and, in reality, we had not a single man upon whom we could rely; under which state of things Pawling's pistols and double-barrelled gun were a matter of some consequence.

We left Ocosingo at a quarter past eight. So little impression did any of our attendants make upon me, that I have entirely forgotten every one of them. Indeed, this was the case throughout the journey. In other countries a Greek muleteer, an Arab boatman, or a Bedouin guide was a companion; here the people had no character, and nothing in which we took any interest except their backs. Each Indian carried, besides his burden, a net bag containing his provisions for the road, viz. a few tortillas, and large balls of mashed Indian corn wrapped in leaves. A drinking cup, being half a calabash, he carried sometimes on the crown of his head. At every stream he filled his cup with water, into which he stirred some of his corn, making a sort of cold porridge; and this throughout the country is the staff of life for the Indian on a journey. In half an hour we passed at some distance on our right large mounds, formerly structures which formed part of the old city. At nine o'clock we crossed the Rio Grande, or Huacachahoul, followed some distance on the bank, and passed three cascades spreading over the rocky bed of the river, unique and peculiar in beauty, and probably many more of the same character were breaking unnoticed and unknown in the wilderness through which it rolled; but, turning up a rugged mountain, we lost sight of it. The road was broken and mountainous. We did not meet a single person, and at three o'clock, moving in a NN.W. direction, we entered the village of Huacachahoul, standing in an open situation, surrounded by mountains, and peopled entirely by Indians, wilder and more savage than any we had yet seen. The men were without hats, but wore their long black hair reaching to their shoulders; and the old men and women, with harsh and haggard features and dark rolling eyes, had a most unbaptized appearance. They gave us no greetings, and their wild but steady glare made us feel a little nervous. A collection of naked boys and girls called Mr. Catherwood " Tata," mistaking him for a padre. We had some misgivings when we put the village behind us, and felt ourselves enclosed in the country of wild Indians. We stopped an hour near a stream, and at half-past six arrived at Chillon, where, to our surprise and pleasure, we found a sub-prefect, a white man, and intelligent, who had travelled to San Salvador, and knew General Morazan. He was very anxious to know whether there was any revolution in Ciudad Real, as, in such case, with a pliancy becoming an office-holder, he wished to give in his adhesion to the new government.

The next morning, at a quarter before seven, we started with a new set of Indians. The road was good to Yahalon, which we reached at ten o'clock. Before entering it we met a young Indian girl with her father, of extraordinary beauty of face, in the costume of the country, but with a modest expression of countenance, which we all particularly remarked as evidence of her innocence and unconsciousness of anything wrong in her appearance. Every village we passed was most picturesque in position, and in this place the church was very effective; as, in the preceding villages, it was undergoing repairs.

Here we were obliged to take another set of Indians, and perhaps we should have lost the day but for the padre, who called off some men working at the church. At a quarter past eleven we set off again; at a quarter before one we stopped at the side of a stream to lunch. At this place a young Indian overtook us, with a very intelligent face, who seated himself beside me, and said, in remarkably good Spanish, that we must beware of the Indians. I gave him some tortillas. He broke off a small piece, and holding it in his fingers, looked at me, and with great emphasis said he had eaten enough; it was of no use to eat; he ate all he could get, and did not grow fat; and thrusting his livid face into mine, told me to see how thin he was. His face was calm, but one accidental expression betrayed him as a maniac; and I now noticed in his face, and all over his body, white spots of leprosy, and started away from him. I endeavoured to persuade him to go back to the village, but he said it made no difference whether he went to the village or not; he wanted a remedio for his thinness.

Soon after we came upon the banks of the river of Yahalon. It was excessively hot, the river as pure as water could be, and we stopped and had a delightful bath. After this we commenced ascending a steep mountain, and when high up saw the poor crazed young Indian standing in the same place on the bank of the river. At half-past five, after a toilsome ascent, we reached the top of the mountain, and rode along the borders of a table-land several thousand feet high, looking down into an immense valley, and turning to the left, around the corner of the forest, entered the outskirts of Tumbala. The huts were distributed among high, rugged, and picturesque rocks, which had the appearance of having once formed the crater of a volcano. Drunken Indians were lying in the path, so that we had to turn out of the way to avoid treading on them. Riding through a narrow passage between these high rocks, we came out upon a corner of the lofty perpendicular table, several thousand feet high, on which stood the village of Tumbala. In front were the church and convent; the square was filled with wild-looking Indians preparing for a fiesta, and on the very corner of the immense table was a high conical peak, crowned with the ruins of a church. Altogether it was the wildest and most extraordinary place we had yet seen, and though not consecrated by associations, for unknown ages it had been the site of an Indian village.

It was one of the circumstances of our journey in this country, that every hour and day produced something new. We never had any idea of the character of the place we were approaching until we entered it, and one surprise followed close upon another. On one corner of the table-land stood the cabildo. The juez was the brother of our silver-dish friend, Padre Solis, as poor and energetic as the padre was rich and inert. At the last village we had been told that it would be impossible to procure Indians for the next day on account of the fiesta, and 'had made up our minds to remain; but my letters from the Mexican authorities were so effective, that immediately the juez held a parley with forty or fifty Indians, and, breaking off occasionally to cuff one of them, our journey was arranged through to Palenque in three days, and the money paid and distributed. Although the wildness of the Indians made us feel a little uncomfortable, we almost regretted this unexpected promptness; but the juez told us we had come at a fortunate moment, for many of the Indians of San Pedro, who were notoriously a bad set, were then in the village, but he could select those he knew, and would send an alguazil of his own with us all the way. As he did not give us any encouragement to remain, and seemed anxious to hurry us on, we made no objections, and in our anxiety to reach the end of our journey, had a superstitious apprehension of the effect of any voluntary delay.

With the little of daylight that remained, he conducted us along the same path trodden by the Indians centuries before, to the top of the cone rising at the corner of the table-land, from which we looked down on one side into an immense ravine several thousand feet in depth, and on the other, over the top of a great mountain range, we saw the village of San Pedro, the end of our next day's journey, and beyond, over the range of the mountains of Palenque, the Lake of Terminos and the Gulf of Mexico. It was one of the grandest, wildest, and most sublime scenes I ever beheld. On the top were ruins of a church and tower, probably once used as a look-out, and near it were thirteen crosses erected over the bodies of Indians, who, a century before, tied the hands and feet of the cura, and threw him down the precipice, and were killed and buried on the spot. Every year new crosses are set up over their bodies, to keep alive in the minds of the Indians the fate of murderers. All around, on almost inaccessible mountain heights, and in the deepest ravines, the Indians have their milpas or corn-patches, living almost as when the Spaniards broke in upon them, and the juez pointed with his finger to a region still occupied by the "unbaptized:" the same strange people whose mysterious origin no man knows, and whose destiny no man can foretell. Among all the wild scenes of our hurried tour, none is more strongly impressed upon my mind than this; but, with the untamed Indians around, Mr. Catherwood was too much excited and too nervous to attempt to make a sketch of it.

At dark we returned to the cabildo, which was decorated with evergreens for the fiesta, and at one end was a table, with a figure of the Virgin fantastically dressed, sitting under an arbour of pine-leaves.

In the evening we visited the padre, the delegate of Padre Solis, a gentlemanly young man from Ciudad Real, who was growing as round, and bade fair to grow as rich out of this village as Padre Solis himself. He and the juez were the only white men in the place. We returned to the cabildo; the Indians came in to bid the juez buenos noches, kissed the back of his hand, and we were left to ourselves.

Before daylight we were roused by an irruption of Indian carriers with lighted torches, who, while we were still in bed, began tying on the covers of our trunks to carry them off. At this place the mechanic arts were lower than in any other we had visited. There was not a rope of any kind in the village; the fastenings of the trunks and the straps to go around the forehead were all of bark strings; and here it was customary for those who intended to cross the mountains to take hammacas or sillas,—the former being a cushioned chair, with a long pole at each end, to be borne by four Indians before and behind, the traveller sitting with his face to the side, and, as the juez told us, only used by very heavy men and padres; and the latter an arm-chair, to be carried on the back of an Indian. We had a repugnance to this mode of conveyance, considering, though unwilling to run any risk, that where an Indian could climb with one of us on his back we could climb alone,—and set out without either silla or hammaca.

Immediately from the village, the road, which was a mere opening through the trees, commenced descending, and very soon we came to a road of palos or sticks, like a staircase, so steep that it was dangerous to ride down them. But for these sticks, in the rainy season the road would be utterly impassable. Descending constantly, at a little after twelve we reached a small stream, where the Indians washed their sweating bodies.

From the banks of this river we commenced ascending the steepest mountain I ever knew. Riding was out of the question; and encumbered with sword and spurs, and leading our mules, which sometimes held back and sometimes sprang upon us, the toil was excessive. Every few minutes we were obliged to stop and lean against a tree or sit down. The Indians did not speak a word of any language but their own. We could hold no communication whatever with them, and could not understand how far it was to the top. At length we saw up a steep pitch before us a rude cross, which we hailed as being the top of the mountain. We climbed up to it, and, after resting a moment, mounted our mules, but, before riding 100 yards, the descent began, and immediately we were obliged to dismount. The descent was steeper than the ascent. In a certain college in our country a chair was transmitted as an heirloom to the laziest man in the senior class. One held it by unanimous consent; but he was seen running down hill, was tried and found guilty, but avoided sentence by the frank avowal that a man pushed him, and he was too lazy to stop himself. So it was with us. It was harder work to resist than to give way. Our mules came tumbling after us; and after a most rapid, hot, and fatiguing descent, we reached a stream covered with leaves and insects. Here two of our Indians left us, to return that night to Tumbala! Our labour was excessive; what must it have been to them! though probably, accustomed to carry loads from their boyhood, they suffered less than we; and the freedom of their naked limbs relieved them from the heat and confinement which we suffered from clothes wet with perspiration. It was the hottest day we had experienced in the country. We had a farther violent descent through woods of almost impenetrable thickness, and at a quarter before four reached San Pedro. Looking back over the range we had just crossed, we saw Tumbala, and the towering point on which we stood the evening before, on a right line, only a few miles distant, but by the road twenty-seven.

If a bad name could kill a place, San Pedro was damned. From the hacienda of Padre Solis to Tumbala, every one we met cautioned us against the Indians of San Pedro. Fortunately, however, nearly the whole village had gone to the fête at Tumbala. There was no alcalde, no alguazils; a few Indians were lying about in a state of utter nudity, and when we looked into the huts the women ran away, probably alarmed at seeing men with pantaloons. The cabildo was occupied by a travelling party, with cargoes of sugar for Tobasco. The leaders of the party and owners of the cargoes were two Mestitzoes, having servants well armed, with whom we formed an acquaintance and tacit alliance. One of the best houses was empty; the proprietor, with his family and household furniture, except reed bedsteads fixed in the ground, had gone to the fiesta. We took possession, and piled our luggage inside.

Without giving us any notice, our men deserted us to return to Tumbala, and we were left alone. We could not speak the language, and could get nothing for the mules or for ourselves to eat; but, through the leader of the sugar party, we learned that a new set of men would be forthcoming in the morning to take us on. With the heat and fatigue I had a violent headache. The mountain for the next day was worse, and, afraid of the effort, and of the danger of breaking down on the road, Mr. C. and Pawling endeavoured to procure a hammaca or silla, which was promised for the morning.

CHAPTER XXXII.

A WILD COUNTRY—ASCENT OF A MOUNTAIN—RIDE IN A SILLA—A PRECARIOUS SITUATION—THE DESCENT—RANCHO OF NOPA—ATTACKS OF MOSQUITOES—APPROACH TO PALENQUE—PASTURE GROUNDS—VILLAGE OF PALENQUE—A CRUSTY OFFICIAL—A COURTEOUS RECEPTION—SCARCITY OF PROVISIONS—SUNDAY—CHOLERA—THE CONVERSION, APOSTASY, AND RECOVERY OF THE INDIANS—RIVER CHACAMAL—THE CARIBS—RUINS OF PALENQUE.

EARLY the next morning the sugar party started, and at five minutes before seven we followed, with silla and men, altogether our party swelled to twenty Indians.

The country through which we were now travelling was as wild as before the Spanish conquest, and without a habitation until we reached Palenque. The road was through a forest so overgrown with brush and underwood as to be impenetrable, and the branches were trimmed barely high enough to admit a man's travelling under them on foot, so that on the backs of our mules we were constantly obliged to bend our bodies, and even to dismount. In some places, for a great distance around, the woods seemed killed by the heat, the foliage withered, the leaves dry and crisp, as if burned by the sun; and a tornado had swept the country, of which no mention was made in the San Pedro papers.

We met three Indians carrying clubs in their hands, naked except a small piece of cotton cloth around the loins and passing between the legs, one of them, young, tall, and of admirable symmetry of form, looking the freeborn gentleman of the woods. Shortly afterwards we passed a stream, where naked Indians were setting rude nets for fish, wild and primitive as in the first ages of savage life.

At twenty minutes past ten we commenced ascending the mountain. It was very hot, and I can give no idea of the toil of ascending these mountains. Our mules could barely clamber up with their saddles only. We disencumbered ourselves of swords, spurs, and all useless trappings; in fact, came down to shirt and pantaloons, and as near the condition of the Indians as we could. First went four Indians, each with a rough oxhide box, secured by an iron chain and large padlock, on his back; then Juan, with only a hat and pair of thin cotton drawers, driving two spare mules, and carrying a double-barrelled gun over his naked shoulders; then ourselves, each one driving before him or leading his own mule; then an Indian carrying the silla, with relief carriers, and several boys bearing small bags of provisions, the Indians of the silla being much surprised at our not using them according to contract and the price paid. Though toiling excessively, we felt a sense of degradation at being carried on a man's shoulders. At that time I was in the worst condition of the three, and the night before had gone to bed at San Pedro without supper, which for any of us was sure evidence of being in a bad way.

We had brought the silla with us merely as a measure of precaution, without much expectation of being obliged to use it: but at a steep pitch, which made my head almost burst to think of climbing, I resorted to it for the first time. It was a large, clumsy arm-chair, put together with wooden pins and bark strings. The Indian who was to carry me, like all the others, was small, not more than five feet six, very thin, but symmetrically formed. A bark strap was tied to the arms of the chair, and, sitting down, he placed his back against the back of the chair, adjusted the length of the strings, and smoothed the bark across his forehead with a little cushion to relieve the pressure. An Indian on each side lifted it up, and the carrier rose on his feet, stood still a moment, threw me up once or twice to adjust me on his shoulders, and set off with one man on each side. It was a great relief, but I could feel every movement, even to the heaving of his chest. The ascent was one of the steepest on the whole road. In a few minutes he stopped and sent forth a sound, usual with Indian carriers, between a whistle and a blast, always painful to my ears, but which I never felt so disagreeably before. My face was turned backward; I could not see where he was going, but observed that the Indian on the left fell back. Not to increase the labour of carrying me, I sat as still as possible; but in a few minutes, looking over my shoulder, saw that we were approaching the edge of a precipice more than a 1,000 feet deep. Here I became very anxious to dismount; but I could not speak intelligibly, and the Indians could or would not understand my signs. My carrier moved along carefully, with his left foot first, feeling that the stone on which he put it down was steady and secure before he brought up the other, and by degrees, after a particularly careful movement, brought both feet up within half a step of the edge of the precipice, stopped, and gave a fearful whistle and blast. I rose and fell with every breath, felt his body trembling under me, and his knees seemed giving way. The precipice was awful, and the slightest irregular movement on my part might bring us both down together. I would have given him a release in full for the rest of the journey to be off his back; but he started again, and with the same care ascended several steps, so close to the edge that even on the back of a mule it would have been very uncomfortable. My fear lest he should break down or stumble was excessive. To my extreme relief, the path turned away; but I had hardly congratulated myself upon my escape before he descended a few steps. This was much worse than ascending; if he fell, nothing could keep me from going over his head; but I remained till he put me down of his own accord. The poor fellow was running down with perspiration, and trembled in every limb. Another stood ready to take me up, but I had had enough. Pawling tried it, but only for a short time. It was bad enough to see an Indian toiling with a dead weight on his back; but to feel him trembling under one's own body, hear his hard breathing, see the sweat rolling down him, and feel the insecurity of the position, made this a mode of travelling which nothing but constitutional laziness and insensibility could endure. Walking, or rather climbing, stopping very often to rest, and riding when it was at all practicable, we reached a thatched shed, where we wished to stop for the night, but there was no water.

We could not understand how far it was to Nopa, our intended stopping-place, which we supposed to be on the top of the mountain. To every question the Indians answered una legua, one league. Thinking it could not be much higher, we continued. For an hour more we had a very steep ascent, and then commenced a terrible descent. At this time the sun had disappeared; dark clouds overhung the woods, and thunder rolled heavily on the top of the mountain. As we descended a heavy wind swept through the forest; the air was filled with dry leaves; branches were snapped and broken, trees bent, and there was every appearance of a violent tornado. To hurry down on foot was out of the question. We were so tired that it was impossible; and, afraid of being caught on the mountain by a hurricane and deluge of rain, we spurred down as fast as we could go. It was a continued descent, without any relief, stony, and very steep. Very often the mules stopped, afraid to go on; and in one place the two spare mules bolted into the thick woods rather than proceed. Fortunately for the reader, this is our last mountain, and I can end honestly with a climax: it was the worst mountain I every encountered in that or any other country, and, under our apprehension of the storm, I will venture to say that no travellers ever descended it in less time. At a quarter before five we reached the plain. The mountain was hidden by clouds, and the storm was now raging above us. We crossed a river, and continuing along it through a thick forest, reached the rancho of Nopa.

It was situated in a circular clearing, about 100 feet in diameter,

44.—RIDING IN A SILLA.

near the river, with the forest around so thick with brush and underwood that the mules could not penetrate it, and with no opening but for the passage of the road through it. The rancho was merely a pitched roof covered with palm-leaves, and supported by four trunks of trees. All around were heaps of snail-shells, and the ground of the rancho was several inches deep with ashes, the remains of fires for cooking them. We had hardly congratulated ourselves upon our arrival at such a beautiful spot, before we suffered such an onslaught of mosquitos as we had not before experienced in the country. We made a fire, and, with appetites sharpened by a hard day's work, sat down on the grass to dispose of a San Pedro fowl; but we were obliged to get up, and, while one hand was occupied with eatables, use the other to brush off the venomous insects. We soon saw that we had bad prospects for the night, lighted fires all around the rancho, and smoked inordinately. We were in no hurry to lie down, and sat till a late hour, consoling ourselves with the reflection that, but for the mosquitos, our satisfaction would be beyond all bounds. The dark border of the clearing was lighted up by fireflies of extraordinary size and brilliancy, darting among the trees, not flashing and disappearing, but carrying a steady light; and, except that their course was serpentine, seeming like shooting stars. In different places there were two that remained stationary, emitting a pale but beautiful light, and seemed like rival belles holding levees. The fiery orbs darted from one to the other; and when one, more daring than the rest, approached too near, the coquette withdrew her light, and the flutterer went off. One, however, carried all before her, and at one time we counted seven hovering around her.

At length we prepared for sleep. Hammocks would leave us exposed on every side to the merciless attacks of the mosquitos, and we spread our mats on the ground. We did not undress. Pawling, with a great deal of trouble, rigged his sheets into a mosquito-net, but it was so hot that he could not breathe under them, and he roamed about or was in the river nearly all night The Indians had occupied themselves in catching snails and cooking them for supper, and then lay down to sleep on the banks of the river; but at midnight, with sharp thunder and lightning, the rain broke in a deluge, and they all came under the shed, and there they lay perfectly naked, mechanically, and without seeming to disturb themselves, slapping their bodies with their hands. The incessant hum and bite of the insects kept us in a constant state of wakefulness and irritation. Our bodies we could protect, but with a covering over the face the heat was insufferable. Before daylight I walked to the river, which was broad and shallow, and stretched myself out on the gravelly bottom, where the water was barely deep enough to run over my body. It was the first comfortable moment I had had. My heated body became cooled, and I lay till daylight. When I rose to dress they came upon me with appetites whetted by a spirit of vengeance. Our day's work had been tremendously hard, but the night's was worse. The morning air, however, was refreshing, and as day dawned our tormentors disappeared. Mr. Catherwood had suffered least, but in his restlessness he had lost from his finger a precious emerald ring, which he had worn for many years, and prized for associations. We remained some time looking for it, and at length mounted and made our last start for Palenque. The road was level, but the woods were still as thick as on the mountain. At a quarter before eleven we reached a path which led to the ruins, or somewhere else. We had abandoned the intention of going directly to the ruins, for, besides that we were in a shattered condition, we could not communicate at all with our Indians, and probably they did not know where the ruins were. At length we came out upon an open plain, and looked back at the range we had crossed, running off to Peten and the country of unbaptized Indians.

As we advanced we came into a region of fine pasture grounds, and saw herds of cattle. The grass showed the effect of early rains, and the picturesque appearance of the country reminded me of many a scene at home; but there was a tree of singular beauty that was a stranger, having a high, naked trunk and spreading top, with leaves of vivid green, covered with yellow flowers. Continuing carelessly, and stopping from time to time to enjoy the smiling view around, and realize our escape from the dark mountains behind, we rose upon a slight table-land and saw the village before us, consisting of one grass-grown street, unbroken even by a mule-path, with a few straggling white houses on each side, on a slight elevation at the further end a thatched church, with a rude cross and belfry before it. A boy could roll on the grass from the church door out of the village. In fact, it was the most dead-and-alive place I ever saw; but, coming from villages thronged with wild Indians, its air of repose was most grateful to us. In the suburbs were scattered Indian huts; and as we rode into the street, eight or ten white people, men and women, came out, more than we had seen since we left Comitan, and the houses had a comfortable and respectable appearance. In one of them lived the alcalde, a white man, about sixty, dressed in white cotton drawers, and shirt outside, respectable in his appearance, with a stoop in his shoulders, but the expression of his face was very doubtful. With what I intended as a most captivating manner, I offered him my passport; but we had disturbed him at his siesta; he had risen wrong side first; and, looking me steadily in the face, he asked me what he had to do with my passport. This I could not answer; and he went on to say that he had nothing to do with it, and did not want to have; we must go to the Prefeto. Then he turned round two or three times in a circle, to show he did not care what we thought of him; and, as if conscious of what was passing in our minds, volunteered to add that complaints had been made against him before, but it was of no use; they couldn't remove him, and if they did he didn't care.

This greeting at the end of our severe journey was rather discouraging, but it was important for us not to have any difficulty with this crusty official; and, endeavouring to hit a vulnerable point, told him that we wished to stop a few days to rest, and should be obliged to purchase many things. We asked him if there was any bread in the village; he answered, "no hay," "there is none;" corn? "no hay;" coffee? "no hay;" chocolate? "no hay." His satisfaction seemed to increase as he was still able to answer "no hay;" but our unfortunate inquiries for bread roused his ire. Innocently, and without intending any offence, we betrayed our disappointment; and Juan, looking out for himself, said that we could not eat tortillas. This he recurred to, repeated several times to himself, and to every new comer said, with peculiar emphasis, they can't eat tortillas. Following it up, he said there was an oven in the place, but no flour, and the baker went away seven years before; the people there could do without bread. To change the subject, and determined not to complain, I threw out the conciliatory remark, that, at all events, we were glad to escape from the rain on the mountains, which he answered by asking if we expected anything better in Palenque, and he repeated with great satisfaction an expression common in the mouths of Palenquians : "tres meses de agua, tres meses de aguaceros y seis meses de nortes," "three months rains, three months heavy showers, and six months north wind," which in that country brings cold and rain.

Finding it impossible to hit a weak point, while the men were piling up the luggage I rode to the prefect, whose reception at that critical moment was most cheering and reviving. With habitual courtesy he offered me a chair and a cigar, and as soon as he saw my passport said he had been expecting me for some time. This surprised me; and he added that Don Patricio had told him I was coming, which surprised me still more, as I did not remember any friend of that name; but soon learned that this imposing cognomen meant my friend Mr. Patrick Walker, of Balize. This was the first notice of Mr. Walker and Captain Caddy I had received since Lieutenant Nicols brought to

Guatimala the report that they had been speared by the Indians. They had reached Palenque by the Balize River and lake of Peten, without any other difficulties than from the badness of the roads, had remained two weeks at the ruins, and left for the Laguna and Yucatan. This was most gratifying intelligence, first, as it assured me of their safety, and second, as I gathered from it that there would be no impediment to our visiting the ruins. The apprehension of being met, at the end of our toilsome journey with a peremptory exclusion had constantly disturbed us more or less, and sometimes weighed upon us like lead.

I returned to make my report, and in regard to the old alcalde, in the language of a ward-meeting manifesto, determined to ask for nothing but what was right, and to submit to nothing that was wrong. In this spirit we made a bold stand for some corn. The alcalde's "no hay" was but too true; the corn-crop had failed, and there was an actual famine in the place. The Indians, with accustomed improvidence, had planted barely enough for the season, and this turning out bad, they were reduced to fruits, plantains, and roots instead of tortillas. Each white family had about enough for its own use, but none to spare. The shortness of the corn-crop made everything else scarce, as they were obliged to kill their fowls and pigs from want of anything to feed them with. The alcalde, who to his other offences added that of being rich, was the only man in the place who had any to spare, and he was holding on for a greater pressure. At Tumbala we had bought good corn at thirty ears for sixpence; here, with great difficulty, we prevailed upon the alcalde to spare us a little at eight ears for sixpence, and these were so musty and worm-eaten that the mules would hardly touch them. At first it surprised us that some enterprising capitalist did not import several dollars' worth from Tumbala; but on going deeper into the matter we found that the cost of transportation would not leave much profit, and, besides, the course of exchange was against Palenque. A few back-loads would overstock the market; for as each white family was provided till the next crop came in, the Indians were the only persons who wished to purchase, and they had no money to buy with. The brunt of the famine fell upon us, and particularly upon our poor mules. Fortunately, however, there was good pasture, and not far off. We slipped the bridles at the door and turned them loose in the streets; but, after making the circuit of the village, they came back in a body, and poked their heads in at the door with an imploring look for corn.

The next day was Sunday, and we hailed it as a day of rest. Heretofore, in all my travels, I had endeavoured to keep it as such; but in this country we had found it impossible. The place was so tranquil, and seemed in such a state of repose, that as the old alcalde passed the door we ventured to wish him a good morning; but again he had got up wrong; and, without answering our greeting, stopped to tell us that our mules were missing, and, as this did not disturb us sufficiently, he added that they were probably stolen; but when he had got us fairly roused and on the point of setting off to look for them, he said there was no danger; they had only gone for water, and would return of themselves.

The village of Palenque, as we learned from the Prefect, was once a place of considerable importance, all the goods imported for Guatimala passing through it; but Balize had diverted that trade and destroyed its commerce, and but a few years before more than half the population had been swept off by the cholera. Whole families had perished, and their houses were desolate and falling to ruins. The church stood at the head of the street, in the centre of a grassy square. On each side of the square were houses with the forest directly upon them; and, being a little elevated in the plaza, we were on a line with the tops of the trees. The largest house on the square was deserted and in ruins. There were a dozen other houses occupied by white families, with whom, in the course of an hour's stroll, I became acquainted. It was but to stop before the door, and I received an invitation. "Pasen adelante, capitan," "Walk in, captain," for which title I was indebted to the eagle on my hat. Each family had its hacienda in the neighbourhood, and in the course of an hour I knew all that was going on in Palenque; i.e. I knew that nothing was going on.

The Prefeto was well versed in the history of Palenque. It is in the province of Tzendales, and for a century after the conquest of Chiapas it remained in possession of the Indians. Two centuries ago, Lorenzo Mugil, an emissary direct from Rome, set up among them the standard of the cross. The Indians still preserve his dress as a sacred relic, but they are jealous of showing it to strangers, and I could not obtain a sight of it. The bell of the church, too, was sent from the holy city. The Indians submitted to the dominion of the Spaniards until the year 1700, when the whole province revolted, and in Chillon, Tumbala, and Palenque they apostatized from Christianity, murdered the priests, profaned the churches, paid impious adoration to an Indian female, massacred the white men, and took the women for their wives. But, as soon as the intelligence reached Guatimala, a strong force was sent against them, the revolted towns were reduced and recovered to the Catholic faith, and tranquillity was restored.

A short distance from Palenque the river Chacamal separates it from the country of the unbaptized Indians, who are here called Caribs. Fifty years ago the Padre Calderon, an uncle of the Prefect's wife, attended by his sacristan, an Indian, was bathing in the river, when the latter cried out in alarm that some Caribs were looking at them, and attempted to fly; but the padre took his cane and went toward them. The Caribs fell down before him, conducted him to their huts, and gave him an invitation to return, and make them a visit on a certain day. On the day appointed the padre went with his sacristan, and found a gathering of Caribs and a great feast prepared for him. He remained with them some time, and invited them in return to the village of Palenque on the day of the fête of St. Domingo. A large party of these wild Indians attended, bringing with them tiger's meat, monkey's meat, and cocoa as presents. They listened to mass, and beheld all the ceremonies of the Church; whereupon they invited the padre to come among them and teach them, and they erected a hut at the place where they had first met him, which he consecrated as a church; and he taught his sacristan to say mass to them every Sunday. As the Prefect said, if he had lived, many of them would probably have been Christianised; but, unfortunately, he died; the Caribs retired into the wilderness, and not one had appeared in the village since.

The ruins lie about eight miles from the village, perfectly desolate. The road was so bad, that, in order to accomplish anything, it was necessary to remain there, and we had to make provision for that purpose. There were three small shops in the village, the stock of all together not worth fifteen pounds; but in one of them we found a pound and a half of coffee, which we immediately secured. Juan communicated the gratifying intelligence that a hog was to be killed the next morning, and that he had engaged a portion of the lard; also, that there was a cow with a calf running loose, and an arrangement might be made for keeping her up and milking her. This was promptly attended to, and all necessary arrangements were made for visiting the ruins the next day. The Indians generally knew the road, but there was only one man in the place who was able to serve as a guide on the ground, and he had on hand the business of killing and distributing the hog, by reason whereof he could not set out with us, but promised to follow.

Towards evening the quiet of the village was disturbed by a crash, and on going out we found that a house had fallen down. A cloud of dust rose from it, and the ruins probably lie as they fell. The cholera had stripped it of tenants, and for several years it had been deserted.

CHAPTER XXXIII.

PREPARATIONS FOR VISITING THE RUINS—A TURN-OUT—DEPARTURE—THE ROAD—RIVERS MICOL AND OTULA—ARRIVAL AT THE RUINS—THE PALACE—A FEU-DE-JOIE—QUARTERS IN THE PALACE—INSCRIPTIONS BY FORMER VISITORS—THE FATE OF BEANHAM—DISCOVERY OF THE RUINS OF PALENQUE—VISIT OF DEL RIO—EXPEDITION OF DUPAIX—DRAWINGS OF THE PRESENT WORK—FIRST DINNER AT THE RUINS—MAMMOTH FIREFLIES—SLEEPING APARTMENTS—EXTENT OF THE RUINS—OBSTACLES TO EXPLORATION—SUFFERING FROM MOSQUITOES.

EARLY the next morning we prepared for our move to the ruins. We had to make provision for housekeeping on a large scale; our culinary utensils were of rude pottery, and our cups the hard shells of some round vegetables, the whole cost, perhaps, amounting to four shillings. We could not procure a water-jar in the place, but the alcalde lent us one free of charge unless it should be broken, and as it was cracked at the time, he probably considered it sold. By the way, we forced ourselves upon the alcalde's affections by leaving our money with him for safe-keeping. We did this with great publicity, in order that it might be known in the village that there was no "plata" at the ruins, but the alcalde regarded it as a mark of special confidence. Indeed, we could not have shown him a greater. He was a suspicious old miser, kept his own money in a trunk in an inner room, and never left the house without locking the street door and carrying the key with him. He made us pay beforehand for everything we wanted, and would not have trusted us half a dollar on any account.

It was necessary to take with us from the village all that could contribute to our comfort, and we tried hard to get a woman; but no one would trust herself alone with us. This was a great privation; a woman was desirable, not, as the reader may suppose, for embellishment, but to make tortillas. These, to be tolerable, must be eaten the moment they are baked; but we were obliged to make an arrangement with the alcalde to send them out daily with the product of our cow.

Our turn-out was equal to anything we had had on the road. One Indian set off with a cowhide trunk on his back, supported by a bark string as the groundwork of his load, while on each side hung by a bark string a fowl wrapped in plantain leaves, the head and tail only being visible. Another had on the top of his trunk a live turkey, with its legs tied and wings expanded, like a spread eagle. Another had on each side of his load strings of eggs, each egg being wrapped carefully in a husk of corn, and all fastened like onions on a bark string.' Cooking utensils and water-jar were mounted on the backs of other Indians, and contained rice, beans, sugar, chocolate, &c.; strings of pork and bunches of plantains were pendent; and Juan carried in his arms our travelling tin coffee-canister filled with lard, which in that country was always in a liquid state.

At half-past-seven we left the village. For a short distance the road was open, but very soon we entered a forest, which continued unbroken to the ruins, and probably many miles beyond. The road was a mere Indian footpath, the branches of the trees beaten down and heavy with the rain, hanging so low that we were obliged to stoop constantly, and very soon our hats and coats were perfectly wet.

From the thickness of the foliage the morning sun could not dry up the deluge of the night before. The ground was very muddy, broken by streams swollen by the early rains, with gulleys in which the mules floundered and stuck fast, in some places very difficult to cross. Amid all the wreck of empires, nothing ever spoke so forcibly the world's mutations as this immense forest shrouding what was anciently a great city. Once it had been a great highway, thronged with people who were stimulated by the same passions that give impulse to human action now; and they are all gone, their habitations buried, and no traces of them left.

In two hours we reached the River Micol, and in half an hour more that of Otula, darkened by the shade of the woods, and breaking beautifully over a stony bed. Fording this, very soon we saw masses of stones, and then a round sculptured stone. We spurred up a sharp ascent of fragments, so steep that the mules could barely climb it, to a terrace so covered, like the whole road, with trees, that it was impossible to make out the form. Continuing on this terrace, we stopped at the foot of a second, when our Indians cried out "El Palacio," "the palace," and through openings in the trees we saw the front of a large building, richly ornamented with stuccoed figures on the pilasters, curious and elegant; trees growing close against it, and their branches entering the doors; in style and effect unique, extraordinary and mournfully beautiful. We tied our mules to the trees, ascended a flight of stone steps forced apart and thrown down by trees, and entered the palace, ranged for a few moments along the corridor and into the courtyard, and after the first gaze of eager curiosity was over, went back to the entrance, and, standing in the doorway, fired a *feu-de-joie* of four rounds each, being the last charge of our firearms. But for this way of giving vent to our satisfaction, we should have made the roof of the old palace ring with a hurrah. It was intended, too, for effect upon the Indians, who had probably never heard such a cannonade before, and almost, like their ancestors in the time of Cortez, regarded our weapons as instruments which spit lightning, and who, we knew, would make such a report in the village as would keep any of their respectable friends from paying us a visit at night.

We had reached the end of our long and toilsome journey, and the first glance indemnified us for our toil. For the first time we were in a building erected by the aboriginal inhabitants, standing before the Europeans knew of the existence of this continent, and we prepared to take up our abode under its roof. We selected the front corridor as our dwelling, turned turkey and fowls loose in the courtyard, which was so overgrown with trees that we could barely see across it; and as there was no pasture for the mules except the leaves of the trees, and we could not turn them loose into the woods, we brought them up the steps through the palace, and turned them into the courtyard also. At one end of the corridor Juan built a kitchen, which operation consisted in laying three stones anglewise, so as to have room for a fire between them. Our luggage was stowed away or hung on poles reaching across the corridor. Pawling mounted a stone about four feet long on stone legs for a table, and with the Indians cut a number of poles, which they fastened together with bark strings, and laid them on stones at the head and foot for beds. We cut down the branches that entered the palace, and some of the trees on the terrace, and from the floor of the palace overlooked the top of an immense forest stretching off to the Gulf of Mexico.

The Indians had superstitious fears about remaining at night among the ruins, and left us alone, the sole tenants of the palace of unknown kings. Little did they who built it think that in a few years their royal line would perish and their race be extinct, their city a ruin, and Mr. Catherwood, Pawling, and I and Juan its sole tenants. Other strangers had been there, wondering like ourselves. Their names were written on the walls, with comments and figures; and even here were marks of those low, grovelling spirits which delight in profaning holy places. Among the names, but not of the latter class, were those of acquaintances: Captain Caddy and Mr. Walker,; and one was that of a countryman, Noah O. Platt, New York. He had gone out to Tobasco as supercargo of a vessel, ascended one of the rivers for logwood, and while his vessel was loading visited the ruins. His account of them had given me a strong desire to visit them long before the opportunity of doing so presented itself.

High up on one side of the corridor was the name of William Beanham, and under it was a stanza written in lead-pencil. By means of a tree with notches cut in it, I climbed up and read the lines. The rhyme was faulty and the spelling bad, but they breathed a deep sense of the moral sublimity pervading these unknown ruins.. The author seemed, too, an acquaintance. I had heard his story in the village. He was a young Irishman, sent by a merchant of Tobasco into the interior for purposes of small traffic; had passed some time at Palenque and in the neighbourhood; and, with his thoughts and feelings turned strongly toward the Indians, after dwelling upon the subject for some time, resolved to penetrate into the country of the Caribs. His friends endeavoured to dissuade him, and the Prefect told him—" You have red hair, a florid complexion, and white skin, and they will either make a god of you, and keep you among them, or else kill and eat you;" but he set off alone and on foot, crossed the river Chacamal, and after an absence of nearly a year returned safe, but naked and emaciated, with his hair and nails long, having been eight days with a single Carib on the banks of a wild river, searching for a crossing-place, and living upon roots and herbs. He built a hut on the borders of the Chacamal River, and lived there with a Carib servant, preparing for another and more protracted journey among them, until at length some boatmen, who came to trade with him, found him lying in his hammock dead, with his skull split open. He had escaped the dangers of a journey which no man in that country dared encounter, to die by the hands of an assassin in a moment of fancied security. His arm was hanging outside, and a book lying on the ground; probably he was struck while reading. The murderers, one of whom was his servant, were caught, and were then in prison in Tobasco. Unfortunately, the people of Palenque had taken but little interest in anything except the extraordinary fact of his visit among the Caribs and his return safe. All his papers and collection of curiosities were scattered and destroyed, and with him died all the fruits of his labours; but, were he still living, he would be the man, of all others, to accomplish the discovery of that mysterious city which had so much affected our imaginations.

As the ruins of Palenque are the first which awakened attention to the existence of ancient and unknown cities in America, and as, on that account, they are perhaps more interesting to the public, it may not be amiss to state the circumstances of their first discovery.

The account is, that in the year 1750, a party of Spaniards travelling in the interior of Mexico penetrated to the lands north of the district of Carmen, in the province of Chiapas, when all at once they found, in the midst of a vast solitude, ancient stone buildings, the remains of a city, still embracing from eighteen to twenty-four miles in extent, known to the Indians by the name of Casas de Piedras. From my knowledge of the country I am at a loss to conjecture why a party of Spaniards were travelling in that forest, or how they could have done so. I am inclined to believe rather that the existence of the ruins was discovered by the Indians, who had clearings in different parts of the forest for their corn-fields, or perhaps was known to them from time immemorial, and on their report the inhabitants were induced to visit them.

The existence of such a city was entirely unknown; there is no mention of it in any book, and no tradition that it had ever been. To this day it is not known by what name it was called, and the only appellation given to it is that of Palenque, after the village near which the ruins stand.

The news of the discovery passed from mouth to mouth, was repeated in some cities of the province, and reached the seat of government; but little attention was paid to it, and the members of the government, through ignorance, apathy, or the actual impossibility of occupying themselves with anything except public affairs, took no measures to explore the ruins, and it was not till 1786, thirty years subsequent to the discovery, that the king of Spain ordered an exploration; on the third of May, 1787, Captain Antonio del Rio arrived at the village, under a commission from the government of Guatimala, and on the 5th he proceeded to the site of the ruined city. In his official report he says, on making his first essay, owing to the thickness of the woods, and a fog so dense that it was impossible for the men to distinguish each other at five paces' distance, the principal building was completely concealed from their view.

He returned to the village, and after concerting measures with the deputy of the district, an order was issued to the inhabitants of Tumbala, requiring 200 Indians with axes and billhooks. On the 17th, seventy-nine arrived, furnished with twenty-eight axes, after which twenty more were obtained in the village; and with these he again moved forward, and immediately commenced felling trees, which was followed by a general conflagration.

The report of Captain Del Rio, with the commentary of Doctor Paul Felix Cabrera, of New Guatimala, deducing an Egyptian origin for the people, through either the supineness or the jealousy of the Spanish government, was locked up in the archives of Guatimala until the time of the revolution, when, by the operation of liberal principles, the original manuscripts came into the hands of an English gentleman long resident in that country, and an English translation was published at London in 1822. This was the first notice in Europe of the discovery of these ruins; and, instead of electrifying the public mind, either from want of interest in the subject, distrust, or some other cause, so little notice was taken of it, that, in 1831, the *Literary Gazette,* a paper of great circulation in London, announced it as a new discovery made by Colonel Galindo, whose unfortunate fate has been before referred to. If a like discovery had been made in Italy, Greece, Egypt, or Asia, within the reach of European travel, it would have created an interest not inferior to the discovery of Herculaneum, or Pompeii, or the ruins of Pæstum.

While the report and drawings of Del Rio slept in the archives of Guatimala, Charles the Fourth of Spain ordered another expedition, at the head of which was placed Captain Dupaix, with a secretary and draughtsman, and a detachment of dragoons. His expeditions were made in 1805, 1806, and 1807, the last of which was to Palenque.

The manuscripts of Dupaix, and the designs of his draughtsman Castenada, were about to be sent to Madrid, which was then occupied by the French army, when the revolution broke out in Mexico; they then became an object of secondary importance, and remained during the wars of independence under the control of Castenada, who deposited them in the Cabinet of Natural History in Mexico. In 1828 M. Baradere disentombed them from the cartons of the museum, where, but for this accident, they might still have remained, and the knowledge of the existence of this city again been lost. The Mexican Congress had passed a law forbidding any stranger not formally authorized to make researches or to remove objects of art from the country; but, in spite of this interdict, M. Baradere obtained authority to make researches in the interior of the republic, with the agreement that after sending to Mexico all that he collected, half should be delivered to him, with permission to transport them to Europe. Afterwards he obtained by exchange the original designs of Castenada; and an authentic copy of the itinerary and descriptions of Captain Dupaix was promised in three months. From divers circumstances, that copy did not reach M. Baradere till long after his return to France, and the work of Dupaix was not published until 1834-5, twenty-eight years after his expedition, when it was brought out in Paris, in four volumes folio, at the price of 800f., with notes and commentaries by M. Alexandre Lenoir, M. Warden, M. Charles Farcy, M. Baradere, and M. De St. Priest.

Lord Kingsborough's ponderous tomes, so far as regards Palenque, are a mere reprint of Dupaix, and the cost of his work is 80*l.* per copy. Colonel Galindo's communications to the Geographical Society of Paris are published in the work of Dupaix, and since him Mr. Waldeck, with funds provided by an association in Mexico, had passed two years among the ruins. His drawings, as he states in a work on another place, were taken away by the Mexican government; but he had retained copies, and before we set out, his work on Palenque was announced in Paris. It, however, has never appeared, and in the meantime Dupaix's is the text-book.

I have two objections to make to this work, not affecting Captain Dupaix, who, as his expedition took place thirty-four years since, is not likely to be affected, if he be even living, but his Paris editors. The first is the very depreciating tone in which mention is made of the work of his predecessor, Del Rio, and, secondly, this paragraph in the introduction:—

"It must be considered that a government only can execute such undertakings. A traveller relying upon his own resources, cannot hope, whatever may be his intrepidity, to penetrate, and, above all, to live in those dangerous solitudes, and, supposing that he succeeds, it is beyond the power of the most learned and skilful man to explore alone the ruins of a vast city, of which he must not only measure and draw the edifices still existing, but also determine the circumference and examine the remains, dig the soil and explore the subterraneous constructions. M. Baradere arrived within fifty leagues of Palenque, burning with the desire of going there; but what could a single man do with domestics or other auxiliaries, without moral force or intelligence, against a people still half savage, against serpents and other hurtful animals, which, according to Dupaix, infest these ruins, and also against the vegetative force of a nature, fertile and powerful, which in a few years re-covers all the monuments and obstructs all the avenues?"

The effect of this is to crush all individual enterprise, and, moreover, it is untrue. All the accounts, founded upon this, represent a visit to these ruins as attended with immense difficulty and danger, to such an extent that we feared to encounter them; but there is no difficulty whatever in going from Europe or the United States to Palenque. Our greatest hardships, even in our long journey through the interior, were from the revolutionary state of the countries and want of time; and as to a residence there, with time to construct a hut or to fit up an apartment in the palace, and to procure stores from the seaboard, those "dangerous solitudes" might be anything rather than unpleasant.

And to show what individuals can accomplish, I state that Mr. Catherwood's drawings include all the objects represented in the work of Dupaix, and others besides which do not appear in that work at all, and have never before been presented to the public; among which is the drawing No. 40, and the large tablets of hieroglyphics, the most curious and interesting pieces of sculpture at Palenque. I add, with the full knowledge that I shall be contradicted by future travellers if I am wrong, that the whole of Mr. C.'s are more correct in proportions, outline, and filling up than his, and furnish more true material for speculation and study. I would not have said thus much but from a wish to give confidence to the reader who may be disposed to investigate and study these interesting remains. As to most of the places visited by us, he will find no materials whatever except those furnished in these pages. In regard to Palenque, he will find a splendid work, the materials of which were procured under the sanction of a commission from government, and brought out with explanations and commentaries by the learned men of Paris, by the side of which this octavo shrinks into insignificance; but I uphold the drawings against these costly folios, and against every other book that has ever been published on the subject of these ruins. The object has been, not to produce an illustrated work, but to present the drawings in such an inexpensive form as to place them within reach of the great mass of the reading community.

But to return to ourselves in the palace. While we were making our observations, Juan was engaged in a business that his soul loved. As with all the mozos of that country, it was his pride and ambition to servir a mano. He scorned the manly occupation of a muleteer, and aspired to that of a menial servant. He was anxious to be left at the village, and did not like the idea of stopping at the ruins, but was reconciled to it by being allowed to devote himself exclusively to cookery. At four o'clock, with a bright sunshine, we sat down to our first dinner. The tablecloth was two broad leaves, each about two feet long, plucked from a tree on the terrace before the door. Our salt-cellar stood like a pyramid, being a case made of husks of corn put together lengthwise, and holding four or five pounds, in lumps from the size of a pea to that of a hen's egg. Juan was as happy as if he had prepared the dinner exclusively for his own eating; and all went merry as a marriage-bell, when suddenly the sky became overcast, and a sharp thunder-clap heralded the afternoon's storm. From the elevation of the terrace, the floor of the palace commanded a view of the top of the forest, and we could see the trees bent down by the force of the wind; very soon a fierce blast swept through the open doors, which was followed instantaneously by heavy rain. The table was cleared by the wind, and, before we could make our escape, was drenched by the rain. We snatched away our plates, and finished our meal as we could.

The rain continued, with heavy thunder and lightning, all the afternoon. In the absolute necessity of taking up our abode among the ruins, we had hardly thought of our exposure to the elements until it was forced upon us. At night we could not light a candle, but the darkness of the palace was lighted up by fireflies of extraordinary size and brilliancy, shooting through the corridors and stationary on the walls, forming a beautiful and striking spectacle. They were of the description with those we saw at Nopa, known by the name of shining beetles, and are mentioned by the early Spaniards, among the wonders of a world where all was new, " as showing the way to those who travel at night." The historian describes them as " somewhat smaller than Sparrows, having two stars close by their Eyes, and two more under their Wings, which gave so great a Light that by it they could spin, weave, write, and paint; and the Spaniards went by night to hunt the Utios or little Rabbits of that country; and a-fishing, carrying these animals tied to their great Toes or Thumbs: and they called them Locuyos, being also of use to save them from the Gnats, which are there very troublesome. They took them in the Night with Firebrands, because they made to the Light, and came when called by their Name; and they are so unwieldy that when they fall they cannot rise again; and the Men stroaking their Faces and Hands with sort of Moisture that is in those Stars, seemed to be afire as long as it lasted."

It always gave us high pleasure to realize the romantic and seemingly half-fabulous accounts of the chroniclers of the conquest. Very often we found their quaint descriptions so vivid and faithful as to infuse the spirit that breathed through their pages. We caught several of these beetles, not, however, by calling them by their names, but with a hat, as school-boys used to catch fireflies. They are more than half an inch long, and have a sharp movable horn on the head; when laid on the back they cannot turn over except by pressing this horn against a membrane upon the front. Behind the eyes are two round transparent substances, full of luminous matter, about as large as the head of a pin, and underneath is a larger membrane containing the same luminous substance. Four of them together threw a brilliant light for several yards around, and by the light of a single one we read distinctly the finely-printed pages of an American newspaper. It was one of a packet, full of debates in Congress, which I had as yet barely glanced over, and it seemed stranger than any incident of our journey to be reading by the light of beetles, in the ruined palace of Palenque, the sayings and doings of great men at home. These things brought up vivid recollections of home, and among the familiar images present were the good beds into which our friends were about that time turning. Ours were set up in the back corridor, fronting the courtyard. This corridor consisted of open doors and pilasters alternately. The wind and rain were sweeping through, and, unfortunately, our beds were not out of reach of the spray. They had been set up with some labour on four piles of stones each, and we could not then change their position. We had no spare articles to put up as screens; but, happily, two umbrellas, tied up with measuring rods and wrapped in a piece of matting, had survived the wreck of the mountain-roads. These Mr. C. and I secured at the head of our beds. Pawling swung a hammock across the corridor so high that the sweep of the rain only touched the foot; and so passed our first night at Palenque. In the morning, umbrellas, bed-clothes, wearing apparel, and hammocks were wet through, and there was not a dry place to stand on. Already we considered ourselves booked for a rheumatism. We had looked to our residence at Palenque as the end of troubles, and for comfort and pleasure, but all we could do was to change the position of our beds to places which promised a better shelter for the next night.

A good breakfast would have done much to restore our equanimity; but, unhappily, we found that the tortillas which we had brought out the day before, probably made of half-mouldy corn, by the excessive dampness were matted together, sour, and spoiled. We went through our beans, eggs, and chocolate without any substitute for bread, and, as often before in time of trouble, composed ourselves with a cigar. Blessed be the man who invented smoking, the soother and composer of a troubled spirit, allayer of angry passions, a comfort under the loss of breakfast, and to the roamer in desolate places, the solitary wayfarer through life, serving for "wife, children, and friends."

At about ten o'clock the Indians arrived with fresh tortillas and milk. Our guide, too, having finished cutting up and distributing the hog, was with them. He was the same who had been employed by Mr. Waldeck, and also by Mr. Walker and Captain Caddy, and was recommended by the Prefect as the only man acquainted with the ruins. Under his escort we set out for a preliminary survey. Of ourselves, leaving the palace, in any direction, we should not have known which way to direct our steps.

In regard to the extent of these ruins. Even in this practical age the imagination of man delights in wonders. The Indians and the people of Palenque say that they cover a space of sixty miles; in a series of well-written articles in our own country they have been set down as ten times larger than New York; and lately I have seen an article in some of the newspapers, referring to our expedition, which represents this city, *discovered* by us, as having been three times as large as London! It is not in my nature to discredit any marvellous story. I am slow to disbelieve, and would rather sustain all such inventions; but it has been my unhappy lot to find marvels fade away as I approached them: even the Dead Sea lost its mysterious charm; and besides, as a traveller and "writer of a book," I know that if I go wrong, those who come after me will not fail to set me right. Under these considerations, not from any wish of my own, and with many thanks to my friends of the press, I am obliged to say that the Indians and people of Palenque really know nothing of the ruins personally, and the other accounts do not rest upon any sufficient foundation. The whole country for miles around is covered by a dense forest of gigantic trees, with a growth of brush and underwood unknown in the wooded deserts of our own country, and impenetrable in any direction except by cutting a way with a machete. What lies buried in that forest it is impossible to say of my own knowledge; without a guide, we might have gone within 100 feet of all the buildings without discovering one of them.

Captain Del Rio, the first explorer, with men and means at command, states in his report, that in the execution of his commission he cut down and burned all the woods; he does not say how far, but, judging from the breaches and excavations made in the interior of the buildings, probably for miles around. Captain Dupaix, acting under a royal commission, and with all the resources such a commission would give, did not discover any more buildings than those mentioned by Del Rio, and we saw only the same; but, having the benefit of them as guides, at least of Del Rio (for at that time we had not seen Dupaix's work), we of course saw things which escaped their observation, just as those who come after us will see what escaped ours. This place, however, was the principal object of our expedition, and it was our wish and intention to make a thorough exploration. Respect for my official character, the special tenour of my passport, and letters from Mexican authorities, gave me every facility. The Prefect assumed that I was sent by my government expressly to explore the ruins; and every person in Palenque except our friend the alcalde, and even he, as much as the perversity of his disposition would permit, was disposed to assist us. But there were accidental difficulties which were insuperable. First, it was the rainy season. This, under any circumstances, would have made it difficult; but as the rains did not commence till three or four o'clock, and the weather was always clear in the morning, it alone would not have been sufficient to prevent our attempting it; but there were other difficulties, which embarrassed us from the beginning, and continued during our whole residence among the ruins. There was not an axe or spade in the place, and, as usual, the only instrument was the machete, which here was like a short and widebladed sword; and the difficulty of procuring Indians to work was greater than at any other place we had visited. It was the season of planting corn, and the Indians, under the immediate pressure of famine, were all busy with their milpas. The price of an Indian's labour was ninepence per day; but the alcalde, who had the direction of this branch of the business, would not let me advance to more than one shilling, and the most he would engage to send was from four to six a day. They would not sleep at the ruins, came late, and went away early; sometimes only two or three appeared, and the same men rarely came twice, so that during our stay we had all the Indians of the village in rotation. This increased very much our labour, as it made it necessary to stand over them constantly to direct their work; and just as one set began to understand precisely what we wanted, we were obliged to teach the same to others; and I may remark that their labour, though nominally cheap, was dear in reference to the work done.

But to return: Under the escort of our guide we had a fatiguing but most interesting day. What we saw does not need any exaggeration. It awakened admiration and astonishment. In the afternoon came on the regular storm. We had distributed our beds, however, along the corridors, under cover of the outer wall, and were better protected, but suffered terribly from mosquitoes, the noise and stings of which drove away sleep. In the middle of the night I took up my mat to escape from these murderers of rest. The rain had ceased, and the moon, breaking through the heavy clouds, with a misty face lighted up the ruined corridor. I climbed over a mound of stones at one end, where the wall had fallen, and, stumbling along outside the palace, entered a lateral building near the foot of the tower, groped in the dark along a low damp passage, and spread my mat before a low doorway at the extreme end. Bats were flying and whizzing through the passage, noisy and sinister; but the ugly creatures drove away mosquitoes. The dampness of the passage was cooling and refreshing; and, with some twinging apprehensions of the snakes and reptiles, lizards and scorpions, which infest the ruins, I fell asleep.

PALACE AT PALENQUE.

CHAPTER XXXIV.

PRECAUTIONS AGAINST THE ATTACKS OF MOSQUITOES—MODE OF LIFE AT PALENQUE—DESCRIPTION OF THE PALACE—PIERS—HIEROGLYPHICS—FIGURES—DOORWAYS—CORRIDORS—COURTYARDS—A WOODEN RELIC—STONE STEPS—TOWERS—TABLETS—STUCCO ORNAMENTS, ETC ETC.—THE ROYAL CHAPEL—EXPLORATIONS—AN ALARM—INSECTS—EFFECT OF INSECT STINGS—RETURN TO THE VILLAGE OF PALENQUE.

At daylight I returned, and found Mr. C. and Pawling sitting on the stones, half dressed, in rueful conclave. They had passed the night worse than I, and our condition and prospects were dismal. Rains, hard work, bad fare, seemed nothing; but we could no more exist without sleep than the "foolish fellow" of Æsop, who, at the moment when he had learned to live without eating, died. In all his travels through the country Pawling had never encountered such hard work as since he met us.

The next night the mosquitoes were beyond all endurance; the slightest part of the body, the tip end of a finger, exposed, was bitten. With the heads covered the heat was suffocating, and in the morning our faces were all in blotches. Without some remedy we were undone. It is on occasions like this that the creative power of genius displays itself. Our beds, it will be remembered, were made of sticks lying side by side, and set on four piles of stones for legs. Over these we laid our pellons and *armas de agua*, or leathern armour against rain, and over these our straw matting. This prevented our enemies invading us from between the sticks. Our sheets were already sewed up into sacks. We ripped one side, cut sticks, and bent them in three bows about two feet high over the frame of the beds. Over these the sheets were stretched, and, sewed down all around, with a small space open at the head, had much the appearance of biers. At night, after a hard day's work, we crawled in. Hosts were waiting for us inside. We secured the open places, when each, with the stump of a lighted candle, hunted and slew, and with a lordly feeling of defiance we lay down to sleep. We had but one pair of sheets apiece, and this was a new way of sleeping under them; but, besides the victory it afforded us over the mosquitoes, it had another advantage; the heat was so great that we could not sleep with our clothes on; it was impossible to place the beds entirely out of the reach of the spray, and the covering, held up a foot or two above us and kept damp, cooled the heated atmosphere within.

In this way we lived: the Indians came out in the morning with provisions, and as the tortillas were made in the alcalde's own kitchen, not to disturb his household arrangements, they seldom arrived till after breakfast.

In the meantime work went on. As at Copan, it was my business to prepare the different objects for Mr. Catherwood to draw. Many of the stones had to be scrubbed and cleaned; and as it was our object to have the utmost possible accuracy in the drawings, in many places scaffolds were to be erected on which to set up the camera lucida. Pawling relieved me from a great part of this labour. That the reader may know the character of the objects we had to interest us, I proceed to give a description of the building in which we lived, called the palace.

A front view of this building is given in the engraving, No. 45. It does not, however, purport to be given with the same accuracy as the other drawings, the front being in a more ruined condition. It stands on an artificial elevation of an oblong form, 40 feet high, 310 feet in front and rear, and 260 feet on each side. This elevation was formerly faced with stone, which has been thrown down by the growth of trees, and its form is hardly distinguishable.

The building stands with its face to the east, and measures 228 feet front by 180 feet deep. Its height is not more than 25 feet, and all around it had a broad projecting cornice of stone. The front contained 14 doorways, about 9 feet wide each, and the intervening piers are between 6 and 7 feet wide. On the left (in approaching the palace) 8 of the piers have fallen down, as has also the corner on the right, and the terrace underneath is cumbered with the ruins. But 6 piers remain entire, and the rest of the front is open.

The engraving, No. 46, represents the ground-plan of the whole. The black lines represent walls still standing; the faint lines indicate remains only, but, in general, so clearly marked that there was no difficulty in connecting them together.

The building was constructed of stone, with a mortar of lime and sand, and the whole front was covered with stucco and painted. The piers were ornamented with spirited figures in bas-relief, one of which is represented in the engraving No. 47. On the top are three hieroglyphics sunk in the stucco. It is enclosed by a richly ornamented border, about 10 feet high and 6 wide, of which only a part now remains. The principal personage stands in an upright position and in profile, exhibiting an extraordinary facial angle of about 45 degrees. The upper part of the head seems to have been compressed and lengthened, perhaps by the same process employed upon the heads of the Chocktaw and Flathead Indians of our own country. The head repre-

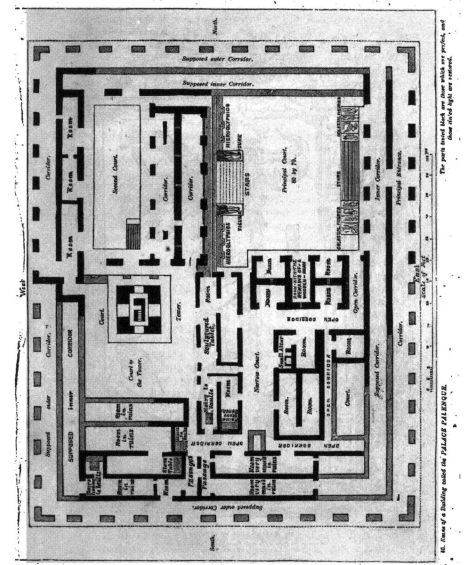

F. Catherwood.

47. BAS-RELIEF IN STUCCO
On one of the Piers of the East Front of the Palace at Palenque.

sents a species of which few are seen in this part of the country at the present time. The head-dress is evidently a plume of feathers. Over the shoulders is a short covering decorated with studs, and a breastplate; part of the ornament of the girdle is broken; the tunic is probably a leopard's skin; and the whole dress no doubt exhibits the costume of this unknown people. He holds in his hand a staff or sceptre, and opposite his hands are the marks of three hieroglyphics, which have decayed or been broken off. At his feet are two naked figures seated cross-legged, and apparently suppliants. A fertile imagination might find many explanations for these strange figures, but no satisfactory interpretation presents itself to my mind. The hieroglyphics doubtless tell its history. The stucco is of admirable consistency, and hard as stone. It was painted, and in different places about it we discovered the remains of red, blue, yellow, black, and white.

The piers which are still standing contained other figures of the same general character, but which, unfortunately, are more mutilated, and from the declivity of the terrace it was difficult to set up the camera lucida in such a position as to draw them. The piers which are fallen were no doubt enriched with the same ornaments. Each one had some specific meaning, and the whole probably presented some allegory or history; and when entire and painted, the effect in ascending the terrace must have been imposing and beautiful.

The principal doorway is not distinguished by its size or by any superior ornament, but is only indicated by a range of broad stone steps leading up to it on the terrace. The doorways have no doors, nor are there the remains of any. Within, on each side, are three niches in the wall, about eight or ten inches square, with a cylindrical stone about two inches in diameter fixed upright, by which, perhaps, a door was secured. Along the cornice outside, projecting about a foot beyond the front, holes were drilled at intervals through the stone; and our impression was, that an immense cotton cloth, running the whole length of the building, perhaps painted in a style corresponding with the ornaments, was attached to this cornice, and raised and lowered like a curtain, according to the exigencies of sun and rain. Such a curtain is used now in front of the piazzas of some haciendas in Yucatan.

The tops of the doorways were all broken. They had evidently been square, and over every one were large niches in the wall on each side, in which the lintels had been laid. These lintels had all fallen, and the stones above formed broken natural arches. Underneath were heaps of rubbish, but there were no remains of lintels. If they had been single slabs of stone, some of them must have been visible and

48. FRONT CORRIDOR OF PALACE.

prominent; and we made up our minds that these lintels were of *wood*. We had no authority for this. It is not suggested either by Del Rio or Captain Dupaix, and perhaps we should not have ventured the conclusion but for the wooden lintel which we had seen over the doorway at Ocosingo; and by what we saw afterward in Yucatan, we were confirmed, beyond all doubt, in our opinion. I do not conceive, however, that this gives any conclusive data in regard to the age of the buildings. The wood, if such as we saw in the other places, would be very lasting; its decay must have been extremely slow, and centuries may have elapsed since it perished altogether.

The building has two parallel corridors running lengthwise on all four of its sides. In front these corridors are about nine feet wide, (Plate 48,) and extend the whole length of the building upward of 200 feet. In the long wall that divides them there is but one door, which is opposite the principal door of entrance, and has a corresponding one on the other side, leading to a courtyard in the rear. The floors are of cement, as hard as the best seen in the remains of Roman baths and cisterns. The walls are about ten feet high, plastered, and on each side of the principal entrance ornamented with medallions, of which the borders only remain; these, perhaps, contained the busts of the royal family. The separating-wall had apertures of about a foot, probably intended for purposes of ventilation. Some were of this form ✢, and some of this ⊤, which have been called the Greek Cross and the Egyptian Tau, and made the subject of much learned speculation.

The ceiling of each corridor was in this form ⊓. The builders were evidently ignorant of the principles of the arch, and the support was made by stones lapping over as they rose, as at Ocosingo, and among the Cyclopean remains in Greece and Italy. Along the top was a layer of flat stone, and the sides, being plastered, presented a flat surface. The long unbroken corridors in front of the palace were probably intended for lords and gentlemen in waiting; or, perhaps, in that beautiful position, which, before the forest grew up, must have commanded an extended view of a cultivated and inhabited plain, the king himself sat in it to receive the reports of his officers, and to administer justice. Under our dominion Juan occupied the front corridor as a kitchen, and the other was our sleeping apartment.

From the centre door of this corridor a range of stone steps, thirty feet long, leads to a rectangular courtyard, eighty feet long by seventy broad. On each side of the steps are grim and gigantic figures, carved on stone in basso-relievo, nine or ten feet high, and in a position slightly inclined backward from the end of the steps to the floor of the corridor. The engraving, No. 49, represents this side of the courtyard, and the one next following; No. 50, shows the figures alone, on a larger scale. They are adorned with rich head-dresses and necklaces, but their attitude is that of pain and trouble. The design and anatomical proportions of the figures are faulty, but there is a force of expression about them which shows the skill and conceptive power of the artist. When we first took possession of the palace this courtyard was encumbered with trees, so that we could hardly see across it, and it was so filled up with rubbish that we were obliged to make excavations of several feet before these figures could be drawn.

On each side of the courtyard the palace was divided into apartments, probably for sleeping. On the right the piers have all fallen down. On the left they are still standing, and ornamented with stucco figures. In the centre apartment, in one of the holes before referred to of the arch, are the remains of a wooden pole about a foot long, which once stretched across, but the rest had decayed. It was the only piece of wood we found at Palenque, and we did not discover this until some time after we had made up our minds in regard to the wooden lintels over the doors. It was much worm-eaten, and probably, in a few years, not a vestige of it will be left.

At the farther side of the courtyard was another flight of stone steps, corresponding with those in front, on each side of which are carved figures, and on the flat surface between are single cartouches of hieroglyphics. The plate, No. 51, represents this side.

The whole courtyard was overgrown with trees, and it was encumbered with ruins several feet high, so that the exact architectural arrangements could not be seen. Having our beds in the corridor adjoining, when we awoke in the morning, and when we had finished the work of the day, we had it under our eyes. Every time we descended the steps, the grim and mysterious figures stared us in the face, and it became to us one of the most interesting parts of the ruins. We were exceedingly anxious to make excavations, clear out the mass of rubbish, and lay the whole platform bare; but this was impossible. It is probably paved with stone or cement; and from the profusion of ornament in other parts, there is reason to believe that many curious and interesting specimens may be brought to light. This agreeable work is left for the future traveller, who may go there better provided with men and materials, and with more knowledge of what he has to encounter; and, in my opinion, if he finds nothing new, the mere spectacle of the courtyard entire will repay him for the labour and expense of clearing it.

The part of the building which forms the rear of the courtyard, communicating with it by the steps, consists of two corridors, the same

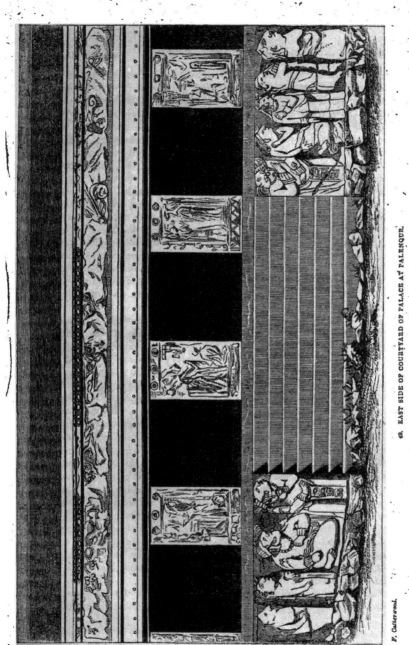

49. EAST SIDE OF COURTYARD OF PALACE AT PALENQUE.

F. Catherwood.

60. COLOSSAL BAS-RELIEFS IN STONE
On the East Side of principal Court of the Palace at Palenque.

61. EAST SIDE OF COURTYARD OF PALACE AT PALENQUE.

as the front, paved, plastered, and ornamented with stucco. The floor of the corridor fronting the courtyard sounded hollow, and a breach had been made in it which seemed to lead into a subterraneous chamber; but in descending, by means of a tree with notches cut in it, and with a candle, we found merely a hollow in the earth, not bounded by any wall.

In the farther corridor the wall was in some places broken, and had several separate coats of plaster and paint. In one place we counted six layers, each of which had the remains of colours. In another place there seemed a line of written characters in black ink. We made an effort to get at them; but, in endeavouring to remove a thin upper stratum, they came off with it, and we desisted.

This corridor opened upon a second courtyard, eighty feet long and but thirty across. The floor of the corridor was ten feet above that of the courtyard, and on the wall underneath were square stones with hieroglyphics sculptured upon them. On the piers were stuccoed figures, but in a ruined condition.

On the other side of the courtyard were two ranges of corridors, which terminated the building in this direction. The first of them is divided into three apartments, with doors opening from the extremities upon the western corridor. All the piers are standing except that on the north-west corner. All are covered with stucco ornaments, and one with hieroglyphics. The rest contain figures in bas-relief, three of which, being those least ruined, are represented in the opposite plates.

The first, No. 52, was enclosed by a border, very wide at the bottom, part of which is destroyed. The subject consists of two figures with facial angles similar to that in the plate before given, plumes of feathers and other decorations for head-dresses, necklaces, girdles, and sandles; each has hold of the same curious baton, part of which is destroyed, and opposite their hands are hieroglyphics, which probably give the history of these incomprehensible personages. The others are more ruined, and no attempt has been made to restore them. One, No. 53, is seated as if to receive an honour, and the other, No. 54, kneeling as if to receive a blow.

So far the arrangements of the palace are simple and easily understood; but on the left are several distinct and independent buildings, as will be seen by the plan, the particulars of which, however, I do not consider it necessary to describe. The principal of these is the tower, on the south side of the second court. This tower is conspicuous by its height and proportions, but on examination in detail it is found unsatisfactory and uninteresting. The base is thirty feet square, and

F. Catherwood.

52. BAS-RELIEF IN STUCCO
On one of the Piers of the West Front of the Palace at Palenque.

F. Catherwood.

53. BAS-RELIEF IN STUCCO
On the West Side of the Palace at Palenque.

F. Catherwood.

54. BAS-RELIEF IN STUCCO
On the West Side of the Palace at Palenque.

it has three stories. Entering over a heap of rubbish at the base, we found within another tower, distinct from the outer one, and a stone staircase, so narrow that a large man could not ascend it. The staircase terminates against a dead stone ceiling, closing all farther passage, the last step being only six or eight inches from it. For what purpose a staircase was carried up to such a bootless termination we could not conjecture. The whole tower was a substantial stone structure, and in its arrangements and purposes about as incomprehensible as the sculptured tablets.

East of the tower is another building with two corridors, one richly decorated with pictures in stucco, and having in the centre the elliptical tablet represented in the engraving opposite. It is four feet long and three wide, of hard stone set in the wall, and the sculpture is in bas-relief. Around it are the remains of a rich stucco border. The principal figure sits cross-legged on a couch ornamented with two leopards' heads; the attitude is easy, the physiognomy the same as that of the other personages, and the expression calm and benevolent. The figure wears around its neck a necklace of pearls, to which is suspended a small medallion containing a face; perhaps intended as an image of the sun. Like every other subject of sculpture we had seen in the country, the personage had earrings, bracelets on the wrists, and a girdle round the loins. The head-dress differs from most of the others at Palenque, in that it wants the plumes of feathers. Near the head are three hieroglyphics.

The other figure, which seems that of a woman, is sitting cross-legged on the ground, richly dressed, and apparently in the act of making an offering. In this supposed offering is seen a plume of feathers, in which the head-dress of the principal person is deficient. Over the head of the sitting personage are four hieroglyphics. This is the only piece of sculptured stone about the palace except those in the courtyard. Under it formerly stood a table, of which the impression against the wall is still visible, and which is given in the engraving in faint lines, after the model of other tables still existing in other places.

At the extremity of this corridor there is an aperture in the pavement, leading by a flight of steps to a platform; from this a door, with an ornament in stucco over it, opens by another flight of steps upon a narrow dark passage, terminating in other corridors, which run transversely. These are called subterraneous apartments; but there are windows opening from them above the ground, and, in fact, they are merely a ground-floor below the pavement of the corridors. In most parts, however, they are so dark that it is necessary to visit them with

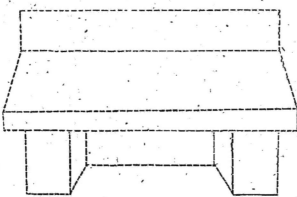

F. Catherwood.

55: OVAL BAS-RELIEF IN STONE,

In the Wall of one of the Apartments of the Palace at Palenque.

F F

candles. There are no bas-reliefs or stucco ornaments; and the only objects which our guide pointed out or which attracted our attention, were several stone tables, one crossing and blocking up the corridor, about eight feet long, four wide and three high. One of these lower corridors had a door opening upon the back part of the terrace, and we generally passed through it with a candle to get to the other buildings. In two other places there were flights of steps leading to corridors above. Probably these were sleeping apartments.

In that part of the plan marked Room No. 1, the walls were more richly decorated with stucco ornaments than any other in the palace; but, unfortunately, they were much mutilated. On each side of the doorway was a stucco figure, one of which, being the most perfect, is given in the engraving, No. 56. Near it is an apartment in which is marked "small altar." It was richly ornamented, like those which will be hereafter referred to in other buildings; and from the appearance of the back wall we supposed there had been stone tablets. In our utter ignorance of the habits of the people who had formerly occupied this building, it was impossible to form any conjecture for what uses these different apartments were intended; but if we are right in calling it a palace, the name which the Indians give it, it seems probable that the part surrounding the courtyards was for public and state occasions, and that the rest was occupied as the place of residence of the royal family; this room with the small altar, we may suppose, was what would be called, in our own times, a royal chapel.

With these helps and the aid of the plan, the reader will be able to find his way through the ruined palace of Palenque; he will form some idea of the profusion of its ornaments, of their unique and striking character, and of their mournful effect, shrouded by trees; and perhaps with him, as with us, fancy will present it as it was before the hand of ruin had swept over it, perfect in its amplitude and rich decorations, and occupied by the strange people whose portraits and figures now adorn its walls.

The reader will not be surprised that, with such objects to engage our attention, we disregarded some of the discomforts of our princely residence. We expected at this place to live upon game, but were disappointed. A wild turkey we could shoot at any time from the door of the palace; but, after trying one, we did not venture to trifle with our teeth upon another; and besides these, there was nothing but parrots, monkeys and lizards, all very good eating, but which we kept in reserve for a time of pressing necessity. The density of the forest and the heavy rains would, however, have made sporting impracticable.

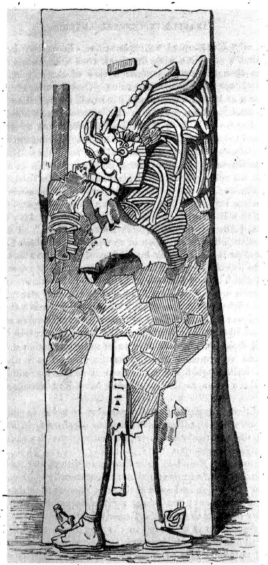

56. BAS-RELIEF IN STUCCO
On the side of a Doorway at the Palace of Palenque.

Once only I attempted an exploration. From the door of the palace, almost on a line with the front, rose a high steep mountain, which we thought must command a view of the city in its whole extent, and perhaps itself contain ruins. (See Frontispiece.) I took the bearing, and, with a compass in my hand and an Indian before me with his machete, from the rear of the last-mentioned building cut a straight line up E. N. E. to the top. The ascent was so steep that I was obliged to haul myself up by the branches. On the top was a high mound of stones, with a foundation-wall still remaining. Back toward the mountain was nothing but forest; in front, through an opening in the trees, we saw a great wooded plain extending to Tobasco and the Gulf of Mexico, and the Indian at the foot of the tree, peering through the branches, turned his face up to me with a beaming expression, and pointing to a little spot on the plain, which was to him the world, cried out, "Alli esta el pueblo," "there is the village." This was the only occasion (with the exception of an aqueduct) on which I attempted to explore, for it was the only time I had any mark to aim at.

Besides the claps of thunder and flashes of lightning, we had one alarm at night. It was from a noise that sounded like the cracking of a dry branch under a stealthy tread, which, as we all started up together, I thought was that of a wild beast, but which Mr. Catherwood, whose bed was nearer, imagined to be that of a man. We climbed up the mound of fallen stones at the end of this corridor, but beyond all was thick darkness. Pawling fired twice as an intimation that we were awake, and we arranged poles across the corridor as a trap, so that even an Indian could not enter from that quarter without being thrown down with some considerable noise and detriment to his person.

In addition to mosquitoes and garrapatas, or ticks, we suffered from another worse insect, called by the natives *niguas*, which, we are told, pestered the Spaniards on their first entry into the country, and which, says the historian, "ate their Way into the Flesh, under the Nails of the Toes, then laid their Nits there within, and multiplied in such manner that there was no ridding them but by Cauteries, so that some lost their Toes, and some their Feet, whereas they should at first have been picked out; but being as yet unacquainted with the Evil, they knew not how to apply the Remedy."

This description is true even to the last clause. We had escaped them until our arrival at Palenque, and being unacquainted with the evil, did not know how to apply the remedy. I carried one in my foot for several days, conscious that something was wrong, but not knowing what, until the nits had been laid and multiplied. Pawling undertook to pick them out with a penknife, which left a large hole in the flesh; and, unluckily, from the bites of various insects my foot became so inflamed that I could not get on shoe or stocking. I was obliged to lie by, and, sitting an entire day with my foot in a horizontal position, uncovered, it was assaulted by small black flies, the bites of which I did not feel at the moment of infliction, but which left marks like the puncture of a hundred pins. The irritation was so great, and the swelling increased so much, that I became alarmed, and determined to return to the village. It was no easy matter to get there. The foot was too big to put in a stirrup, and, indeed, to keep it but for a few moments in a hanging position made it feel as if the blood would burst through the skin, and the idea of striking it against a bush makes me shudder even now. It was indispensable, however, to leave the place. I sent in to the village for a mule, and on the tenth day after my arrival at the ruins hopped down the terrace, mounted, and laid the unfortunate member on a pillow over the pommel of the saddle. This gave me, for that muddy road, a very uncertain seat. I had a man before me to cut the branches, yet my hat was knocked off three or four times, and twice I was obliged to dismount; but in due season, to my great relief, we cleared the woods. After the closeness and confinement of the forest, coming once more into an open country quickened every pulse.

As I ascended to the table-land on which the village stood, I observed an unusual degree of animation, and a crowd of people in the grass-grown street, probably some fifteen or twenty, who seemed roused at the sight of me, and presently three or four men on horseback rode toward me. I had borne many different characters in that country, and this time I was mistaken for three padres who were expected to arrive that morning from Tumbala. If the mistake had continued I should have had dinner enough for six at least; but unluckily it was soon discovered, and I rode on to the door of our old house. Presently the alcalde appeared, with his keys in his hands and in full dress, i.e. his shirt was inside of his pantaloons; and I was happy to find that he was in a worse humour at the coming of the padres than at our arrival; indeed, he seemed now rather to have a leaning toward me, as one who could sympathise in his vexation at the absurdity of making such a fuss about them. When he saw my foot, too, he really showed some commiseration, and endeavoured to make me as comfortable as possible. The swelling had increased very much. I was soon on my back, and, lying perfectly quiet, by the help of a medicine-chest, starvation, and absence of irritating causes, in two days and nights I reduced the inflammation very sensibly.

CHAPTER XXXV.

A VOICE FROM THE RUINS—BUYING BREAD—ARRIVAL OF PADRES—CURA OF PALENQUE—CARD PLAYING—SUNDAY—MASS—A DINNER PARTY—MEMENTOS OF HOME—DINNER CUSTOMS—RETURN TO THE RUINS—A MARKED CHANGE—TERRIFIC THUNDER—A WHIRLWIND—A SCENE OF THE SUBLIME AND TERRIBLE.

The third day I heard from the ruins a voice of wailing. Juan had upset the lard, and every drop was gone. The imploring letter I received roused all my sensibilities; and, forgetting everything in the emergency, I hurried to the alcalde's, and told him a hog must die. The alcalde made difficulties, and to this day I cannot account for his concealing from me a fact of which he must have been aware, to wit, that on that very night a porker had been killed. Very early the next morning I saw a boy passing with some strings of fresh pork, hailed him, and he guided me to a hut in the suburbs, but yesterday the dwelling of the unfortunate quadruped. I procured the portion of some honest Palenquian, and returned, happy in the consciousness of making others so. That day was memorable, too, for another piece of good fortune; for a courier arrived from Ciudad Real with despatches for Tobasco, and a back-load of bread on private account. As soon as the intelligence reached me, I despatched a messenger to negotiate for the whole stock. Unfortunately, it was sweetened, made up into diamonds, circles, and other fanciful forms, about two inches long and an inch thick, to be eaten with chocolate, and that detestable lard was oozing out of the crust. Nevertheless, it was bread; and placing it carefully on a table, with a fresh cheese, the product of our cow, I lay down at night full of the joy that morning would diffuse over the ruins of Palenque; but, alas! all human calculations are vain. In my first sleep I was roused by a severe clap of thunder, and detected an enormous cat on the table. While my boot was sailing toward her with one bound she reached the wall, and disappeared under the eaves of the roof. I fell asleep again; she returned, and the consequences were fatal.

The padres were slow in movement; and after keeping the village in a state of excitement for three days, this morning they made a triumphal entry, escorted by citizens, and with a train of more than 100 Indians, carrying hammocks, chairs, and luggage. The villages of Tumbalá and San Pedro had turned out 200 or 300 strong, and carried them on their backs and shoulders to Nopa, where they were met by a deputation from Palenque, and transferred to the village. It is a glorious thing in that country to be a padre, and next to being a padre oneself is the position of being a padre's friend. In the afternoon I visited them, but after the fatigues of the journey they were all asleep, and the Indians around the door were talking in low tones so as not to disturb them. Inside were enormous piles of luggage, which showed the prudent care the good ecclesiastics took of themselves. The siesta over, very soon they appeared, one after the other, in dresses, or rather undresses, difficult to describe, but certainly by no means clerical; neither of them had coat or jacket. Two of them were the curas of Tumbala and Ayalon, whom we had seen on our journey. The third was a Franciscan friar from Ciudad Real, and they had come expressly to visit the ruins. All had suffered severely from the journey. The cura of Ayalon was a deputy to Congress, and in Mexico many inquiries had been made of him about the ruins, on the supposition that they were in his neighbourhood, which erroneous supposition he mentioned with a feeling reference to the intervening mountains. The padre of Tumbala was a promising young man of twenty-eight, and weighed at that time about seventeen stone, or 240 pounds: a heavy load to carry about with him over such roads as they had traversed; but the Dominican friar suffered most, and he sat sideways in a hammock, with his vest open, wiping the perspiration from his chest. They were all intelligent men, and, in fact, the circumstance of their making the journey for no other purpose than to visit the ruins was alone an indication of their superior character. The Congress man we had seen on our way through his village, and then were struck with his general knowledge, and particularly with his force of character. He had borne an active part in all the convulsions of the country from the time of the revolution against Spain, of which he had been an instigator; and ever since, to the scandal of the Church party, stood forth as a Liberal; he had played the soldier as well as priest, laying down his blood-stained sword after a battle to confess the wounded and dying; twice wounded, once chronicled among the killed, an exile in Guatimala, and with the gradual recovery of the Liberal party restored to his place and sent as a deputy to Congress, where very soon he was to take part in new convulsions. They were all startled by the stories of mosquitoes, insects, and reptiles at the ruins, and particularly by what they had heard of the condition of my foot.

While we were taking chocolate the cura of Palenque entered. At the time of our first arrival he was absent at another village under his charge, and I had not seen him before. He was more original in his appearance than either of the others, being very tall, with long black hair, an Indian face and complexion, and certainly four-fifths Indian blood. Indeed, if I had seen him in Indian costume, and what that is the reader by this time understands, I should have taken him for a "puro," or Indian of unmixed descent. His dress was as unclerical as his appearance, consisting of an old straw hat, with the rim turned up before, behind, and at the sides, so as to make four regular corners, with a broad blue velvet riband for a hatband, both soiled by long exposure to wind and rain. Beneath this were a check shirt, an old blue silk neckcloth with yellow stripes, a striped roundabout jacket, black waistcoat, and pantaloons made of bedticking, not meeting the waistcoat by two inches, the whole tall figure ending below in yellow buckskin shoes. But under this outré appearance existed a charming simplicity and courtesy of manner, and when he spoke his face beamed with kindness. The reception given him showed the good feeling existing among the padres; and after some general conversation, the chocolate-cups were removed, and one of the padres went to his chest, whence he produced a pack of cards, which he placed upon the table. He said that he always carried them with him, and it was very pleasant to travel with companions, as, wherever they stopped, they could have a game at night. The cards had evidently done much service, and there was something orderly and systematic in the preliminary arrangements, that showed the effect of regular habits and a well-trained household. An old Indian servant laid on the table a handful of grains of corn and a new bundle of paper cigars. The grains of corn were valued at six-pence. I declined joining in the game, whereupon one of the reverend fathers kept aloof to entertain me, and the other three sat down to Monté, still taking part in the conversation. Very soon they became abstracted, and I left them playing as earnestly as if the souls of unconverted Indians were at stake. I had often heard the ill-natured remark of foreigners, that two padres cannot meet in that country without playing cards, but it was the first time I had seen its verification; perhaps (I feel guilty in saying so) because, except on public occasions, it was the first time I had ever seen two padres together. Before I left them the padres invited me to dine with them the next day, and on returning to my own quarters I found that Don Santiago, the gentleman who gave them the dinner, and, next to the Prefect, the principal inhabitant, had called upon me with a like invitation, which I need not say I accepted.

The next day was Sunday; the storm of the night had rolled away, the air was soft and balmy, the grass was green, and, not being obliged to travel, I felt what the natives aver, that the mornings of the rainy season were the finest in the year. It was a great day for the little church at Palenque. The four padres were there, all in their gowns and surplices, all assisted in the ceremonies, and the Indians from every hut in the village went to mass. This over, all retired, and in a few minutes the village was as quite as ever.

At twelve o'clock I went to the house of Don Santiago to dine. The three stranger padres were there, and most of the guests were assembled. Don Santiago, the richest man in Palenque, and the most extensive merchant, received us in his tienda or shop, which was merely a few shelves with a counter before them in one corner, and his whole stock of merchandise was worth perhaps four to six pounds; but Don Santiago was entirely a different style of man from one in such small business in America or Europe; courteous in manners, and intelligent for that country; he was dressed in white pantaloons and red slippers, a clean shirt, with an embroidered bosom, and braces, which probably cost more than all the rest of his habiliments, and were not to be hidden under coat and waistcoat. In this place, which had before seemed to me so much out of the world, I was brought more directly in contact with home than at any other I visited. The chair on which I sat came from New York; also a small looking-glass, two pieces of American "cottons," and the remnant of a box of vermicelli, of the existence of which in the place I was not before informed. The most intimate foreign relations of the inhabitants were with New York, through the port of Tobasco. They knew a man related to a family in the village who had actually been at New York, and a barrel of New York flour, the bare mention of which created a yearning, had once reached the place. In fact, New York was more familiar to them than any other part of the world, except the capital. Don Santiago had a copy of Zavala's tour in the United States, which, except a few volumes of the lives of saints, was his library, and which he knew almost by heart; and they had kept up with our political history so well as to know that General Washington was not president, but General Jackson.

The padre of Tumbala, he of 240 pounds' weight, was somewhat of an exquisite in dress for that country, and had brought with him his violin. He was curious to know the state of musical science in my country, and whether the government supported good opera companies; regretted that I could not play some national airs, and entertained himself and the company with several of their own.

In the meantime the padre of Palenque was still missing, but, after being sent for twice, made his appearance. The dinner was, in fact, his; but, on account of want of conveniences in the convent from his careless housekeeper, was given by his friend Don Santiago on his behalf, and the answer of the boy sent to call him was, that he had forgotten all about it. He was absent and eccentric enough for a genius, though he made no pretensions to that character. Don Santiago told us that he once went to the padre's house, where he found inside a cow and a calf; the cura, in great perplexity, apologised, saying that he could not help himself, they would come in; and considered it a capital idea when Don Santiago suggested to him the plan of driving them out.

As soon as he appeared the other padres rallied him upon his forgetfulness, which they insisted was all feigned; they had won sixteen dollars of him the night before, and said that he was afraid to come. He answered in the same strain that he was a ruined man. They offered him his revenge, and forthwith the table was brought out, cards and grains of corn were spread upon it as before, and while the padre of Tumbala played the violin, the other three played Monté. Being Sunday, in some places this would be considered rather irregular; at least, to do so with open doors would be considered setting a bad example to children and servants; and, in fact, considering myself on a pretty sociable footing, I could not help telling them that in my country they would all be read out of Church. The padre Congress man had met an Englishman in Mexico who told him the same thing, and also the manner of observing the Sunday in England, which they all thought must be very stupid.

Perhaps upon less ground than this the whole Spanish American priesthood has at times been denounced as a set of unprincipled gamblers, but I have too warm a recollection of their many kindnesses to hold them up in this light. They were all intelligent and good men, who would rather do benefits than an injury; in matters connected with religion they were most reverential, laboured diligently in their vocations, and were without reproach among their people. By custom and education they did not consider that they were doing wrong. From my agreeable intercourse with them, and my regard for their many good qualities, I would fain save them from denunciations of utter unworthiness which might be cast upon them. Nevertheless, it is true that dinner was delayed, and all the company kept waiting until they had finished their game of cards.

The table was set in an unoccupied house adjoining. Every white man in the village, except the Prefect and alcalde, were present; the former being away at his hacienda, and the latter, from the sneering references he made to it, I suspected was not invited. In all there were fifteen or sixteen, and I was led to the seat of honour at the head of the table. I objected, but the padres seated me perforce. After the gentlemen were seated, it was found that, by sitting close, there was room for some ladies, and after the arrangements for the table were completed, they were invited to take seats. Unluckily, there was only room for three, who sat all together on my left. In a few minutes I felt very much as if the dinner was got up expressly for me. It was long since I had seen such a table, and I mourned in spirit that I had not sent notice for Mr. Catherwood to come to the village accidentally in time to get an invitation. But it was too late now; there was no time for reflection; every moment the dinner was going. In some places my position would have required me to devote myself to those on each side of me; but at Palenque they devoted themselves to me. If I stopped a moment my plate was whipped away, and another brought, loaded with something else. It may seem unmannerly, but I watched the fate of certain dishes, particularly some dolces or sweetmeats, hoping they would not be entirely consumed, as I purposed to secure all that should be left to take with me to the ruins. Wine was on the table, which was recommended to me as coming from New York, but this was not enough to induce me to taste it. There was no water, and, by-the-way, water is never put on the table, and never drunk until after the dolces, which come on as the last course, when it is served in a large tumbler, which passes round for each one to sip from. It is entirely irregular and ill-bred to ask for water during the meal. Each guest, as he rose from the table, bowed to Don Santiago, and said "Muchas gratias," which I considered in bad taste, and not in keeping with the delicacy of Spanish courtesy, as the host ought rather to thank his guests for their society than they to thank him for his dinner. Nevertheless, as I had more reason to be thankful than any of them, I conformed to the example set me. After dinner my friends became drowsy, and retired to siesta. I found my way back to Don Santiago's house, where, in a conversation with the ladies, I secured the remains of the dolces, and bought out his stock of vermicelli.

In the morning, my foot being sufficiently recovered, I rode up to the house of the padres to escort them to the ruins. They had passed the evening sociably at cards, and again the padre of Palenque was wanting. We rode over to his house, and waited while he secured carefully on the back of a tall horse a little boy, who looked so wonderfully like him, that, out of respect to his obligation of celibacy, people felt delicate in asking whose son he was. This done, he tied an extra pair of shoes behind his own saddle, and we set off with the adios of all the village. The padres intended to pass the night at the ruins, and had a train of fifty or sixty Indians loaded with beds, bedding, provisions, sacate for mules, and multifarious articles, down to a white earthen washbowl; besides which, more favoured than we, they had four or five women.

Entering the forest, we found the branches of the trees, which had been trimmed on my return to the village, again weighed down by the rains; the streams were very bad; the padres were well mounted, but no horsemen, dismounted very often, and under my escort we got lost; but at eleven o'clock, very much to the satisfaction of all, our long, strange-looking, straggling party reached the ruins. The old palace was once more alive with inhabitants.

There was a marked change in it since I left; the walls were damp, the corridors wet; the continued rains were working through cracks and crevices, and opening leaks in the roof; saddles, bridles, boots, shoes, &c. were green and mildewed, and the guns and pistols covered with a coat of rust. Mr. Catherwood's appearance startled me. He was wan and gaunt; lame, like me, from the bites of insects; his face was swollen, and his left arm hung with rheumatism as if paralysed.

We sent the Indians across the courtyard to the opposite corridor, where the sight of our loose traps might not tempt them to their undoing, and selecting a place for that purpose, the catres were set up immediately, and with all the comforts of home the padres lay down for an hour's rest. I had no ill-will toward these worthy men; on the contrary, the most friendly feeling; but, to do the honours of the palace, I invited them to dine with us. Catherwood and Pawling objected, and they would have done better if left to themselves; but they appreciated the spirit of the invitation, and returned me muchas gratias. After their siesta I escorted them over the palace, and left them in their apartment. Singularly enough, that night there was no rain, so that, with a hat before a candle, we crossed the courtyard and paid them a visit; we found the three reverend gentlemen sitting on a mat on the ground, winding up the day with a comfortable game at cards, and the Indians asleep around them.

The next morning, with the assistance of Pawling and the Indians to lift and haul them, I escorted them to the other buildings, heard some curious speculations, and at two o'clock, with many expressions of good-will, and pressing invitations to their different convents, they returned to the village.

Late in the afternoon the storm set in with terrific thunder, which at night rolled with fearful crashes against the walls, while the vivid lightning flashed along the corridors. The padres had laughed at us for their superior discrimination in selecting a sleeping-place, and this night their apartment was flooded. From this time my notebook contains memoranda only of the arrival of the Indians, with the time that the storm set in, its violence and duration, the deluges of rain, and the places to which we were obliged to move our beds. Every day our residence became more wet and uncomfortable. On Thursday, the 30th of May, the storm opened with a whirlwind. At night the crash of falling trees rang through the forest, rain fell in deluges, the roaring of thunder was terrific, and as we lay looking out, the aspect of the ruined palace, lighted by the glare of lightning such as I never saw in this country, was awfully grand; in fact, there was too much of the sublime and terrible. The storm threatened the very existence of the building; and, knowing the tottering state of the walls, for some moments we had apprehensions lest the whole should fall and crush us. In the morning the courtyard and the ground below the palace were flooded, and by this time the whole front was so wet that we were obliged to desert it and move to the other side of the corridor. Even here we were not much better off; but we remained until Mr. Catherwood had finished his last drawing; and on Saturday, the 1st of June, like rats leaving a sinking ship, we broke up and left the ruins. Before leaving, however, we will present a description of the remaining buildings.

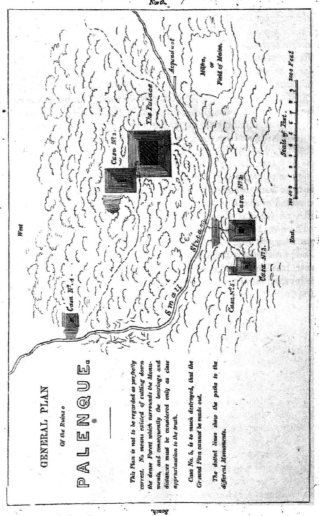

CHAPTER XXXVI.

PLAN OF THE RUINS—PYRAMIDAL STRUCTURE—A BUILDING—STUCCO ORNAMENTS—HUMAN FIGURES—TABLETS—REMARKABLE HIEROGLYPHICS—RANGE OF PILLARS—STONE TERRACE—ANOTHER BUILDING—A LARGE TABLET—A CROSS—CONJECTURES IN REGARD TO THIS CROSS—BEAUTIFUL SCULPTURE—A PLATFORM—CURIOUS DEVICES—A STATUE—ANOTHER PYRAMIDAL STRUCTURE SURMOUNTED BY A BUILDING—CORRIDORS—A CURIOUS BAS-RELIEF—STONE TABLETS, WITH FIGURES IN BAS-RELIEF—TABLETS AND FIGURES—THE ORATORIO—MORE PYRAMIDAL STRUCTURES AND BUILDINGS—EXTENT OF THE RUINS—THESE RUINS THE REMAINS OF A POLISHED AND PECULIAR PEOPLE—ANTIQUITY OF PALENQUE.

The plan opposite, No. 57, indicates the position of all the buildings which have been discovered at Palenque. There are remains of others in the same vicinity, but so utterly dilapidated that we have not thought it worth while to give any description of them, nor even to indicate their places on the plan.

From the palace no other building is visible. Passing out by what is called the subterraneous passage, you descend the south-west corner of the terrace, and at the foot immediately commence ascending a ruined pyramidal structure, which appears once to have had steps on all its sides. These steps have been thrown down by the trees, and it is necessary to clamber over stones, aiding the feet by clinging to the branches. The ascent is so steep, that if the first man displaces a stone it bounds down the side of the pyramid, and woe to those behind! About half-way up, through openings in the trees, is seen the building represented in the engraving No. 58. The height of the structure on which it stands is 110 feet on the slope. The engraving represents the actual condition of the building, surrounded and overgrown by trees, but no description and no drawing can give effect to the moral sublimity of the spectacle. From the multiplicity of engravings required to illustrate the architecture and arts of this unknown people, we have felt obliged to omit many striking and picturesque views, for fear of wearying the reader. The ruins and the forest made the deep and abiding impression upon our minds; but our object is to present the building as restored, as subjects for speculation and comparison with the architecture of other lands and times. The supposed restorations were made after a careful examination, and in each case the reader will see precisely what we had to guide us in making them. I must remark, however, that the buildings are the only parts which we attempted to restore; the specimens of sculpture and stuccoed ornaments were drawn as we found them.

59. CASA No. 1, IN RUINS.

Elevation showing the Building, and the Pyramid on which it stands.

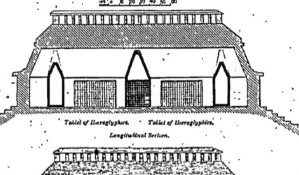
Tablet of Hieroglyphics.   Tablet of Hieroglyphics.
Longitudinal Section.

Front Elevation.

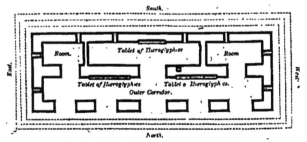
159. Plan of No. 1, CASAS DE PIEDRA, PALENQUE.

Scale of feet.

F. Catherwood.

G G

The engraving, No. 59, represents the same building cleared from forest and restored, and, according to our division, marked on the plan No. 1. In the plate are given the ground-plan (beginning at the bottom), the front elevation, a section showing the position of tablets within, and the front elevation on a smaller scale, with the pyramidal structure on which it stands.

The building is 76 feet in front and 25 feet deep. It has five doors and six piers, all standing. The whole front was richly ornamented in stucco, and the corner piers are covered with hieroglyphics, each of which contains 96 squares. The four piers are ornamented with human figures, two on each side, facing each other, which are represented in the following engravings in the order in which they stand upon the piers.

The first, No. 60, is that of a woman with a child in her arms; at least we suppose it to be intended for a woman from the dress. It is enclosed by an elaborate border, and stands on a rich ornament. The head is destroyed. Over the top are three hieroglyphics, and there are traces of hieroglyphics broken off in the corner. The other three following are of the same general character; each probably had an infant in the arms, and over each are hieroglyphics.

At the foot of the two centre piers, resting on the steps, are two stone tablets with what seemed interesting figures, but so encumbered with ruins that it was impossible to draw them.

The interior of the building is divided into two corridors, running lengthwise, with a ceiling rising nearly to a point, as in the palace, and paved with large square stones. The front corridor is seven feet wide. The separating wall is very massive, and has three doors, a large one in the centre, and a smaller one on each side. In this corridor, on each side of the principal door, is a large tablet of hieroglyphics, each thirteen feet long and eight feet high, and each divided into 240 squares of characters or symbols. Both are set in the wall so as to project three or four inches. In one place a hole had been made in the wall close to the side of one of them, apparently for the purpose of attempting its removal, by which we discovered that the stone is about a foot thick. The sculpture is in bas-relief. The tablets are represented in the engravings, Nos. 64, 65.

The construction of the tablets was a large stone on each side, and smaller ones in the centre, as indicated by the dark lines in the engravings.

In the right-hand tablet one line is obliterated by water that has trickled down for an unknown length of time, and formed a sort of stalactite or hard substance, which has incorporated itself with the

F. Catherwood.

60. BAS-RELIEF IN STUCCO
On one of the Piers of No. 1, Casas de Piedra, Palenque

F. Catherwood.
61. BAS-RELIEF IN STUCCO, PALENQUE.
Pier No. 2, north. No. 1, Casas de Piedra.

62.—BAS-RELIEF IN STUCCO, PALENQUE.
Pier No. 3. No. 1, Casas de Piedra.

F. Catherwood.   63. BAS-RELIEF IN STUCCO, PALENQUE.
Pier No. 4.   No. 1, Casas de Piedra.

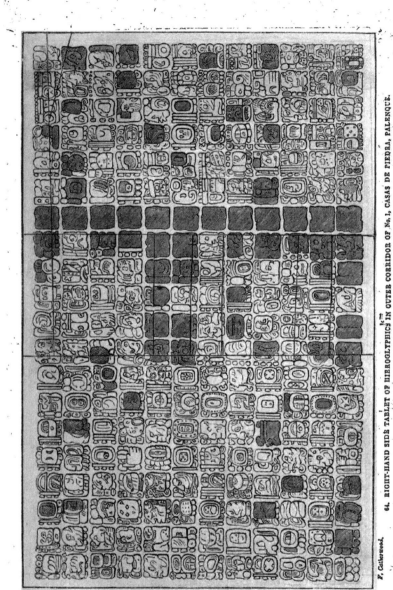

64. RIGHT-HAND SIDE TABLET OF HIEROGLYPHICS IN OUTER CORRIDOR OF No. 1, CASAS DE PIEDRA, PALENQUE.

65. OUTER CORRIDOR OF NO. 1, CASAS DE PIEDRA, PALENQUE.

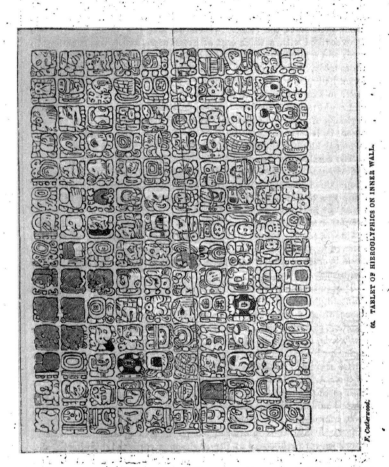

64. TABLET OF HIEROGLYPHICS ON INNER WALL.

stone, and which we could not remove, though perhaps it might be detached by some chemical process. In the other tablet, nearly one half of the hieroglyphics are obliterated by the action of water and decomposition of the stone. When we first saw them both tablets were covered with a thick coat of green moss, and it was necessary to wash and scrape them, clear the lines with a stick, and scrub them thoroughly, for which last operation a pair of blacking-brushes that Juan had picked up in my house at Guatimala, and disobeyed my order to throw away upon the road, proved exactly what we wanted and could not have procured. Besides this process, on account of the darkness of the corridor, from the thick shade of the trees growing before it, it was necessary to burn candles or torches, and to throw a strong light upon the stones while Mr. Catherwood was drawing.

The corridor in the rear is dark and gloomy, and divided into three apartments. Each of the side apartments has two narrow openings, about three inches wide and a foot high. They have no remains of sculpture, or painting, or stuccoed ornaments. In the centre apartment, set in the back wall, and fronting the principal door of entrance, is another tablet of hieroglyphics, four feet six inches wide and three feet six inches high. The roof above it is tight; consequently it has not suffered from exposure, and the hieroglyphics are perfect, though the stone is cracked lengthwise through the middle, as indicated in the engraving, No. 66.

The impression made upon our minds by these speaking but unintelligible tablets I shall not attempt to describe. From some unaccountable cause they have never before been presented to the public. Captains Del Rio and Dupaix both refer to them, but in very few words, and neither of them has given a single drawing. Acting under a royal commission, and selected, doubtless, as fit men for the duties entrusted to them, they cannot have been ignorant or insensible of their value. It is my belief they did not give them because in both cases the artists attached to their expedition were incapable of the labour, and the steady, determined perseverance required for drawing such complicated, unintelligible, and anomalous characters. As at Copan, Mr. Catherwood divided his paper into squares; the original drawings were reduced, and the engravings corrected by himself, and I believe they are as true copies as the pencil can make: the real written records of a lost people. The Indians call this building an escuela or school, but our friends the padres called it a tribunal of justice, and these stones, they said, contained the tables of the law.

There is one important fact to be noticed. The hieroglyphics are the same as were found at Copan and Quirigua. The intermediate

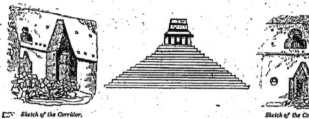

Sketch of the Corridor. Sketch of the Corridor.

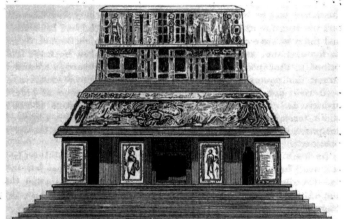

Front Elevation.

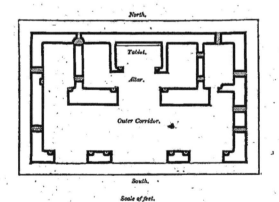

67. Plan of No. 2, CASAS DE PIEDRA, PALENQUE.

country is now occupied by races of Indians speaking many different languages, and entirely unintelligible to each other; but there is room for the belief that the whole of this country was once occupied by the same race, speaking the same language, or, at least, having the same written characters.

There is no staircase or other visible communication between the lower and upper parts of this building, and the only way of reaching the latter was by climbing a tree which grows close against the wall, and the branches of which spread over the roof. The roof is inclined, and the sides are covered with stucco ornaments, which, from exposure to the elements, and the assaults of trees and bushes, are faded and ruined, so that it was impossible to draw them; but enough remained to give the impression that, when perfect and painted, they must have been rich and imposing. Along the top was a range of pillars eighteen inches high and twelve apart, made of small pieces of stone laid in mortar, and covered with stucco, crowning which is a layer of flat projecting stones, having somewhat the appearance of a low open balustrade.

In front of this building, at the foot of the pyramidal structure, is a small stream, part of which supplies the aqueduct before referred to. Crossing this, we come upon a broken stone terrace about 60 feet on the slope, with a level esplanade at the top, 110 feet in breadth, from which rises another pyramidal structure, now ruined and overgrown with trees; it is 134 feet high on the slope, and on its summit is the building marked No. 2, like the first, shrouded among trees, but presented in the engraving, No. 67, as restored. The plate contains, as before, the ground-plan, front elevation, section, and front elevation on a smaller scale, with the pyramidal structure on which it stands.

This building is 50 feet front, 31 feet deep, and has three doorways. The whole front was covered with stuccoed ornaments. The two outer piers contain hieroglyphics; one of the inner piers is fallen, and the other is ornamented with a figure in bas relief, but faded and ruined.

The interior, again, is divided into two corridors running lengthwise, with ceilings as before, and pavements of large square stones, in which forcible breaches have been made, doubtless by Captain Del Rio, and excavations underneath. The back corridor is divided into three apartments, and opposite the principal door of entrance is an oblong enclosure, with a heavy cornice or moulding of stucco, and a doorway richly ornamented over the top, but now much defaced; on each side of the doorway was a tablet of sculptured stone, which, however, has been removed. Within, the chamber is thirteen feet wide and seven feet

deep. There was no admission of light except from the door; the sides were without ornament of any kind, and in the back wall, covering the whole width, was the tablet given in the engraving, No. 68. It was ten feet eight inches wide, six feet four inches in height, and consisted of three separate stones. That on the left, facing the spectator, is still in its place. The middle one has been removed and carried down the side of the structure, and now lies near the bank of the stream. It was removed many years ago by one of the inhabitants of the village, with the intention of carrying it to his house; but, after great labour, with no other instruments than the arms and hands of Indians, and poles cut from trees, it had advanced so far, when its removal was arrested by an order from the government forbidding any farther abstraction from the ruins. We found it lying on its back near the banks of the stream, washed by many floods of the rainy season, and covered with a thick coat of dirt and moss. We had it scrubbed and propped up, and probably the next traveller will find it with the same props under it which we placed there. In the engraving it is given in its original position on the wall. The stone on the right is broken, and, unfortunately, altogether destroyed; most of the fragments have disappeared; but, from the few we found among the ruins in the front of the building, there is no doubt that it contained ranges of hieroglyphics corresponding in general appearance with those of the stone on the left.

The tablet, as given in the engraving, contains only two-thirds of the original. In Del Rio's work it is not represented at all. In Dupaix it is given, not, however, as it exists, but as made up by the artist in Paris, so as to present a perfect picture. The subject is reversed, with the cross in the centre, and on each side a single row of hieroglyphics, only eight in number. Probably, when Dupaix saw it (thirty-four years before), it was entire, but the important features of six rows of hieroglyphics on each side of the principal figures, each row containing seventeen in a line, do not appear. This is the more inexcusable in his publishers, as in his report Dupaix expressly refers to these numerous hieroglyphics; but it is probable that his report was not accompanied by any drawings of them.

The principal subject of this tablet is the cross. It is surmounted by a strange bird, and loaded with indescribable ornaments. The two figures are evidently those of important personages. They are well drawn, and in symmetry of proportion are perhaps equal to many that are carved on the walls of the ruined temples in Egypt. Their costume is in a style different from any heretofore given, and the folds would seem to indicate that they were of a soft and pliable texture, like cotton. Both are looking toward the cross, and one seems in the act of making an offering, apparently of a child: all speculations on the subject are of course entitled to little regard, but perhaps it would not be wrong to ascribe to these personages a sacerdotal character. The hieroglyphics doubtless explain all. Near them are other hieroglyphics, which reminded us of the Egyptian mode of recording the name, history, office, or character of the persons represented. This tablet of the cross has given rise to more learned speculations than perhaps any others found at Palenque. Dupaix and his commentators, assuming for the building a very remote antiquity, or, at least, a period long antecedent to the Christian era, account for the appearance of the cross by the argument that it was known and had a symbolical meaning among ancient nations long before it was established as the emblem of the Christain faith. Our friends the padres, at the sight of it, immediately decided that the old inhabitants of Palenque were Christians, and by conclusions which are sometimes called jumping, they fixed the age of the buildings in the third century.

There is reason to believe that this particular building was intended as a temple, and that the enclosed inner chamber was an adoratorio, or oratory, or altar. What the rites and ceremonies of worship may have been, no one can undertake to say.

The upper part of this building differs from the first. As before, there was no staircase or other communication inside or out, nor were there the remains of any. The only mode of access was, in like manner, by climbing a tree, the branches of which spread across the roof. The roof was inclined, and the sides were richly ornamented with stucco figures, plants, and flowers, but mostly ruined. Among them were the fragments of a beautiful head and of two bodies, in justness of proportion and symmetry approaching the Greek models. On the top of this roof is a narrow platform, supporting what, for the sake of description, I shall call two stories. The platform is but two feet ten inches wide, and the superstructure of the first story is seven feet five inches in height; that of the second eight feet five inches, the width of the two being the same. The ascent from one to the other is by square projecting stones, and the covering of the upper story is by flat stones laid across and projecting over. The long sides of this narrow structure are of open stucco work, formed into curious and indescribable devices, human figures with legs and arms spreading and apertures between; and the whole was once loaded with rich and elegant ornaments in stucco relief. Its appearance at a distance must have been that of a high, fanciful lattice. Altogether, like the rest of the architecture and ornaments, it was perfectly unique, different from the

F. Catherwood.

69. STONE STATUE IN FRONT OF CASA, No. 2.

works of any other people with which we were familiar, and its uses and purposes entirely incomprehensible. Perhaps it was intended as an observatory. From the upper gallery, through openings in the trees growing around, we looked out over an immense forest, and saw the Lake of Terminos and the Gulf of Mexico.

Near this building was another interesting monument, which had been entirely overlooked by those who preceded us in a visit to Palenque, and I mention this fact in the hope that the next visitor may discover many things omitted by us. It lies in front of the building, about forty or fifty feet down the side of the pyramidal structure. When we first passed it with our guide it lay on its face, with its head downward, and half buried by an accumulation of earth and stones. The outer side was rough and unhewn, and our attention was attracted by its size; our guide said it was not sculptured; but, after he had shown us everything that he had knowledge of, and we had discharged him, in passing it again we stopped and dug around it, and discovered that the under surface was carved. The Indians cut down some saplings for levers, and rolled it over. The engraving, No. 69, represents this monument. It is the only statue that has ever been found at Palenque. We were at once struck with its expression of serene repose, and its strong resemblance to Egyptian statues, though in size it does not compare with the gigantic remains of Egypt. In height it is ten feet six inches, of which two feet six inches were underground. The head-dress is lofty and spreading; there are holes in the place of ears, which were perhaps adorned with earrings of gold and pearls. Round the neck is a necklace, and pressed against the breast by the right hand is an instrument apparently with teeth. The left hand rests on a hieroglyphic, from which descends some symbolical ornament. The lower part of the dress bears an unfortunate resemblance to the modern pantaloons, but the figure stands on what we have always considered a hieroglyphic, analogous again to the custom in Egypt of recording the name and office of the hero or other person represented. The sides are rounded, and the back is of rough stone. Probably it stood imbedded in a wall.

From the foot of the elevation on which the last-mentioned building stands, their bases almost touching, rises another pyramidal structure of about the same height, on the top of which is the building marked No. 3. Such is the density of the forest, even on the sides of the pyramidal structure, that, though in a right line, but a short distance apart, one of these buildings cannot be seen from the other.

The engraving, No. 70, represents this building as restored, not

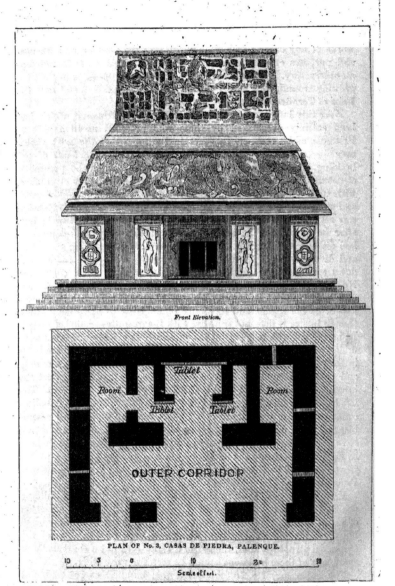

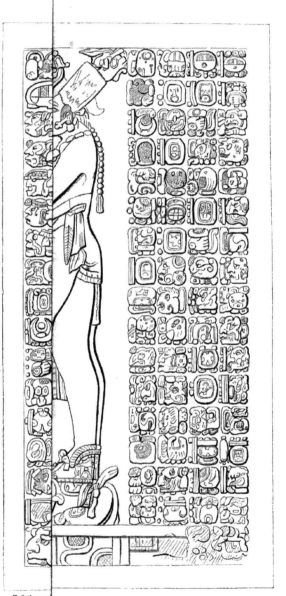

F. Catherwood

from any fancied idea of what it might have been, but from such remains and indications that it was impossible to make anything else of it. It is thirty-eight feet front and twenty-eight feet deep, and has three doors. The end piers are ornamented with hieroglyphics in stucco, two large medallions in handsome compartments, and the intermediate ones with bas-reliefs, also in stucco; in general character similar to those before-given, and for that reason, not to multiply engravings, they are omitted.

The interior, again, is divided into two corridors, about nine feet wide each, and paved with stone. The engraving, No. 71, represents the front corridor, with the ceiling rising nearly to a point, and covered at the top with a layer of flat stones. In several places on each side are holes, which are found also in all the other corridors; they were probably used to support poles for scaffolding while the building was in process of erection, and had never been filled up. At the extreme end, cut through the wall, is one of the windows before referred to, which have been the subject of speculation from analogy to the letter Tau.

The back corridor is divided into three apartments. In the centre, facing the principal door of entrance, is an enclosed chamber similar to that which in the last building we have called an oratory or altar. Its outline is seen in the engraving. The top of the doorway was gorgeous with stuccoed ornaments, and on the piers at each side were stone tablets in bas-relief. Within, the chamber was four feet seven inches deep and nine feet wide. There were no stuccoed ornaments or paintings, but set in the back wall was a stone tablet covering the whole width of the chamber, nine feet wide and eight feet high.

The tablet is given in the engraving, No. 72, and I beg to call to it the particular attention of the reader, as the most perfect and most interesting monument in Palenque. Neither Del Rio nor Dupaix has given any drawing of it, and it is now for the first time presented to the public. It is composed of three separate stones, the joints in which are shown by the blurred lines in the engraving. The sculpture is perfect, and the characters and figures stand clear and distinct on the stone. On each side are rows of hieroglyphics. The principal personages will be recognised at once as the same who are represented in the tablet of the cross. They wear the same dress, but here both seem to be making offerings. Both personages stand on the backs of human beings, one of whom supports himself by his hands and knees, and the other seems crushed to the ground by the weight. Between them, at the foot of the tablet, are two figures, sitting cross-legged, one bracing himself with his right hand on the

F. Catherwood. 71. CASA No. 3, FRONT CORRIDOR.

ground, and with the left supporting a square table; the attitude and action of the other are the same, except that they are in reverse order. The table also rests upon their bended necks, and their distorted countenances may, perhaps, be considered expressions of pain and suffering. They both are clothed in leopard-skins. Upon this table rest two batons crossed, their upper extremities richly ornamented, and supporting what seems a hideous mask, the eyes widely expanded, and the tongue hanging out. This seems to be the object to which the principal personages are making offerings.

The pier on each side of the doorway contained a stone tablet, with figures carved in bas-relief, which are represented in the two following engravings, Nos. 73, 74. These tablets, however, have been removed from their place to the village, and set up in the wall of a house as ornaments. They were the first objects which we saw, and the last which Mr. Catherwood drew. The house belonged to two sisters, who have an exaggerated idea of the value of these tablets; and, though always pleased with our coming to see them, made objections to having them copied. We obtained permission only by promising a copy for them also, which, however, Mr. Catherwood, worn out with constant labour, was entirely unable to make. I cut out of Del Rio's book the drawings of the same subjects, which I thought, being printed, would please them better; but they had examined Mr. Catherwood's drawing in its progress, and were not at all satisfied with the substitute. The moment I saw these tablets I formed the idea of purchasing them, and carrying them home as a sample of Palenque, but it was some time before I ventured to broach the subject. They could not be purchased without the house; but that was no impediment, for I liked the house also. It was afterward included among the subjects of other negotiations which were undetermined when I left Palenque.

The two figures stand facing each other, the first on the right hand, fronting the spectator. The nose and eyes are strongly marked, but altogether the development is not so strange as to indicate a race entirely different from those which are known. The head-dress is curious and complicated, consisting principally of leaves of plants with a large flower hanging down; and among the ornaments are distinguished the beak and eyes of a bird, and a tortoise. The cloak is a leopard's skin, and the figure has ruffles around the wrists and ankles.

The second figure, standing on the left of the spectator, has the same profile which characterises all the others at Palenque. Its head-dress is composed of a plume of feathers, in which is a bird holding a fish in its mouth; and in different parts of the head-dress there are three.

F. Catherwood.

73. BAS-RELIEF ON SIDE OF DOORWAY LEADING TO ALTAR, PALENQUE.

76. BAS-RELIEF ON SIDE OF DOORWAY LEADING TO ALTAR, PALENQUE.

other fishes. The figure wears a richly-embroidered tippet, and a broad girdle, with the head of some animal in front, sandals, and leggings: the right hand is extended in a prayerful or deprecating position, with the palm outward. Over the heads of these mysterious personages are three cabalistic hieroglyphics.

We considered the oratorio or altar the most interesting portion of the ruins of Palenque; and in order that the reader may understand it in all its details, the plate, No. 75, is presented, which shows distinctly all the combinations of the doorway, with its broken ornaments, the tablets on each side; and within the doorway is seen the large tablet on the back of the inner wall. The reader will form from it some idea of the whole, and of its effect upon the stranger, when, as he climbs up the ruined pyramidal structure, on the threshold of the door, this scene presents itself. We could not but regard it as a holy place, dedicated to the gods, and consecrated by the religious observances of a lost and unknown people. Comparatively, the hand of ruin has spared it, and the great tablet, surviving the wreck of elements, stands perfect and entire. Lonely, deserted, and without any worshippers at its shrine, the figures and characters are distinct as when the people who reared it went up to pay their adorations before it. To us it was all a mystery; silent, defying the most scrutinising gaze and reach of intellect. Even our friends the padres could make nothing of it.

Near this, on the top of a pyramidal structure, was another building entirely in ruins, which apparently had been shattered and hurled down by an earthquake. The stones were strewn on the side of the pyramid, and it was impossible even to make out the ground-plan.

Returning to No. 1, and proceeding south, at a distance of 1,500 feet, and on a pyramidal structure 100 feet high from the bank of the river, is another building, marked on the plan No. 4, 20 feet front, and 18 feet deep, but unfortunately in a ruined condition. The whole of the front wall has fallen, leaving the outer corridor entirely exposed. Fronting the door, and against the back wall of the inner corridor, was a large stucco ornament, representing a figure sitting on a couch; but a great part has fallen, or been taken off and carried away.* The body of the couch, with tigers' feet, is all that now remains. The outline of two tigers' heads and of the sitting personage is seen on the wall. The loss or destruction of this ornament is more to be regretted, as from what remains it appears to have been superior in execution to any other stucco relief in Palenque. The body of the couch is entire, and the leg and foot hanging down

* By Monsieur de Walderk.

ADORATORIO OR ALTAR, CASA No. 3, PALENQUE.

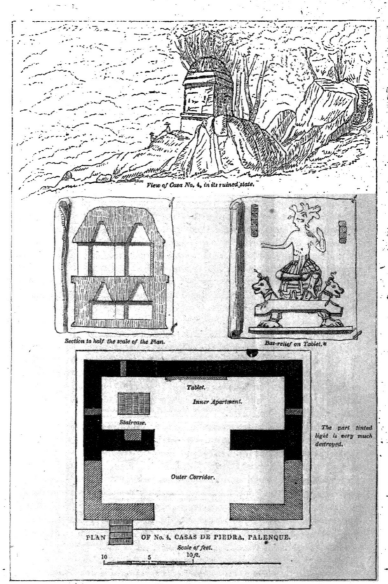

ANTIQUITY OF PALENQUE.

the side are elegant specimens of art and models for study. The plate, No. 76, represents this relief, and also a plan, section, and general view of the building.

We have now given, without speculation or comment, a full description of the ruins of Palenque. We repeat what was stated in the beginning, there may be more buildings, but, after a close examination of the vague reports current in the village, we are satisfied that no more have ever been discovered; and from repeated inquiries of Indians who had traversed the forest in every direction in the dry season, we are induced to believe that no more exist. The whole extent of ground covered by those as yet known, as appears by the plan, is not larger than twenty to thirty acres. In stating this fact I am very far from wishing to detract from the importance or interest of the subject. I give our opinion, with the grounds of it, and the reader will judge for himself how far these are entitled to consideration. It is proper to add, however, that considering the space now occupied by the ruins as the site of palaces, temples, and public buildings, and supposing the houses of the inhabitants to have been, like those of the Egyptians and the present race of Indians, of frail and perishable materials, and, as at Memphis and Thebes, to have disappeared altogether, the city may have covered an immense extent.

The reader is, perhaps, disappointed, but we were not. There was no necessity for assigning to the ruined city an immense extent, or an antiquity coeval with that of the Egyptians or of any other ancient and known people. What we had before our eyes was grand, curious, and remarkable enough. Here were the remains of a cultivated, polished, and peculiar people, who had passed through all the stages incident to the rise and fall of nations; reached their golden age, and perished, entirely unknown. The links which connected them with the human family were severed and lost, and these were the only memorials of their footsteps upon earth. We lived in the ruined palace of their kings; we went up to their desolate temples and fallen altars; and wherever we moved we saw the evidences of their taste, their skill in arts, their wealth and power. In the midst of desolation and ruin we looked back to the past, cleared away the gloomy forest, and fancied every building perfect, with its terraces and pyramids, its sculptured and painted ornaments, grand, lofty, and imposing, and overlooking an immense inhabited plain; we called back into life the strange people who gazed at us in sadness from the walls; pictured them, in fanciful costumes and, adorned with plumes of feathers, ascending the terraces of the palace and the steps leading to the temples; and often we imagined a scene of unique and gorgeous beauty and magnificence, realizing the creations of Oriental poets, the very spot which fancy would have selected for the "Happy Valley" of Rasselas. In the romance of the world's history nothing ever impressed me more forcibly than the spectacle of this once great and lovely city, overturned, desolate, and lost; discovered by accident, overgrown with trees for miles around, and without even a name to distinguish it. Apart from everything else, it was a mourning witness to the world's mutations.

"Nations melt
From Power's high pinnacle, when they have felt
The sunshine for a while, and downward go."

As at Copan, we shall not at present offer any conjecture in regard to the antiquity of these buildings, merely remarking that at ten leagues' distance is a village called Las Tres Cruces, or the Three Crosses, from three crosses which, according to tradition, Cortez erected at that place when on his conquering march from Mexico to Honduras by the lake of Peten. Cortez, then, must have passed within twenty or thirty miles of the place now called Palenque. If it had been a living city, its fame must have reached his ears, and he would probably have turned aside from his road to subdue and plunder it. It seems, therefore, but reasonable to suppose that it was at that time desolate and in ruins, and even the memory of it lost.

CHAPTER XXXVII.

DEPARTURE FROM THE RUINS—BAD ROAD—AN ACCIDENT—ARRIVAL AT THE VILLAGE—A FUNERAL PROCESSION—NEGOTIATIONS FOR PURCHASING PALENQUE—MAKING CASTS—FINAL DEPARTURE FROM PALENQUE—BEAUTIFUL PLAIN—HANGING BIRDS' NESTS—A SITIO—ADVENTURE WITH A MONSTROUS APE—HOSPITALITY OF PADRES—LAS PLAYAS—A TEMPEST—MOSQUITOES—A YOUTHFUL MERCHANT—ALLIGATORS—ANOTHER FUNERAL—DISGUSTING CEREMONIALS.

Among the Indians who came out to escort us to the village was one whom we had not seen before, and whose face bore a striking resemblance to those delineated on the walls of the buildings. In general the faces of the Indians were of an entirely different character, but he might have been taken for a lineal descendant of the perished race. The resemblance was perhaps purely accidental, but we were anxious to procure his portrait. He was, however, very shy, and unwilling to be drawn. Mr. Catherwood, too, was worn out, and in the confusion of removing, we postponed it upon his promising to come to us at the village, but we could not get hold of him again.*

We left behind our kitchen furniture, consisting of the three stones which Juan put together the first day of our residence, vessels of pottery and calabashes, and also our beds, for the benefit of the next comer. Everything susceptible of injury from damp was rusty or mouldy, and in a ruinous condition; we ourselves were not much better; and with the clothes on our backs far from dry, we bade farewell to the ruins. We were happy when we reached them, but our joy at leaving them burst the bounds of discretion, and broke out into

---

* There have lately been exhibited in the United States, and in England, two little Indian children, called by those who have the charge of them, *Aztec Lilliputians*, and said to have been brought from the mysterious city mentioned to Mr. Stephens and myself, by the Padre of Santa Cruz del Quiché, as related in the first part of this book. The story told of their capture, in the published account of them, it is scarcely worth while to refute, and I will only say, that in my opinion, it has not even the semblance of truth. In the case of the children, however, (after many times examining their countenances with great attention,) I am strongly of opinion, that they are descendants of the race who built the Palace at Palenque, and erected the various extensive and costly buildings which I afterwards made drawings of in Yucatan. If they be not descendants of these ancient builders, the profiles of their faces bear the most extraordinary likeness to the sculptured figures, and to the Indian whose portrait I was so anxious to obtain on the last day of my stay at Palenque. I afterwards saw some others of the same race, both men and women, exceedingly well-proportioned, but different from the tribes usually met with, very shy and taciturn, and said to follow in secret the pagan rites of their ancestors.

I have every reason to believe that the mysterious city mentioned by the Padre is a reality, and that it lies buried in the recesses of the mountainous country inhabited by the Lacandones, or unbaptized Indians, but I have no reason for believing that any one has yet penetrated to it.—F.C.

extravagances poetical, which, however, fortunately for the reader, did not advance much beyond the first line:—

"Adios, Las Casas de Piedra."

The road was worse than at any time before; the streams were swollen into rivers, and along the banks were steep, narrow gulleys, very difficult to pass. At one of these, after attempting to ascend with my macho, I dismounted. Mr. Catherwood was so weak that he remained on the back of his mule; and after he had crossed, just as he reached the top, the mule's strength gave way, and she fell backward, rolling over in the stream with Mr. Catherwood entirely under. Pawling was behind, and at that time in the stream. He sprang off and extricated Mr. Catherwood, unhurt, but very faint, and, as he was obliged to ride in his wet clothes, we had great apprehensions for him. At length we reached the village, when, exhausted by hard and unintermitted labour, he gave up completely, and took to bed and the medicine chest. In the evening nearly all my friends of the dinner-party came to see us. That one day had established an intimacy. All regretted that we had had such an unfortunate time at the ruins, wondered how we had lived through it, and were most kind in offers of services. The padre remained after the rest, and went home with a lantern in the midst of one of those dreadful storms which had almost terrified us at the ruins.

The next day again was Sunday. It was my third Sunday in the village, and again it was emphatically a day of rest. In the afternoon a mournful interruption was given to the stillness of the place by the funeral of a young Indian girl, once the pride and beauty of the village, whose portrait Mr. Waldeck had taken to embellish his intended work on Palenque. Her career, as often happens with beauty in higher life, was short, brilliant, and unhappy. She had married a young Indian, who abandoned her and went to another village. Ignorant, innocent, and unconscious of wrong, she was persuaded to marry another, drooped, and died. The funeral procession passed our door. The corpse was borne on a rude bier, without coffin, in a white cotton dress, with a shawl over the head, and followed by a slender procession of women and children only. I walked beside it, and heard one of them say, "Bueno Christiano, to attend the funeral of a poor woman." The bier was set down beside the grave, and in lifting the body from it the head turned on one side, and the hands dropped; the grave was too short, and as the dead was laid within, the legs were drawn up. Her face was thin and wasted, but the mouth had a sweetness of expression which seemed to express that she had died with a smile of forgiveness for him who had injured her. I could not turn my eyes from her placid but grief-worn countenance, and so touching was its expression that I could almost have shed tears. Young, beautiful, simple, and innocent, abandoned and dead, with not a mourner at her grave. All seemed to think that she was better dead: she was poor, and could not maintain herself. The men went away, and the women and children with their hands scraped the earth upon the body. It was covered up gradually and slowly; the feet stuck out, and then all was buried but the face. A small piece of muddy earth fell upon one of the eyes, and another on her sweetly smiling mouth, changing the whole expression in a moment; death was now robed with terror. The women stopped to comment upon the change; the dirt fell so as to cover the whole face except the nose, and for two or three moments this alone was visible. Another brush covered this, and the girl was buried. The reader will excuse me. I am sorry to say that if she had been ugly, I should, perhaps, have regarded it as an every-day case of a wife neglected by her husband; but her sweet face speaking from the grave created an impression which even yet is hardly effaced.

But to return to things more in my line. We had another long journey before us. Our next move was for Yucatan. From Mr. Catherwood's condition I had great fear that we should not be able to accomplish what we purposed; but, at all events, it was necessary to go down to the sea coast. There were two routes, either by Tobasco or the Laguna, to Campeachy, and war again confronted us. Both Tobasco and Campeachy were besieged by the Liberals, or, as they were called, the Revolutionists. The former route required three days' journey by land, the latter one short day; and as Mr. C. was not able to ride, this determined us. In the meantime, while waiting for his recovery, and so as not to rust and be utterly useless when I returned home, I started another operation, viz. the purchase of the city of Palenque. I am bound to say, however, that I was not bold enough to originate this, but fell into it accidentally, in a long conversation with the Prefect about the richness of the soil, the cheapness of land, its vicinity to the seaboard and the United States, and easy communication with New York. He told me that a merchant of Tobasco, who had visited the place, had proposed to purchase a tract of land and establish a colony of emigrants, but he had gone away and never returned. He added, that for two years a government order from the State of Chiapas, to which the region belonged, had been lying in his hands for the sale of all land in the vicinity, lying within certain limits; but there were no purchasers, and no sales were ever made. Upon inquiry I learned that this order, in its terms, embraced the ground occupied by the ruined city. No exception whatever was made in favour of it. He showed me the order, which was imperative; and he said that if any exception was intended, it would have been so expressed; wherefore he considered himself bound to receive an offer for any portion of the land. The sale was directed to be by appraisement, the applicant to name one man, the Prefect another, and, if necessary, they two to name a third; and the application, with the price fixed and the boundaries, was to be sent to Ciudad Real for the approval of the governor and a deed.

The tract containing the ruins consisted of about 6,000 acres of good land, which, according to the usual appraisement, would cost about 300*l.*, and the Prefect said that it would not be valued any higher on account of the ruins. I resolved immediately to buy it. I would fit up the palace and re-people the old city of Palenque. But there was one difficulty: by the laws of Mexico no stranger can purchase lands unless married to a hija del pais, or daughter of the country. This, by-the-way, is a grand stroke of policy, holding up the most powerful attraction of the country to seduce men from their natural allegiance, and radicate them in the soil; and it is taking them where weak and vulnerable; for, when wandering in strange countries, alone and friendless, buffeted and battered, with no one to care for him, there are moments when a lovely woman might root the stranger to any spot on earth. On principle I always resisted such tendencies, but I never before found it to my interest to give way. The ruined city of Palenque was a most desirable piece of property.

The case was embarrassing and complicated. Society in Palenque was small; the oldest young lady was not more than fourteen, and the prettiest woman, who already had contributed most to our happiness (she made our cigars), was already married. The house containing the two tablets belonged to a widow lady and a single sister, good-looking, amiable, and both about forty. The house was one of the neatest in the place. I always liked to visit it, and had before thought that, if passing a year at the ruins, it would be delightful to have this house in the village for recreation and occasional visits. With either of these ladies would come possession of the house and the two stone tablets; but the difficulty was that there were two of them, both equally interesting and equally interested. I am particular in mentioning these little circumstances, to show the difficulties that attended every step of our enterprise in that country. There was an alternative, and that was to purchase in the name of some other person; but I did not know any one I could trust. At length, however, I hit upon Mr.

Russell, the American consul at Laguna, who was married to a Spanish lady, and already had large possessions in the country; and I arranged with the Prefect to make the purchase in his name. Pawling was to accompany me to the Laguna, for the purpose of procuring and carrying back evidence of Mr. Russell's co-operation and the necessary funds, and was to act as my agent in completing the purchase. The Prefect was personally anxious to complete it. The buildings, he said, were fast going to decay, and in a few years more would be mounds of ruins. In that country they were not appreciated or understood, and he had the liberal wish that the tablets of hieroglyphics particularly might find their way to other countries, be inspected and studied by scientific men, and their origin and history be ascertained. Besides, he had an idea that immense discoveries were still to be made and treasures found, and he was anxious for a thorough exploration, in which he should himself co-operate. The two tablets which I had attempted to purchase were highly prized by the owners, but he thought they could be secured by purchasing the house, and I authorized him to buy it at a fixed price.

In my many conversations with the Prefect I had broached the subject of making casts from the tablets. Like every other official whom I met, he supposed that I was acting under a commission from my government, which idea was sustained by having in my employ a man of such character and appearance as Pawling, though every time I put my hand in my pocket I had a feeling sense that the case was far otherwise. In the matter of casts he offered every assistance, but there was no plaster-of-Paris nearer than the Laguna or Campeachy, and perhaps not there. We had made an experiment at the ruins by catching in the river a large quantity of snails and burning the shells, but it did not answer. He referred us to some limestone in the neighbourhood, but this would not do. Pawling knew nothing of casting. The idea had never entered his mind before, but he was willing to undertake this. Mr. Catherwood, who had been shut up in Athens during the Greek Revolution, when it was besieged by the Turks, and in pursuing his artistical studies had perforce made castings with his own hands, gave him written instructions, and it was agreed that when he returned with the credentials from Mr. Russell he should bring back plaster-of-Paris, and, while the proceedings for completing the purchase were pending, should occupy himself in this new branch of business.

On the fourth of June we took our final departure from Palenque. Don Santiago sent me a farewell letter, enclosing, according to the custom of the country, a piece of silk, the meaning of which I did not understand, but learned that it was meant as a pledge of friendship, which I reciprocated with a penknife. The Prefect was kind and courteous to the last; even the old Alcalde, drawing a little daily revenue from us, was touched. Every male inhabitant came to the house to bid us farewell and wish us to return; and before starting we rode round and exchanged adios with all their wives: good, kind, and quiet people, free from all agitating cares, and aiming only at an undisturbed existence in a place which I had been induced to believe the abode of savages and full of danger.

In order to accompany us, the cura had postponed for two days a visit to his hacienda, which lay on our road. Pawling continued with us for the purpose before mentioned, and Juan according to contract. I had agreed to return him to Guatimala. Completely among strangers, he was absolutely in our power, and followed blindly, but with great misgivings asked the padre where we were taking him. His impression was that he was setting out for my country, and he had but little expectation of ever seeing Guatimala again.

From the village we entered immediately upon a beautiful plain, picturesque, ornamented with trees, and extending five or six days' journey to the Gulf of Mexico. The road was very muddy, but, open to the sun in the morning, was not so bad as we feared. On the borders of a piece of woodland were singular trees, with tall trunks, the bark very smooth, and the branches festooned with hanging birds'-nests. The bird was called the jagua, and built in this tree, as the padre told us, to prevent serpents from getting at the young. The cura, notwithstanding his strange figure, and a life of incident and danger, was almost a woman in voice, manner, tastes, and feelings. He had been educated at the capital, and sent as a penance to this retired curacy. The visit of the padres had for the first time broken the monotony of his life. In the political convulsions of the capital he had made himself obnoxious to the church government by his liberal opinions; but unable, as he said, to find in him any tangible offence, his superiors had called him up on a charge of polluting the surplice, founded on the circumstance that, in the time of the cholera, when his fellow-creatures were lying all around him in the agonies of death, in leaning over their bodies to administer the sacrament, his surplice had been soiled by saliva from the mouth of a dying man. For this he was condemned to penance and prayers, from midnight till daybreak, for two years in the cathedral, deprived of a good curacy, and sent to Palenque.

At half-past two we reached his sitio, or small hacienda. In the apprehension of the afternoon's rain, we would have continued to the end of our afternoon's journey; but the padre watched carefully the appearance of the sky, and, after satisfying himself that the rain would not come on till late, positively forbade our passing on. His sitio was what would be called at home a "new" place, being a tract of wild land of I do not know what extent, but some large quantity, which had cost him five pounds, and about as much more to make the improvements, which consisted of a hut made of poles and thatched with corn-husks, and a cocina or kitchen at a little distance. The stables and outhouses were a clearing bounded by a forest so thick that cattle could not penetrate it, and on the roadside by a rude fence. Altogether, in that mild climate, the effect was good; and it was one of those occasions which make a man feel, away from the region of fictitious wants, how little is necessary for the comforts of life. The furniture of the hut consisted of two reed bedsteads, a table, and a bench, and in one corner was a pile of corn. The cura sent out for half-a-dozen fresh pine-apples; and while we were refreshing ourselves with them we heard an extraordinary noise in the woods, which an Indian boy told us was made by "un animal." Pawling and I took our guns, and, entering a path in the woods, as we advanced the noise sounded fearful, but all at once it stopped. The boy opened a way through thickets of brush and underwood, and through an opening in the branches I saw on the limbs of a high tree a large black animal with fiery eyes. The boy said it was not a mico or monkey, and I supposed it to be a catamount. I had barely an opening through which to take aim, fired, and the animal dropped below the range of view; but, not hearing him strike the ground, I looked again, and saw him hanging by his tail, and dead, with the blood streaming from his mouth. Pawling attempted to climb the tree; but it was fifty feet to the first branch, and the blood trickled down the trunk. Wishing to examine the creature more closely, we sent the boy to the house, whence he returned with a couple of Indians. They cut down the tree, which fell with a terrible crash, and still the animal hung by its tail. The ball had struck him in the mouth and knocked out the fore teeth, passed out at the top of his back between his shoulders, and must have killed him instantly. The tenacity of his tail seemed marvellous, but was easily explained. It had no grip, and had lost all muscular power, but was wound round the branch with the end under so that the weight of the body tightened the coil, and the harder the strain, the more secure was the hold. It was not a monkey, but so near a connexion that I would not have shot him if I had known it. In fact, he was even more nearly related to the human family, being called a monos or ape, and measured six feet including the tail; very muscular, and in a struggle would have been more than a match for a man; and the padre said they were known to have attacked women. The Indians carried him up to the house and skinned him; and when lying on his back, with his skin off and his eyes staring, the padre cried out, "es hombre," it is a man, and I almost felt liable to an indictment for homicide. The Indians cooked the body, and I contrived to preserve the skin as a curiosity, for its extraordinary size; but, unluckily, I left it on board a Spanish vessel at sea.

In the meantime the padre had a fowl boiled for dinner. Three guests at a time were not too much for his open hospitality, but they went beyond his dinner-service, which consisted of three bowls. There was no plate, knife, fork, or spoon, and for the cura himself not even a bowl. The fowl was served in an ocean of broth, which had to be disposed of first. Tortillas and a small cake of fresh cheese composed the rest of the meal. The reader will perhaps connect such an entertainment with vulgarity of manners; but the cura was a gentleman, and made no apologies, for he gave us the best he had. We had sent our carriers on before, the padre gave us a servant as a guide, and at three o'clock we bade him farewell. He was the last padre whom we met, and put a seal upon the kindness we had received from all the padres of that country.

At five o'clock, by a muddy road, through a picturesque country, remarkable only for swarms of butterflies with large yellow wings, which filled the air, we reached Las Playas. This village is the head of navigation of the waters that empty in this direction into the Gulf of Mexico. The whole of the great plain to the sea is intersected by creeks and rivers, some of them in the summer dry, and on the rising of the waters overflowing their banks. At this season the plain on one side of the village was inundated, and seemed a large lake. The village was a small collection of huts upon what might be called its banks It consisted of one street or road, grass-grown and still as at Palenque, at the extreme end of which was the church, under the pastoral care of our friend the padre. Our guide, according to the directions of the padre, conducted us to the convent, and engaged the sexton to provide us with supper. The convent was built of upright sticks, with a thatched roof, mud floor, and furnished with three reed bedsteads and a table.

At this place we were to embark in a canoe, and had sent a courier a day beforehand with a letter from the Prefect to the juez, to have one ready for us. The juez was a portly mulatto, well dressed, and very civil, had a canoe of his own, and promised to procure us two bogadores or rowers in the morning. Very soon the mosquitoes made alarming demonstrations, and gave us apprehensions of a fearful night. To make a show of resistance, we built a large fire in the middle of the convent. At night the storm came on with a high wind, which made it necessary to close the doors. For two hours we had a tempest of wind and rain, with terrific thunder and lightning. One blast burst open the door and scattered the fire, so that it came very near burning down the convent. Between the smoke and mosquitoes, it was a matter of debate which of the two to choose,—suffocation or torture. We preferred the former, and had the latter besides, and passed a miserable night.

The next morning the juez came to say that the bogadores were not ready, and could not go that day. The price which he named was about twice as much as the cura told us we ought to pay, besides possol (balls of mashed Indian corn), tortillas, honey, and meat. I remonstrated, and he went off to consult the mozos, but returned to say that they would not take less, and, after treating him with but little of the respect due to office, I was obliged to accede; but I ought to add, that throughout that country, in general, prices are fixed, and there is less advantage taken of the necessity of travellers than in most others. We were loth to remain, for, besides the loss of time and the mosquitoes, the scarcity of provisions was greater than at Palenque.

The sexton bought us some corn, and his wife made us tortillas. The principal merchant in the place, or, at least, the one who traded most largely with us, was a little boy about twelve years old, who was dressed in a petate or straw hat. He had brought us some fruit, and we saw him coming again with a string over his naked shoulder, dragging on the ground what proved to be a large fish. The principal food of the place was young alligators. They were about a foot and a half long, and at that youthful time of life were considered very tender. At their first appearance on the table they had not an inviting aspect, but—ce n'est que le premier pas qui coûte—they tasted better than the fish, and they were the best food possible for our canoe voyage, being dried and capable of preservation.

Go where we will, to the uttermost parts of the earth, we are sure to meet one acquaintance. Death is always with us. In the afternoon was the funeral of a child. The procession consisted of eight or ten grown persons, and as many boys and girls. The sexton carried the child in his arms, dressed in white, with a wreath of flowers around its head. All were huddled around the sexton, walking together; the father and mother with him; and even more than in Costa Rica I remarked, not only an absence of solemnity, but cheerfulness and actual gaiety, from the same happy conviction that the child had gone to a better world. I happened to be in the church as they approached, more like a wedding than a burial party. The floor of the church was earthen, and the grave was dug inside, because, as the sexton told me, the father was rich and could afford to pay for it, and the father seemed pleased and proud that he could give his child such a burial-place. The sexton laid the child in the grave, folded its little hands across its breast, placing there a small rude cross, covered it over with eight or ten inches of earth, and then got into the grave and stamped it down with his feet. He then got out and threw in more, and, going outside of the church, brought back a pounder, being a log of wood about four feet long and ten inches in diameter, like the rammer used among us by paviors, and again taking his place in the grave, threw up the pounder to the full swing of his arms, and brought it down with all his strength over the head of the child. My blood ran cold. As he threw it up a second time I caught his arm and remonstrated with him, but he said that they always did so with those buried inside the church; that the earth must be all put back, and the floor of the church made even. My remonstrances seemed only to give him more strength and spirit. The sweat rolled down his body, and when perfectly tired with pounding he stepped out of the grave. But this was nothing. More earth was thrown in, and the father laid down his hat, stepped into the grave, and the pounder was handed to him. I saw him throw it up twice and bring it down with a dead, heavy noise. I never beheld a more brutal and disgusting scene. The child's body must have been crushed to atoms.

Toward evening the mosquitoes began their operations. Pawling and Juan planted sticks in the ground outside the convent, and spread sheets over them for nets; but the rain came on and drove them within, and we passed another wretched night. It may be asked how the inhabitants live. I cannot answer. They seemed to suffer as much as we, but at home they might have conveniences which we could not carry in travelling. Pawling suffered so much, and heard such dreadful accounts of what we should meet with below, that, in a spirit of impetuosity and irritation, he resolved not to continue any further. From the difficulty and uncertainty of communications, however, I strongly apprehended that in such case all the schemes in which he was concerned must fall through and be abandoned, as I was not willing to incur the expense of sending materials, subject to delays and uncertainties, unless in special charge, and once more he changed his purpose.

I had but one leave-taking, and that was a trying one. I was to bid farewell to my noble macho. He had carried me more than 2,000 miles, over the worst roads that mule ever travelled. He stood tied to the door of the convent; saw the luggage, and even his own saddle, carried away by hand, and seemed to have a presentiment that something unusual was going on. I had often been solicited to sell him, but no money could have tempted me. He was in poorer condition than when we reached Palenque. Deprived of corn, and exposed to the dreadful rains, he was worse than when worked hard and fed well every day, and in his drooping state seemed to reproach me for going away and leaving him forlorn. I threw my arms around his neck; his eyes had a mournful expression, and at that moment he forgot the angry prick of the spur. I laid aside the memory of a toss from his back and ineffectual attempts to repeat it, and we remembered only mutual kind offices and good-fellowship. Tried and faithful companion, where are you now? I left him, with two others, tied at the door of the convent, to be taken by the sexton to the Prefect at Palenque, there to recover from the debilitating influence of the early rains, and to roam on rich pasture-grounds, untouched by bridle or spur, until I should return to mount him again.

CHAPTER XXXVIII.

EMBARKATION—AN INUNDATED PLAIN—RIO CHICO—THE USUMASINTA—RIO PALISADA—YUCATAN—MORE REVOLUTIONS—VESPERS—EMBARKATION FOR THE LAGUNA—SHOOTING ALLIGATORS—TREMENDOUS STORM—BOCA CHICO—LAKE OF TERMINOS—A CALM, SUCCEEDED BY A TEMPEST—ARRIVAL AT THE LAGUNA.

At seven o'clock we went down to the shore to embark. The boatmen whom the juez had consulted, and for whom he had been so tenacious, were his honour himself and another man, who, we thought, was hired as the cheapest help he could find in the village. The canoe was about forty feet long, with a toldo or awning of about twelve feet at the stern, and covered with matting. All the space before this was required by the boatmen to work the canoe, and, with all our luggage under the awning, we had but narrow quarters. The seeming lake on which we started was merely a large inundated plain, covered with water to the depth of three or four feet; and the juez in the stern, and his assistant before, walking in the bottom of the canoe, with poles against their shoulders, set her across. At eight o'clock we entered a narrow, muddy creek, not wider than a canal, but very deep, and with the current against us. The setting-pole could not touch the bottom, but it was forked at one end, and, keeping close to the bank, the bogador or rower fixed it against the branches of overhanging trees and pushed, while the juez, whose pole had a rude hook, fastened it to other branches forward, and pulled. In this way, with no view but that of the wooded banks, we worked slowly along the muddy stream. In turning a short bend, suddenly we saw on the banks eight or ten alligators, some of them twenty feet long, huge, hideous monsters, appropriate inhabitants of such a stream, and, considering the frailty of our little vessel, not very attractive neighbours. As we approached, they plunged heavily into the water, sometimes rose in the middle of the stream, and swam across or disappeared. At half past twelve we entered the Rio Chico or Little River, varying from 200 to 500 feet in width, deep, muddy, and very sluggish, with wooded banks of impenetrable thickness. At six o'clock we entered the great Usumasinta, 500 or 600 yards across, one of the noblest rivers in Central America, rising among the mountains of Peten, and emptying into the lake of Terminos.

At this point, the three provinces of Chiapas, Tobasco, and Yucatan meet, and the junction of the waters of the Usumasinta and the Rio

Chico presents a singular spectacle. Since leaving the sheet of water before the Playas we had been ascending the stream, but now, continuing in the same direction and crossing the line of junction, we came from the ascending current of the Rio Chico into the descending flow of the Usumasinta. Working out into the middle and looking back, we saw the Usumasinta and Rio Chico coming together, and forming an angle of not more than forty degrees, one running up and the other down. Amid the wildness and stillness of the majestic river, and floating in a little canoe, the effect was very extraordinary; but the cause was obvious.*

At this time, away from the wooded banks, with the setting-poles at rest, and floating quietly on the bosom of the noble Usumasinta, our situation was pleasant and exciting. A strong wind sweeping down the river drove away the mosquitoes, and there were no gathering clouds to indicate rain. We had expected to come to for the night, but the evening was so clear that we determined to continue. Unfortunately, we were obliged to leave the Usumasinta, and, about an hour after dark, turned to the north into the Rio Palisada. The whole great plain from Palenque to the Gulf of Mexico is broken by creeks and streams. The Usumasinta in its stately course receives many, and sends off others to find their way by separate channels to the sea.

Leaving the broad expanse of the Usumasinta, with its comparative light, the Rio Palisada, narrow, and with a dark line of forest on each side, had an aspect fearfully ominous of mosquitoes. Unfortunately, at the very beginning we brushed against the bank, and took on board enough to show us the bloodthirsty character of the natives. Of course that night afforded us little sleep.

At daylight we were still dropping down the river. This was the region of the great logwood country. We met a large bungo with two masts moving against the stream, set up by hauling and pushing on the branches of trees, on her way for a cargo. As we advanced, the banks of the river in some places were cleared and cultivated, and had whitewashed houses, and small sugar-mills turned by oxen, and canoes were lying on the water; altogether the scene was pretty, but with the richness of the soil suggesting the idea how beautiful this country might be made.

At two o'clock we reached the Palisada, situated on the left bank of the river, on a luxuriant plain elevated some fifteen or twenty feet.

---

* The Usumasinta being at this time of the year at a higher level than the Rio Chico and the adjacent plains of Las Playas, the waters of the great Usumasinta flow up the latter river until the level is restored. At other seasons of the year both rivers flow downwards in the same direction. I have recently observed the same phenomenon, but on a much larger scale, at the junction of the Columbia and Willamette Rivers, in Oregon Territory.—F.C.

Several bungoes lay along the bank, and in front was a long street, with large and well-built houses. This, our first point, was in the State of Yucatan, then in revolution against the government of Mexico. Our descent of the river had been watched from the bank, and before we landed we were hailed, asked for our passports, and directed to present ourselves immediately to the alcalde The intimation was peremptory, and we proceeded forthwith to the alcalde. Don Francisco Hebreu was superior to any man I had yet found at the head of a municipality; in fact, he was chief of the Liberal party in that section of the state, and, like all the other officials in the Mexican provinces, received us with the respect due to an official passport of a friendly nation. We were again in the midst of a revolution, but had not the remotest idea what it was about. We were most intimately acquainted with Central American politics, but this was of no more use to us than a knowledge of Texan politics would be to a stranger in the United States. For several months the names of Morazan and Carrera had rung in our ears like those of our own candidates for the presidency at a contested election; but we had passed the limits of their world, and were obliged to begin anew.

For eight years the Central party had maintained the ascendency in Mexico, during which time, as a mark of the *sympathy* between neighbouring people, the Liberal or Democratic party had been ascendant in Central America. Within the last six months the Centralists had overturned the Liberals in Central America, and during the same time the Liberalists had almost driven out the Centralists in Mexico. Along the whole coast of the Pacific the Liberals were in arms, waging a strong revolutionary war, and threatening the capital, which they afterwards entered, but, after great massacre and bloodshed, were expelled. On the Atlantic side, the states of Tobasco and Yucatan had declared their independence of the General Government, and in the interior of both states the officials of the Central Government had been driven out. The seaports of Tobasco and Campeachy, garrisoned by Central troops, still held out, but they were at that time blockaded and besieged on land by the Federal forces. All communications by sea and land were cut off, their supplies were short, and Don Francisco thought they would soon be obliged by starvation to surrender.

The revolution seemed of a higher tone, for greater cause, and conducted with more moderation than in Central America. The grounds of revolt here were the despotism of the Central Government, which, far removed by position, and ignorant of the condition and resources of the country, used its distant provinces as a quartering place for rapacious officers, and a source of revenue for money to be squandered in the capital. One little circumstance showed the impolicy and inefficiency of the laws. On account of high duties, smuggling was carried to such an extent on the coast that many articles were regularly sold at the Palisada for much less than the duties.

The revolution, like all others in that country, began with pronunciamentos, *i.e.* declarations of the municipality, or what we should call the corporation of a town, in favour of any particular party. The Palisada had made its pronunciamento but two weeks before, the Central officers had been turned out, and the present alcalde was hardly warm in his place. The change, however, had been effected with a spirit of moderation and forbearance, and without bloodshed. Don Francisco, with a liberality unusual, spoke of his immediate predecessor as an upright but misguided man, who was not persecuted, but then living in the place unmolested. The Liberals, however, did not expect the same treatment at the hands of the Centralists. An invasion had been apprehended from Tobasco. Don Francisco had his silver and valuables packed up, and kept his bungo before the door to save his effects and family, and the place was alive with patriots brushing up arms and preparing for war.

Don Francisco was a rich man; had a hacienda of 30,000 head of cattle, logwood plantations, and bungoes, and was rated at 200,000 dollars. The house in which he lived was on the bank of the river, newly built, 150 feet front, and had cost him 20,000 dollars, or 4,000*l.* While we were with him, dinner was about being served, in a liberal style of housekeeping unusual in that country, and, with the freedom of a man who felt sure that he could not be taken unawares, he asked us to join him at table. Don Francisco had never travelled farther than Tobasco and Campeachy, but he was well acquainted with Europe and the United States, geographically and politically; indeed, he was one of the most agreeable companions and best-informed men we met in that country. We remained with him all the afternoon, and toward evening moved our chairs outside in front of the house, which at evening was the regular gathering-place of the family. The bank of the river was a promenade for the people of the town, who stopped to exchange greetings with Don Francisco and his wife; a vacant chair was always at hand, and from time to time one took a seat with us. When the vesper bell struck, conversation ceased, all rose from their seats, made a short prayer, and when it was over turned to each other with a buenos noces, good evening, reseated themselves, and renewed the conversation. There was always something imposing in the sound of the vesper bell, presenting the idea of an immense multitude of people at the same moment offering up a prayer.

During the evening a courier arrived with despatches for Don Francisco, bringing intelligence that a town which had "pronounced" in favour of the Liberals had pronounced back again, which seemed to give both him and his wife much uneasiness. At ten o'clock an armed patrol came for orders, and we retired to what we much needed, a good night's rest.

In the morning, Don Francisco, half in jest and half in earnest, told us of the uneasiness we had given his wife. Pawling's Spanish, and constant use of idioms well known as belonging to the city of Mexico, had excited her suspicions; she said he was not an American, but a Mexican from the capital, and she believed him to be a spy of the Centralists. Pawling did not like the imputation; he was a little mortified at this visible mark of long absence from his country, and not at all flattered at being taken for a Mexican. Don Francisco laughed at it, but his wife was so pertinacious, that, if it had not been for the apparent propriety of my being attended by one perfectly familiar with the language of the country, I believe, in the state of apprehension and distrust, Pawling would have lost the benefit of his birthright, and been arrested as a spy.

We passed the next day in a quiet lounge and in making arrangements for continuing our journey, and the next day after, furnished with a luxurious supply of provisions-by the señora, and accompanied to the place by Don Francisco, we embarked on board a bungo for the Laguna. The bungo was about fifteen tons burden, flat-bottomed, with two masts and sails, and loaded with logwood. The deck was covered with mangoes, plantains, and other fruits and vegetables, and so encumbered, that it was impossible to move. The stern had movable hatches. A few tiers of logwood had been taken out, and the hatches put over so as to give us a shelter against rain; a sail was rigged into an awning to protect us from the sun, and in a few minutes we pushed off from the bank.

We had as passengers two young Central Americans from Peten, both under twenty, and flying on account of the dominion of the Carrera party. Coming, as we did, direct from Central America, we called each other countrymen. We soon saw that the bungo had a miserable crew. Up river the men were called bogadores or rowers; but here, as they were on board a bungo with sails, and going down to the seacoast, they called themselves marineros, or sailors. The patron, or master, was a mild, inoffensive, and inefficient man, who prefaced all his orders to his breechless marineros with the conciliatory words—"Señores, haga me el favor;" "Gentlemen, do me the favour."

Below the town commenced an island, about four leagues in length, at the end of which, on the main land, was a large clearing and farming establishment, with canoes lying on the water. All travelling here is along the river, and in canoes. From this place there were no habitations; the river was very deep, the banks densely wooded, with the branches spreading far over.

Very soon we came to a part of the river where the alligators seemed to enjoy undisturbed possession. Some lay basking in the sun on mudbanks, like logs of driftwood, and in many places the river was dotted with their heads. The Spanish historian says, that "They swim with their Head above the water, gaping at whatsoever they see, and swallow it, whether Stick, Stone, or living Creature, which is the true reason of their swallowing Stones; and not to sink to the bottom, as some say, for they have no need to do so, nor do they like it, being extraordinary Swimmers; for the Tail serves instead of a Rudder, the Head is the Prow, and the Paws the Oars, being so swift as to catch any other fish as it swims. An hundred Weight and a half of fresh Fish has been found in the Maw of an Alligator, besides what was digested; in another was an Indian Woman, whole, with her Cloaths, whom he had swallowed the Day before, and another with a pair of Gold Bracelets, with Pearls, the Enamel gone off, and Part of the Pearls dissolved, but the Gold entire."

Here they still maintained their dominion. Accidents frequently happen; and at the Palisada, Don Francisco told us that a year before a man had had his leg bitten off, and was drowned. Three were lying together at the mouth of a small stream which emptied into the river. The patron told us that at the end of the last dry season upward of 200 had been counted in the bed of a pond emptied by this stream. The boatmen of several bungoes went in among them with clubs, sharp stakes, and machetes, and killed upward of sixty. The river itself, discoloured, with muddy banks, and a fiery sun beating upon it, was ugly enough; but these huge and ugly monsters, neither fish nor flesh, made it absolutely hideous. The boatmen called them enemigos de los Christianos, by which they mean enemies of mankind. In a canoe it would have been unpleasant to disturb them, but in the bungo we brought out our guns and made indiscriminate war. One monster, twenty-five or thirty feet long, lay on the arm of a gigantic tree, which projected forty or fifty feet, the lower part covered with water, but the whole of the alligator was visible. He was hit just under the white line; he fell off, and with a tremendous convulsion, reddening the water with a circle of blood, turned over on his back, dead. A boatman and one of the Peten lads got into a canoe to bring him alongside. The canoe was small and tottering, and had not proceeded fifty yards before it dipped, filled, upset, and threw them both into the water. At that moment there were perhaps twenty alligators in sight on the banks and swimming in different parts of the river. We could do nothing for the man and boy, and the old bungo, which before hardly moved, seemed to start forward purposely to leave them to their fate. Every moment the distance between us and them increased, and on board all was confusion; the patron cried out in agony to the señores, and the señores, straining every nerve, turned the bungo into the bank, and got the masts foul of the branches of the trees, which held her fast. In the meantime our friends in the water were not idle. The Peten lad struck out vigorously toward the shore, and we saw him seize the branch of a tree, which projected fifty feet over the water, so low as to be within reach, haul himself up like a monkey, and run along it to the shore. The marinero, having the canoe to himself, turned her bottom upward, got astride, and paddled down with his hands. Both got safely on board, and, apprehension over, the affair was considered a good joke.

In the meantime, our masts had become so locked in the branches of the trees that we carried away some of our miserable tackling in extricating them; but at length we were once more in the middle of the river, and renewed our war upon los enemigos de los Christianos. The sun was so hot that we could not stand outside the awning, but the boatmen gave us notice when we could have a shot. Our track down the river will be remembered as a desolation and scourge. Old alligators, by dying injunction, will teach the rising generation to keep the head under water when the bungoes are coming. We killed perhaps twenty, and others are probably at this moment sitting on the banks with our bullets in their bodies, wondering how they came there. With rifles we could have killed at least a hundred.

At three o'clock the regular afternoon storm came on, beginning with a tremendous sweep of wind up the river, which turned the bungo round, drove her broadside up the stream, and before we could come to at the bank we had a deluge of rain. At length we made fast, secured the hatch over the place prepared for us, and crawled under. It was so low that we could not sit up, and, lying down, there was about a foot of room above us. On our arrival at the Palisada we considered ourselves fortunate in finding a bungo ready, although she had already on board a full load of logwood from stem to stern. Don Francisco said it would be too uncomfortable, and wished us to wait for a bungo of his own; but delay was to us a worse evil, and I made a bargain to have a portion of the logwood taken out behind the mainmast, so as to admit of a hatch on deck, and give room below. But we had not given any personal superintendence; and when we came on board, though the logwood seemed of a rather-hard species for sleeping on, we did not discover the extreme discomfort of the place until forced below by the rain. Even the small place engaged, and paid for accordingly, we had not to ourselves. The Peten lads crawled under with us, and the patron and señores followed. We could not drive them out into a merciless rain, and all lay like one mass of human flesh, animated by the same spirit of suffering, irritation, and helplessness. During this time the rain was descending in a deluge; the thunder rolled fearfully over our heads; lightning flashed in through the crevices of our dark burrowing-place, dazzling and blinding our eyes; and we heard near us the terrific crash of a falling tree, snapped by the wind, or, as we, then, supposed, shivered by lightning.

Such was our position. Sometimes the knots in the logwood fitted well into the curves and hollows of the body, but in general they were just where they should not be. We thought we could not be worse off, but very soon we found our mistake, and looked back upon ourselves as ungrateful murmurers without cause. The mosquitoes claimed us as waifs, and in murderous swarms found their way under the hatches, humming and buzzing—

> "Fee, faw, fum,
> I smell the blood of an Englishman,
> Dead or alive I will have some."

I now look back upon our troubles at that place with perfect equanimity; but at the moment, with the heat and confinement, we were in anything but an amiable humour, and at ten o'clock broke out furious, upbraided the patron and his lazy señores for not reaching the mouth of the river before night, as is usually done, and as he had been charged by the alcalde to do, and insisted upon his hauling out into the stream.

The rain had ceased, but the wind was still furious, and dead a-head. By the misty light we saw a large bungo, with one sail set, seemingly flying up the river like a phantom. We made the patron haul out from the bank, but we could not keep the river, and, after a few zigzag movements, were shot across to the opposite side, where we brought upon us new and more hungry swarms. Here we remained an hour longer, when the wind died away, and we pushed out into the stream. This was a great relief. The señores, though more used to the scourge of mosquitoes than we, suffered quite as much. The clouds rolled away, the moon broke out, and, but for the abominable insects, our float down the wild and desolate river would have been an event to live in memory; as it was, not one of us attempted to sleep; and I verily believe a man could not have passed an entire night on the banks and lived.

At daylight we were still in the river. Very soon we reached a small lake, and, making a few tacks, entered a narrow passage called the Boca Chica, or Little Mouth. The water was almost even with the banks, and on each side were the most gigantic trees of the tropical forests, their roots naked three or four feet above the ground, gnarled, twisted, and interlacing each other, grey and dead-looking, and holding up, so as to afford an extended view under the first branches, a forest of vivid green. At ten o'clock we passed the Boca Chica, and entered the lake of Terminos. Once more in salt water, and stretching out under full sail, on the right we saw only an expanse of water; on the left was a border of trees with naked roots, which seemed growing out of the water; and in front, but a little to the left, and barely visible, a long line of trees, marking the island of Carmen, on which stood the town of Laguna, our port of destination. The passage into the lake was shoal and narrow, with reefs and sandbars, and our boatmen did not let slip the chance of running her ashore. Their efforts to get her off capped the climax of stupidity and laziness; one or two of them pushing on poles at a time, as if they were shoving off a row-boat, and then stopping to rest and giving up to others. Of what could be done by united force they seemed to have no idea; and, after a few ineffectual efforts, the patron said we must remain till the tide rose. We had no idea of another night on board the bungo, and took entire command of the vessel. This we were entitled to do from the physical force we brought into action, and we were altogether four able-bodied and desperate men. Juan's efforts were gigantic. From the great surface exposed, the mosquitoes had tormented him dreadfully, and he was even more disgusted with the bungo than we. We put two of the men into the water to heave against the bottom with their shoulders, and ourselves bearing on poles all together, we shoved her off into deep water. With a gentle breeze we sailed smoothly along until we could distinguish the masts of vessels at the Laguna rising above the island, when the wind died away entirely, and left us under a broiling sun in a dead calm.

At two o'clock we saw clouds gathering, and immediately the sky became very black, the harbinger of one of those dreadful storms which even on dry land were terrible. The hatches were put down, and a tarpaulin spread over for us to take refuge under. The squall came on so suddenly that the men were taken unawares, and the confusion on board was alarming. The patron, with both hands extended, and a most beseeching look, begged the señores to take in sail; and the señores, all shouting together, ran and tumbled over the logwood, hauling upon every rope but the right one. The mainsail stuck half way up, and would not come down; and while the patron and all the men were shouting and looking up at it, the marinero who had been upset in the canoe, with tears of terror actually streaming from his eyes, and a start of desperation, ran up the mast by the rings, and, springing violently upon the top one, holding fast by a rope, brought the sail down with a run. A hurricane blew through the naked masts, a deluge of rain followed, and the lake was lashed into fury; we lost sight of everything. At the very beginning, on account of the confusion on board, we determined not to go under the hatch; if the bungo swamped, the logwood cargo would carry her to the bottom like lead. We disencumbered ourselves of boots and coats, and brought out life-preservers ready for use. The deck of the bungo was about three feet from the water, and perfectly smooth, without anything to hold on by; and, to keep from being blown or washed away, we lay down and took the whole brunt of the storm. The atmosphere was black; but by the flashes we saw the bare poles of another bungo, tossed, like ourselves, at the mercy of the storm. This continued more than an hour, when it cleared off as suddenly as it came up, and we saw the Laguna crowded with more shipping than we had seen since we left New York. In our long inland journey we had almost forgotten the use of ships, and the very sight of them seemed to bring us into close relations with home. The squall having spent its fury, there was now a dead calm. The men took to their sweeps, but made very little headway; and, with the port in full sight, we had great apprehensions of another night on board, when another squall came on, not so violent, but blowing directly from the harbour. Tremendous rain accompanied it. We made two or three tacks under a close-reefed foresail; the old bungo seemed to fly through the water; and, when, under full way, the anchor, or, to speak more correctly, stone, was thrown out at some distance below the shipping, and brought us up all standing. There were breakers between us and the shore, and we hallooed to some men to come and take us off, but they answered that the breakers were too rough. The rain came on again, and for half an hour we stowed ourselves away under hatches.

As soon as it cleared off we were on deck, and in a little time we saw a fine jolly-boat, with a cockswain and four men, coasting along the shore against a rapid current, the men at times jumping into the water, and hauling by ropes fixed for the purpose. We hailed them in English, and the cockswain answered in the same language, that it was too rough, but after a consultation with the sailors they pulled towards us, and took Mr. Catherwood and me on board. The cockswain was the mate of a French ship, and spoke English. His ship was to sail the next day, and he was going to take in some large turtles which lay on the beach waiting for him. As soon as we struck, we mounted the shoulders of two square-built French sailors, and were set down on shore, and perhaps in our whole tour we were never so happy as at that moment in being rid of the bungo.

The town extended along the bank of the lake. We walked the whole length of it, saw numerous and well-filled stores, cafés, and even barbers' shops, and at the extreme end reached the American consul's. Two men were sitting on the portico, of a most home-like appearance. One was Don Carlos Russell, the consul. The face of the other was familiar to me; and learning that we had come from Guatimala, he asked news of me, which I was most happy to give him in person. It was Captain Fensley, whose acquaintance I had made in New York, when seeking information about that country, and with whom I had spoken of sailing to Campeachy; but at the moment I did not recognise him, and in my costume from the interior it was impossible for him to recognise me. He was direct from New York, and gave the first information we had received in a long time from that place, with budgets of newspapers, burdened with suspension of specie payments and universal ruin. Some of my friends had been playing strange antics; but in the important matters of marriages and deaths I did not find anything to give me either joy or sorrow.

Don Carlos Russell, or Mr. Charles Russell, was a native of Philadelphia, married to a Spanish lady of large fortune, and, though long absent, received us as one who had not forgotten his home. His house, his table, all that he had, even his purse, were at our service. Our first congratulations over, we sat down to a dinner which rivalled that of our friend of Totonicapan. We could hardly believe ourselves the same miserable beings who had been a few hours before tossing on the lake, in dread alike of the bottom and of another night on board the bungo. The reader must have gone through what we had to form any idea of our enjoyment.

CHAPTER XXXIX.

LAGUNA—JOURNEY TO MERIDA—SISAL—A NEW MODE OF CONVEYANCE—VILLAGE OF HUNUCAMA—ARRIVAL AT MERIDA—ASPECT OF THE CITY—FÊTE OF CORPUS DOMINI—THE CATHEDRAL—THE PROCESSION—BEAUTY AND SIMPLICITY OF THE INDIAN WOMEN—PALACE OF THE BISHOP—THE THEATRE—JOURNEY TO UXMAL—HACIENDA OF VAYALQUEX—VALUE OF WATER—CONDITION OF THE INDIANS IN YUCATAN—A PECULIAR KIND OF COACH—HACIENDA OF MUCUYCHE—A BEAUTIFUL GROTTO.

THE town of Laguna stands on the island of Carmen, which is about seven leagues long, and which, with another island about four leagues in length, separates the lake of Terminos from the Gulf of Mexico. It is the dépôt of the great logwood country in the interior, and a dozen vessels were then in port awaiting cargoes for Europe and the United States. The town is well built and thriving; its trade has been trammelled by the oppressive regulations of the Central government, but it had made its pronunciamento, disarmed and driven out the garrison, and considered itself independent, subject only to the State government of Yucatan. The anchorage is shoal, but safe, and easy of access for vessels not drawing over twelve or thirteen feet of water.

We could have passed some time with satisfaction in resting and strolling over the island, but our journey was not yet ended. Our next move was for Merida, the capital of Yucatan. The nearest port was Campeachy, 120 miles distant, and the voyage was usually made by bungo, coasting along the shore of the open sea. With our experience of bungoes this was most disheartening. Nevertheless, this would have been our unhappy lot, but for the kindness of Mr. Russell and Captain Fensley. The latter was bound directly to New York, and his course lay along the coast of Yucatan. Personally he was disposed to do all in his power to serve us, but there might be some risk in putting into port to land us. Knowing his favourable disposition, we could not urge him; but Mr. Russell was his consignee, and by charter-party had a right to detain him ten days, and intended to do so; but he offered to load him in two days upon condition of his taking us on board, and, as Campeachy was blockaded, landing us at Sisal, sixty miles beyond, and the seaport of Merida. Captain Fensley assented, and we were relieved from what at the time we should have considered a great calamity.

On Saturday morning at seven o'clock we bade farewell to Mr. Russell, and embarked on board the Gabrielacho. Pawling accompanied us outside the bar, and we took leave of him as he got on board the pilot-boat to return. We had gone through such rough scenes together since he overtook us at the foot of the Sierra Madre, that it may be supposed we did not separate with indifference. Juan was still with us, for the first time at sea, and wondering where we should take him next.

The Gabrielacho was a beautiful brig of about 160 tons, built under Captain Fensley's own direction, one half belonging to himself, and fitted up neatly and tastefully as a home. He had no house on shore; one daughter was at boarding-school in the United States, and the rest of his family, consisting of his wife and a little daughter about three years old, was with him on board. Since his marriage seven years before, his wife had remained but one year on shore, and she determined not to leave him again as long as he followed the seas; while he was resolved that every voyage should be the last, and looked forward to the consummation of every sailor's hopes, a good farm. His daughter Vicentia, or poor Centy, as she called herself, was the pet of all on board; and we had twelve passengers, interesting to the Aldermen of New York, being enormous turtles, one of which the captain hoped would gladden the hearts of the fathers of the city at their next annual dinner.

The reader cannot realize the satisfaction with which we found ourselves in such comfortable quarters on board this brig. We had an afternoon squall, but we considered ourselves merely passengers, and, with a good vessel, master, and crew, laughed at a distant bungo crawling close along the shore, and for the first time feared that the voyage would end too soon. Perhaps no captain ever had passengers so perfectly contented under storm or calm. Oh you who cross the Atlantic in packet-ships, complaining of discomforts, and threaten to publish the captain because the porter does not hold out, may you one day be caught on board a bungo loaded with logwood!

The wear and tear of our wardrobe was manifest to the most indifferent observer: and Mrs. Fensley, pitying our ragged condition, sewed on our buttons, darned, patched, and mended us, and put us in order for another expedition. On the third morning, Captain Fensley told us we had passed Campeachy during the night, and, if the wind held, would reach Sisal that day. At eight o'clock we came in sight of the long low coast, and moving steadily toward it, at a little before dark anchored off the port, about two miles from the shore. One brig was lying there, a Spanish trader, bound to Havana, and the only vessel in port. The anchorage is an open roadstead, outside of the breakers, which is considered perfectly safe except during a north-east storm, when Spanish vessels always slip their cables and stand out to sea.

In the uncertainty whether what we were going to see was worth the trouble, and the greater uncertainty of a conveyance when we wanted it, it was trying to leave a good vessel which in twenty days might carry us home. Nevertheless, we made the exertion. It was dusk when we left the vessel. We landed at the end of a long wooden dock, built out on the open shore of the sea, where we were challenged by a soldier. At the head of the pier was a guard and custom-house, where an officer presented himself to escort us to the commandant. On the right, near the shore, was an old Spanish fortress with turrets. A soldier, barely distinguishable on the battlements, challenged us; and passing the quartel, we were challenged again. The answer, as in Central America, was "Patria libre." The tone of the place was warlike, the Liberal party dominant. The revolution, as in all the other places, had been conducted in a spirit of moderation; but when the garrison was driven out, the commandant, who had been very tyrannical and oppressive, was taken, and the character of the revolution would have been stained by his murder, but he was put on board a bungo and escaped. We were well received by the commandant; and Captain Fensley took us to the house of an acquaintance, where we saw the captain of the brig in the offing, which was to sail in eight days for Havana, and no other vessel was expected for a long time. We made arrangements for setting out the next day for Merida, and early in the morning accompanied the captain to the pier, saw him embark in a bungo, waited till he got on board, and saw the brig, with a fine breeze and every sail set, stand out into the ocean for home. We turned our backs upon it with regret. There was nothing to detain us at Sisal. Though prettily situated on the sea-shore, and a thriving place, it was merely the dépôt of the exports and imports of Merida. At two o'clock we set out for the capital.

We were now in a country as different from Central America as if separated by the Atlantic, and we began our journey with an entirely new mode of conveyance. It was in a vehicle called a calêche, built somewhat like the old-fashioned cab, but very large, cumbersome, made for rough roads, without springs, and painted red, green, and yellow. One cow-hide trunk for each was strapped on behind, and above them, reaching to the top of the calêche, was secured a pile of sacate for the horses. The whole of this load, with Mr. Catherwood and me, was drawn by a single horse, having a rider on his back. Two other horses followed for change, harnessed, and each with a boy riding him. The road was perfectly level, and on a causeway a little elevated above the plain, which was stony and covered with scrub-trees. At first it seemed a great luxury to roll along in a wheel carriage; but, with the roughness of the road, and the calêche being without springs, in a little while this luxury began to be questionable.

After the magnificent scenery of Central America, the country was barren and uninteresting, but we perceived the tokens of a rich interior, in large carts drawn by mules five abreast, with high wheels six or eight feet apart, and loaded with hemp, bagging, wax, honey, and ox and deer skins. The first incident of the road was changing horses, which consisted in taking out the horse in the shafts and putting in one of the others, already in a sweat. This occurred twice; and at one o'clock we entered the village of Hunucama, pleasantly situated, embowered among trees, with a large plaza, at that time decorated with an arbour of evergreens all around, preparatory to the great fête of Corpus Christi, which was to be celebrated the next day. Here we took three fresh horses; and changing them as before, and passing two villages, through a vista two miles long saw the steeples of Merida, and at six o'clock rode into the city. The houses were well built, with balconied windows, and many had two stories. The streets were clean, and the people in them well dressed, animated, and cheerful in appearance; calêches fancifully painted and curtained, having ladies in them handsomely dressed, without hats, and their hair ornamented with flowers, gave it an air of gaiety and beauty that, after the sombre towns through which we had passed, was fascinating and almost poetic. No place had yet made so agreeable a first impression; and there was a hotel in a large building kept by Doña Micaela, driving up to which we felt as if by some accident we had fallen upon a European city.

I had met casually in New York a Spanish gentleman of Merida, who told me he was the proprietor of the ruins of Uxmal. As yet I knew nothing of the position or character of my friend, but I soon found that everybody in Merida knew Don Simon Peon. In the evening we called at his house. It was a large, aristocratic looking mansion of dark grey stone, with balconied windows, occupying nearly the half of one side of the plaza. Unfortunately, he was then at Uxmal; but we saw his wife, father, mother, and sisters, the house being a family residence, and the different members of it having separate haciendas. They had heard from him of my intended visit, and received me as an acquaintance. Don Simon was expected back in a few days, but, in the hope of finding him at Uxmal, we determined to go on immediately. Doña Joaquina, his mother, promised to make all necessary arrangements for the journey, and to send a servant with us. It was long since we passed so pleasant an evening; we saw many persons who in appearance and manner would do credit to any society, and left with a strong disposition to make some stay in Merida.

The plaza presented a gay scene. It was the eve of the fête of El Corpus. Two sides of the plaza were occupied by corridors, and the others were adorned with arbours of evergreens, among which lights were interspersed. Gay parties were promenading under them, and along the corridors and in front of the houses were placed chairs and benches for the use of the promenaders, and all who chose to take them.

The city of Merida contains about 20,000 inhabitants. It is founded on the site of an old Indian village, and dates from a few years after the conquest. In different parts of the city are the remains of Indian buildings. As the capital of the powerful State of Yucatan, it had always enjoyed a high degree of consideration in the Mexican confederacy, and throughout the republic is famed for its sabios or learned men. The State of Yucatan had declared its independence of Mexico; indeed, its independence was considered achieved. News had been received of the capitulation of Campeachy and the surrender of the Central garrison. The last remnant of despotism was rooted out, and the capital was in the first flush of successful revolution, the pride of independence. Removed by position, it was manifest that it would be no easy matter for Mexico to reconquer it; and probably, like Texas, it is a limb for ever lopped from that great, but feeble and distracted republic. It was pleasant to find that political animosities were not cherished with the same ferocity; and Centralists and Liberals met like men of opposite parties at home.

The next day was the fête of Corpus Domini throughout all Spanish America, the greatest in the Catholic Church. Early in the morning, at the tolling of the bell, we went to the Cathedral, which, with the palace of the bishop, occupied one entire side of the plaza. The interior was grand and imposing, having a vaulted roof of stone, and two rows of lofty stone pillars; the choir was in the centre, the altar richly adorned with silver; but the great attraction was in the ladies kneeling before the altars, with white or black veils laid over the top of the head, some of them of saintlike purity and beauty, in dress, manners, and appearance realizing the pictures of Spanish romance. Indeed, the Spanish ladies appear nowhere so lovely as in church.

The associations of one of my acquaintances having turned out so well, I determined to present a letter of introduction from friends in New York to Don Joaquin Gutierrez, whose family name stood high in Merida, and who, to my surprise, spoke English quite as well as we did. He had gone the rounds of society in Europe and the United States, and, like a good citizen, had returned to marry one of the belles and beauties of his own country. His family was from Merida, but he himself was resident at Campeachy; and, being a prominent Centralist, had left that city on account of its blockade by the Federalists, and in apprehensions of excesses that might be committed against obnoxious individuals should the place fall into their hands. From his house we went to the plaza to see the procession. After those we had seen in Guatimala this was inferior, and there were no devils; but the gathering of people under the arbour and in the corridors presented a beautiful spectacle. There was a large collection of Indians, both men and women, the best looking race we had seen, and all were neatly dressed. In the whole crowd there was not a single garment that was not clean that day, and we were told that any Indian too poor to appear in a fitting dress that morning, would be too proud to appear at all. The Indian women were really handsome: all were dressed in white, with a red border around the neck, sleeves, and hem of their garments, and their faces had a mild, contented, and amiable expression; the higher class were seated under the arbours before the doors of the houses and along the corridors, elegantly attired, without hats, and with veils or flowers in their hair, combining an elegance of appearance with simplicity of manners that almost made the scene one of poetic beauty; and they had an air of gaiety and freedom from disquietude, so different from the careworn faces of Guatimala, that they seemed as if what God intended them to be, happy. In fact, at this place it would have been no hardship to comply with the condition of purchasing Palenque; and yet perhaps some of the effect of this strong impression was only the result of comparison.

After the procession Don Joaquin proposed to call either upon the bishop or a lady who had a beautiful daughter. The bishop was the greatest man in Merida, and lived in the greatest style; but, determined to make the best of our day in Merida, we chose the other branch of the alternative. In the evening, however, we called upon him. His palace was adjoining the Cathedral, and before the door was a large cross; the entrance was through a courtyard with two rows of corridors. We ascended to a second flight, and entered an ante-room, where we were received by a well-dressed official, who notified the bishop of our coming, and shortly afterward conducted us through three stately saloons with high ceilings and lighted with lamps, in one of which was a chair of state covered with red damask, which was carried up on the wall behind and ceiling over it. From the last, a door opened into a large room elegantly fitted up as a sleeping apartment, in one corner of which was a silver wash-hand basin with a silver pitcher; and in the centre, not a movable, or not very easily moved, sat the bishop, a man several feet round, handsomely dressed, and in a chair made to fit, stuffed, and covered with red morocco, neither pinching him nor permitting him to roll, with a large, firmly secured projecting ear-piece on each side, to catch his head during the siesta. It had arms broad enough to support books and papers, and seemed the work of a man of genius. The lines of the bishop's face, however, indicated a man of high tone and character, and his conversation sustained the impression. He was a Centralist, and a great politician; and spoke of letters from generals, sieges, blockades, and battles, in tones which brought up a vivid picture of some priestly warrior or grand master of the Temple. In conclusion, he said that his influence, his house, and his *table* were at our service, asked us to name a day for dining with him, and said he would invite some friends to meet us. We had many trials in our journey, and it was not the least to decline this invitation; but we had some hope that we might be able to share his hospitality on our return from Uxmal.

From the bishop's palace we went to the theatre, a large building built expressly for the purpose, with two rows of boxes and a pit. The upper tier of boxes was private. The prima donna was a lady who sat next me at dinner at the hotel; but I had better employment than attending to the performance, in conversation with ladies who would have graced any circle. One of them told me that there was to be a tertulia and a dance at a country-house near the town in a few days, and to forego this was a harder trial than the loss of the bishop's dinner. Altogether, the evening at the theatre consummated the satisfaction of the only day we passed in Merida, so that it remains impressed on my mind in bright relief to months of dulness.

The morning at half-past six we set out for Uxmal on horseback, escorted by a servant of Señor Peon, with Indians before us, one of whom carried a load not provided by us, in which a box of claret was conspicuous. Leaving the city, we entered upon a level stony road, which seemed one bed of limestone, cut through a forest of scrub-trees. At the distance of a league we saw through a vista in the trees a large hacienda belonging to the Peon family, the entrance to which was by a handsome gate into a cattle-yard. The house was built of stone, and had a front of about 150 feet, with an arcade running the whole length. It was raised about 20 feet, and at the foot was a large water-trough extending the whole length, about 10 feet wide and of the same depth, filled with water for cattle. On the left was a flight of stone steps, leading to a stone platform on which the hacienda stood. At the end of this structure was an artificial reservoir or tank, also built of stone and cemented, about 150 feet square, and perhaps 20 feet deep. At the foot of the wall of the tank was a plantation of henniken, a species of aloe, from the fibres of which hemp is made. The style of the house, the strong and substantial character of the reservoir, and its apparent costliness, gave an imposing character to the hacienda.

At this place our Indian carriers left us, and we took others from the hacienda, with whom we continued three leagues further to another hacienda of the family of much the same character, where we stopped to breakfast. This over, we set out again, and by this time it had become desperately hot.

The road was very rough, over a bed of stone thinly covered, with barely soil enough for the growth of scrub-trees; our saddles were of a new fashion, and most painfully trying to those unused to them; the heat was very oppressive, and the leagues very long, till we reached another hacienda, a vast, irregular pile of buildings of dark grey stone, that might have been the castle of a German baron in feudal times. Each of these haciendas had an Indian name; this was called the hacienda of Vayalquex, and it was the only one of which Doña Joaquina, in speaking of our route, had made any particular mention. The entrance was by a large stone gateway, with a pyramidal top, into a long lane, on the right of which was a shed, built by Don Simon since his return from the United States as a ropewalk for manufacturing hemp raised on the hacienda; and there was one arrangement which added very much to the effect, and which I did not observe anywhere else: the cattle-yard and water-tanks were on one side and out of sight. We dismounted under the shade of noble trees in front of the house, and ascended by a flight of broad stone steps to a corridor thirty feet wide, with large mattings, which could be rolled up, or dropped as an awning for protection against the sun and rain. On one side the corridor was continued around the building, and on the other it conducted to the door of a church having a large cross over it, and within ornamented with figures like the churches in towns, for the tenants of the hacienda. The whole establishment was lordly in its appearance. It had 1,500 Indian tenants, bound to the master by a sort of feudal tenure, and, as the friends of the master, escorted by a household servant, the whole was ours.

We had fallen unexpectedly upon a state of things new and peculiar. The peninsula of Yucatan, lying between the bays of Campeachy and Honduras, is a vast plain. Cape Catoche, the north-eastern point of

FEUDAL RELATIONS IN YUCATAN.

the peninsula, is but fifty-one leagues from San Antonio, the western extremity of the island of Cuba, which is supposed at a remote period to have formed part of the American Continent. The soil and atmosphere are extremely dry; along the whole coast, from Campeachy to Cape Catoche, there is not a single stream or spring of fresh water. The interior is equally destitute; and water is the most valuable possession in the country. During the season of rains, from April to the end of October, there is a superabundant supply; but the scorching sun of the next six months dries up the earth, and unless water were preserved, man and beast would perish, and the country be depopulated. All the enterprise and wealth of the landed proprietors, therefore, are exerted in procuring supplies of water, as without it the lands are worth nothing. For this purpose each hacienda has large tanks and reservoirs, constructed and kept up at great expense, to supply water for six months to all dependent upon it; and this creates a relation with the Indian population, which places the proprietor somewhat in the position of a lord under the old feudal system.

By the act of independence, the Indians of Mexico, as well as the white population, became free. No man can buy and sell another, whatever may be the colour of his skin; but as the Indians are poor, thriftless, and improvident, and never look beyond the immediate hour, they are obliged to attach themselves to some hacienda which can supply their wants; and, in return for the privilege of using the water, they come under certain obligations of service to the master, which place him in a lordly position; and this state of things, growing out of the natural condition of the country, exists, I believe, nowhere in Spanish America except in Yucatan. Each hacienda has its major-domo, who attends to all the details of the management of the estate, and in the absence of the master is his viceroy, and has the same powers over the tenants. At this hacienda the major-domo was a young Mestitzo, and had fallen into his place in an easy and natural way, by marrying his predecessor's daughter, who had just enough white blood to elevate the dulness of the Indian face into one of softness and sweetness; and yet it struck me that he thought quite as much of the place he got with her as of herself.

It would have been a great satisfaction to pass several days at this lordly hacienda; but, not expecting anything to interest us on the road, we had requested Doña Joaquina to hurry us through, and the servant told us that the señora's orders were to conduct us to another hacienda of the family, about two leagues beyond, to sleep. At the moment we were particularly loth to leave, on account of the fatigue of the previous ride. The servant suggested to the major-domo to llamar un coché; in English, to "call a coach," which the latter proposed to do if we wished it. We made a few inquiries, and said, unhesitatingly and peremptorily, in effect, "Go call a coach, and let a coach be called." The major-domo ascended by a flight of stone steps outside to the belfry of the church, whither we followed him; and, turning round with a movement and tone of voice that reminded us of a Mussulman in a minaret calling the faithful to prayers, he called for a coach. The roof of the church, and of the whole pile of buildings connected, was of stone cemented, firm and strong as a pavement. The sun beat intensely upon it, and for several minutes all was still. At length we saw a single Indian trotting through the woods toward the hacienda, then two together, and in a quarter of an hour there were twenty or thirty. These were the horses; the coaches were yet growing on the trees. Six Indians were selected for each coach, who, with a few minutes' use of the machete, cut a bundle of poles, which they brought up to the corridor to manufacture into coaches. This was done, first, by laying on the ground two poles about as thick as a man's wrist, ten feet long and three feet apart. These were fastened by cross-sticks tied with strings of unspun hemp, about two feet from each end; grass hammocks were secured between the poles, bows bent over them, and covered with light matting, and the coaches were made. We placed our ponchas at the head for pillows, crawled inside, and lay down. The Indians took off little cotton shirts covering the breast, and tied them around their petates as hatbands. Four of them raised up each coach, and placed the end of the poles on little cushions on their shoulders. We bade farewell to the major-domo and his wife, and, feet first, descended the steps, and set off on a trot, while an Indian followed leading the horses. In the great relief we experienced, we forgot our former scruples against making beasts of burden of men. They were not troubled with any sense of indignity or abasement, and the weight was not much. There were no mountains; only some little inequalities which brought the head lower than the heels, and they seldom stumbled. In this way they carried us about three miles, and then laid us down gently on the ground. Like the Indians in Merida, they were a fine-looking race, with a good expression of countenance, cheerful, and even merry in their toil. They were amused at us because we could not talk with them. There is no diversity of Indian languages in Yucatan; the Maya is universal, and all the Spaniards speak it.

Having wiped off the perspiration and rested, they took us up again; and, lulled by the quiet movement and the regular fall of the Indians' feet upon the ear, I fell into a doze, from which I was roused by stopping at a gate, on entering which I found we were advancing to a range of white stone buildings, standing on an elevation about twenty feet high, which by measurement afterwards I found to be 360 feet long, with an imposing corridor running the whole length; and on the extreme right of the building the platform was continued 100 or 200 feet, forming the top of a reservoir, on which there was a windlass with long arms; and Indian women, dressed in white, were moving round in a circle, drawing water and filling their water-jars. This was called the hacienda of Mucuyche. We entered, as usual, through a large cattle-yard. At the foot of the structure on which the building stood, running nearly the whole length, was a gigantic stone tank, about eight or ten feet wide, and of the same depth, filled with water. We were carried up an inclined stone platform, about the centre of the range of buildings, which consisted of three distinct sets, each 120 feet front. In that on the left was the church, the door of which was open, and an old Indian was then lighting candles at the altar for vesper prayers. In front, setting a little back, were the apartments of the major-domo, and at the other end of the range, the mansion of the master, in the corridor of which we were set down, and crawled out of our coaches. There was something monstrously aristocratic in being borne on the shoulders of tenants from such a hacienda as that we had left to this stately pile. The whole appearance of things gave an idea of country residence upon a scale of grand hospitality, and yet we learned, to our astonishment, that most of the family had never seen it.

We had an hour of daylight, which I could have employed very satisfactorily on the spot, but the servant urged us to go immediately and see a cenote. What a cenote was we had no idea, and Mr. C, being much fatigued, turned into a hammock; but, unwilling to lose anything where all was strange and unexpected, I followed the servant, crossed the roof of the reservoir, cemented as hard as stone, passed on to an open tank built of stones, covered with cement inside and out, about 150 square, and 20 feet deep, filled with water, in which twenty or thirty Indians were swimming; and, descending to the foot of the tank, at the distance of about a hundred yards, came to a large opening in the ground, with a broad flight of more than fifty steps; descending which, I saw unexpectedly a spectacle of such extraordinary beauty, that I sent the servant back to tell Mr. Catherwood to come to me forthwith, if he had to be carried in his hammock. It was a large cavern or grotto, with a roof of broken, overhanging rock, high enough to give an air of wildness and grandeur, impenetrable at midday to the sun's rays, and at the bottom, water pure as crystal, still and deep, resting upon a bed of white limestone rock. It was the very creation of romance; a bathing-place for Diana and her nymphs. Grecian poet never imagined so beautiful a scene. It was almost a profanation, but in a few minutes we were swimming around the rocky basin with feelings of boyish exultation, only regretting that such a freak of nature was played where so few could enjoy its beauties. On a nobleman's estate in England it would be above all price. The bath reinvigorated our frames. It was after dark when we returned; hammocks were waiting for us, and very soon we were in a profound sleep.

F. Catherwood

17.—CENOTE.

CHAPTER XL.

JOURNEY RESUMED—ARRIVAL AT UXMAL—HACIENDA OF UXMAL—MAJOR-DOMOS—ADVENTURES OF A YOUNG SPANIARD—VISIT TO THE RUINS OF UXMAL—FIRST SIGHT OF THE RUINS—CHARACTER OF THE INDIANS—DETAILS OF HACIENDA LIFE—A DELICATE CASE—ILLNESS OF MR. CATHERWOOD—BREAKING UP.

At daybreak the next morning, with new Indians and a guide on horseback from the hacienda, we resumed our journey. The surface of the country was the same, limestone with scrub-trees. There was not soil enough to absorb the water, which rested in puddles in the hollows of the stones At nine o'clock we reached another hacienda, smaller than the last, but still having a lordly appearance, where, as before, the women were drawing water by a wheel. The major-domo expressed his sense of the honour conferred upon him by our visit, and his anxiety to serve us, gave us a breakfast of milk, tortillas and wild honey, and furnished us with other Indians and a guide. We mounted again; very soon the sun became intensely hot; there were no trees to shade us, and we suffered excessively. At half-past twelve we passed some mounds of ruins a little off the road, but the sun was so scorching that we could not stop to examine them, and at two o'clock we reached Uxmal. Little did I think, when I made the acquaintance of my unpretending friend in New York, that I should ride upwards of fifty miles on his family estates, carried by his Indians, and breakfasting, dining, and sleeping at his lordly haciendas, while the route marked out for our return would bring us to others, one of which was larger than any we had seen. The family of Peon, under the Spanish dominion, had given governors to the province of Yucatau. On the establishment of independence, its present head, a staunch Royalist, retired in disgust from all kinds of employment, and the whole of the large family estates were managed by the Señora Doña Joaquina. Unfortunately, Don Simon had left for Merida, and we had missed him on the way. Moreover, owing to the heat of the sun and our awkward saddles, we arrived at the end of this triumphal march in a dreadfully jaded and forlorn condition, and perhaps we never dismounted more utterly worn out and uncomfortable.

The hacienda of Uxmal was built of dark grey stone, ruder in appearance and finish than any of the others, with a greater appearance of antiquity, and at a distance looked like an old baronial castle. A year before it had been given to Don Simon by his father, and he was making large repairs and additions to the building, though, as his family never visited it, and he only for a few days at a time, for what purpose I could not conceive. It had its cattle-yard in front, with tanks of water around, some with green vegetation on the top, and there was an unwholesome sensation of dampness. It had, too, its church, which contained a figure of Nuestro Señor, "Our Lord," revered by the Indians of all the haciendas around, the fame of which had reached the household servants at Merida, and which was the first object that attracted the attention of our guide. The whole hacienda was immediately at our disposal; but, worn down with heat and fatigue, we took at once to our hammocks.

The hacienda had two major-domos, one a Mestitzo, who understood the language and business, and in the other we found an acquaintance, or, at least, what seemed so, for about the time that we left New York he was a waiter at Delmonico's Hotel. It was a strange encounter at this out-of-the-way place, to be brought into close connexion with this well-known restaurant, which in that country seemed the seat of art and fountain of happiness. He was a young Spaniard from Catalonia, who, with a friend, having taken part in some defeated insurrection, fled to Cuba, whence, on the point of being discovered, they escaped to New York, penniless. Ignorant of the language, with no means of getting a livelihood, both were received by Delmonico as waiters at his restaurant, where the friend rose to be head chocolate-maker; but he was languishing as simple waiter, when Don Simon proposed to him to go to Uxmal. Without knowing where he was going, except that it was to some part of Spanish America, or what was to be his business, he found himself in a retired place, surrounded by Indians whose language he could not understand, and having no one near him with whom he could exchange a word except the major-domo. These major-domos form a class in Yucatan who need sharp looking after. Like the Scotch servant applying for a place, they are not particular about wages, and are satisfied with what they can pick up about the house. This is the character of most of the major-domos; and the position of the young man, being white, intelligent, and honest, had advantages in that country, as Don Simon intended to give him, as soon as he understood the business, a superintendence over the major-domos of three or four haciendas; but, unfortunately, he wanted energy, felt the want of society and the loneliness of his situation, remembered scenes of enjoyment with his friend and other waiters, and at Uxmal talked of the opera; and when at dinner-time he drew a feeling picture of Delmonico's saloon, we sympathised with him cordially.

In the afternoon, rested and refreshed, we set out for a walk to the ruins. The path led through some noble woods, in which there were many tracks, and our Indian guide lost his way. Mr. C., being unwell, returned to the hacienda. We took another road, and, emerging suddenly from the woods, to my astonishment came at once upon a large open field strewed with mounds of ruins, and vast buildings on terraces, and pyramidal structures, grand and in good preservation, richly ornamented, without a bush to obstruct the view, and in picturesque effect almost equal to the ruins of Thebes; for these, standing on the flat valley of the Nile, and extending on both sides of the river, nowhere burst in one view upon the sight. Such was the report I made to Mr. Catherwood on my return, who, lying in his hammock unwell and out of spirits, told me I was romancing; but early the next morning we were on the ground, and his comment was that the reality exceeded my description.

The place of which I am now speaking was beyond all doubt once a large, populous and highly civilized city, and the reader can nowhere find one word of it on any page of history. Who built it, why that spot was chosen away from water or any of those natural advantages which have determined the sites of cities whose histories are known, what led to its abandonment and destruction, no man can tell. The only name by which it is known is that of the hacienda on which it stands. In the oldest deed belonging to the Peon family, which goes back 140 years, the buildings are referred to, in the boundaries of the estate, as Las Casas de Piedra. This is the only ancient document or record in existence in which the place is mentioned at all, and there are no traditions except the wild superstitions of Indians in regard to particular buildings. The ruins were all exhumed; within the last year the trees had been cut down and burned, and the whole field of ruins was in view, enclosed by the woods and planted with corn.

We passed a most interesting and laborious day, and at evening returned to the hacienda to mature our plans for a thorough exploration; but, unfortunately, during the night Mr. Catherwood, I believe affected by the immensity of the work, had a violent attack of fever, which continued upon him in the morning, with a prospect of serious illness.

It was Monday, and very early all the Indians of the hacienda, according to their obligation to the master, presented themselves to receive directions from the major-domo for the day's work. In remaining about the house I had an opportunity of learning somewhat of hacienda discipline and the character of the Indians.

The hacienda of Uxmal is ten leagues or thirty miles square, but only a small portion is cultivated, and the rest is a mere roaming-ground for cattle. The Indians are of two classes: vaceros, or tenders of cattle and horses, who receive two pounds ten shillings per year, with five almudas of maize per week; and labradores or labourers, who are also called Luneros, from their obligation, in consideration of their drinking the water of the hacienda, to work for the master without pay on Lunes or Monday. These last constitute the great body of the Indians; and, besides their obligation to work on Monday, when they marry and have families, and, of course, need more water, they are obliged to clear, sow, and gather twenty micates of maize for the master, each micate being twenty-four square yards. When the bell of the church is struck five times, every Indian is obliged to go forthwith to the hacienda, and, for sixpence a day and a ration of three halfpence-worth of maize, do whatever work the master or his delegate, the major-domo, may direct. The authority of the master or his delegate over these is absolute. He settles all disputes between the Indians themselves, and punishes for offences, acting both as judge and executioner. If the major-domo punish an Indian unreasonably, the latter may complain to his master; and if the master refuse to give him redress, or himself punishes an Indian unreasonably, the latter may apply for his discharge. There is no obligation upon him to remain on the hacienda unless he is in debt to the master, but, practically, this binds him hand and foot. The Indians are all improvident, anticipate their earnings, never have two days' provisions in store, and never keep any accounts. A dishonest master may always bring them in debt, and generally they are really so. If able to pay off the debt, the Indian is entitled to his immediate discharge; but if not, the master is obliged to give him a writing to the effect following: "Whatever señor wishes to receive the Indian named ———, can take him, provided he pays me the debt he owes me." If the master refuses him this paper, the Indian may complain to the juez. When he has obtained it, he goes round to the different haciendas until he finds a proprietor who is willing to purchase the debt, with a mortgage upon him until it is paid. The account is settled, and the master gives the Indian a writing of this purport: "The account of my former servant ——— being adjusted, which is twenty dollars, and having paid me the said debt, I, his present master, give him this receipt;" and with this he enters into the service of a new master. There is but little chance of his ever paying off the smallest debt. He will never work merely to clear off the incumbrance, considers all he can get on his body clear gain, and virtually from the time he receives his first dollar, goes through life in bondage, varied only by an occasional change of masters. In general they are mild, amiable and very docile; bear no malice; and when one of them is whipped and smarting under stripes, with tears in his eyes he makes a bow to the major-domo, and says, "Buenos tarde, señor;" "good evening, sir." But they require to be dealt with sternly, and kept at a distance; are uncertain, and completely the creatures of impulse; and one bad Indian or a bad Mestitzo may ruin a whole hacienda. They inherit all the indolence of their ancestors, are wedded to old usages, and unwilling to be taught anything new. Don Simon has attempted to introduce improvements in agriculture, but in vain; they cannot work except in their own old way. Don Simon brought out the common churn from the United States, and attempted to introduce the making of butter and cheese; but the Indians could not be taught the use of them, the churns were thrown aside, and hundreds of cows wander in the woods unmilked. The master is not obliged to maintain the Indian when sick; though, as he derives a profit from his labour, it is his interest to do so; and, on broad grounds, as it is an object always to increase his labradores, it is his interest to treat them in such a manner as to acquire among the Indians a reputation as a good master.

In the course of the morning I visited many of the huts of the Indians. They were built in an oblong form, of round poles set upright in the ground and thatched, and some appeared clean and comfortable. The men were all away at work, and all day there was a procession of women in white cotton dresses moving from the gate to the well and drawing water. It was pleasant to find that marriage was considered proper and expedient, conducing to good order and thrift certainly, and probably to individual happiness. Don Simon encouraged it; he did not like to have any single men on the estate, and made every young Indian of the right age take unto himself a wife. When, as often happened, the Indian, in a deprecating tone, said, "No tengo muger," "I have no wife," Don Simon looked through the hacienda, and found one for him. On his last visit he made four matches, and the day before our arrival the Delmonico major-domo had been to the nearest village to escort the couples and pay the padre for marrying them, the price being six shillings each. He was afraid to trust them with the money, for fear they would spend it and not get married.

The old major-domo was energetic in carrying out the views of his master on this important subject, and that day a delicate case was brought before him. A young Indian girl brought a complaint against a married woman for slander. She said that she was engaged to be married to a young man whom she loved and who loved her, and the married woman had injured her fair fame by reporting that she was already in " an interesting situation;" she had told the young man of it, said that all the women in the hacienda saw it, and taunted him with marrying such a girl; and now she said the young man would not have her. The married woman was supported by a crowd of witnesses, and it must be admitted that appearances were very much against the plaintiff; but the old major-domo, without going into the merits at all, decided in her favour on broad grounds. Indignant at a marriage being prevented, he turned to the married woman and asked, What was it to her?, what right had she to meddle? what if it were true?—it was none of her business. Perhaps the young man knew it, and was party to it, and still intended to marry the girl, and they might have lived happily but for her busy tongue; and, without more ado, he brought out a leather whip cut into long lashes, and with great vigour began applying it to the back of the indiscreet communicator of unwelcome tidings. He wound up with an angry homily on busy-bodies, and then upon women generally, who, he said, made all the difficulties on the hacienda, and but for them the men would be quiet enough. The matrons of the hacienda stood aghast at this unexpected turn of things; and, when the case was dismissed, all crowded around the victim and went away with her, giving such comfort as they could. The young girl went away alone; the hearts of her sex were steeled against her: in savage as in civilized life,

"Every wo a tear may claim,
Except an erring sister's shame."

In the afternoon Mr. Catherwood's fever left him, but in a very low state. The hacienda was unhealthy at this season; the great troughs and tanks of water around the house were green, and, with the regular afternoon rains, induced fatal fevers. Mr. Catherwood's constitution was already severely shattered. Indeed, I became alarmed, and considered it indispensable for him to leave the hacienda, and, if possible, the country altogether. To carry out other plans, we intended at all events to return. We made a calculation that, by setting out the next morning we could reach the Spanish brig in time to embark for Havana, and in ten minutes' consultation we determined to break up and go home. Immediately we communicated our purpose to the major-domo, who ascended to the belfry of the church and called a coach, to be ready at two o'clock the next morning.

CHAPTER XLI.

RUINS OF UXMAL—A LOFTY BUILDING—MAGNIFICENT VIEW FROM ITS DOORWAY—PECULIAR SCULPTURED ORNAMENTS—ANOTHER BUILDING, CALLED BY THE INDIANS THE HOUSE OF THE DWARF—AN INDIAN LEGEND—THE HOUSE OF THE NUNS—THE HOUSE OF TURTLES—THE HOUSE OF PIGEONS—THE GUARD-HOUSE—ABSENCE OF WATER—THE HOUSE OF THE GOVERNOR—TERRACES—*Wooden* LINTELS—DETAILS OF THE HOUSE OF THE GOVERNOR—DOORWAYS—CORRIDORS—A BEAM OF WOOD, INSCRIBED WITH HIEROGLYPHICS—SCULPTURED STONES, &c.

In the meantime I returned for one more view of the ruins. Mr. Waldeck's work on these ruins had appeared before we left the United States. It was brought out in Paris in a large folio edition, with illustrations fancifully and beautifully coloured, and contains the result of a year's residence at Merida and eight days at Uxmal. At the time of his visit the ruins were overgrown with trees, which, within the last year had been cleared away, and the whole was laid bare and exposed to view. In attempting a description of these ruins, so vast a work rises up before me that I am at a loss where to begin. Arrested on the very threshold of our labours, I am unable to give any general plan; but, fortunately, the whole field was level, clear of trees, and in full sight at once. The first view stamped it indelibly upon my mind, and Mr. Catherwood's single day was well employed.

The first object that arrests the eye on emerging from the forest is the building represented on the right hand of the engraving, No. 78. Drawn off by mounds of ruins and piles of gigantic buildings, the eye returns and again fastens upon this lofty structure. It was the first building I entered. From its front doorway I counted sixteen elevations, with broken walls and mounds of stones, and vast, magnificent edifices, which at that distance seemed untouched by time and defying ruin. I stood in the doorway when the sun went down, throwing from the buildings a prodigious breadth of shadow, darkening the terraces on which they stood, and presenting a scene strange enough for a work of enchantment.

This building is 68 feet long. The elevation on which it stands is built up solid from the plain, entirely artificial. Its form is not pyramidal, but oblong and rounding, being 240 feet long at the base, and 120 broad, and it is protected all around, to the very top, by a wall of square stones. Perhaps the high ruined structures at Palenque, which we have called pyramidal, and which were so ruined that we could not make them out exactly, were originally of the same shape. On the east side of the structure is a broad range of stone steps, between 8 and 9 inches high, and so steep that great care is necessary in ascending and descending; of these we counted 101 in their places. Nine were wanting at the top, and perhaps 20 were covered with

F. Catherwood.

78, UXMAL.—HOUSE OF THE NUNS, AND HOUSE OF THE DWARF.

rubbish at the bottom. At the summit of the steps is a stone platform 4½ feet wide, running along the rear of the building. There is no doorway in the centre, but at each end a doorway opens into an apartment 18 feet long and 9 wide, and between the two is a third apartment of the same width, and 34 feet long. The whole building is of stone; inside, the walls are of polished smoothness; outside, up to the height of the door, the stones are plain and square; above this line there is a rich cornice or moulding, and from this to the top of the building all the sides are covered with rich and elaborate sculptured ornaments, forming a sort of arabesque. The style and character of these ornaments were entirely different from those of any we had ever seen before, either in that country or any other; they bore no resemblance whatever to those of Copan or Palenque, and were quite as unique and peculiar. The designs were strange and incomprehensible, very elaborate, sometimes grotesque, but often simple, tasteful, and beautiful. Among the intelligible subjects are squares and diamonds, with busts of human beings, heads of leopards, and compositions of leaves and flowers, and the ornaments known everywhere as *grecques*. The ornaments, which succeed each other, are all different; the whole form an extraordinary mass of richness and complexity, and the effect is both grand and curious. And the construction of these ornaments is not less peculiar and striking than the general effect. There were no tablets or single stones, each representing separately and by itself an entire subject; but every ornament or combination is made up of separate stones, on each of which part of the subject was carved, and which was then set in its place in the wall. Each stone, by itself, was an unmeaning fractional part; but, placed by the side of others, helped to make a whole, which without it would be incomplete. Perhaps it may, with propriety, be called a species of sculptured mosaic.

From the front door of this extraordinary building a pavement of hard cement, 22 feet long by 15 broad, leads to the roof of another building, seated lower down on the artificial structure, as shown in the engraving. There is no staircase or other visible communication between the two; but, descending by a pile of rubbish along the side of the lower one, and groping around the corner, we entered a doorway in front 4 feet wide, and found inside a chamber 12 feet high, with corridors running the whole breadth, of which the front one was 7 feet 3 inches deep, and the other 3 feet 9 inches. The inner walls were of smooth and polished square stones, and there was no inner door or means of communication with any other place. Outside the doorway was loaded with ornaments, and the whole exterior was the same as that of the building described above. The steps leading from the doorway to the foot of the structure were entirely destroyed.

The Indians regard these ruins with superstitious reverence. They will not go near them at night, and they have the old story that immense treasure is hidden among them. Each of the buildings has its name given to it by the Indians. This is called the Casa del Enano, or House of the Dwarf, and it is consecrated by a wild legend, which, as I sat in the doorway, I received from the lips of an Indian, as follows :—

There was an old woman who lived in a hut on the very spot now occupied by the structure on which this building is perched, and opposite the Casa del Gobernador (which will be mentioned hereafter), who went mourning that she had no children. In her distress she one day took an egg, covered it with a cloth, and laid it away carefully in one corner of the hut. Every day she went to look at it, until one morning she found the egg hatched, and a criatura, or creature, or baby, born. The old woman was delighted, and called it her son, provided it with a nurse, took good care of it, so that in one year it walked and talked like a man; and then it stopped growing. The old woman was more delighted than ever, and said he would be a great lord or king. One day she told him to go to the house of the gobernador and challenge him to a trial of strength. The dwarf tried to beg off, but the old woman insisted, and he went. The guard admitted him, and he flung his challenge at the gobernador. The latter smiled, and told him to lift a stone of three arrobas, or seventy-five pounds, at which the little fellow cried, and returned to his mother, who sent him back to say that if the gobernador lifted it first, he would afterwards. The gobernador lifted it, and the dwarf immediately did the same. The gobernador then tried him with other feats of strength, and the dwarf regularly did whatever was done by the gobernador. At length, indignant at being matched by a dwarf, the gobernador told him that, unless he made a house in one night higher than any in the place, he would kill him. The poor dwarf again returned crying to his mother, who bade him not to be disheartened, and the next morning he awoke and found himself in this lofty building. The gobernador, seeing it from the door of his palace, was astonished, and sent for the dwarf, and told him to collect two bundles of cogoiol, a wood of a very hard species, with one of which he, the gobernador, would beat the dwarf over the head, and *afterwards* the dwarf should beat him with the other. The dwarf again returned crying to his mother; but the latter told him not to be afraid, and put on the crown of his head a tortillita de trigo, a small thin cake of wheat flour. The trial was made in the presence of all the great men in the city. The gobernador broke the whole of his bundle over the dwarf's head without hurting the little fellow in the least. He then tried to avoid the trial on his own head, but he had given his word in the presence of his officers, and was obliged to submit. The second blow of the dwarf broke his skull in pieces, and all the spectators hailed the victor as their new gobernador. The old woman then died; but at the Indian village of Mani, seventeen leagues distant, there is a deep well, from which opens a cave that leads under ground an immense distance to Merida. In this cave, on the bank of a stream, under the shade of a large tree, sits an old woman with a serpent by her side, who sells water in small quantities, not for money, but only for a criatura or baby to give the serpent to eat; and this old woman is the mother of the dwarf. Such is the fanciful legend connected with this edifice; but it hardly seemed more strange than the structure to which it referred.

The other building indicated in the plate is called by a name which may originally have had some reference to the vestals who, in Mexico, were employed to keep burning the sacred fire; but I believe in the mouths of the Indians of Uxmal it has no reference whatever to history, tradition, or legend, but is derived entirely from Spanish associations. It is called Casa de las Monjas, or House of the Nuns, or the Convent. It is situated on an artificial elevation about fifteen feet high. Its form is quadrangular, and one side, according to my measurement, is ninety-five paces in length. It was not possible to pace all around it, from the masses of fallen stones which encumber it in some places, but it may be safely stated at 250 feet square. Like the house of the dwarf, it is built entirely of cut stone, and the whole exterior is filled with the same rich, elaborate, and incomprehensible sculptured ornaments.

The principal entrance is by a large doorway into a beautiful patio or courtyard, grass-grown, but clear of trees, and the whole of the inner façade is ornamented more richly and elaborately than the outside, and in a more perfect state of preservation. On one side the combination was in the form of diamonds, simple, chaste, and tasteful; and at the head of the courtyard two gigantic serpents, with their heads broken and fallen, were winding from opposite directions along the whole façade.

In front, and on a line with the door of the convent, is another building, on a lower foundation, of the same general character, called Casa de Tortugas, from sculptured turtles over the doorway. This building had in several places huge cracks, as if it had been shaken by an earthquake. It stands nearly in the centre of the ruins, and the top commands a view all round of singular but wrecked magnificence.

Beyond this, a little to the right, approached by passing over mounds of ruins, was another building, which at a great distance attracted our attention by its conspicuous ornaments. We reached it by ascending two high terraces. The main building was similar to the others, and along the top ran a high ornamented wall in this form, from which it was called Casa de Palomos, or House of Pigeons, and at a distance it looked more like a row of pigeon-houses than anything else.

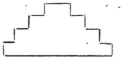

In front was a broad avenue, with a line of ruins on each side, leading beyond the wall of the convent to a great mound of ruins, which probably had once been a building with which it was connected; and beyond this is a lofty building in the rear, to which this seemed but a vestibule or porter's lodge. Between the two was a large patio or courtyard, with corridors on each side, and the ground of the courtyard sounded hollow. In one place the surface was broken, and I descended into a large excavation, cemented, which had probably been intended as a granary. At the back of the courtyard, on a high, broken terrace, which it was difficult to climb, was another edifice more ruined than the others, but which, from the style of its remains and its commanding position, overlooking every other building except the house of the dwarf, and apparently having been connected with the distant mass of ruins in front, must have been one of the most important in the city, perhaps the principal temple. The Indians called it the quartel or guard-house. It commanded a view of other ruins not contained in the enumeration of those seen from the house of the dwarf; and the whole presented a scene of barbaric magnificence, utterly confounding all previous notions in regard to the aboriginal inhabitants of this country, and calling up emotions which had not been wakened to the same extent by anything we had yet seen.

There was one strange circumstance connected with these ruins. No water had ever been discovered; and there was not a single stream, fountain, or well, known to the Indians, nearer than the hacienda, a mile and a half distant. The sources which supplied this element of life had disappeared; the cisterns were broken, or the streams dried up. This, as we afterward learned from Don Simon, was an object of great interest to him, and made him particularly anxious for a thorough exploration of the ruins. He supposed that the face of the country had not changed, and that somewhere under ground must exist great wells, cisterns, or reservoirs, which supplied the former inhabitants of the city with water. The discovery of these wells or reservoirs would, in that region, be like finding a fountain in the desert, or, more poetically, like finding money. The supply of water would be boundless. Luneros without number might draw from it, and the old city be repeopled without any new expense for wells or tanks.

While I was making the circuit of these ruins, Mr. Catherwood proceeded to the Casa del Gobernador, which title, according to the naming of the Indians, indicates the principal building of the old city, the residence of the governor, or royal house. It is the grandest in position, the most stately in architecture and proportions, and the most perfect in preservation of all the structures remaining at Uxmal.

The plate, No. 79, represents the ground-plan, with the three ranges of terraces on which it stands. The first terrace is 600 feet long and five feet high. It is walled with cut stone, and on the top is a platform 20 feet broad, from which rises another terrace 15 feet high. At the corners this terrace is supported by cut stones, having the faces rounded so as to give a better finish than with sharp angles. The great platform above is flat and clear of trees, but abounding in green stumps of the forest but lately cleared away, and now planted, or, rather, from its irregularity, sown with corn, which as yet rose barely a foot from the ground. At the south-east corner of this platform is a row of round pillars 18 inches in diameter and 3 or 4 feet high, extending about 100 feet along the platform; and these were the nearest approach to pillars or columns that we saw in all our exploration of the ruins of that country. In the middle of the terrace, along an avenue leading to a range of steps, was a broken, round pillar, inclined and falling, with trees growing around it. It was part of our purpose to make an excavation in this platform, from the impression that underneath would be found a vault, forming part of the immense reservoirs for supplying the city with water.

In the centre of the platform, at a distance of 205 feet from the border in front, is a range of stone steps more than 100 feet broad, and 35 in number, and ascending to a third terrace, 15 feet above the last, and 35 feet from the ground, and which, being elevated on a naked plain, formed a most commanding position. The erection of these terraces alone was an immense work. On this third terrace, with its principal doorway facing the range of steps, stands the noble structure of the Casa del Gobernador. The façade measures 320 feet. Away from the region of dreadful rains, and the rank growth of forest which smothers the ruins of Palenque, it stands with all its walls erect, and almost as perfect as when deserted by its inhabitants. The whole building is of stone, plain up to the moulding that runs along the tops of the doorway, and above filled with the same rich, strange, and elaborate sculpture, among which is particularly conspicuous the ornament before referred to as *la grecque*. There is no rudeness or barbarity in the design or proportions; on the contrary,

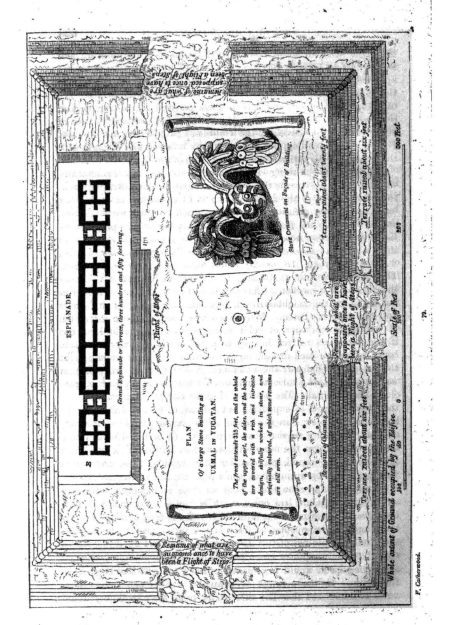

the whole wears an air of architectural symmetry and grandeur; and as the stranger ascends the steps and casts a bewildered eye along its open and desolate doors, it is hard to believe that he sees before him the work of a race in whose epitaph, as written by historians, they are called ignorant of art, and said to have perished in the rudeness of savage life. If it stood at this day on its grand artificial terrace in Hyde Park or the Garden of the Tuileries, it would form a new order, I do not say equalling, but not unworthy to stand side by side with the remains of Egyptian, Grecian, and Roman art.

But there was one thing which seemed in strange want of conformity with all the rest. It was the first object that had arrested my attention in the house of the dwarf, and which I had marked in every other building. I have mentioned that at Ocosingo we saw a wooden beam, and at Palenque the fragment of a wooden pole; at this place *all the lintels had been of wood, and throughout the ruins most of them were still in their places over the doors.* These lintels were heavy beams, 8 or 9 feet long, 18 or 20 inches wide, and 12 or 14 thick. The wood, like that at Ocosingo, was very hard, and rang under the blow of the machete. As our guide told us, it was of a species not found in the neighbourhood, but came from the distant forests near the lake of Peten. Why wood was used in the construction of buildings otherwise of solid stone seemed unaccountable; but if our guide was correct in regard to the place of its growth, each beam must have been carried on the shoulders of eight Indians, with the necessary relief carriers, a distance of 300 miles; consequently, it was rare, costly, and curious, and for that reason may have been considered ornamental. The position of these lintels was most trying, as they were obliged to support a solid mass of stone wall 14 or 16 feet high, and 3 or 4 in thickness. Once, perhaps, they were strong as stone, but they showed that they were not as durable, and contained within them the seeds of destruction. Most, it is true, were in their places, sound, and harder than lignum vitæ; but others were perforated by worm-holes; some were cracked in the middle, and the walls, settling upon them, were fast overcoming their remaining strength; and others had fallen down altogether. In fact, except in the House of the Nuns, the greatest destruction was from the decay and breaking of these wooden beams. If the lintels had been of stone, the principal buildings of this desolate city would at this day be almost entire; or, if the edifices had been still occupied under a master's eye, a decaying beam would have been replaced, and the buildings saved from ruin. In the moment of greatness and power, the builders never contemplated that the time would come when their city would be a desolation.

The Casa del Gobernador stands with its front to the east. In the centre, and opposite the range of steps leading up to the terrace, are three principal doorways. The middle one is 8 feet 6 inches wide, and 8 feet 10 inches high; the others are of the same height, but two feet less in width. The centre doorway opens into an apartment 60 feet long and 27 feet deep, which is divided into two corridors by a wall 3½ feet thick, with a doorway of communication between, of the same size with the doorway of entrance. The plan is the same as that of the corridor in front of the palace at Palenque, except that here the corridor does not run the whole length of the building, and the back corridor has no doorway of egress. The floors are of smooth square stone, the walls of square blocks nicely laid and smoothly polished. The ceiling forms a triangular arch without the keystone, as at Palenque △; but, instead of the rough stones overlapping or being covered with stucco, the layers of stone are bevelled as they rise, and present an even and polished surface. Throughout, the laying and polishing of the stones are as perfect as under the rules of the best modern masonry.

In this apartment we determined to take up our abode, once more in the palace of an unknown king, and under a roof tight as when sheltering the heads of its former occupants. Different from ruins in the Old World, where every fragment is exaggerated by some prating cicerone, in general, in this country, the reality exceeded our expectations. When we left Captain Fensley's brig we did not expect to find occupation for more than two or three days. But a vast field of interesting labour was before us, and we entered upon it with the advantages of experience, the protection and kind assistance of the proprietor, and within reach of comforts not procurable at any other place. We were not buried in the forest as at Palenque. In front of our doorway rose the lofty House of the Dwarf, seeming almost to realize the Indian legend, and from every part of the terrace we looked over a field of ruins.

From the centre apartment the divisions on each wing corresponded exactly in size and finish, the details of which appear in the plan, and the same uniformity was preserved in the ornaments. Throughout, the roof was tight, the apartments were dry, and to speak understandingly, a *few hundred pounds expended in repairs* would have restored it, and made it fit for the re-occupation of its royal owners. In the apartment marked A the walls were coated with a very fine plaster-of-Paris, equal to the best seen on walls in this country. The rest were all of smooth polished stone. There were no paintings, stucco ornaments, sculptured tablets, or other decorations whatever.

In the apartment marked B we found what we regarded as a most interesting object. It was a *beam of wood*, about ten feet long, and very heavy, which had fallen from its place over the doorway, and for some purpose or other been hauled inside the chamber into a dark corner.* On the face was a line of characters carved or stamped, almost obliterated, but which we made out to be hieroglyphics, and, so far as we could understand them, similar to those at Copan and Palenque. Several Indians were around us, with an idle curosity watching all our movements; and, not wishing to call their attention to it, we left it with an Indian at the moment sitting upon it. Before we were out of the doorway we heard the ring of his machete from a blow which, on rising, he had struck at random, and which chipped off a long shaving within a few inches of the characters. It almost gave us a shivering fit, and we did not dare tell him to spare it, lest from ignorance, jealousy, or suspicion, it should be the means of ensuring its destruction. I immediately determined to secure this mystical beam. Compelled to leave in haste, on my arrival at Merida Don Simon kindly promised to send it to me, together with a sculptured stone which formed one of the principal ornaments in all the buildings. The latter is now in my possession, but the former has never arrived. In the multitude of regrets connected with our abrupt departure from these ruins, I cannot help deploring the misfortune of not being assured of the safety of this beam. By what feeble light the pages of American history are written! There are at Uxmal no "idols," as at Copan; not a single stuccoed figure or carved tablet, as at Palenque. Except this beam of hieroglyphics, though searching earnestly, we did not discover any one absolute point of resemblance; and the wanton machete of an Indian may destroy the only link that can connect them together.

It was our purpose to present full drawings of the exterior of this building, and, in fact, of all the others. The plate, No. 80, represents one division, with its sculptured ornaments, or what I have called mosaic. As at Copan, Mr. Catherwood was obliged to make several attempts before he could comprehend the subject so, as to copy the characters. The drawing was begun late in the afternoon, was unfinished when we left to return to the hacienda, and, unfortunately, Mr. C. was never able to resume it. It is presented in the state given by the last touches of the pencil on the spot, wanting many of the minute characters with which the subject was charged, and without any attempt to fill them in. The reader will see how utterly insufficient any verbal description must be, and he will be able to form from it some idea of the imposing exterior of the building. The exterior of every building in Uxmal was ornamented in the same elaborate

* Mr. Waldeck informs me that he had caused this beam to be hidden away.—F. C.

manner. The part represented in the engraving embraces about twenty feet of the Casa del Gobernador. The whole exterior of this building presents a surface of 700 feet; the Casa de las Monjas is 2,000 feet, and the extent of sculptured surface exhibited by the other buildings we are not able to give. Complete drawings of the whole would form one of the most magnificent series ever offered to the public, and such

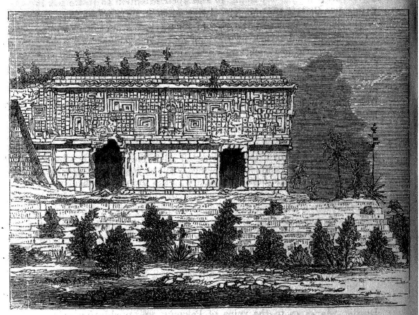

F. Catherwood.   80. SCULPTURED FRONT OF THE CASA DEL GOBERNADOR.

it is yet our hope one day to be able to present. The reader will be able to form some idea of the time, skill, and labour required for making them; and, more than this, to conceive the immense time, skill, and labour required for carving such a surface of stone, and the wealth, power, and cultivation of the people who could command such skill and labour for the mere decoration of their edifices. Probably all these ornaments have a symbolical meaning; each stone is part of an allegory or fable, hidden from us, inscrutable under the light of the feeble torch we may burn before it, but which, if ever revealed, will show that the history of the world yet remains to be written.

CHAPTER XLII.

EXPLORATION FINISHED—WHO BUILT THESE RUINED CITIES?—OPINION OF DUPAIX—THESE RUINS BEAR NO RESEMBLANCE TO THE ARCHITECTURE OF GREECE AND ROME—NOTHING LIKE THEM IN EUROPE—DO NOT RESEMBLE THE KNOWN WORKS OF JAPAN AND CHINA—NEITHER THOSE OF HINDU—NO EXCAVATED TEMPLES FOUND—THE PYRAMIDS OF EGYPT, IN THEIR ORIGINAL STATE, DO NOT RESEMBLE WHAT ARE CALLED THE PYRAMIDS OF AMERICA—THE TEMPLES OF EGYPT NOT LIKE THOSE OF AMERICA—SCULPTURE NOT THE SAME AS THAT OF EGYPT—PROBABLE ANTIQUITY OF THESE RUINS—ACCOUNTS OF THE SPANISH HISTORIANS—THESE CITIES PROBABLY BUILT BY THE RACES INHABITING THE COUNTRY AT THE TIME OF THE SPANISH CONQUEST—THESE RACES NOT YET EXTINCT.

We have now finished the exploration of ruins. And here I would be willing to part, and leave the reader to wander alone and at will through the labyrinth of mystery which hangs over these ruined cities; but it would be craven to do so, without turning for a moment to the important question, Who were the people that built these cities?

Since their discovery, a dark cloud has been thrown over them in two particulars. The first is in regard to the immense difficulty and danger, labour and expense, of visiting and exploring them. It will appear from these pages that the accounts have been exaggerated; and, as regards Palenque and Uxmal at least, the only places which have been brought before the public at all, there is neither difficulty in reaching nor danger in exploring them.

The second is in regard to the age of the buildings; but here the cloud is darker, and not so easily dispelled.

I will not recapitulate the many speculations that have already been presented. The most irrational, perhaps, is that of Captain Dupaix, who gives to the ruins of Palenque an antediluvian origin; and, unfortunately for him, he gives his reason, which is the accumulation of earth over the figures in the courtyard of the palace. His visit was thirty years before ours; and, though he cleared away the earth, the accumulation was again probably quite as great when we were there. At all events, by his own showing, the figures were not entirely buried. I have a distinct recollection of the condition of those monuments, and have no scruple in saying that, if entirely buried, one Irishman, with the national weapon that has done such service on our canals, would in three hours remove the whole of this antediluvian deposit. I shall not follow the learned commentaries upon this suggestion of Captain Dupaix, except to remark that much learning and research have been expended upon insufficient or incorrect data, or when a bias has been given by a statement of facts; and, putting ourselves in the same category with those who have furnished these data, for the benefit of explorers and writers who may succeed us I shall narrow down this question to a ground even yet sufficiently broad, viz. a comparison of these remains with those of the architecture and sculpture of other ages and people.

I set out with the proposition that they are not Cyclopean, and do not resemble the works of Greek or Roman; there is nothing in Europe like them. We must look, then, to Asia and Africa.

It has been supposed that at different periods of time vessels from Japan and China have been thrown upon the western coast of America. The civilization, cultivation, and science of those countries are known to date back from a very early antiquity. Of Japan I believe some accounts and drawings have been published, but they are not within my reach; of China, during the whole of her long history, the interior has been so completely shut against strangers that we know but little of her ancient architecture. Perhaps, however, that time is close at hand. At present we know only that they have been a people not given to change; and if their ancient architecture be the same with their modern, it bears no resemblance whatever to these unknown ruins.

The monuments of India have been made familiar to us. The remains of Hindu architecture exhibit immense excavations in the rock, either entirely artificial or made by enlarging natural caverns, supported in front by large columns cut out of the rock, with a dark and gloomy interior.

Among all these American ruins there is not a single excavation. The surface of country, abounding in mountain sides, seems to invite it; but, instead of being under ground, the striking feature of these ruins is, that the buildings stand on lofty artificial elevations; and it can hardly be supposed that a people emigrating to a new country, with that strong natural impulse to perpetuate and retain under their eyes memorials of home, would have gone so directly counter to national and religious associations.

In sculpture, too, the Hindus differ entirely. Their subjects are far more hideous, being in general representations of human beings distorted, deformed, and unnatural, very often many-headed, or with three or four arms or legs thrown out from the same body.

Lastly we come to the Egyptians The point of resemblance upon which the great stress has been laid is the pyramid. The pyramidal form is one which suggests itself to human intelligence in every country as the simplest and surest mode of erecting a high structure upon a solid foundation. It cannot be regarded as a ground for assigning a common origin to all people among whom structures of that character are found, unless the similarity is preserved in its most striking features. The pyramids of Egypt are peculiar and uniform, and were invariably erected for the same uses and purposes, so far as those uses and purposes are known. They are all square at the base, with steps rising and diminishing until they come to a point. The nearest approach to this is at Copan; but even at that place there is no entire pyramid standing alone and disconnected, nor one with four sides complete, but only two, or, at most, three sides, and intended to form part of other structures. All the rest, without a single exception, were high elevations, with sides so broken that we could not make out their form, which, perhaps, were merely walled around, and had ranges of steps in front and rear, as at Uxmal, or terraces or raised platforms of earth, at most of three or four ranges, not of any precise form, but never square, and with small ranges of steps in the centre. Besides, the pyramids of Egypt are known to have interior chambers, and, whatever their other uses, to have been intended and used as sepulchres. These, on the contrary, are of solid earth and stone. No interior chambers have ever been discovered, and probably none exist. And the most radical difference of all is, the pyramids of Egypt are complete in themselves; the structures of this country were erected only to serve as the foundations of buildings. There is no pyramid in Egypt with a palace or temple upon it; there is no pyramidal structure in this country without; at least none from whose condition any judgment can be formed.

But there is one farther consideration, which must be conclusive. The pyramids of Egypt, as I have considered them, and as they stand now, differ most materially from the original structures. Herodotus says that in his time the great pyramid was coated with stone, so as to present a smooth surface on all its sides from the base to the top. The second pyramid of Ghizeh, called the Pyramid of Cephrenes, in its present condition, presents on the lower part ranges of steps, with an accumulation of angular stones at the base, which originally filled up the interstices between the steps, but have fallen down. In the upper part the intermediate layers are still in their places, and the sides present a smooth surface to the top. There is no doubt that originally every pyramid in Egypt was built with its sides perfectly smooth. The steps formed no part of the plan. It is in this state only that they ought to be considered, and in this state any possible

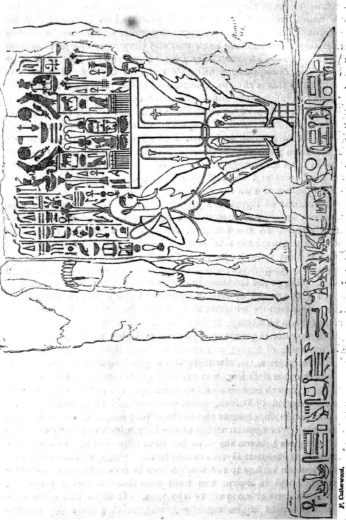

81. EGYPTIAN HIEROGLYPHICS

resemblance between them and what are called the pyramids of America, ceases.

Next to the pyramids, the oldest remains of Egyptian architecture, such as the temple of Abousimboul in Nubia, like those of the Hindus, are excavations in the rock, from which it has been supposed that the Egyptians derived their style from that people. In later times they commenced erecting temples above ground, retaining the same features of gloomy grandeur, and remarkable for their vastness and the massiveness of the stone used in their construction. This does not seem to have been aimed at by the American builders. Among all these ruins we did not see a stone worthy of being laid on the walls of an Egyptian temple. The largest single blocks were the "idols," or " obelisks" as they have been called, of Copan and Quirigua; but in Egypt stones large as these are raised to a height of twenty or thirty feet and laid in the walls, while the obelisks which stand as ornaments at the doors, towering, a single stone, to the height of ninety feet, so overpower them by their grandeur, that, if imitations, they are the feeblest ever attempted by aspiring men.

Again, as to sculpture.* The idea of resemblance in this particular has been so often and so confidently expressed, and the drawings in these pages have so often given the same impression, that I almost hesitate to declare the total want of similarity. What the differences are I will not attempt to point out; but, that the reader may have the whole subject before him at once, I have introduced a plate, No. 81, of Egyptian sculpture taken from the side of the great monument at Thebes, known as the Vocal Memnon, and I think, by comparison with the engravings before presented, it will be found that there is no resemblance whatever. If there be any at all striking, it is only that the figures are in profile, and this is equally true of all good sculpture in bas-relief.

There is, then, no resemblance in these remains to those of the Egyptians; and, failing here, we look elsewhere in vain. They are different from the works of any other known people, of a new order, and entirely and absolutely anomalous: they stand alone.

I invite to this subject the special attention of those familiar with the arts of other countries; for, unless I am wrong, we have a conclusion far more interesting and wonderful than that of connecting the builders of these cities with the Egyptians or any other people. It is the spectacle of a people skilled in architecture, sculpture, and drawing, and, beyond doubt, other more perishable arts, and possessing the cultivation and refinement attendant upon these, not derived from the Old World, but originating and growing up here, without models or masters, having a distinct, separate, independent existence; like the plants and fruits of the soil, indigenous.

I shall not attempt to inquire into the origin of this people, from what country they came, or when, or how; I shall confine myself to their works and to the ruins.

I am inclined to think that there are not sufficient grounds for the belief in the great antiquity that has been ascribed to these ruins; that they are not the works of people who have passed away, and whose history has become unknown; but, opposed as is my idea to all previous speculations, that they were constructed by the races who occupied the country at the time of the invasion by the Spaniards, or of some not very distant progenitors.

And this opinion is founded, first, upon the appearance and condition of the remains themselves. The climate and rank luxuriance of soil are most destructive to all perishable materials. For six months every year exposed to the deluge of tropical rains, and with trees growing through the doorways of buildings and on the tops, it seems impossible that, after a lapse of two or three thousand years, a single edifice could now be standing.

The existence of wooden beams, and at Uxmal in a perfect state of preservation, confirms this opinion. The durability of wood will depend upon its quality and exposure. In Egypt, it is true, wood has been discovered sound and perfect, and certainly 3,000 years old; but even in that dry climate none has ever been found in a situation at all exposed. It occurs only in coffins in the tombs and mummy-pits of Thebes, and in wooden cramps connecting two stones together, completely shut in and excluded from the air.

Secondly, my opinion is founded upon historical accounts. Herrera, perhaps the most reliable of the Spanish historians, says of Yucatan: "The whole country is divided into eighteen districts, and in all of them were so many and such stately Stone Buildings that it was amazing, and the greatest Wonder is, that having no Use of any Metal, they were able to raise such Structures, which seem to have been Temples, for their Houses were always of Timber and thatched. In those Edifices were carved the Figures of naked Men, with Earrings after the Indian manner, Idols of all Sorts, Lions, Pots or Jarrs," &c.; and again, "After the parting of these lords, for the space of twenty years there was such plenty through the Country, and the People multiplied so much, that old Men said the whole Province looked like one Town, and then they applied themselves to build more Temples, which produced so great a number of them."

Of the natives he says, "They *flattened their Heads and Foreheads*, *their Ears bor'd with Rings in them.* Their Faces were generally good, and not very brown, *but without Beards,* for they scorched them when young, that they might not grow. Their Hair was *long like Women,* and in Tresses, with which they made a Garland about the Head, and a *little Tail hung behind.*" " The prime Men wore a *Rowler eight Fingers broad round about them* instead of Breeches, and *going several times round the Waist, so that one end of it hung before and the other behind,* with fine Feather-work, and had large *square Mantles knotted on their Shoulders,* and *Sandals* or *Buskins* made of Deer's Skins." The reader almost sees here, in the flatted heads and costumes of the natives, a picture of the sculptured and stuccoed figures at Palenque, which, though a little beyond the present territorial borders of Yucatan, was perhaps once a part of that province.

Besides the glowing and familiar descriptions given by Cortez of the splendour exhibited in the buildings of Mexico, I have within my reach the authority of but one eye-witness. It is that of Bernal Diaz de Castillo, a follower and sharer in all the expeditions attending the conquest of Mexico.

Beginning with the first expedition, he says, " On approaching Yucatan, we perceived a large town at the distance of two leagues from the coast, which, from its size, it exceeding any town in Cuba, we named Grand Cairo." Upon the invitation of a chief, who came off in a canoe, they went ashore, and set out to march to the town, but on their way were surprised by the natives, whom, however, they repulsed, killing fifteen. " Near the place of this ambuscade," he says, " were three buildings *of lime and stone,* wherein were idols of clay with *diabolical countenances,*" &c. " The buildings of *lime and stone,* and the gold, gave us a high idea of the country we had discovered."

In fifteen days' farther sailing, they discovered from the ships a large town, with an inlet, and went ashore for water. While filling their casks they were accosted by fifty Indians, "dressed in cotton mantles," who " by signs invited us to their town." Proceeding thither, they "arrived at some large and very well-constructed buildings of *lime and stone,* with figures of *serpents* and of *idols* painted upon the walls."

In the second expedition, sailing along the coast, they passed a low island, about three leagues from the main, where, on going ashore, they found " two buildings of lime and stone, well constructed, each with steps, and an altar placed before certain hideous figures, the representations of the gods of these Indians."

His third expedition was under Cortez, and in this his regard for truth and the reliance that may be placed upon him are happily shown in the struggle between deep religious feeling and belief in the evidence of his senses, which appears in his comment upon Gomara's account of their first battle. "In his account of this action, Gomara says that, previous to the arrival of the main body under Cortez, Francisco de Morla appeared in the field upon a grey dappled horse, and that it was one of the holy apostles, St. Peter or St. Jago, disguised under his person. I say that all our works and victories are guided by the hand of our Lord Jesus Christ, and that in this battle there were so many enemies to every one of us, that they could have buried us under the dust they could have held in their hands, but that the great mercy of God aided us throughout. What Gomara asserts may be the case, and I, sinner as I am, was not permitted to see it. What I did see was Francisco de Morla riding in company with Cortez and the rest, upon a chestnut horse. But although I, unworthy sinner that I am, was unfit to behold either of these apostles, upward of 400 of us were present. Let their testimony be taken. Let inquiry also be made how it happened that, when the town was founded on that spot, it was not named after one or other of these holy apostles, and called St. Jago de la Vittoria or St. Pedro de la Vittoria, as it was Santa Maria, and a church erected and dedicated to one of these holy saints. Very bad Christians were we, indeed, according to the account of Gomara, who, when God sent us his apostles to fight at our head, did not every day after acknowledge and return thanks for so great a mercy!"

Setting out on their march to Mexico, they arrived at Cempoal, entering which, he says, "We were surprised with the beauty of the buildings." "Our advanced guard having gone to the great square, the buildings of which had been lately whitewashed and *plastered, in which art these people are very expert,* one of our horsemen was so struck with the splendour of their appearance in the sun, that he came back in full speed to Cortez to tell him that the walls of the houses were of silver."

As they approached the territory of Mexico, he continues, "Appearances demonstrated that we had entered a new country, for the *temples were very lofty,* and, together with the *terraced dwellings* and the houses of the cacique, being *plastered* and whitewashed, appeared very well, and resembled some of our towns in Spain."

Farther on he says, "We arrived at a kind of fortification, built of *lime and stone,* of so strong a nature that nothing but tools of iron could have any effect upon it. The people informed us that it was built by the Tlascalans, on whose territory it stood, as a defence against the incursions of the Mexicans."

At Tehuacingo, after a sanguinary battle, in which the Indians " drew off and left the field to them, who were too much fatigued to follow," he adds, "As soon as we found ourselves clear of them, we returned thanks to God for his mercy, and, entering a *strong and spacious temple,* we dressed our wounds with the fat of Indians."

Approaching the city of Mexico, he gives way to a burst of enthusiasm. " We could compare it to nothing but the enchanted scenes we had read of in Amadis de Gaul, from the *great towers,* and *temples,* and other *edifices of lime and stone* which seemed to rise up out of the water."

" We were received by great lords of that country, relations of Montezuma, who conducted us to our lodgings there, in *palaces* magnificently built *of stone,* the timber of which was cedar, with *spacious courts* and apartments furnished with canopies of the *finest cotton.* The whole was ornamented with *works of art painted,* and *admirably plastered* and whitened, and it was rendered more delightful by numbers of beautiful birds."

" The palace in which we were lodged was very light, airy, clean, and pleasant, the entry being through a great court."

Montezuma, in his first interview with Cortez, says, " The Tlascalans have, I know, told you that I am like a god, and that all about me is gold, and silver, and precious stones; but you now see that I am mere flesh and blood, and that my *houses are built like other houses, of lime, and stone, and timber.*"

"At the great square we were astonished at the crowds of people and the regularity which prevailed, and the vast quantities of merchandise."

" The entire square was enclosed in piazzas."

" From the square we proceeded to the great temple, but before we entered it we made a circuit through a number of *large courts,* the smallest of which appeared to me to contain more ground than the great square of Salamanca, with double enclosures, *built of lime and stone,* and the *courts* paved with large white *cut* stones, or, where not paved, they were *plastered and polished.*"

" The ascent to the great temple was by *a hundred and fourteen steps.*"

" From the platform on the summit of the temple, Montezuma, taking Cortez by the hand, pointed out to him the different parts of the city and its vicinity, all of which were commanded from that place." " We observed also the temples and adoratories of the adjacent cities, built in the form of *towers* and *fortresses,* and others on the causeway, all whitewashed and wonderfully brilliant."

"The noise and bustle of the market-place could be heard almost a league off, and *those who had been at Rome and Constantinople* said that for convenience, regularity, and population they had never seen the like."

During the siege he speaks of being "quartered in a *lofty temple;*" "marching *up the steps of the temple;*" "*some lofty temples* which we now battered with our artillery;" "the *lofty temples* where Diego Velasquez and Salvatierra were posted;" "the *breaches* which they had made in the *walls;*" "*cut stone* taken from the buildings from the terraces."

Arrived at the great temple, instantly above 4,000 Mexicans rushed up into it, who for some time prevented them from ascending. "Although the cavalry several times attempted to charge, the stone pavements of the courts of the temple were so smooth that the horses could not keep their feet, and fell." "Their numbers were such that we could not make any effectual impression or *ascend the steps*. At length we *forced our way up*. Here Cortez showed himself the man that he really was. What a desperate engagement we then had! Every man of us was covered with blood."

"They drove us *down six, and even ten of the steps;* while others who were in the corridors, or within side of the railings and concavities of the great temple, shot such clouds of arrows at us that we could not maintain our ground," "began our retreat, every man of us being wounded, and forty-six of us left dead on the spot. I have often seen this engagement represented in the *paintings* of the natives both of Mexico and Tlascala, and *our ascent into the great temple*."

"We proceeded to another town called Terrayuco, but which we named the town of the *serpents,* on account of the *enormous figures of those animals* which we found in their temples, and which they worshipped as gods."

Again: "In this garden our whole force lodged for the night. I certainly never had seen one of such magnificence; and Cortez and the treasurer Alderete, after they had walked through and examined it, declared that it was admirable, and equal to any they had ever seen in Castille."

"I and ten more soldiers were posted as a guard upon a *wall of lime and stone.*"

"When we arrived at our quarters at Jacuba it rained heavily, and we remained under it for two hours in some *large enclosed courts.* The general, with his captains, the treasurer, our reverend father, and many others of us, mounted to the *top of the temple,* which commanded all the lake."

"We crossed the water up to our necks at the pass they had left open, and followed them until we came to a place where were *large temples* and *towers of idols.*"

"As Cortez now lodged at Cuejoacan, in large buildings with white walls, very well adapted for scribbling on, there appeared every morning libels against him in prose and verse. I recollect the words of one only:—

'Que trista esta el alma mea
Hasta que la parte vea'

How anxious I am for a share of the plunder."

"When our party (for I went with Sandoval) arrived at Tustepeque, I took up my lodgings in the summit of a *tower in a very high temple*, partly for the fresh air and to avoid the mosquitoes, which were very troublesome below, and partly to be near Sandoval's quarters." "We pursued our route to the city of Chiapas, in the same province with Palenque, and a city it might be called, from the regularity of its streets and houses. It contained not less than 4,000 families, not reckoning the population of the many dependent towns in its neighbourhood." "We found the whole force of Chiapas drawn up to receive us. Their troops were adorned with plumage."

"On our arrival we found it too closely built to be safely occupied by us, and we therefore pitched our camp in the open field. In their *temples* we found idols of a horrid figure."

Now it will be recollected that Bernal Diaz wrote to do justice to himself and others of the "true conquerors," his companions in arms, whose fame had been obscured by other historians not actors and eye-witnesses; all his references to building are incidental; he never expected to be cited as authority upon the antiquities of the country. The pettiest skirmish with the natives was nearer his heart than all the edifices of lime and stone which he saw, and it is precisely on that account that his testimony is the more valuable. It was written at a time when there were many living who could contradict him if incorrect or false. His "true history" never was impeached; on the contrary, while its style was considered rude and inelegant, its fidelity and truth have been acknowledged by all contemporaneous and subsequent historians. In my opinion it is as true and reliable as any work of *travels* on the countries through which he fought his way. It gives the hurried and imperfect observations of an unlettered soldier, whose sword was seldom in its scabbard, surrounded by dangers, attacking, retreating, wounded, and flying, with his mind constantly occupied by matters of more pressing moment.

The reader cannot fail to be struck with the general resemblance between the objects described by him and the scenes referred to in these pages. His account presents to my mind a vivid picture of the ruined cities which we visited, as they once stood, with *buildings of lime and stone, painted* and *sculptured ornaments,* and *plastered; idols, courts, stone walls,* and *lofty temples with high ranges of steps.*

But if this be not sufficient, I have farther and stronger support. After the siege of Mexico, on the re-entry of the Spaniards, a ruthless and indiscriminate destruction fell upon every building and monument in the city. No memorials of the arts of the Mexicans were left; but in the year 1790, two statues and a flat stone, with sculptured characters relative to the Mexican calendar, were discovered and dug up from among the remains of the great Teocalli in the plaza of the city of Mexico. The statues excited great interest among the Mexican Indians, and the priests, afraid of their relapsing into idolatry, and to destroy all memorials of their ancient rites, buried them in the court of the Franciscan convent. The calendar was fixed in a conspicuous place in the wall of the Cathedral, where it now stands. In the centre, and forming the principal subject of this calendar, is a face, published in Humboldt's work, which in one particular bears so strong a resemblance to that called the mask, in Plate No. 72 of this volume, as to suggest the idea that they were intended for the same. There are palpable differences, but perhaps the expression of the eyes is changed and improved in the engraving published, and, at all events, in both the peculiar and striking feature is that of the tongue hanging out of the mouth. The calendar is in bas-relief, and the sculpture is very good.*

And, lastly, among the hieroglyphical paintings which escaped destruction from monkish fanaticism are certain Mexican manuscripts now in the libraries of Dresden and Vienna. These have been published in Humboldt's work, and in that of Lord Kingsborough, and, on a careful examination, we are strongly of the opinion that the characters are the same with those found on the monuments and tablets at Copan and Palenque. For the sake of comparison I have introduced again the engraving No. 82, of the top of the altar at Copan, and another from a hieroglyphical manuscript published in Humboldt's work. Differences, it is true, are manifest; but it must be borne in mind that in the former the characters are carved on stone, and in the latter written on paper (made of the Agave Mexicana). Probably, for this reason, they want the same regularity and finish; but, altogether, the reader cannot fail to mark the strong similarity, and this similarity cannot be accidental. The inference is, that the Aztecs or Mexicans,

* Vues de las Cordilleras, vol. xiii p 276.

CENTRAL AMERICAN AND MEXICAN HIEROGLYPHICS. 539

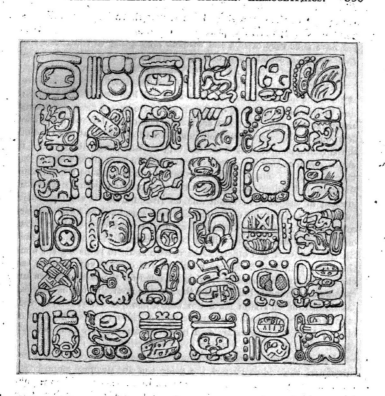

at the time of the conquest, had the same written language with the people of Copan and Palenque.

I have thus very briefly, and without attempting to controvert the opinions and speculations of others, presented our own views upon the subject of these ruins. As yet we perhaps stand alone in these views, but I repeat my opinion, that we are not warranted in going back to any ancient nation of the Old World for the builders of these cities; that they are not the work of people who have passed away and whose history is lost, but that there are strong reasons to believe them the creations of the same races who inhabited the country at the time of the Spanish conquest, or some not very distant progenitors. And I would remark, that we began our exploration without any theory to support. Our feelings were in favour of going back to a high and venerable antiquity. During the greater part of our journey we were groping in the dark, in doubt and uncertainty, and it was not until our arrival at the ruins of Uxmal that we formed our opinion of their comparatively modern date. Some are beyond doubt older than others; some are known to have been inhabited at the time of the Spanish conquest, and others, perhaps, were really in ruins before; and there are points of difference which as yet cannot very readily be explained; but in regard to Uxmal, at least, we believe that it was an existing and inhabited city at the time of the arrival of the Spaniards. Its desolation and ruin since are easily accounted for. With the arrival of the Spaniards the sceptre of the Indians departed. In the city of Mexico every house was razed to the ground, and, beyond doubt, throughout the country every gathering-place or stronghold was broken up, the communities scattered, their lofty temples thrown down, and their idols burned, the palaces of the caciques ruined, the caciques themselves made bondmen; and, by the same ruthless policy which from time immemorial has been pursued in a conquered country, all the mementoes of their ancestors and lost independence were destroyed or made odious in their eyes. And, without this, we have authentic accounts of great scourges which swept over, and for a time depopulated and desolated, the whole of Yucatan.

It perhaps destroys much of the interest that hangs over these ruins to assign to them a modern date; but we live in an age whose spirit is to discard phantasms and arrive at truth, and the interest lost in one particular is supplied in another scarcely inferior; for, the nearer we can bring the builders of these cities to our own times, the greater is our chance of knowing all. Throughout the country the convents are rich in manuscripts and documents written by the early fathers, caciques, and Indians, who very soon acquired the knowledge of

Spanish and the art of writing. These have never been examined with the slightest reference to this subject; and I cannot help thinking that some precious memorial is now mouldering in the library of a neighbouring convent, which would determine the history of some one of these ruined cities; moreover, I cannot help believing that the tablets of hieroglyphics will yet be read. No strong curiosity has hitherto been directed to them; vigour and acuteness of intellect, knowledge and learning, have never been expended upon them. For centuries the hieroglyphics of Egypt were inscrutable, and, though not perhaps in our day, I feel persuaded that a key surer than that of the Rosetta stone will be discovered. And if only three centuries have elapsed since any one of these unknown cities was inhabited, the race of the inhabitants is not extinct. Their descendants are still in the land, scattered, perhaps, and retired, like our own Indians, into wildernesses which have never yet been penetrated by a white man, but not lost; living as their fathers did, erecting the same buildings of "lime and stone," "with ornaments of sculpture and plastered," "large courts," and "lofty towers with high ranges of steps," and still carving on tablets of stone the same mysterious hieroglyphics; and if, in consideration that I have not often indulged in speculative conjecture, the reader will allow one flight, I turn to that vast and unknown region, untraversed by a single road, wherein fancy pictures that mysterious city seen from the topmost range of the Cordilleras, of unconquered, unvisited, and unsought aboriginal inhabitants.

In conclusion, I am at a loss to determine which would be the greatest enterprise,—an attempt to reach this mysterious city, to decipher the tablets of hieroglyphics, or to wade through the accumulated manuscripts of three centuries in the libraries of the convents.

CHAPTER XLIII.

JOURNEY TO MERIDA—VILLAGE OF MOONA—A POND OF WATER, A CURIOSITY—ABOULA—INDIAN RUNNERS—MERIDA—DEPARTURE—HUNUCAMA—SIEGE OF CAMPEACHY—EMBARKATION FOR HAVANA—INCIDENTS OF THE PASSAGE—FOURTH OF JULY AT SEA—SHARK-FISHING—GETTING LOST AT SEA—RELIEVED BY THE HELEN MARIA—PASSAGE TO NEW YORK—ARRIVAL—CONCLUSION.

But to return to ourselves. At three, by the light of the moon, we left Uxmal by the most direct road for Merida, Mr. Catherwood in a coché and I on horseback, charged with a letter from the junior majordomo to his compatriot and friend, Delmonico's head chocolate-maker. As I followed Mr. C. through the woods, borne on the shoulders of Indians, the stillness broken only by the shuffle of their feet, and under my great apprehensions for his health, it almost seemed as if I were following his bier. At the distance of three leagues we entered the village of Moona, where, though a fine village, having white people and Mestitzoes among its inhabitants, travellers were more rare than in the interior of Central America. We were detained two hours at the casa real, waiting for a relief coché At a short distance beyond, my guide led me out of the road to show me a pond of water, which in that country was a curiosity. It was surrounded by woods; wild cattle were drinking on the borders, and started like deer at our approach. At the distance of four leagues we reached the village of Aboula, with a plaza enclosed by a rough picket-fence, a good casa real and fine old alcalde, who knew our servant as belonging to the Peon family.

There was no intermediate village, and he undertook to provide us with relief Indians to carry the coché through to Merida, twenty-seven miles. It was growing late, and I went on before with a horse for change, to reach Merida in time to make arrangements for a calêche the next day.

Toward evening it rained hard. At dark I began to have apprehension of leaving Mr. Catherwood behind, sent the servant on to secure the calêche, and dismounted to wait. I was too dreadfully fatigued to ride back, and sat down in the road; by degrees I stretched myself on a smooth stone, with the bridle around my wrist, and, after a dreamy debate whether my horse would tread on me or not, fell asleep. I was roused by a jerk which nearly tore my arm off, and saw coming through the woods Indian runners with blazing pine torches, lighting the way for the coché, which had an aspect so funereal that it almost made me shudder. Mr. C. had had his difficulties. After carrying him about a league, the Indians stopped, laid him down, and, after an animated conversation, took him up, went on, but in a little while laid him down again, and, thrusting their heads under the cover of the coché, made him an eager and clamorous address, of which he did not understand one word. At length he picked up dos pesos, or two dollars, and gathered that they wanted two dollars more. As the alcalde had adjusted the account, he refused to pay, and, after a noisy wrangle, they quietly took him up on their shoulders, and began trotting back with him to the village. This made him tractable, and he paid the money, threatening them as well as he could with vengeance; but the amusing part was that they were right. The alcalde had made a mistake in the calculation; and, on a division and distribution on the road, by hard pounding and calculating, each one knowing what he ought to receive himself, they discovered that they had been paid two dollars short. The price was a shilling per man for the first, and ninepence for every subsequent league, besides two shillings for making the coché; so that, with four men for relief, it was eight shillings for the first league, and six shillings for every subsequent one; and a calculation of the whole amount for nine leagues was rather complicated.

It was half-past one when we reached Merida, and we had been up and on the road since two in the morning. Fortunately, with the easy movement of the coché, Mr. C. had suffered but little. I was tired beyond all measure; but I had, what enabled me to endure any degree of fatigue, a good cot, and was soon asleep.

The next morning we saw my friend Don Simon, who was preparing to go back and join us. He promised, if we returned, to go down with us and assist in a thorough exploration of the ruins. The Spanish vessel was to sail the next day. Toward evening, after a heavy rain, as the dark clouds were rolling away, and the setting sun was tinging them with a rich golden border, we left Merida. At eleven o'clock we reached Hunucama, and stopped in the plaza two hours to feed the horses. While here, a party of soldiers arrived from the port, waving pine torches, having just returned victorious from the siege of Campeachy. They were all young, ardent, well-dressed, and in fine spirits, and full of praises of their general, who, they said, had remained at Sisal to attend a ball, and was coming on as soon as it was over. Resuming our journey, in an hour more we met a train of calêches, with officers in uniform. We stopped, congratulated the general upon his victory at Campeachy; inquired for a United States' sloop-of-war which we had heard was there during the blockade; and, with many interchanges of courtesy, but without seeing a feature of each other's faces, resumed our separate roads. An hour before daylight we reached Sisal, at six o'clock we embarked on board the Spanish brig *Alexandre* for Havana, and at eight we were under way.

It was the 24th of June; and now, as we thought, all our troubles were ended. The morning was fine. We had eight passengers, all Spanish; one of whom, from the interior, when he came down to the shore and saw the brig in the offing, asked what animal it was. From my great regard for the captain, I will not speak of the brig or of its condition, particularly the cabin, except to say that it was Spanish. The wind was light; we breakfasted on deck, making the top of the companion-way serve as a table under an awning. The captain told us we should be in Havana in a week.

Our course lay along the coast of Yucatan toward Cape Catoche. On Sunday the 28th, we had made, according to the brig's reckoning, about 150 miles, and were then becalmed. The sun was intensely hot, the sea of glassy stillness, and all day a school of sharks was swimming round the brig. From this time we had continued calms, and the sea was like a mirror, heated and reflecting its heat. On the 4th of July there was the same glassy stillness, with light clouds, but fixed and stationary. The captain said we were incantado or enchanted, and really it almost seemed so. We had expected to celebrate this day by dining with the American consul in Havana; but our vessel lay like a log, and we were scorching, and already pinched for water; the bare thought of a 4th of July dinner meanwhile making Spanish ship-cookery intolerable. We had read through all the books in the mate's library, consisting of some French novels translated into Spanish, and a history of awful shipwrecks. To break the monotony of the calm, we had hooks and lines out constantly for sharks; the sailors called them, like the alligators, ennemigos de los Christianos, hoisted them on deck, cut out their hearts and entrails, and then threw them overboard. We were already out ten days, and growing short of provisions; we had two young sharks for dinner. Apart from the associations, they were not bad—quite equal to young alligators; and the captain told us that in Campeachy they were regularly in the markets, and eaten by all classes. In the afternoon they gathered around us fearfully. Everything that fell overboard was immediately snapped up; and the hat of a passenger which fell from his head had hardly touched the water before a huge fellow turned over on his side, opened his ugly mouth above the water, and swallowed it: luckily, the man was not under it. Toward evening we caught a leviathan, raised him four or five feet out of the water with the hook, and the sailors, leaning over, beat his brains with the capstan bars till he was motionless; then fastening a rope with a slipnoose under his fins, with the ship's tackle they hoisted him on deck. He seemed to fill half the side of the vessel. The sailors opened his mouth, and fastened the jaws apart with a marlinspike, turned him over on his back, ripped him open, and tore out his heart and entrails. They then chopped off about a foot of his tail and threw him overboard; what he did I will not mention, lest it should bring discredit upon other parts of these pages which the reader is disposed to think may be true; but the last we saw of him he seemed to be feeling for his tail.

In the afternoon of the next day we crossed a strong current setting to north-west, which roared like breakers; soundings before 120 fathoms; during the evening there was no bottom, and we supposed we must have passed Cape Catoche.

On the 6th, 7th, 8th, 9th, 10th, 11th, and 12th, there was the same dead calm, with a sea like glass and intense heat. We were scant of provisions, and alarmed for entire failure of water. The captain was a noble Spaniard, who comforted the passengers by repeating every morning that we were enchanted, but for several days he had been uneasy and alarmed. He had no chronometer on board. He had been thirty years trading from Havana to different ports in the Gulf of Mexico, and had never used one; but out of soundings, among currents, with nothing but the log, he could not determine his longitude, and was afraid of getting into the Gulf Stream, and being carried past Havana. Our chronometer had been nine months in hard use, jolted over severe mountain roads, and, as we supposed, could not be relied upon. Mr. Catherwood made a calculation with an old French table of logarithms which happened to be on board, but with results so different from the captain's reckoning that we supposed it could not be correct. At this time our best prospect was that of reaching Havana in the midst of the yellow fever season, sailing from there in the worst hurricane month, and a quarantine at Staten Island.

On the 13th of July everything on board was getting scarce, and with crew and passengers twenty in number, we broached our last cask of water. The heat was scorching, and the calm and stillness of the sea were fearful. All said we were enchanted; and the sailors added, half in earnest, that it was on account of the heretics; sharks more numerous than ever; we could not look over the side of the vessel without seeing three or four, as if waiting for prey.

On the 14th the captain was alarmed. The log was thrown regularly, but could not give his position. Toward evening we saw an enormous monster, with a straight black head ten feet out of water, moving directly toward us. The captain, looking at it from the rigging with a glass, said it was not a whale. Another of the same kind appeared at the stern, and we were really nervous; but we were relieved by hearing them spout, and seeing a column of water thrown into the air. At dark they were lying huge and motionless on the surface of the water.

On the 15th, to our great joy, a slight breeze sprang up in the morning, and the log gave three miles an hour. At twelve o'clock we took the latitude, which was in 25° 10′, N, and found that in steering *southward* at the rate of three miles an hour by the log, we were fifty-five miles to the northward of the reckoning of the day before. The captain now believed that we were in the midst of the Gulf Stream, had been so, perhaps, two or three days, and were then 200 or 300 miles past Havana. Mr Catherwood's chronometer gave 88° longitude; but this was so far out of the way by our dead reckoning, that, with our distrust of the chronometer, we all disregarded it, and the captain especially. We were then in a very bad position, short of provisions and water, and drifted past our port. The captain called aft passengers, sailors, cook, and cabin-boy, spread the chart on the companion-way, and pointed out our supposed position, saying, that he wished to take the advice of all on board as to what was best to be done. The mate sat by with the log-book to take notes. All remained silent until the cook spoke, and said that the captain knew best; the sailors and passengers assented; for, although we considered it all uncertain, and that we were completely lost, we believed that he knew better than anybody else. The captain pointed out the course of the Gulf Stream, said it would be impossible to turn back against it, and, having a light, favourable breeze, recommended that we should follow the stream, and bear up for New Providence for a supply of provisions and water. All assented, and so we put about from the south, and squared the yards for the north-east. At that moment we considered ourselves farther from Havana than when we started.

With most uncomfortable feelings we sat down to a scanty meal. Supposing that we were in the Gulf Stream and in the track of vessels, the captain sent a man aloft to look out for a sail, who very soon, to our great joy, reported a brig to leeward. We hoisted our flag, and bore down upon her. As we approached she answered our signal, and with a glass we recognised the American ensign. In an hour we were nearly within hailing distance; the captain could not speak English, and gave me the speaking-trumpet; but fancying, from his movements, that our countryman did not like the Spanish colours, and afraid of some technical irregularity in my hail, which would make us an object of suspicion, we begged him to lower the jolly-boat. This was lying on the deck, with her bottom upward, and her seams opened by the sun. The water poured into her, and before we were fifty yards from the brig she was half full. We sat up on the gunwale, and two of the men had as much as they could do to keep her afloat, while we urged the others to pull. Sharks were playing around us, and for a few moments we wished to be back on board the old brig. A breeze seemed to strike the vessel, which for two or three minutes kept steadily on; but, to our great relief, she hove to and took us on board. Our Spanish colours, and our irregular movement in attempting to board without hailing, had excited suspicion, and the sailors said we were pirates; but the captain, a long, cool-headed down-easter, standing on the quarter with his hands in his pockets, and seeing the sinking condition of our boat, said, "Them's no pirates." The brig was the Helen Maria, of North Yarmouth, Sweetzer, master, from Tobasco, and bound to New York! The reader cannot imagine the satisfaction with which I greeted on the high seas a countryman bound for New York. My first question was whether he could take us on board, next for provisions and water for our friends, and then where we were. He showed us his observation for the day. We were about 400 miles from the spot we supposed. The current which sets up between Cape Catoche and Cape Antonio the captain had taken for the Gulf Stream. If we had attended to Mr. C.'s chronometer we should not have been far out of the way. As it was, we were perfectly lost; and if we had not met this vessel, I do not know what would have become of us. The captain was but seven days from Tobasco, with a wind that had carried away one of his sails, and had lost one of his men. He had no surplus of provisions, particularly with two additional passengers; but he sent on board what he could, and a supply of water. We returned, told the captain, much to his surprise and astonishment, of his position, not more than 200 miles from Sisal, and bade all hands farewell. They were not sorry to get rid of us, for the absence of two mouths was an object; and though perhaps, in their hearts, they thought their bad luck was on account of the heretics, it was pleasant, that with all our vexations, parting thus on the wide ocean, we shook hands with captain, passengers, sailors, cook, and cabin-boy, having no unkind feeling with any one on board.

Our new vessel had a full cargo of logwood, the deck being loaded even with the quarter, and stowed so close that the cabin-door was taken off, and the descent was over a water-cask; but the change from the Spanish to the American vessel was a strange transition. The former had a captain, two mates, and eight sailors; the latter one mate and three sailors, with plank over the deck-load for sailors to run on, an enormous boom mainsail, and a tiller instead of a wheel, sweeping the whole quarter-deck, and at times requiring two men to hold it. In the evening we had two or three hours of calm; we were used to it, but the captain was annoyed; he detested a calm; he had not had one since he left Tobasco; he could bear anything but a calm. In the evening the charm was broken by a squall. The captain hated to take in sail, held on till the last moment, and then, springing from the tiller, hauled on the ropes himself, and was back again at the rudder, all in a flash. Mr. C. and I were so well pleased with the change that we were in no hurry; and, noticing the shortness of hands, and stumbling over logwood, we suggested to the captain that if he lost another man he would have difficulty in carrying his vessel into port; but he put this down at once by swearing that, if he lost every hand on board, the mate and he could carry her in themselves, deck-load and all.

On the 31st of July we arrived at New York, after an absence of nearly ten months, and nine without receiving any intelligence whatever from our friends at home. In the hope of making another journey with the reader to Yucatan, I now bid the reader farewell.

THE END.

R. CLAY, PRINTER, BREAD STREET HILL.

A LIST OF
NEW WORKS AND NEW EDITIONS

PUBLISHED BY

ARTHUR HALL, VIRTUE, & CO.,
25, PATERNOSTER ROW, LONDON.

Now Ready, with ILLUSTRATIONS, in Three Volumes 8vo., cloth,

THE

HOMES OF THE NEW WORLD:
IMPRESSIONS OF AMERICA.

BY FREDRIKA BREMER.—TRANSLATED BY MARY HOWITT.

"Really, the Swedish lady, on the whole, writes so pleasantly, so good-naturedly, so lovingly, and ingenuously, that we cannot indicate one tithe of the good things—of the rough sketches, numerous points, pleasing anecdotes, pretty stories, personal experiences of the authoress, that abound in these volumes."—*Critic.*

"A voluminous and valuable work, forming the best filled picture of the lights and shades, the absurdities and the amenities of American life."—*Morning Advertiser.*

"Here we have sound, clear views, on the public and private life in America, mixed with expressions of comprehensive human kindness, and close family affection."—*Standard.*

"Such a delineation of America and the Americans as was never before written."—*Bell's Messenger.*

"One charming characteristic is the honesty of purpose and largeness of heart in which all the letters—for that is the form of the work—have been composed. Many things were not at all in accordance with her own views; but there is no caricature, no intolerance, but an earnest and usually very successful endeavour to understand what it really was, and to appreciate the good that it contained."—*Atlas.*

"In this delightful series of letters, full of intelligence and kindly sympathy, a really new world of gentleness and refinement is opened out to us."—*Britannia.*

"Suffice it to say, that while she missed none of the celebrities of civilised life in the new world, she contrived to make personal acquaintance also with life in the bush, and that she was not so much engrossed by the intellectual brilliancy of the North, as to lose sight of the sufferings to which degraded humanity is subjected in the South."—*John Bull.*

"The leading characteristic of this book of letters from America is personal. There are elaborate descriptions of scenery, but the scenery itself is subordinate to the personal impression it makes upon the writer. There are many sketches of individuals and domestic life—'the *homes* of the New World' predominate in the volumes. The successive sketches of home life open up some remarkable views and thoughts as respects women in America; favourable in a few, rather depreciatory in the mass, and singular in the rising independence of the sex—that is, as regards professional pursuits or public display on the platform or in semi-public meetings. The parts relating to the South and its slavery are among the most interesting of the book."—*Spectator.*

"This work, which is comprised in a series of letters written to her relatives in Sweden during the period of her sojourn in America, evinces considerable power of humour, description, and observation, and worthily sustains the reputation of Miss Bremer as a chaste and simple writer, remarkable for clearness of expression and fulness of illustration. It is impossible to read it without being delighted with its force, originality, and variety. The author, no doubt, is very discursive, but the enchantment of her moral enthusiasm carries us insensibly through all the mazes of her digressions. Her criticisms are distinguished by mildness, justice, and refined observation; her portraits by liveliness of colouring, and fidelity of representation."—*Morning Post.*

"Her statements and opinions on the subject of slavery will be read with intense interest on both sides of the Atlantic. The slaveholders must acknowledge that evidence on this question has never been given in a kinder and more impartial spirit."—*The Friend.*

"Europe, but especially America, owes her a debt of gratitude. The slave has found in her a fearless, a pathetic, and a potent pleader, and her zeal is uniformly tempered with discretion. Public men have found, in Miss Bremer, an enlightened and a candid critic on their doings, and the country a warm but wise and discriminating eulogist. She prognosticates for the States a glorious future. Her general reviews, prepared expressly for her Pastor and for the Queen Dowager of Sweden, are the most complete, accurate, and comprehensive bird's-eye digest of American affairs that has yet appeared in the English tongue."—*British Banner.*

ARTHUR HALL, VIRTUE, & CO., 25, PATERNOSTER ROW.

Illustrated Works by W. H. Bartlett.

This day is published, price 12s. cloth, or 21s. morocco,

THE PILGRIM FATHERS;
OR, THE FOUNDERS OF NEW ENGLAND IN THE REIGN OF JAMES I.
BY W. H. BARTLETT.
With Twenty-eight Engravings on Steel and numerous Woodcuts.

In super-royal 8vo., price 16s. cloth gilt,

PICTURES FROM SICILY.
Illustrated with Thirty-three Engravings on Steel and several Woodcuts.

"As a work of reference it is of the highest utility; as an ornamental book it is unsurpassed; and as a guide to the traveller it has no equal in the English language."—*Observer.*

"This is a very handsome and pleasing pictorial handbook of the beauties of Sicily. The illustrations do honour alike to the artist, engraver, and publishers —and the style is, generally speaking, graphic and faithful * * * with an interest beyond its pictorial claims."—*Athenæum.*

THIRD EDITION, in super-royal 8vo., 12s. cloth gilt, or 21s. morocco gilt,

WALKS ABOUT JERUSALEM AND ITS ENVIRONS.
BY W. H. BARTLETT.
Illustrated by Twenty-four Engravings on Steel, Two Maps, and many Superior Woodcuts.

"We have, at length, in this attractive volume, the *desideratum* of a complete picturesque guide to the topography of Jerusalem."—*Patriot.*

"The volume is well got up in point of embellishments, and contains much valuable matter, with illustrations beautifully executed."—*Ch. of England Mag.*

"Our impression is, that Jerusalem was never before so successfully delineated."—*Evangelical Mag.*

FOURTH EDITION, in super-royal 8vo., price 12s. cloth gilt, or 21s. morocco gilt,

FORTY DAYS IN THE DESERT,
ON THE TRACK OF THE ISRAELITES; or, a Journey from Cairo by Wady Feiran to Mount Sinai and Petra. By W. H. BARTLETT. Illustrated with Twenty-seven Engravings on Steel, a Map, and numerous Woodcuts.

"Mr. Bartlett has made a book, pleasant in letterpress, as well as attractive in its illustrations—delicately-finished line engravings of subjects particularly well chosen."—*Athenæum.*

"The author presents, in this volume, one of the most picturesque accounts of the route across the wilderness of sand we have ever read."—*Morning Herald.*

SECOND EDITION, in super-royal 8vo., 16s. cloth gilt, or 28s. morocco elegant,

GLEANINGS ON THE OVERLAND ROUTE.
By the Author of "Walks about Jerusalem," "Forty Days in the Desert," &c. Illustrated by Twenty-eight Steel Plates and Maps, and Twenty-three Woodcuts.

"The reader will find abundance of interesting and amusing information in the volume. As a work of art, it possesses very considerable merit."—*Chambers's Journal.*

"The present work is as excellent as his former productions, for its lively and picturesque narrative, and for the exquisite engravings by which it is illustrated."—*Athenæum.*

THIRD EDITION, in super-royal 8vo., price 16s. cloth gilt, 28s. morocco gilt,

THE NILE BOAT;
Or, GLIMPSES OF THE LAND OF EGYPT. Illustrated by Thirty-five Steel Engravings and Maps, with numerous Woodcuts. By W. H. BARTLETT, Author of "Walks about Jerusalem," &c.

THIRD EDITION, in super-royal 8vo., price 14s. cloth, gilt edges, or 26s. morocco elegant,

FOOTSTEPS OF OUR LORD AND HIS APOSTLES,
IN SYRIA, GREECE, AND ITALY. A Succession of Visits to the Scenes of New Testament Narrative. With Twenty-three Steel Engravings, and several Woodcuts.

ARTHUR HALL, VIRTUE, & CO., 25, PATERNOSTER ROW.

Works in Preparation.

I.
ROME.—REGAL AND REPUBLICAN.
A History for Families. By JANE M. STRICKLAND. Edited by AGNES STRICKLAND, Authoress of "Lives of the Queens of England." [*Shortly.*

II.
JULIAN; or, THE CLOSE OF THE CENTURY.
By L. F. BUNGENER. Author of "History of the Council of Trent."

III.
NEW WORK BY THE REV. DR. CUMMING.
THE COMFORTER.
Uniform with "The Finger of God." By the Rev. JOHN CUMMING, D.D.

IV.
MODERN ROMANISM.
A View of the Proceedings, &c., of the Council of Trent. By B. B. WOODWARD, Esq., B.A.

V.
EVENINGS IN MY TENT.
By the Rev. N. DAVIS. In 8vo., with Illustrations.

VI.
RAILWAY READING.
DRESS AS A FINE ART.
By Mrs. MERRIFIELD. Reprinted from the "Art-Journal," with Additions and numerous Illustrations.

VII.
RAILWAY READING.
JACK AND THE TANNER.
By the Author of "Mary Powell."

VIII.
AN ABRIDGMENT OF
OLD AND NEW TESTAMENT HISTORY AND GEOGRAPHY.
By J. T. WHEELER, F.R.G.S. For the Use of Schools. 18mo.

IX.
TALES OF MANY LANDS.
By Miss M. F. TYTLER. With Cuts. New Edition.

X.
MOWBRAY'S TREATISE ON
DOMESTIC AND ORNAMENTAL POULTRY.
Plates. New Edition, enlarged.

XI.
THOUGHTS AND SKETCHES IN VERSE.
By CAROLINE DENT.

XII.
A CATECHISM OF FAMILIAR THINGS.
By EMILY E. WILLEMENT. New and Improved Edition. 12mo.

XIII.
PEACE IN BELIEVING.
A Memoir of ISABELLA CAMPBELL. New Edition.

XIV.
ENGLISH STORIES OF THE OLDEN TIME.
By MARIA HACK. New Edition.

ARTHUR HALL, VIRTUE, & CO., 25, PATERNOSTER ROW.

Works by the Author of "MARY POWELL."

"Whenever we open a volume by the author of 'Mary Powell,' we know at once that we have a work in our hands that is sure to be distinguished by its purity. There may be more or less of amusement—more or less of interest, of pleasantness, or instruction, and these are never wanting; but one thing is sure to abound—namely, an unaffected and a healthy purity."—CHURCH AND STATE GAZ.

I.

Published this day, price 7s. 6d., post 8vo.,
CHERRY AND VIOLET: A TALE OF THE GREAT PLAGUE.
In Antique.

II.

Recently published, price 7s. 6d., post 8vo., cloth,
THE PROVOCATIONS OF MADAME PALISSY.
WITH COLOURED FRONTISPIECE BY WARREN.

"One of the most graceful of stories gracefully told, something to touch the heart, to call up a quiet smile, and to summon a tear even into manly eyes. We do not remember ever having met with a book at once so natural, so clever, and so emphatically 'delicious.'"—*Church and State Gazette.*

"It is a long time since we have met with a book of such truly excellent characteristics as are apparent in every page of this volume."—*Bell's Messenger.*

"On the basis of the true history of Palissy, the writer has framed the present work; has given a very spirited sketch of his labours; has exhibited the extravagances, amounting to crimes, of a man of genius driving on in the pursuit of his darling object; and has depicted—as the title promises—with a good deal of power, the plagues of a wife who has such a husband."—*Christian Observer.*

III.

Recently published, with FRONTISPIECE, &c., price 7s. 6d., cloth antique,
THE COLLOQUIES OF EDWARD OSBORNE,
CITIZEN AND CLOTH-WORKER OF LONDON.

"This is a pleasant little volume, relating the fortunes of a London apprentice in the sixteenth century."—*Athenæum.*

"The domestic history of the household of a citizen of London, nearly 400 years ago, is most delightfully told, and there is a reality about the book which renders every page of it interesting."—*Atlas.*

IV.

Second Edition, with PORTRAIT, &c., price 7s. 6d., cloth antique,
YE HOUSEHOLD OF SIR THOS. MORE.
LIBELLUS A MARGARETA MORE,
QUINDECIM ANNOS NATA, CHELSEIÆ INCEPTUS.

"It ends with musical melancholy, a strain of exquisitely simple beauty, referring to the judicial slaying of one of England's worthiest sons. There are some fine portraits ably limned herein. There are family pictures so graphically described that they possess the mind for ever."—*Church and State Gazette.*

V.

Handsomely bound and gilt, with ILLUMINATIONS,
QUEENE PHILIPPA'S GOLDEN BOOKE.

VI.

YE MAIDEN AND MARRIED LIFE OF MARY POWELL,
AFTERWARDS MISTRESS MILTON.

"This is a charming little book; and whether we regard its subject, cleverness, or delicacy of sentiment and expression—to say nothing of its type and orthography—it is likely to be a most acceptable present to young or old, be their peculiar taste for religion, morals, poetry, history, or romance."—*Christian Observer.*

VII.

In preparation,
YE CHRONICLE OF MERRIE ENGLAND, REHEARSED UNTO HER PEOPLE.

VIII.

CLAUDE THE COLPORTEUR.
With Coloured Frontispiece after WARREN, uniform with "Madame Palissy."

ARTHUR HALL, VIRTUE, & CO., 25, PATERNOSTER ROW.

DR. CUMMING'S NEW VOLUME OF LECTURES.

In preparation, uniform with "APOCALYPTIC SKETCHES."

THE TENT AND ALTAR;
OR, SKETCHES OF PATRIARCHAL TIMES.

New Edition, in fcap. price 9s. full cloth, gilt,
THE CHURCH BEFORE THE FLOOD.

New Edition, revised and enlarged, in two volumes, price 9s. each, bound in cloth, full gilt,
FORESHADOWS;
Or, Lectures on Our Lord's Miracles and Parables as Earnests of the Age to come. With Designs by JOHN FRANKLIN.

Ninth Edition, fcap. 8vo. cloth, 3s.
"IS CHRISTIANITY FROM GOD?"
A Manual of Christian Evidences for Scripture Readers, Sunday School Teachers, City Missionaries, and Young Persons.

Ninth Thousand, in fcap. 8vo. 9s. cloth, elegantly gilt, or 13s. morocco extra,
PROPHETIC STUDIES;
Or, Lectures on the Prophet Daniel.

Sixteenth Thousand, in 3 vols. 9s. each, cloth gilt,
APOCALYPTIC SKETCHES;
Or, Lectures on the Book of Revelation, and on the Seven Churches. Delivered in Exeter Hall, and at Crown Court Church. New Editions, revised and corrected, with Indexes.

Fifth Edition, fcap. 8vo., 3s. cloth, with gilt edges,
OUR FATHER;
A Manual of Family Prayers for General and Special Occasions. With short Prayers for spare Minutes, and Passages for Reflection.

DR. CUMMING ON THE NEW TESTAMENT.

Now complete, in cloth, price 5s., with FRONTISPIECE,

SABBATH EVENING READINGS ON ST. MATTHEW.

IN THE SAME SERIES,

ST. MARK.
Shortly, complete in cloth, price 3s. 6d.

ST. LUKE.
To be published in Numbers, commencing January 1.

THE BOOK OF REVELATION.
Complete. SECOND EDITION, 7s. 6d.

Just published, price 2s. 6d. neatly bound, THIRD EDITION,

THE FINGER OF GOD,
BY THE REV. JOHN CUMMING, D.D.

"It deals with subjects on which true Christians now have not two opinions, and on which the most opposite of the most ultra of partizans ought not to disagree.... It therefore addresses itself to a wide class, and it is evidently intended for all professing Christians, irrespective of denomination."—*Church and State Gazette.*

"A work which well proves that the author can be eloquent upon other topics besides those of the Romish Controversy and Apocalyptic Interpretation. Indeed, for our own part, we like him better on a subject like the present. There are some truly eloquent and graceful passages in the little volume before us, which must commend themselves to every reader."—*Critic.*

"A work not of great magnitude, but of great interest. This work will amply repay perusal. Notwithstanding occasional evidences of rapid composition, it contains many instances of great beauty of thought."—*Church of Scotland Review.*

"A little volume which abounds in beauties both of thought, style, and illustration."—*The Church Journal.*

"Eloquent, demonstrative, and useful."—*Wesleyan Methodist Magazine.*

Published this day, price 2s. 6d., uniform with the above,

CHRIST OUR PASSOVER;
OR, THOUGHTS ON THE ATONEMENT.

Tenth Thousand, post 8vo. cloth, price 6s., a Cheap Edition of

THE CELEBRATED PROTESTANT DISCUSSION,
BETWEEN THE REV. JOHN CUMMING, D.D., AND DANIEL FRENCH, ESQ., BARRISTER-AT-LAW. HELD AT HAMMERSMITH IN 1839.

"No clergyman's library can be complete without it."—*Bell's Messenger.*
"A compendium of argument."—*Gentleman's Magazine.*
"The subject (*pro* and *con*) is all but exhausted."—*Church and State Gazette.*

ARTHUR HALL, VIRTUE, & CO., 25, PATERNOSTER ROW.

Recent Publications.

THIRD EDITION, in foolscap 8vo., price 7s. 6d. bound in cloth, with VIGNETTE and FRONTISPIECE, uniform with "Proverbial Philosophy,"

BALLADS FOR THE TIMES.

NOW FIRST COLLECTED.

Geraldine, American Lyrics, Hactenus, A Modern Pyramid, A Thousand Lines, and other Poems.

By MARTIN F. TUPPER, D.C.L., F.R.S.

"With smoothness of measure, Mr. Tupper's design is always excellent, and his versification is brought to bear upon things of no transient interest. It is one of the best characteristics of his labours, that he does not write for praise, but for the benefit of his fellow-men—not merely for time, but for eternity."—*Bell's Messenger.*

THE OLD FOREST RANGER:

Or, Wild Sports in India, on the Neigherry Hills, in the Jungles, and on the Plains. By Major WALTER CAMPBELL, of Skipness. New Edition, with Illustrations on Steel. Price 8s. in post 8vo., cloth gilt.

"Truly, the popularity which it has gained is well deserved. The great variety of field-sports which it describes, with all the exciting accompaniment of terrible dangers and hairbreadth escapes, and the lively humorous tone in which they are narrated, are enough to stir the blood of the most phlegmatic reader; and we can easily believe with what rapturous delight sportsmen of all kinds, but especially old Indians whose memories are refreshed by the tale, are likely to follow the 'Old Forest Ranger' on his venturesome expeditions."—*John Bull.*

"Full of wild adventures and most amusing incidents, of which thousands who 'have no stomach for the fight' like to hear."—*Art Journal.*

"In a word, 'The Old Forest Ranger' may now be reckoned among our modern standard works."—*The Advertiser.*

RAILWAY READING.

LEGENDS OF OLD LONDON.

By J. Y. AKERMAN, ESQ., F.S.A. Price 2s. 6d., post 8vo.

"There is a smack of the good old city about his descriptions, which should recommend them to all such novel readers as have a spice of antiquarianism in their nature; while 'The Foster Son,' 'The Alderman,' both contain passages of powerful writing, which, twenty years ago, might have made a stir."—*Athenæum*, 1842.

"An extremely amusing volume for railway reading. * * * They show familiar acquaintance with the habits and manners of our ancestors."—*Critic.*

"A little volume of antiquarian tales, cleverly told; and in general sufficiently truthful as a picture of the society they represent."—*London Weekly Paper.*

Also, uniform, price 1s. 6d. each,

THE CROCK OF GOLD. By MARTIN F. TUPPER, ESQ.
THE TWINS. By MARTIN F. TUPPER, ESQ.
HEART. By MARTIN F. TUPPER, ESQ.

Or, complete in cloth, price 5s., neatly bound,

THE DOUBLE CLAIM. By Mrs. T. K. HERVEY.
TOIL AND TRIAL. By Mrs. CROSLAND.
HUMBOLDT'S LETTERS TO A LADY. By Dr. STEBBING.

THE FARMER'S ASSISTANT AND AGRICULTURIST'S CALCULATOR.

By JOHN GRIEVE. New and enlarged Edition. In Fcap. cloth, price 4s.

"This is a very valuable work, by a thoroughly practical man. It should be in the hands of every farmer, land-steward, farm-steward, drainer, and land-surveyor. We have learned more from it on the theory and practice of drainage, as well as the advantages of it, than from any work we have ever read. We trust the author will be no stranger to the public, and that the public will acknowledge him as one of its benefactors."—*Edinburgh Witness.*

THE EARTH AND ITS INHABITANTS.

By MARGARET E. DARTON. With Coloured Frontispiece. In crown 8vo., price 5s. cloth lettered.

"The design of this little volume, which is executed with considerable ability and success, is to render the study of geography less dry, by presenting the facts to the mind of the pupil in an attractive and entertaining form."—*John Bull.*

"One of the handsomest elementary works that ever came into our hands. * * * It is also true to its purpose; successful in realizing it, and as good as it is novel in character."—*Nonconformist.*

ARTHUR HALL, VIRTUE, & CO., 25, PATERNOSTER ROW.

RODWELL'S CHILD'S FIRST STEP TO ENGLISH HISTORY.

New Edition, Revised and Continued by JULIA CORNER, with numerous Illustrations. Fifth Edition, 16mo., cloth, price 2s. 6d.

"This little work is admirably fitted to convey to the minds of children the most important historical facts in the annals of their own country, being couched in plain and simple language, with the ideas lucidly expressed. Any difficult word or technical expression that occurs is cleared up in a little conversation which is appended to each chapter."—*Educational Times.*

BASES OF BELIEF;

An Examination of Christianity, as a Divine Revelation, by the Light of Recognised Facts and Principles. In Four Parts. By EDWARD MIALL, M.P. New Edition, 8vo., price 10s. 6d.

"We have read this work with interest and satisfaction. In clearness of statement, conclusiveness of argument, and power of expression, it has no superior among publications of its class, and very few equals. * * The book is alike admirable for thought and for language. As a piece of argumentative writing, it does credit not only to the name it bears, but to the august assembly in which he has been called to speak and act."—*British Banner.*

"We predict a wide circulation for this volume; and we trust that the labour bestowed upon it may be requited by an incalculable amount of benefit, not only to his own generation, but to succeeding ages."—*New Quarterly Review.*

MEMORIALS OF EARLY CHRISTIANITY.

By J. G. MIALL. With numerous Illustrations. Fcap. cloth, price 5s.

SAINT PAUL.

Five Discourses by the Rev. A. MONOD, of Paris. Translated by the Rev. W. G. BARRETT. 18mo., cloth, price 2s.

"Written in an earnest and practical style."—*Britannia.*

"The whole conception of St. Paul's character is exceedingly faithful; and the manner in which these discourses are written, and, we may add, translated, makes them both interesting and instructive."—*Patriot.*

"The volume may be taken as a superior specimen of French preaching,—brilliant and pathetic."—*British Banner.*

HIPPOLYTUS, AND THE CHRISTIAN CHURCH,

At the commencement of the Third Century: with a copious Analysis of the newly-discovered MS., and a translation of all its most important parts, from the original Greek. By W. ELFE TAYLER, author of "Popery: its Character and Crimes." Fcap. cloth, 3s. 6d.

"Well and truly executed, and the importance of the volume can hardly be estimated too highly."—*Church and State Gazette.*

"Mr. Tayler here puts forth his strength, and brings it to bear on some of the follies of the present day. It need hardly be said, that a work constituted on this plan cannot fail to be of special value."—*Christian Witness.*

THE CELT, THE ROMAN, AND THE SAXON:

A History of the Early Inhabitants of Britain, down to the Conversion of the Anglo-Saxons to Christianity. Illustrated by the Ancient Remains brought to light by recent research. By THOMAS WRIGHT, Esq., M.A., F.S.A. With numerous Engravings. Price 8s. in post 8vo.

ROSALIE;

Or, THE TRUTH SHALL MAKE YOU FREE. An Authentic Narrative. By Mademoiselle R. B. de P——. With Introduction by the Rev. JOSEPH RIDGEWAY. Price 3s. 6d., neatly bound.

NINEVEH AND PERSEPOLIS:

An HISTORICAL SKETCH of ANCIENT ASSYRIA and PERSIA, with an Account of the recent Researches in those countries. By W. S. W. VAUX, M.A., of the British Museum. Third Edition, post 8vo., with numerous Illustrations, price 8s. bound in cloth, or 17s. morocco antique.

A MANUAL OF THE ANATOMY AND PHYSIOLOGY OF THE HUMAN MIND.

By the Rev. J. CARLILE, D.D., of Dublin and Parsonstown. Fcap., price 5s., cloth.

ARTHUR HALL, VIRTUE, & CO., 25, PATERNOSTER ROW.

SCRIPTURE CLASS BOOKS.
ANALYSIS AND SUMMARY OF THE OLD AND NEW TESTAMENT HISTORY AND GEOGRAPHY,

And of the LAWS OF MOSES, with a Connexion between the Old and New Testaments, a Harmony of the Gospels, a continuous History of St. Paul, and Introductory Outlines of their Geography, Critical and Political History, Authenticity, and Inspiration, with Copious Notes, Chronological Tables, &c. By J. T. WHEELER, F.R.G.S. Author of " Analysis of Herodotus and Thucydides." New Editions, in 2 vols. post 8vo. cloth, price 5s. 6d. each.

A NEW SCRIPTURE ATLAS,

To illustrate the above; comprising Five Coloured Maps, a large View of Jerusalem, and Plan of the Ancient City, with an Analysis and Summary of the Historical Geography of the Bible, and a copious Index. Price 7s. 6d. small folio, neatly bound.

THE AUTOBIOGRAPHY OF WILLIAM JERDAN;

With his Literary, Political, and Social Reminiscences and Correspondence, during the last Forty Years, as Editor of the "Sun" Newspaper, 1812-17, and of the "Literary Gazette," 1817-50, in connexion with most of the Eminent Persons who have been distinguished in the past half century as Statesmen, Poets, Authors, Men of Science, Artists, &c. Now complete in four volumes, post 8vo., cloth, with Portraits and Vignettes, price 21s.

" Such a book, written by a man whose hand has been familiar with the use of the pen for more than half a century, and when the greater portion of that period is spent in intercourse with the intellectual celebrities of the times, becomes of undoubted value, and possesses necessarily those intrinsic qualities which remind us of the enchanting pages of Boswell. It is a most charming volume, and independent of its personal value, and its reminiscences of dead and living friends, it is the history of a literary man's struggles through the world, and in which a deep, and at times a profoundly painful, interest will be felt. —*The Weekly Dispatch*.

" This first instalment of what we are to expect from the veteran *litterateur* in the performance of his life-shrift has much of the interest which attaches to the Confessions of Rousseau, and in the easy flow of its captivating narrative is not unlike that favourite masterpiece. The vivid interchange of occurrences in remote early life, with their influence on subsequent fortune and mental development, has here a peculiar charm; and in none of his previous writings has the pen of Mr. Jerdan put forth such powers of unconscious fascination. The curtain falls with graceful effect, and the impression on the reader is that of kindly sympathy with his interesting narrator, wonder at the stories of personal anecdote displayed, as well as the untiring energy of the young adventurer on the threshold of life, and pleasant anticipations of the volumes that are to follow."—*Globe*.

Eighteenth Edition, pp. 800, 8vo., cloth, price 21s.,
LAURIE'S INTEREST TABLES.

TABLES OF SIMPLE INTEREST FOR EVERY DAY IN THE YEAR, at Six different Rates, from £1 to £100, &c. By JAMES LAURIE.

Also,

A VOLUME AT HIGHER RATES. Tables of Simple Interest at 5, 6, 7, 8, 9½, per cent. per annum. Third Edition, uniform with the above, price 7s.

" In the great requisites of simplicity of arrangement and comprehensiveness, we have seen none better adapted for general use."—*M'Culloch's Commercial Dictionary*, Edit. 1832, p. 674.

NEW GIFT BOOK FOR ALL SEASONS.

New and cheaper Edition, complete in One Volume, handsomely bound and gilt, price One Guinea,

PILGRIMAGES TO ENGLISH SHRINES.
BY MRS. S. C. HALL.
With Notes and Illustrations by F. W. Fairholt, F.S.A.

"Descriptions of such Shrines come home with deep interest to all hearts—all English hearts—particularly when they are done with the earnestness which distinguishes Mrs. Hall's writings. That lady's earnestness and enthusiasm are of the right sort—felt for freedom of thought and action, for taste, and for genius winging its flight in a noble direction. They are displayed, oftentimes most naturally, throughout the attractive pages of this volume."—*Observer*.

" Mrs. Hall's talents are too well known to require our commendation of her 'Pilgrimages,' which are every way worthy of the beautiful woodcuts that illustrate almost every page; and this is very high praise indeed."—*Standard*.

" The illustrations are very effective; and the whole work, externally and internally, is worthy of the patronage of all who love to be instructed as well as amused."—*Church and State Gazette*.

" The book is a pleasant one; a collection of a great deal of curious information about a number of curious places and persons, cleverly and readily put together, and combined into an elegant volume."—*Guardian*.

*** The separate Volumes of the former Edition may still be had to complete sets.

ARTHUR HALL, VIRTUE, & CO., 25, PATERNOSTER ROW.

WEDDING, BIRTHDAY, OR NEW YEAR'S PRESENT.

With numerous Engravings, price £1 6s. cloth gilt,

A GUIDE TO FAMILY DEVOTION.

BY THE REV. ALEXANDER FLETCHER, D.D.

Containing 730 Services, each including a Hymn, a Prayer, a Portion of Scripture, and appropriate Reflections,

BEING ONE FOR THE MORNING AND EVENING OF EVERY DAY IN THE YEAR.

Selections from Testimonials of Christian Ministers in favour of the REV. A. FLETCHER'S " GUIDE TO FAMILY DEVOTION."

I have great pleasure in bearing testimony to the worth of "Fletcher's Family Devotion." It is admirably adapted to accomplish the sacred purpose for which it is intended. The genial warmth of true spirituality pervades it throughout; and it may safely be recommended, both for the judgment and piety by which it is characterized, to earnest-minded Christians of every denomination. Great as its circulation already is, I should be glad to find it increased, and increasing. Yours very faithfully,

Parsonage, St. James's, Hampstead-road.

Extract from a letter by the Rev. J. HARRIS, *D.D., Author of "Mammon."*

The conception and arrangement of the work are admirable; and, as far as I have had an opportunity of judging, the execution of it equals the plan. I have read various parts of it attentively; and while I have not met with anything which I could wish to have been omitted, most unfeignedly can I say that I have found much calculated to inspire and sustain devotion.

Epsom.

A superficial survey of it ["A Guide to Family Devotion"] is sufficient to manifest that its plan is the most complete of any with which I am acquainted, embracing everything which the service of the family altar requires, or admits of; while its execution is also such as to entitle it to commendation, and secure for it the circulation and use which it deserves.

Birmingham.

I consider it a vast advantage to persons who begin housekeeping, if unaccustomed to extemporaneous prayer, to have such a help to devotion as your work affords. Many, especially females, have felt considerable difficulty in conducting family worship, for want of a selection of Scriptures adapted to family reading: this difficulty your work meets, and cannot but be appreciated by a large class of the Christian community. The work appears to me to be executed devotionally, which, in my opinion, is a strong recommendation to its excellency. With many sincere wishes for its success,

Surrey Chapel House.

On examination, I am much pleased with it ["A Guide to Family Devotion"], and feel, when I am called to leave my family, that I leave for its use a good substitute behind me.

Weigh House.

The evangelical strain of the prayers gives them an advantage over most other forms which have been published for families: I mean not only the savour of evangelical feeling and motive with which they are imbued, but the frequent addresses which are intermingled to each Divine Person of the Triune Jehovah. I trust that your labours will lead many families to a practical use and enjoyment of the glorious privileges of the Gospel.

Late Vicar of St. Stephen's, Coleman-street.

Letters have also been received from the following Clergymen:—Rev. W. B. COLLYER, D.D., Peckham; Rev. J. MORRISON, D.D., Chelsea; Rev. JAMES PARSONS, York; Rev. SAMUEL RANSOM, Hackney; Rev. A. THOMSON, Coldstream; &c. &c. In addition to which, upwards of One Hundred of the most influential Clergymen of America have testified, by letter, their high commendation of the excellence and great utility of the above-named Work.

Extract from a Notice of the Thirtieth Edition (see "The Times," Sept. 27).

"Our attention has lately been called to an advertisement of a book of "Family Devotion, containing the Morning and Evening Service of a Family for every Day throughout the Year." According to the Advertisement, this new Order of Morning and Evening Prayer daily throughout the year is already in the thirtieth edition of 1000 each. 30,000 copies of a book of Common Prayer for Dissenters, recommended by twenty-five ministers, whose names are given, and who include some of the most prominent of the day, cannot be dispersed throughout England without working some considerable change in the minds of probably 200,000 persons."

ARTHUR HALL, VIRTUE, & CO., 25, PATERNOSTER ROW.

Neatly printed in Foolscap 8vo., cloth lettered, price 2s. 6d. each vol.,

A SELECT LIBRARY OF THEOLOGICAL WORKS;

WITH A CHOICE SELECTION OF

Sacred Poetry and Sermon Literature of the Seventeenth Century.

EDITED BY THE REV. R. CATTERMOLE, B.D., AND THE REV. H. STEBBING, D.D.

TO WHICH ARE PREFIXED

ORIGINAL ESSAYS, MEMOIRS, NOTES, &c.

By Dr. PYE SMITH, ROBERT SOUTHEY, Esq., JAMES MONTGOMERY, Esq., Dr. CROLY, the Rev. W. TROLLOPE, and others.

The Series comprises the following important Works:—

Jeremy Taylor's Liberty of Prophesying; showing the Unreasonableness of prescribing to other Men's Faith; and the Iniquity of persecuting differing Opinions.

Cave's Lives of the Apostles and the Fathers, 2 vols.

Bates's Spiritual Perfection Unfolded and Enforced; with an Introductory Essay, by the Rev. JOHN PYE SMITH, D.D.

Bishop Hall's Treatises, Devotional and Practical.

Baxter's Dying Thoughts.

Jeremy Taylor's Select Sermons.

Butler's Analogy of Religion, Natural and Revealed, to the Constitution and Course of Nature: to which are added Two Brief Dissertations. With a Memoir of the Author, by the Rev. GEORGE CROLY, LL.D.

Dr. Watt's Lyric Poems. With a Biographical Essay, by ROBERT SOUTHEY, Esq., LL.D.

Beveridge's Private Thoughts. To which is added, the Necessity of Frequent Communion, 2 vols.

Cave's Primitive Christianity. With an Historical Account of Paganism under the First Christian Emperors; and the Lives of Justin Martyr and St. Cyprian. 2 vols.

Archbishop Leighton's Expositions of the Creed, the Lord's Prayer, and the Ten Commandments, &c., &c.

Sermons, selected from the Works of the most Eminent Divines of the Sixteenth and Seventeenth Centuries. 3 vols.

The Hon. Robert Boyle on the Veneration due to God—on Things above Reason —and on the Style of the Holy Scriptures. With an Essay, by H. ROGERS, Esq.

Vicesimus Knox's Christian Philosophy.

Howe's Select Treatises. With a Memoir, by THOMAS TAYLOR, Author of "The Life of Cowper," "Memoirs of Bishop Heber," &c.

Sacred Poetry of the Seventeenth Century, 2 vols., including the whole of Giles Fletcher's "Christ's Victory and Triumph," with copious selections from Spenser, Davies, Sandys, P. Fletcher, Wither, Bishop King, Quarles, Herbert, and Milton.

Jeremy Taylor's Life of Christ. With an Introductory Essay to each Part, by the Rev. H. STEBBING, D.D., 3 vols.

Locke on the Reasonableness of Christianity. With an Appendix, containing an Analysis of the First and Second Vindications, &c.

Bishop Butler's Fifteen Sermons, preached at the Rolls Chapel; and Charge to the Clergy of Durham in 1751. With an Appendix by BISHOP HALIFAX.

Bishop Horne's Commentary on the Psalms, with Life of the Author, by the Rev. W. JONES, of Nayland; and an Introductory Essay, by JAMES MONTGOMERY, Esq., 3 vols.

Jeremy Taylor's Holy Living and Holy Dying, with a Sketch of his Life and Times, by the Rev. GEORGE CROLY, LL.D., 2 vols.

ARTHUR HALL, VIRTUE, & CO., 25, PATERNOSTER ROW.

NEW WORK OF THE REV. JOHN CUMMING, D.D.

In one volume quarto, price £1 1s., cloth gilt, gilt edges,
DAILY FAMILY DEVOTION;
OR, GUIDE TO FAMILY WORSHIP.
BY THE REV. JOHN CUMMING, D.D.,
Minister of the Scottish National Church, Crown Court, Russell Street, Covent Garden.

This work, consisting of a Hymn, a portion of Scripture, and an appropriate Prayer, for the Morning and Evening of every Day in the Year, is designed to introduce or facilitate the practice of Family Worship; and, by constructing the daily prayers on the passage of Scripture selected for reading, greater variety, interest, and practical use are associated with the exercise.

A Second Edition, with Twenty-four Engravings. Price £1 5s.

Complete in one vol., super-royal, price 18s., cloth lettered,
BUNYAN'S PILGRIM'S PROGRESS.
PICTORIAL EDITION.

A splendidly-illustrated Edition, in super-royal 8vo., comprising upwards of Eighty Engravings on Wood, by the Messrs. WHIMPER, from designs by Artists of celebrity. Also, Nine elegant Engravings on Steel, a Portrait, and Fac-simile of JOHN BUNYAN'S Will.

Uniform with the above, in one vol., 12s. cloth,
THE HOLY WAR.
PICTORIAL EDITION.

A most beautiful work, and forming an appropriate companion to the "Pictorial Pilgrim's Progress." With numerous splendid Illustrations, designed expressly for this work.

In one vol., super-royal 8vo., cloth, £1 5s.,
THE WORKS OF JOSEPHUS.
PICTORIAL EDITION.

With an Introductory Essay, by the Rev. HENRY STEBBING, D.D., author of the "History of the Christian Church," &c., &c. Illustrated by Eighty fine Woodcuts, from designs by MELVILLE. Also, Eleven Engravings on Steel, and a Portrait of the Author.

In one vol., super-royal 8vo., cloth, 18s.,
THE WORKS OF THE REV. JOHN NEWTON,
Late Rector of the united Parishes of St. Mary Woolnoth and St. Mary Woolchurch-Haw, London. With a Portrait.
Also, a LIFE OF THE AUTHOR, by the Rev. RICHARD CECIL; and an INTRODUCTION, by the Rev. FRANCIS CUNNINGHAM, Vicar of Lowestoft.

In four vols., imperial 8vo., cloth, £3 3s.,
THE PRACTICAL WORKS OF RICHARD BAXTER.
THE ONLY COMPLETE EDITION.

Reprinted, without abridgment, from the Original collected Edition. With an Introductory Essay on the Genius and Writings of BAXTER, by ROBERT PHILIP, and a Fine Portrait of BAXTER.

Beautifully printed in super-royal 8vo., in three large volumes cloth gilt, each containing upwards of eleven hundred pages, £3 3s.,
FOXE'S ACTS AND MONUMENTS OF THE CHURCH.
PICTORIAL EDITION.

With an Introductory Essay; and the whole carefully Revised and Edited by the Rev. JOHN CUMMING, D.D. Illustrated with numerous Wood Engravings, by Eminent Artists, together with a Series of highly-finished Portraits of the leading Characters connected with the Reformation, and other illustrative Plates.

ARTHUR HALL, VIRTUE & CO., 25, PATERNOSTER ROW.

On the 1st of January, 1854, will be published Part I., price 1s.,

A DICTIONARY OF TERMS IN ART.

EDITED AND ILLUSTRATED BY
F. W. FAIRHOLT, F.S.A.,

Author of "Costume in England," &c., Hon. Memb. of the Soc. of Antiquaries of Normandy, Poitiers, and Picardy; and Corresponding Memb. of the Soc. of Antiquaries of Scotland.

ILLUSTRATED BY THREE HUNDRED ENGRAVINGS ON WOOD.

The plan embraced in the present Work includes all such terms as are generally employed in painting, sculpture, and engraving, whether descriptive of real objects or principles of action; it will thus include the Æsthetics of Art, as well as their practical results. But as it is desirable to make this an useful hand-book for all persons interested in Art, all such terms, ancient or modern, as may be used in describing the contents of a museum or picture-gallery will be explained. Thus, the technical terms for antique vases or mediæval pottery, sacred and domestic implements, as well as for costume, civil and military, armour, arms, &c., will be included; all which form the component parts of a picture, or may be included in its description; an analysis of colours and artistic implements; a brief notice of the saints and their symbols; such manufacturing processes as call Art to their aid, or such terms in architecture and the cognate arts as are necessarily used in Art. Thus, while this Dictionary exhibits a somewhat wide range of subject, the restrictive limit embodied in its title will prevent its resemblance to any other; giving it a completeness and utility as a general reference-book to all students or amateurs of the Fine Arts.

☞ The Work will be closely-printed in post octavo, and not exceed Twelve Parts, at One Shilling.

In Parts at One Shilling, Monthly, to be completed in two vols. super-royal 8vo.,

A CYCLOPÆDIA OF USEFUL ARTS,

MECHANICS, MANUFACTURES, MINING, AND CIVIL ENGINEERING.
EDITED BY CHARLES TOMLINSON.

WITH TWO THOUSAND ENGRAVINGS.

This Work includes detailed accounts of the principal Manufacturing Processes, Mechanical Inventions, and Chemical Operations in actual use, either in Great Britain, the continent of Europe, or the United States. The descriptive portions will be illustrated and explained by about two thousand Diagrams and Engravings made expressly for the Work, mostly copied from the actual working machinery, by the permission of the patentees and owners. In these volumes, the utmost care will be taken so to simplify and methodically arrange the various subjects treated upon, that every step of the most complicated manufacture may be clearly traced, from the first collection of the raw material to the completion of the finished product. In reference to the construction of Machinery, each distinctive stage of improvement will be pointed out and explained, and the various failures and misconceptions of scientific men exhibited, to serve as beacons for future inventors. In the Mining and Chemical departments, Historical and Geological Notices will be introduced whenever the importance of the subject may require them; while nothing will be omitted that can render the CYCLOPÆDIA OF ART a valuable Book of Reference, and an indispensable Companion to the Manufacturer, the Miner, the Chemist, the Engineer, and the Scientific Workman. This Work contains an Original Essay on

THE GREAT EXHIBITION OF 1851,

Illustrated by beautifully executed Steel Engravings of the Exterior and Interior of the Building, as well as numerous Woodcuts, and Descriptions of some of the most important Mechanical Inventions and Machines submitted to public inspection in that magnificent structure; thus rendering the Work a permanent record of the highest efforts and most valuable productions of the Mechanical and Scientific genius of every country in the civilised world.

The First Volume, price £1 1s., cloth gilt, is now ready.

CRITICAL NOTICES.

"We have had repeated occasions to speak favourably of this book. It still sustains its character, and is evidently an honest, as well as an able book."—*The Builder*

"The information is communicated in the clearest language, and, in every instance we have examined, is *brought down to the present time*; so that we have a just representation, not of the state of any art some years ago, but of its condition in the present year. * * * * Our limits do not enable us in the present number to give any further specimen here of this interesting work. It is a cheap work, and one of great value to the industrial classes, and, indeed, to every one who is desirous— and who is not?—of obtaining a just and comprehensive acquaintance with the industrial arts."—*The Artizan*.

ARTHUR HALL VIRTUE, & CO., 25, PATERNOSTER ROW.

In Parts, at 3s. each, containing Three Plates; or complete in four volumes, handsomely bound and gilt, price £2 2s. each,

THE VERNON GALLERY:
A COLLECTION OF FIRST-CLASS LINE ENGRAVINGS;
Being copies of the Paintings presented to the Nation by the late ROBERT VERNON, Esq.
WITH DESCRIPTIVE TEXT, BY S. C. HALL, ESQ.
Vols. I. to III. are now ready.

Under the Patronage of Her Most Gracious Majesty, His Royal Highness Prince Albert, K.G., &c.

PROOF IMPRESSIONS
OF THE ENGRAVINGS OF THE
PICTURES IN THE VERNON GALLERY.

Of these highly-finished and most popular Plates only a few sets now remain unsold: they have been largely patronised by the Nobility and Gentry of Great Britain, as well as by the connoisseurs of Fine Art throughout the continent of Europe. Their merits have secured for them a place in the Gallery of every collector of eminence; and there is no doubt but that their value will in a few years be greatly enhanced, by the impossibility of procuring additional copies.

These Plates are published in Parts. Parts 1 to 36 contain Two Engravings in each: the succeeding Parts comprise Three in each. A handsome Portfolio is given every twelve months, and explanatory letter-press accompanies each volume. They may be obtained in three sizes; viz.:—

Artists' Proofs, folio grand eagle . . . . £2 2 0 per Part.
Unlettered Proofs, folio columbier . . . .   1 1 0   ,,
Lettered Proofs, quarto grand eagle . . . . 0 10 6   ,,

The attention of the trade, and that of persons interested in the establishment of "Fine Art Distributions," is particularly called to this Series of Engravings; they comprise about One Hundred and Fifty Plates, being beautifully-executed Copies of Modern Pictures by British Artists, are printed in the best style, upon India paper, and are, from their excellence, their variety, and their price, especially adapted for the purpose of such enterprises. The Proprietors, anxious to extend the taste for Engravings, will be disposed to meet the wishes of any person connected with these undertakings, by furnishing a selection upon liberal terms.

In one vol., price £2 10s., cloth gilt,

THE WILKIE GALLERY:
WITH NOTICES BIOGRAPHICAL AND CRITICAL.

The Engravings are accompanied by original critical notices, from the pen of an artist whose abilities peculiarly qualify him to explain and illustrate those numerous points of excellence with which the compositions of WILKIE abound. The work contains a Biography of the Painter, written expressly for the WILKIE GALLERY.

The Volume contains Forty-four beautiful Engravings in line; average size, 6¼ by 9¼ inches.

In one vol. 8vo., 22s. cloth gilt, with Forty-two Illustrations by "Phiz,"

LEWIS ARUNDEL; or, THE RAILROAD OF LIFE.
BY FRANK E. SMEDLEY (FRANK FAIRLEGH).

"The task of the reviewer becomes a pleasant one when such works as the one before us is forced upon his perusal. We must once more commend the taste and talent of the author of 'Lewis Arundel.'"—*Weekly Times.*

"The best tale going is 'Lewis Arundel,' by the author of 'Frank Fairlegh.' It displays a great deal of that sort of feeling for which we can find no better term than gentlemanly."—*Cambridge Chronicle.*

BY THE AUTHOR OF "LEWIS ARUNDEL."
Complete in one vol. 8vo., 16s. cloth gilt,

FRANK FAIRLEGH; or, SCENES FROM THE LIFE OF A PRIVATE PUPIL.
With Thirty Illustrations, by GEORGE CRUIKSHANK.

"Its fame is very likely to be more durable than that of the majority of works of the kind."—*Bell's Life in London.*

"There is no writer of fiction since Sir Walter Scott who has so well deserved popularity as the author of this story."—*Exeter Gazette.*

ARTHUR HALL, VIRTUE, & CO., 25, PATERNOSTER ROW.

Lightning Source UK Ltd.
Milton Keynes UK
UKHW022018270122
397848UK00003B/125